SATELLITES AND COMMISSARS

PRINCETON STUDIES IN

INTERNATIONAL HISTORY AND POLITICS

Series Editors
Jack L. Snyder
Marc Trachtenberg
Fareed Zakaria

———————————————

Recent Titles:

SATELLITES AND COMMISSARS

STRATEGY AND CONFLICT IN THE POLITICS OF SOVIET-BLOC TRADE

Randall W. Stone

PRINCETON UNIVERSITY PRESS   PRINCETON AND OXFORD

Second printing, and first paperback printing, 2002
Paperback ISBN 0-691-09598-1

*The Library of Congress has cataloged the cloth edition
of this book as follows*

Stone, Randall W., 1966–
Satellites and commissars : strategy and conflict in the politics
of Soviet-Bloc trade / Randall W. Stone.
p.   cm. — (Princeton studies in international history and politics)
Includes bibliographical references and index.
ISBN 0-691-04414-7 (cloth : alk. paper)
1. Trade adjustment assistance—Soviet Union.   2. Europe, Eastern—
Foreign economic relations—Soviet Union.   3. Europe, Eastern—
Foreign relations—Soviet Union.   I. Title.   II. Series.
HF1421.S76   1995
337.47—dc20   95-17510

British Library Cataloging-in-Publication Data is available

This book has been composed in Times Roman

Printed on acid-free paper. ⊚

www.pup.princeton.edu

Printed in the United States of America

3   5   7   9   10   8   6   4   2

To Martha and Henry, with love

Contents

Tables

Preface

THE RESEARCH on which this book is based began with the ambition to extend the contemporary study of international political economy into the region that was then dominated by the Soviet Union. It appeared to me a serious short-coming of the research program that it rarely ventured into this unfriendly terrain, ceding it instead as a realm for the naked exercise of power, where the finer considerations of international cooperation were unlikely to find much purchase. At the same time I was motivated by a sense that much of what passed for explanation in the field of Soviet politics was generally inadequate. Studies of this region have tended to be dominated by concepts and theoretical concerns peculiar to it, which have seemed irrelevant or uninteresting to students of other countries. Rigorous, empirical testing has been the exception, rather than the norm. This book aims to make a contribution toward bridging the chasm that has emerged between studies of the area and recent theoretical developments in political science and economics.

My starting point is to insist that explanations are inadequate if they lack microfoundations; that is, if they fail to give a coherent account of how patterns of behavior follow from the motivations of the basic units of analysis, whether these be individuals, groups, or states. To focus on the choices made by rational actors is not to deny the importance of unintended consequences or of collectively suboptimal decisions. Rather, it is to argue that such phenomena have to be explained as the result of choices made by individuals or groups seeking to achieve their objectives.

Indeed, explaining suboptimal outcomes is a major concern of this study. The central puzzles are the persistent failures of socialist allies to cooperate in the economic realm, and the apparent paradox of a great power that fails to defend its own interests. My explanations, however, are firmly grounded in the notion of individual self-interest. The title of this book, *Satellites and Commissars*, captures the units of analysis most central to my argument. I claim that the East European states were pursuing their individual interests when they undermined cooperative agreements that would have yielded benefits for all. Moreover, I argue that the paralysis of Soviet policy was the product of rational adaptation by myriads of low-level officials to the constraints imposed by Soviet institutions. The failures of these institutions cannot be understood apart from the incentives that they imposed on the officials who betrayed them.

I was extremely fortunate to embark on this project at a time when a vast array of new sources of information was becoming available in Russia and Eastern Europe. Indeed, because of secrecy rules and a variety of incentives to withhold information, it would have been impossible to conduct this research before the collapse of the Soviet bloc. Because the new information is so startling, and because so many of the novel claims of this book depend on it, it is important at the outset to describe the new sources. First, this book is based on recorded interviews with ninety firsthand witnesses, and numerous less important conversations, conducted in Moscow, Warsaw, Prague, and Budapest. Second, it is based on six major collections of primary-source documents located in Moscow, Warsaw, and Prague.

The interviews represent an unprecedented degree of access to Soviet and East European foreign trade officials. Five of the officials had ranked as deputy premiers, two had been Central Committee secretaries, and seven more had held the rank of minister. Many others had intimate knowledge of foreign trade negotiations. I located the officials by searching for surviving members of the countries' delegations to key meetings of the Council for Mutual Economic Assistance (CMEA) where major integration programs had been discussed, so the respondents had firsthand knowledge of the negotiations described in the case studies. I interviewed Russians in Russian, Poles in Polish or Russian, and Czechs and Hungarians in Russian or German. In the text that follows, I do not cite any interviews without giving the source by name; an appendix to the book lists the major positions the respondents have held.

The quality of the interviews was extraordinary. At the time they were conducted, former Soviet and East European officials were still actively engaged with the past but had almost liberated themselves from their fear of it. They spoke with great interest about their subject matter, which for most of them had been a life's work, yet they spoke with a self-critical, even in some cases a cynical, distance from it, and uncovered the shortcomings and errors of the past with an almost feverish intensity. Many of the officials I interviewed spoke with an eagerness born of pent-up experiences and stories that had never before been shared with a nonparticipant. Most had limited experiences with Americans, and very few had ever been interviewed for academic purposes. The interviews usually lasted several hours, and in some instances I was able to meet a subject two or three times. In the process I was able to draw on a vast wealth of experience and information.

I chose to conduct open-ended interviews rather than survey-style interviews for two reasons. First, open-ended interviews are the best strategy to assure that no relevant explanatory variable has been left unexamined. In an open-ended conversation an experienced respondent is unlikely to allow an obvious oversight to go unnoticed. As a result, I can now claim that a large number of knowledgeable witnesses have concurred with the major arguments of this work. Second, open-ended interviews are much more informative than surveys. Respondents were often able to provide detailed information about incidents that I would never have thought to ask about. Since my study covered a large span of years, and the memories of respondents varied, I allowed the respondents themselves to help guide me through their recollections.

In Moscow I had access to three major sources of documents: (1) the CMEA Archive; (2) the archive of the Institute for the Economy of the World Socialist System (IEMSS), now renamed the Institute for International Economic and Political Studies (IMEPI); and (3) a portion of the holdings of the International Research Institute for Problems of Management (MNIIPU). I used the CMEA Archive by arrangement with the Central State Archive for the National Economy (TsGANKh), and I had unrestricted access. The CMEA Archive is a rich collection of seventy thousand boxes (fifty million pages) of documents that were declassified in 1992 and cover the period from 1949 to 1991. My research traced the international negotiations over each integration program from beginning to end. Some meetings were recorded only in protocols, but in many cases stenographic records were preserved as well, together with background reports, the legal documents that had been adopted, and the texts of speeches. The legal documents are illuminating, because under CMEA procedure, successive versions contain notations that record the "particular opinions" of the various countries. By tracing the evolution of these documents over time, one is able to reconstruct stages of negotiation.

The IMEPI Archive is a rich storehouse of confidential memos prepared by the Institute between 1965 and 1992 on every aspect of East European affairs, and addressed to high-ranking officials in a number of important Soviet organizations. Many are addressed to the Central Committee of the Communist Party of the Soviet Union (CPSU); others to the State Planning Commission (Gosplan), the office of the Permanent Representative to the CMEA, and various ministries. The memos were classified DSP (for qualified personnel only) or higher, which allowed the authors to be fairly candid in their opinions. The rules of political correctness and tact reserved for censored materials for general publication were relaxed for confidential internal memos. Since the memos are addressed to particular officials, the researcher has an unusual amount of information about how high in the bureaucracy their influence reached, and how widely they were circulated. In some cases, notations indicated that particular reports were written in response to personal inquiries by the addressees, which serves as confirmation that the recipients had some concern about the subject matter. In almost every case, the report contains information about the author or authors and the date of writing.

The MNIIPU collection was particularly valuable in preparing chapter 8, on the Comprehensive Program for Scientific and Technical Progress, because the researchers at MNIIPU played an unusually important role in preparing Soviet position papers for the program. The documents in the collection included numerous proposals and reports prepared by MNIIPU, correspondence with the Central Committee and other Soviet organizations, and numerous protocols of negotiating sessions. Most important, it included a series of drafts of the treaty text, which demonstrated the modifications that were made in the basic document in the course of negotiations with the East Europeans.

In Warsaw I had access to two major sources of documents: (1) the archive of the Polish Planning Commission, now known as the Central Office for Planning (CUP); and (2) the archive of the Office for Progress in Science, Technology, and Implementation (UPNTiW), now known as the Committee for Scientific Research (KBN). I had restricted access to the CUP Archive, but I was able to view numerous classified documents on Soviet-Polish coordination of planning from 1969 to 1991. The documents included protocols of negotiating sessions, the approved plan for 1986–90, extensive correspondence between Warsaw and Moscow, and numerous internal memos used to brief negotiators, to report on progress, and to issue instructions. From this documentation it was possible to reconstruct the outlines of Soviet-Polish trade negotiations. The KBN materials shed a great deal of light on the politics of science and technology in the Soviet bloc. The materials included internal and external audits of the ministry charged with implementing the Comprehensive Program for Scientific and Technical Progress, protocols of Soviet-Polish negotiating sessions, and extensive correspondence between Polish ministries regarding the Program.

Finally, in Prague I had access to the archive of the State Planning Commission (SPK). The archive unfortunately contains only materials dating from 1987; all earlier materials have been transferred to the state archive system, and the present intention is to keep them classified for twenty years. Subject to this restriction, however, the materials in the archive are very complete. They include protocols and minutes of most of the trade-negotiating sessions, as well as internal reports, briefing papers, and long-term planning documents. In some cases the materials are in the form of abbreviated stenographic records, which help to preserve the flavor of the negotiating sessions. From these materials, it was possible to reconstruct a very detailed picture of the trade negotiations surrounding the last two five-year plans, and to witness the changes in the Soviet bargaining position toward the end of the 1980s. I had unrestricted access to the collection.

An unusual feature of this study was that documents and interviews could be used to corroborate each other. While in Moscow I was able to interview the authors of key documents that were used as blueprints for Soviet integration initiatives. In Poland and Czechoslovakia I interviewed the officials who wrote many of the documents on trade with the Soviet Union, and who participated in most of the negotiations that these documents described. As a result, I was able to use the interviews to fill in the context and significance of particular agreements or disputes, and use documents to fill in the gaps in the respondents' memories. Overlapping interviews and documents increased the value of each immeasurably.

This work would not have been possible without the support and encouragement of a large number of people and institutions. I wish to thank my dissertation advisers—Timothy Colton, Stanley Hoffmann, and Robert Keohane—whose careful reading of numerous drafts and insightful comments added a great deal to the quality of the manuscript. Robert Keohane deserves particular credit as an early intellectual influence and the model of a dedicated teacher. I also wish to thank others who read drafts and made important methodological or substantive contributions: James Alt, Jo Andrews, Seweryn Bialer, Wojciech Bienkowski, Stanisław Długosz, Mark Elder, Judith Goldstein, Joel Hellman, Antoni Kaminski, Gary King, Robert Legvold, Michael Loriaux, Lisa Martin, Andrew Moravcsik, Alec Nove, Maciej Perczyński, Kenneth Shepsle, Jack Snyder, Jozef Soldaczuk, Eugeniusz Tabaczyński, Helmut Wagner, Celeste Wallander, and an anonymous reviewer. Although I would not claim their endorsement of my thesis, I am confident that their criticisms have significantly refined it. Of course, any mistakes or oversights in the work are entirely my own.

I thank Norma and Robert Koenig, who read the entire manuscript and made many valuable suggestions. Thanks are due as well to the staff at Princeton University Press: Malcolm DeBevoise, my editor, who encouraged me to pursue the project, and Rita Bernhard, my copyeditor, who did an admirable job of reconciling my prose with the strictures of English grammar.

I wish to express my deepest gratitude to all the individuals in Russia, Poland, Czechoslovakia, and Hungary who consented to grant interviews, and whose names are listed in the appendix. They received no compensation for their time and effort beyond the hope of making some contribution to understanding.

My appreciation and thanks go to the administrators and librarians of several archival collections, who made my research possible and took pains to make the experience enjoyable. In Moscow I wish to thank the staffs of TsGANKh, IMEPI (formerly IEMSS), MNIIPU, and TsKhSD (the archive of the former Central Committee). In Warsaw I thank the staffs of the CUP Archive and the International Department of the KBN. In Prague I thank the staff of the SPK Archive.

A number of institutions supported this work financially and materially. I was the guest of the Institut Mezhdunarodnykh Ekonomicheskikh i Politicheskikh Issledovanii of the Russian Academy of Sciences in Moscow, of the Szkoła Główna Handlowa in Warsaw, and of the Prognostický Ústav of the Czech and Slovak Academy of Sciences in Prague. Each of these institutions was extremely helpful in arranging interviews and access to archives, and each provided me with the same stipend that is extended to its own graduate students. I owe a particular debt of gratitude to Nataliia N. Abaken and Inna V. Lisitskaia, who helped me in countless ways in Moscow, and to Alena Nešporová, whose assistance proved invaluable in Prague. Financial support for various stages of the research and writing was provided by the Social Science Research Council, the International Research and Exchanges Board, the Fulbright-Hays Program of the U.S. Department of Education, the Minda de Gunzburg Center for European Studies of Harvard University, the Russian Research Center of Harvard University, the Fund for Peace, the Soviet Peace Fund, and the National Science Foundation. The manuscript was written while I was in residence at the Russian Research Center of Harvard University and the Thomas J. Watson, Jr., Institute for International Studies of Brown University. The views expressed, of course, are those of the author and do not necessarily reflect the opinions of any of these institutions.

Abbreviations

AES	Atomnaia elektrostantsiia [Russian: nuclear power plant]
AN SSSR	Akademiia nauk SSSR [Russian: USSR Academy of Sciences]
CC	Central Committee
CMEA	Council for Mutual Economic Assistance
CPC	Communist Party of Czechoslovakia
CPSU	Communist Party of the Soviet Union
CSSR	Czechoslovak Socialist Republic
CUP	Centralny urząd planowaniia [Polish: Central Planning Office]
DTsPS	Dolgosrochnye tselevye programmy sotrudnichestva [Russian: Long-Term Target Programs for Cooperation]
GDR	German Democratic Republic
GKNT	Gosudarstvennyi komitet po nauke i tekhnike [Russian: State Committee for Science and Technology]
Gosplan	Gosudarstvennyi komitet planovaniia [Russian: State Planning Commission]
Gossnab	Gosudarstvennyi komitet material'no-tekhnicheskogo snabzheniia [Russian: State Commission for Material and Technical Supply]
GSPiS	Główna szkoła planowania i statystyki [Polish: Main School of Planning and Statistics]
HSWP	Hungarian Socialist Workers' Party
IEMSS	Institut ekonomiki mirovoi sotsialisticheskoi sistemy [Russian: Institute for the Economy of the World Socialist System]
IMEPI	Institut mezhdunarodnykh ekonomicheskikh i politicheskikh issledovanii [Russian: Institute for International Economic and Political Studies (formerly IEMSS)]
Ispolkom	Ispolnitel'nyi komitet [Russian: Executive Committee]
KBN	Komitet badan naukowych [Polish: Committee for Scientific Research]
KNTS	Komitet po nauchno-tekhnicheskomu sotrudnichestvu [Russian: (CMEA) Committee for Cooperation in Science and Technology]
KP NTP	Kompleksnaia programma nauchno-technicheskogo progresa [Russian: Comprehensive Program for Progress in Science and Technology]

KSOPD	Komitet po sotrudnichestvu v oblasti planovoi deiatel'nosti [Russian: (CMEA) Committee for Cooperation in Planning]
MIEP MSS	Mezhdunarodnyi institut ekonomicheskikh problem mirovoi sotsialisticheskoi sistemy [Russian: International Institute for Economic Problems of the World Socialist System]
MNIIPU	Mezhdunarodnyi nauchno-issledovatel'skii institut problem upravleniia [Russian: International Management Research Institute]
NIK	Najwyzsza izba kontroli [Polish: Supreme Inspection Commission]
PRP	People's Republic of Poland
PUWP	Polish United Workers' Party
RVPH	Council for Mutual Economic Assistance (Czech abbr.)
RWPG	Council for Mutual Economic Assistance (Polish abbr.)
SED	Sozialistische Einheitspartei Deutschlands [German: Socialist Unity Party of Germany]
SEV	Sovet ekonomicheskogo vzaimopomoshchi [Russian: Council for Mutual Economic Assistance]
SPIM	Sovmestnyi plan integratsionnykh meropriiatii [Russian: Joint Plan of Integration Measures]
SPK	Statni planovaci komise [Czech: State Planning Commission]
SRR	Socialist Republic of Romania
TsGANKh	Tsentral'nyi gosudarstvennyi arkhiv narodnogo khoziaistva SSSR [Russian: Central State Archive of the National Economy of the USSR]
UPNTiW	Urząd postępu naukowo-technicznego i wdrożen [Polish: Office for Progress in Science, Technology, and Implementation]
VIA	Vnější integračné akcí [Czech: Foreign integration projects, i.e., joint investments]
VLK	Výbor lidové kontroly [Czech: People's Control Commission]

Part One

THEORY AND HISTORY

CHAPTER 1

A Principal-Agent Theory of Soviet
Bargaining Failure

THE COLLAPSE of Soviet power in Eastern Europe has unleashed a flood of new information, which is compelling observers to revise their settled opinions on many aspects of Soviet foreign policy. Soviet-bloc politics played itself out under a shroud of secrecy and disinformation that was designed to project the myth of a monolithic communist bloc, united in purpose and action. Hints of dissension spilled out periodically in the socialist press, particularly at times of upheaval in Eastern Europe such as 1956 in Hungary, 1968 in Czechoslovakia, and 1981 in Poland. Yet there was much that these hints left obscure, and many of them were deceptive. With the opening of archives across Eastern Europe and Russia, and the removal of the sanctions that formerly prevented candid interviews with communist officials, an important chapter in the history of Europe can now be rewritten.

New evidence demonstrates that the Soviet Union's control over its satellites was much weaker than was believed during the years of the cold war. The East Europeans waged a covert campaign over several decades to rebuff Soviet proposals for economic integration, to fill official documents with loopholes, and to avoid implementing agreements that had been signed. This campaign succeeded even though the Soviet Union paid a handsome subsidy to its satellites in the form of skewed prices for machinery and raw materials. In return for its largess, the Soviet Union sought to extract concessions on a series of objectives intended to improve the political and economic viability of the alliance, such as industrial policy, technological development, and infrastructure investment. Economic integration with Eastern Europe was a primary foreign policy objective of the Soviet leadership, one that was reaffirmed by every party congress and that absorbed a great deal of the time and energy of top officials. The Soviet Union wielded enormous economic, political, and military power, and led a strategic alliance of like-minded and dependent socialist states. Why, then, was the Soviet policy of economic integration with Eastern Europe such a conspicuous failure? What explains the inability of the Soviet leadership to use political resources to political effect?

The answer must be sought on two levels. At the level of strategy, bargaining theory identifies several variables that determine the performance of negotiators: resolve, credibility, linkage, and monitoring. The record of Soviet–East European negotiations over economic integration demonstrates a pervasive failure of Soviet bargaining strategy along each of these dimensions. Low-level Soviet negotiators failed to drive hard bargains, compromising the hard-won agreements that had been forged at higher levels. Central authorities were unable to make binding commitments to the satellites, so the East Europeans were not inclined to participate in projects whose success depended on Soviet promises. Soviet negotiators were unable to create effective linkages between their bargaining resources and the concessions they sought to win. Finally, Soviet officials did not monitor the satellites' behavior closely enough to identify infractions of agreements when they occurred, and this omission encouraged the satellites to engage in wholesale evasion. At one level, the defects of Soviet bargaining strategy explain the failures of the policy.

Explaining the emergence of an ineffective bargaining strategy, however, requires us to take a closer look at the bargainer, and to descend to the level of the incentives facing individuals. I argue that Soviet policy toward Eastern Europe was crippled by the incoherence of Soviet institutions: systemic management failures undermined the Soviet Union's ability to bargain with its client states. The responsibility of bargaining with the satellites was superimposed on the existing economic plan for each organization, and subtle objectives were therefore crowded out by compelling incentives to concentrate on quantitative quotas. The procedure of ratcheting quotas upward to meet each organization's production frontier, meanwhile, created incentives for economic actors to suppress information. These perverse incentives might have been overcome had each level of the Soviet hierarchy not wielded such absolute power that it was unable to make credible commitments to the levels below. Because such commitments could not be made, however, Soviet officials faced incentives to smother uncomfortable information, to ignore violations of international agreements, to avoid conflict with Soviet allies—in short, to do everything but vigorously pursue the national interest.

This claim represents a substantial revision of past interpretations of Soviet–East European relations. Although no serious observer has failed to notice the marked changes in Soviet politics between the Stalin and Gorbachev eras, it has generally been assumed that the dictatorial or totalitarian elements that lingered in Soviet politics made the Soviet bureaucracy more effective than those of the hapless Western democracies.[1] Instead, I argue the reverse: the fewer restraints imposed on superiors, the weaker the commitments made to subordinates and the more incoherent the resulting policy. When the principal is unconstrained, and therefore unable to make credible commitments, the agents face incentives to suppress information and to base their behavior on evaluation parameters rather than on their own specialized knowledge. The result is fragmentation, policy drift, and broken promises.

[1]Fainsod, *How Russia is Ruled*, pp. 386–89.

Although high-level Soviet leaders repeatedly tried to advance the cause of economic integration, the Soviet bureaucracy consistently allowed itself to be manipulated and outmaneuvered by the East Europeans. The satellites plotted their own orbits and extracted ever-growing subsidies from their patron.

FORTY YEARS OF DISINTEGRATION

The politics of trade in the Soviet bloc swirled and eddied around the opportunities created by the distorted prices mandated by the Council for Mutual Economic Assistance. Trade prices in the Soviet bloc were based on world prices quoted in London or Zurich but were calculated according to complex formulas that ensured that they diverged from the prices prevailing on capitalist markets. Commodities such as oil, which appreciated rapidly on world markets, were generally underpriced in the Soviet bloc. Meanwhile, Soviet-bloc machinery was generally overpriced because it was treated as if it were comparable to Western machinery, although it in fact lagged far behind Western products in quality. Using artificial prices meant, unfortunately, that each trade transaction involved opportunity costs to one side or the other, because a better buying or selling price could always be obtained on the world market. Naturally, the East European satellites tailored their negotiating positions to the opportunities offered by the distorted prices. As a result, opportunities were missed for expanded trade, specialization, and investment that might have revitalized the socialist economies.

According to an arrangement that became more costly to the Soviet Union as time went on, the USSR exported the lion's share of the raw materials and energy consumed by the East European satellites, and received payment in the form of machinery. Consequently, the Soviet Union exported primarily subsidized goods and imported primarily overpriced goods in return, offering its satellites a substantial net subsidy. Attempts to measure the subsidy have been complicated by shortcomings in the available data, but thirty years of debate has led to a broad consensus that the subsidy was real and very costly.[2] Numerous East European scholars have disputed the thesis that the Soviet Union

[2]The debate began when Mendershausen presented evidence that the Soviet Union practiced price discrimination against its satellites ("Terms of Trade," *Review of Economics and Statistics* [May 1959]). In response, Holzman argued that all the CMEA countries practiced price discrimination against one another ("Soviet Foreign Trade Pricing," *Review of Economics and Statistics* [May 1962]).

Sandor Ausch, a Hungarian economist, used official East European figures to show that trade prices in the CMEA exceeded world prices in 1964 in all categories, but that the difference was 25.9 percent for machines and only 15.4 percent for raw materials, which meant that raw materials were relatively underpriced. He carefully avoided the conclusion that there was a trade subsidy (Ausch, *Theory and Practice*, p. 85). Using a different method of estimating prices in a study spanning the years 1960 to 1978, Marrese and Vanous found that Soviet-bloc prices of

subsidized its trade.[3] The new availability of interviews with the participants in trade negotiations, however, should put such objections to rest. Forty-five Polish, Czechoslovak, and Hungarian foreign trade officials interviewed in 1992 unanimously concurred that their countries had received substantial subsidies from the Soviet Union because of the skewed prices of fuels, raw materials, and engineering products. Asked to identify the most important issue in bilateral trade negotiations in open-ended interviews, trade officials invariably identified the commodity structure of trade. With some nuances of interpretation, each official responded that the mix of goods determined the terms of trade, and that some goods, including most machinery, were overpriced relative to others, including most raw materials and energy sources.[4]

Anatol Dikij, who supervised the Polish office for bilateral negotiations with the Soviet Union in the 1980s, explained that the Polish side collected "definite rents." Dikij cited a Soviet estimate that the subsidy to Poland in the 1980s was 1.5 to 2 billion rubles per year, and indicated that this was broadly consistent with a Polish analysis prepared by the Central Planning Office in 1988.[5] Stanisław Długosz, deputy chairman of the Polish Planning Commission, and the chief Polish trade negotiator with the Soviet Union in the 1980s, put the matter simply:

---

machinery, equipment, and manufactured consumer goods substantially exceeded world levels, and that prices of fuels and other raw materials were at or below world levels in every year. Again, this meant that raw materials were relatively underpriced. Their central conclusion that there was a Soviet trade subsidy has become widely accepted, but the Marrese and Vanous estimate that "the Soviet Union has implicitly transferred resources equivalent to $87.2 billion to Eastern Europe during 1960–80" remains controversial (Marrese and Vanous, *Soviet Subsidization of Trade*, p. 3). The Marrese-Vanous methodology has been criticized. Marer argues that quality differences should not be taken into account in estimating the Soviet trade subsidy, because they are difficult to measure (Marer, "The Political Economy"). A recent study has shown, however, that fairly precise estimates of these quality differentials can be obtained by employing extensive surveys of Hungarian foreign trade enterprise executives (Oblath and Tarr, "The Terms of Trade Effects," pp. 75–93). Oblath and Tarr estimate that the discontinuation of trade subsidies on 1 January 1991 moved the terms of trade against Hungary by 30 percent, costing Hungary $1.7 billion in 1991 alone.

[3]A significant recent work to take this position is that of Laszlo Csaba. In *Eastern Europe in the World Economy* (Cambridge: Cambridge University Press, 1990), Csaba argues that the uncertainty surrounding the subsidy was so great that neither side knew who was benefiting and who was losing.

[4]The appendix comprises a list of interviews. Each of the East European trade officials was asked the same questions about the trade subsidy, and each gave roughly the same account of its major features. Former Soviet officials confirmed the view of their counterparts (interviews with Iurii Pekshev, 3.10.1992; Oleg Rybakov, 3.9.1992; and Leonid Krasnov, 2.27.1992). These views were corroborated during numerous interviews with academics of the former Institute for the Economy of the World Socialist System (IEMSS) and the international CMEA institute (MIEP MSS).

[5]Interview with Anatol Dikij, 6.2.1992.

Trade [with the Soviet Union] was profitable for the socialist countries because of the structure of trade, since we received raw materials and paid with equipment and consumer goods. In terms of prices, we got better prices for our machinery than we paid for raw materials.[6]

Zdeněk Šedivý, who occupied the same position in the Czechoslovak Planning Commission from 1968 to 1983, concurred:

If you take Czechoslovak-Soviet relations from a macroeconomic point of view, they were profitable for the Czechoslovak side. . . . If Czechoslovakia exported 80 percent machinery, equipment and consumer goods, and imported only 20 percent, then the difference was 60 percent. . . . From the point of view of terms of trade, this was profitable for the whole [postwar] period.[7]

Istvan Hetenyi, who served as deputy and first deputy chairman of the Hungarian Planning Commission from 1964 to 1980, argued that the same analysis applied to Hungarian-Soviet relations:

The fact that we imported oil and exported machinery was very favorable. You can see it in our budget, because we introduced world market prices for domestic prices, so the state budget got some 10 billion forints [in taxes paid by foreign trade enterprises] from oil imports. Well, we paid some export subsidies as well, but the net balance was some 30 to 40 billion forints. At that time, that was about one billion dollars.[8]

In the Hungarian case, the difference between the foreign trade taxes and subsidies that converted domestic prices into CMEA prices provides a rough approximation of the trade subsidy.

The chief political consequence of offering a trade subsidy and tying it to distorted prices was that it politicized what should have been essentially a technical matter: the process of determining the commodity composition of trade. In order to increase the national share of the Soviet trade subsidy, each East European country sought to increase the volume of its subsidized imports and overpriced exports, whereas the Soviet Union sought to hold the line. Efficiency issues were lost in the scramble for unilateral advantage. How much steel the alliance really needed, or who could produce it at the lowest

[6]Interview with Stanisław Długosz, 5.21.92. Długosz was first deputy minister of foreign trade from 1972 to 1980. As deputy chairman of the Planning Commission from 1980 to 1991, he directed Polish trade policy with socialist countries.

[7]Interview with Zdeněk Šedivý, 6.30.1992. Šedivý was deputy chairman of the Czechoslovak State Planning Commission from July 1968 until 1983, and directed Czechoslovak trade policy toward socialist countries.

[8]Interview with Istvan Hetenyi, 9.3.1992. Hetenyi was a department director in the Czechoslovak State Planning Commission from 1958 to 1964, deputy chairman supervising the CMEA and foreign trade departments from 1964 to 1973, and first deputy chairman supervising general operations from 1973 to 1980. He was minister of finance from 1980 to 1986.

cost, were secondary matters; the only important consideration was whether the CMEA price made steel a profitable commodity to export. As a result, a number of Soviet initiatives to improve the efficiency of the bloc shattered against the inflexible structure of price distortions. The countries could agree that there were shortages of certain products throughout the region, and that it would be desirable to expand their production. However, when it was time to draw up a plan, each country lobbied to produce the overpriced items, and when it was time to implement it, each conveniently neglected to produce the subsidized goods.

The poor quality of East European machinery exports, naturally, was a flashpoint of contention. The satellites had no plausible alternative market. East European machines could be sold in the West in limited quantities, but only at a steep discount from their CMEA prices. Nevertheless, the satellites exported the same models to the Soviet Union without modification for many years, cut corners by using poor-quality materials, and provided a poor assortment of goods. Furthermore, they withheld their best products for export to the less forgiving markets of the West, and sold second-rate goods to the other socialist countries. Consequently, one of the Soviet Union's most important bargaining objectives was to induce its trading partners to invest in improving their products. This would have required the East Europeans to make substantial investments, however, and the satellites resisted. The Soviet Union launched a plethora of programs to raise quality standards, to promote new products, and to develop science and technology. In principle, the satellites applauded these initiatives, but in detail, they fought to retain outmoded models and resist technological progress.

In the last two decades of Soviet power, four major programs were negotiated with the East Europeans. Each was launched with a major speech by the Soviet general secretary. Each involved the participation of thousands of officials, the diversion of billions of rubles, and the investment of several years of negotiation. Every major Soviet integration initiative failed, however, because the satellites filled them with exceptions and maneuvered to avoid implementing onerous requirements. Each program became an embarrassing setback for Soviet foreign policy. Integration initiatives invariably contained provisions designed to revise the terms of trade in favor of the Soviet Union, and the satellites made every effort to boycott these points during implementation. It was too costly to oppose every Soviet proposal outright, however, so the East Europeans sought opportunities to evade their obligations by stealth, and to frustrate Soviet objectives through attrition. When necessary, they did not hesitate to sign agreements with no intention of carrying them out.

As the East European satellites gradually discovered, however, a strategy that is individually rational can have unintended consequences that are extremely damaging to collective interests. Many of the cooperative projects proposed by the Soviet Union posed collective-action problems. Joint construction projects, joint investments in research and development, and international specialization schemes, for example, offered the promise of joint gains from more efficient use of resources, but could only succeed if they could attract broad participation. They relied, therefore, on the efforts of each participant to minimize the effects of uncertainty and mistrust. The dominant East European strategy, however, was essentially covert: it was to evade linkages and retaliation in order to maximize the subsidy reaped in bilateral trade with the Soviet Union. The satellites relied on any difficulties or unforeseen contingencies that might complicate the enforcement of agreements. Their guerrilla tactics, however, riddled the Soviet plans with holes, which created bottlenecks in production and slowed cooperation to a crawl; potential joint gains were squandered. Witnessing the pervasive failure of common ventures, the East Europeans felt little inclination to invest in them. In an ironic twist, the perverse incentives created by the Soviet trade subsidy became an insuperable obstacle to East European integration.

THE BLACK BOX OF BARGAINING THEORY

It is possible to predict unique outcomes for many bargaining situations by making certain restrictive assumptions, but there exist broad classes of strategic situations for which the distributional outcomes are indeterminate.[9] This is why bargaining is problematic. Exerting a bit more effort could always change the outcome; being a bit more flexible just might lead to agreement. Bargaining remains more an art than a science, governed by rules that are far from transparent. Bargaining theorists, however, have identified bargaining characteristics and strategies that influence both the likelihood of achieving cooperation and the distribution of benefits. Although this is an extensive and disputatious literature, four variables can be isolated that consistently appear most central: resolve, credibility, linkage, and monitoring.[10] An explanation of the failure of Soviet bargaining strategy should be sought first in an analysis of Soviet performance along these dimensions.

Resolve. Resolve is the willingness of a bargainer to forego the benefits of agreement in order to press for a more favorable deal in the future. This has traditionally been modeled in one of two ways. First, it can be represented as the willingness to risk the breakdown of bargaining, leading to no agreement.[11] In this case, the relative resolve of two bargainers depends on the size

---

[9]Nash, "Equilibrium Points." For a discussion of the uses and limitations of Nash equilibria, see Kreps, *Game Theory.*

[10]The seminal contribution to this genre of theory was made by Schelling in *Strategy of Conflict* (Oxford: Oxford University Press, 1960).

[11]This formulation was proposed by Zeuthen in 1930 (Harsanyi, "Bargaining," in Eatwell, Milgate and Newman, eds., *The New Palgrave,* pp. 60–62).

of the benefits that each will receive from a particular agreement point, and the two sides' attitudes toward risk. More recent attempts to model bargaining formally have concentrated on the fact that bargaining creates delays, as in the metaphor of a "war of attrition." In these models, the cost to each party of failing to reach an agreement in each period is the benefit that is foregone in that period, and the potential gain is discounted because it comes in the future. One recent treatment of international bargaining concludes that the more the players discount future gains, the more easily they can reach agreement, because the cost of disagreement in the present overwhelms the accumulating cost of concessions adding up in future periods.[12] Whether failure to agree is modeled as a risk or a delay, the outcome depends on the characteristics of the bargainers, and in particular on their attitudes toward risk and delay.

Credibility. Credibility is the ability to make commitments that will be believed. The ability to make credible commitments is essential in order to reach cooperative solutions to mixed-motive games, such as the prisoners' dilemma. In this familiar example, there are joint gains to be had if the two parties can cooperate, but each has an incentive to cheat, and each will suffer if he or she cooperates while the other cheats unilaterally. The equilibrium outcome in single play is conflict, rather than cooperation. A cooperative equilibrium can be reached in repeated play, however, if both sides can credibly commit to cooperate. Credible promises and threats make it possible to reach cooperative outcomes in a wide range of situations. In many instances, however, multiple equilibrium outcomes exist that are consistent with joint improvements of welfare, but that have very different distributional consequences.[13] In such situations, the credibility of the threats and promises made by the bargainers has a decisive influence on which outcomes are chosen, and on the final distribution of benefits.

Linkage. Linkage is a commitment to treat two or more issues jointly rather than separately. In principle, it should often be possible to resolve disputes by introducing additional dimensions of interest to both parties. This expands the set of possible solutions, and creates cooperative equilibria where only noncooperative ones may have previously existed.[14] (Of course, it is also possible to reduce potentially cooperative situations to deadlock by introducing additional issues.) In order to be effective, however, linkages must be credible. The party pursuing a strategy of linkage must be able to make a commitment that the linked issue will not be resolved in isolation, and that any threats or promises made in the linked issue area will indeed be carried out.[15] Further-

[12]Fearon, "Cooperation and Bargaining." The war-of-attrition model is drawn from biology, where it describes the dynamics of two animals struggling over a prize (Riley, "Strong Evolutionary Equilibrium." Cited in Alesina and Drazen, "Why are Stabilizations Delayed?").

[13]Krasner, "Life on the Pareto Frontier," in Baldwin, ed., *Neorealism and Neoliberalism.*

[14]Sebenius, "Negotiation Arithmetic."

[15]Stein, "The Politics of Linkage."

more, linkages have important distributional consequences. In many cases, one set of equilibria would emerge if each of the issues were settled in isolation, and another set would emerge that redistributed benefits if the issues were linked. The ability of states to pursue credible linkage strategies, therefore, has an important influence on bargaining outcomes.

Monitoring. The initiation of cooperation may create opportunities for one party to exploit another. Thus, although two parties may initially agree to cooperate, the agreement becomes unstable as new opportunities emerge. The solution is to create a mechanism that compensates for the changing incentives, usually by imposing costs on the actor who violates the agreement. Under conditions of perfect information, no agreement would be struck that allowed cheating to occur, and every equilibrium solution would be self-enforcing. Given imperfect information, however, enforcement mechanisms will be flawed, and a certain amount of cheating is bound to take place. Consequently, bargaining will concern not only prospective agreements but also the implementation of existing ones. In this second stage of bargaining, the ability of each party to monitor the implementation of agreements by the other side will be a critical asset.

These four variables provide a powerful vocabulary for describing bargaining behavior, and as later chapters will show, the shortcomings of Soviet policy fall along these four dimensions. An elegant description, however, is far from an explanation. Bargaining theory treats resolve, credibility, linkage, and monitoring as causal variables: they are the input that is needed for the theory to predict distributive outcomes. But from where do these all-important endowments come? Bargaining theory continues to treat the protagonist—the bargainer—as a black box, a sort of inscrutable basic datum that cannot be analyzed, but whose characteristics are all-important. Distributional outcomes ultimately depend on the preferences and strategies of the bargainers, but these considerations are exogenous. I will argue, however, that the factors that lead to bargaining power need not remain exogenous. To take the analysis further, we need to take a closer look at the protagonist of our drama: the bargainer. I will argue that the key to understanding a negotiator's behavior is to identify his or her role as the agent of some principal. Understanding the incentives created by the relationship between a bargaining agent and a principal makes it possible to supply the input necessary to construct an explanation of bargaining performance.

Principal-agent relationships play a role in almost every arena in which bargaining appears. Labor contracts are not negotiated by unions and firms, but by the employees of unions and firms. International negotiations are usually conducted by agents, rather than by sovereigns; even when heads of state meet directly, each continues to represent certain constituencies and to be held accountable in certain ways. Almost every negotiator is constrained in some way by the principals he or she represents. It is these constraints that ensure that the negotiator is a fair representative and does not pursue a private agenda. If the constraints are inappropriate, however, they may prevent, rather than motivate, good performance.

Most discussions of principal-agent relationships and bargaining have focused on the ratification of agreements and the effect that the need for ratification has on bargaining. For example, if the ratifying body will only accept an extremely favorable agreement, the agent can make a credible commitment not to make concessions, which strengthens the agent's bargaining power.[16] Alternatively, if there is uncertainty about the principal's reservation price (the worst bargain that the principal will accept), agents should be motivated to hold out for a better bargain. Again, this strengthens the agent's resolve but also leads to a lower probability of reaching an agreement.[17] Since these approaches have focused on the exercise of a veto by the principal, they have left the impression that the principal-agent relationship generally reinforces a negotiator's bargaining characteristics. As will be shown in the next section, however, the incentives created by principal-agent relationships may have entirely different consequences.

INSIDE THE BLACK BOX: AGENTS OF THE SOVIET UNION

The typical Soviet foreign trade negotiator was the head of an economic organization: an enterprise, branch ministry, or division of the State Planning Commission (Gosplan). The most important source of incentives constraining such an individual was the State Plan, the fundamental instrument of control over the planned economy, which determined everything from the number of ball bearings that went into a fighter aircraft to the topics of reports prepared by an elite research institute. The Plan was the basic measure of organizational performance, and individual tenure, promotion, and bonuses depended on meeting its quantitative indicators. For tasks that readily lent themselves to quantification, the Plan was an effective management tool, which presided over the rapid industrialization of the Soviet economy and victory in World War II. Central planning was poorly adapted, however, to tasks that required subtlety, independent judgment, and the exercise of discretion.

Recent developments in principal-agent theory have focused on the importance of credible commitments. Specifically, efforts to elicit performance from agents who are expected to carry out complex tasks depend on the credibility of the commitments that their principals make to them.[18] The difficulty

---

[16]Putnam, "Diplomacy and Domestic Politics."

[17]Lax and Sebenius, "Negotiating through an Agent."

[18]Kreps, "Corporate Culture and Economic Theory"; Willliamson, *Economic Institutions of Capitalism*; Milgrom and Roberts, *Economics, Organization and Management*; Laffont and Tirole, *A Theory of Incentives*.

in the Soviet case is that Soviet officials exercised such domination over their subordinates, and had so little recourse to defend themselves from their superiors' whims. Under such circumstances, it was very difficult to make the kind of credible commitments to one's subordinates that would allow them to reveal compromising information or to take appropriate risks. Safeguards common in bureaucracies, such as established procedures and appeals processes, were weak or nonexistent. In the absence of credible commitments to procedural fairness, the biases of the Plan asserted themselves, undermining Soviet negotiators' incentives to project resolve, credibility, linkage, and monitoring.

Moral Hazard and Adverse Selection

Principal-agent relationships present dilemmas for principals because of two problems related to asymmetric information: moral hazard and adverse selection. Moral hazard arises when the principal is able to determine only certain facts about an agent's performance, and not others. For example, the principal can determine the total cost of production, but not the amount of effort that the agent expended to reduce cost. We assume that rational agents incur some disutility for each unit of effort they expend. This does not mean that all agents are lazy and dishonest, but rather that there are always alternative uses for time, and that, on average, agents prefer to follow their own priorities rather than those of their principals. Consequently, principals must find incentives to motivate their agents to perform well. Adverse selection, on the other hand, arises when the agent has private information about some state of the world, such as the quality of a product or the technical difficulty of achieving some outcome.[19] The agent has incentives to misrepresent the privately known parameter in order to extract additional incentive payments (rents) from the principal. The principal, therefore, must offer incentives to induce the agent to reveal valuable private information.

Jean-Jacques Laffont and Jean Tirole draw together several decades of progress on these issues in an important new study of the economics of regulation.[20] They demonstrate that principals typically face trade-offs between efforts to motivate performance, on the one hand, and attempts to recapture the rents extracted by the highest-performing agents, on the other. The optimal incentive scheme recognizes this trade-off, and offers a menu of contracts with both high and low levels of incentive payments, which induces high

---

[19]A classic discussion of adverse selection is Akerlof, "The Market for Lemons," pp. 488–500.

[20]Laffont and Tirole, *A Theory of Incentives.* I follow Laffont and Tirole's notation where possible.

performers to declare themselves. To illustrate the problem, imagine a stylized situation in which the state fully reimburses an enterprise for its cost of production, and offers an additional incentive payment to motivate the management to keep costs down. The situation is characterized by moral hazard and adverse selection, so we assume that the enterprise's cost of production (C) is directly observable, but is determined by the enterprise's privately known technological parameter (β) and the hidden level of effort exerted by the enterprise manager (E):

$$C = \beta - E$$

If β is high, the enterprise is inefficient and cost will be high; increased effort, however, can compensate for inefficient technology.

The manager prefers to minimize E, so the principal (the ministry that manages the relevant industry, the State Planning Commission, etc.) must offer incentives to elicit performance. The principal therefore offers a contract something like the following, where a direct transfer to the enterprise (T) depends on a fixed payment (A) and some proportion (B) of the realized cost:

$$T = A - BC$$

At the extreme where $B = 0$, the principal is offering a cost-plus contract (the principal reimburses cost and then pays a transfer of A). If $B = 1$, the principal is offering a fixed-price contract (the principal pays a flat rate of A and requires the agent to bear the full cost).[21] The greater the proportion (B) of cost borne by the agent, the more "high-powered" is the contract, and therefore the greater the incentive to cut costs.

The principal's dilemma is that no pairing of a payment and a cost-sharing rule will be appropriate for all enterprises, since technological parameters vary. If B is large (a high-powered incentive), then inefficient enterprises will face strong incentives to minimize cost. Efficient enterprises, however, will enjoy substantial rents, because they can offer low cost with little effort, and a weaker incentive would have sufficed to motivate the level of performance that they achieve. If B is small (a low-powered incentive scheme, which is closer to a cost-plus contract), the efficient enterprise receives lower rents, but the inefficient enterprise fails to control costs. From the principal's point of view, the ideal solution is to induce the enterprises to reveal their technological parameters and offer customized incentive schemes. Efficient enterprises, however, are reluctant to reveal themselves, because their rents depend on holding private information. In theory, the enterprises can be induced to reveal their parameters if they are offered a menu of contracts that guarantees higher levels of rent to more efficient enterprises. Each enterprise chooses the

---

[21] The principal reimburses cost and pays a net transfer, so the gross transfer is $C + T$. If the principal offers a fixed price contract, $T = A - C$. The gross transfer is therefore $C + (A - C) = A$.

contract that maximizes its own rent, and the more efficient enterprises choose more high-powered incentives.[22] The resulting outcome is less efficient than the one the principal would impose if he or she enjoyed perfect information, but it leads to more cost reduction and lower rents than are possible under any single contract given asymmetric information.

At first glance this may not appear much like the system of incentives actually employed in the Soviet Union, where enterprises faced fixed production quotas, and cost accounting was underdeveloped. Certainly it is true that Soviet planning underemphasized cost and often offered weak incentives for performance. (In fact, however, all empirical cases of regulation and procurement diverge from the optimum, and this does not make the theory less powerful as an analytical tool that demonstrates how suboptimal incentives affect the behavior of agents.) This abstract schema does, however, capture some essential dynamics of the Soviet system. Although the Soviet plan was a regime of fixed quotas and full reimbursement, the informal planning process embodied some elements of incentive payments and cost sharing. Quotas were renegotiated at one- and five-year intervals, and planners used negotiations as a means of eliciting information from enterprises about their technological potential. Enterprise managers could be induced to accept higher quotas, for example, in return for additional investments, materials, or labor. Since the bargaining concerned inputs and outputs, it was essentially a discussion of cost. Instead of profits, managers pursued organizational slack: surplus materials, machinery, and labor that would make it easier to meet goals in the future and easier to divert resources for private purposes.[23] In principle, planners were willing to offer higher levels of rent to more efficient producers, if that would allow them to identify the more efficient types and motivate them to achieve higher performance. Managers might be willing to behave in ways that revealed their efficiency parameters in return for higher bonuses, and to secure promotions. However, Soviet institutions exacerbated two types of incentive distortions that typically arise under incentive contracts: the crowding-out effect and the ratchet effect. Since trade negotiators were embedded in the Plan, these effects weakened Soviet bargaining strategies, reducing the potential for resolve, credibility, linkage, and monitoring.

---

[22]The principle of incentive compatibility requires that the rent offered to an enterprise with each technological parameter be sufficient to guarantee that such an enterprise would choose the appropriate contract, but not great enough to induce enterprises with less efficient technology to seek to masquerade as efficient types. This requirement ensures that the optimal menu of contracts leaves more rent to the enterprise than would be the case if the principal had knowledge about the enterprise's technology. This rent is, in a sense, a payment to the enterprise to reveal its private information. See John O. Ledyard, "Incentive Compatibility," in Eatwell, Milgate, and Newman, *The New Palgrave.*

[23]For the classic statement of this position, see Berliner, *Factory and Manager in the USSR.* pp. 75–76, passim. Berliner refers to organizational slack as a "safety factor."

The crowding-out effect. This is a distortion of incentives that arises when a principal seeks to motivate an agent to divide his or her time or efforts efficiently among several tasks, but is unable to assess how the agent apportions the work. If the employer attempts to use incentive pay to motivate the employee to work hard, the incentives will determine how the employee's efforts are apportioned. If the employee receives higher marginal compensation for certain activities than for others, it is rational for the employee to expend all of his or her effort in the most rewarding activity.[24] In terms of the preceding discussion, the enterprise's cost function now includes terms representing such additional objectives as quality control (S), resolve in bargaining with foreign countries (R), and effort expended in monitoring the performance of the satellites' contractual obligations (M):

$$C = \beta - E + S + R + M$$

Each of the additional demands on the enterprise increases the final cost of production, either by requiring additional investment, by creating delays, or by reducing the amount of effort that can be devoted to holding down costs. If the principal can measure quality, bargaining resolve, and monitoring independently, this represents no difficulty. The principal simply constructs an incentive scheme that motivates the agent to choose the optimal division of effort. If these parameters are the agent's private information, however, incentives that motivate the agent to hold down costs will tend to crowd out other useful activities.[25]

This is a common problem in all sorts of employment situations, where an employee faces a complex or evolving set of objectives. The typical solution is to write an incomplete contract, in which the employee pledges to exercise diligence and good judgment, and the employer pledges to follow a fair and predictable procedure in evaluating the employee's performance. This solution is only available, however, if the employer is able to make binding procedural commitments; otherwise, the employee has incentives to second-guess the employer and concentrate on fulfilling the objectives that are most closely linked to evaluation.[26] The failure of superior officials to make credible commitments in the Soviet bureaucracy ensured that efforts devoted to quality, bargaining, and monitoring were effectively crowded out.

The ratchet effect. The problem with relying on optimal contracts to induce agents to reveal their technology is that the principal must be able to make a commitment that he or she will not exploit tomorrow the information gained today.[27] Inferring each enterprise's technology from its choice of incentives,

---

[24]Milgrom and Roberts, *Economics, Organization and Management*, pp. 228–32.

[25]For an extensive discussion of this effect, as well as of certain conditions under which it does not apply, see Laffont and Tirole, *A Theory of Incentives*, chap. 4.

[26]Milgrom and Roberts, *Economics, Organization and Management*, pp. 402–3.

[27]Laffont and Tirole, *A Theory of Incentives*, chap. 9; Milgrom and Roberts, *Economics, Organization and Management*, pp. 232–36.

the planner could set quotas for future periods that expropriated the rent enjoyed by each enterprise. Foreseeing such an outcome, rational managers will conceal their technology by imitating inefficient types. In fact, it has been observed that central planners routinely escalated production targets to try to capture the slack and underutilized capacity that they knew was hidden in the system. The better an organization performed, the higher its quotas were set in the next Plan. In response, economic managers at all levels hoarded resources and misrepresented production capacity to ensure that they would be able to meet future targets.[28]

Indeed, industrial ministries often revised their enterprises' production plans mid-year in order to redistribute orders to surplus producers, thereby meeting their own plan targets for the percentage of enterprises that successfully fulfilled the Plan. These revisions had to be allowed in the planning process to provide some flexibility in meeting unforeseen circumstances and alleviating shortages, but the consequence was disastrous for enterprise-level incentives. A survey of ninety-five enterprises in the Novosibirsk region revealed that they had received 1,554 changes to their production plans in one year, without any compensating changes in the targets for surpluses that were used to calculate bonuses.[29] This clearly undermined any incentive that bonuses might provide to reveal efficiency, since the surplus production was effectively confiscated in the form of increased plan targets. The center's effort to elicit information by paying bonuses, therefore, was undermined because the center was unable to make commitments on behalf of intervening levels of the bureaucracy. As a consequence of the incentives created by ratcheting, lower levels of the hierarchy attempted to withhold from higher levels all the information that would be necessary to set appropriate production targets.

CONSEQUENCES FOR INTERNATIONAL BARGAINING

Resolve. Bargaining involves the expenditure of time and effort, and the diversion of valuable employees from other tasks. The resolution of bargaining, therefore, is usually modeled as a trade-off between continued bargaining costs and additional concessions. In the Soviet bureaucracy, however, efforts devoted to bargaining had to compete with another trade-off. Powerful incentives to meet quantitative production targets crowded out effort on all other fronts, including bargaining with the East European allies. Less efficient organizations, in particular, which felt intense pressure to increase productivity, had little time to waste in international negotiations. More efficient organiza-

[28]Weitzman, "The 'Ratchet Principle,'" pp. 302–8; Hewett, *Reforming the Soviet Economy,* pp. 183–91.

[29]*Pravda,* November 12, 1973. Cited in Nove, *The Soviet Economic System,* p. 107.

tions, however, had no incentive to perform better than their less efficient counterparts. Doing so would simply reveal their superior technology and expose them to escalating plan targets. If they were able to demonstrate that the Poles really could make certain concessions, for example, they would then face pressure to extract the same concessions from the Czechs and Hungarians, at increasing cost of time and effort. It was preferable for superiors to believe that the agreements reached represented the outer boundary of feasible cooperation, rather than a comfortable margin of organizational slack.

The resolve of Soviet negotiators fell off dramatically as discussion moved from quantities of goods to issues of quality control. The Plan could measure performance in terms of tons of coal, millions of rubles, or thousands of pairs of shoes, but it could not measure anything that was not captured in official statistics. Indeed, because of the excessive cost of gathering detailed micro-economic information, the most important plan targets were often set in tons. As a result, sheet steel and glass were made too heavy and paper was made too thick. After one enterprise struggled in vain for permission to produce lighter pipe that was less wasteful, *Pravda* lamented, "What isn't planned in tons! Pipe, rolling-mill and other equipment, and even in one instance plastic dolls! Yet everybody knows that this contradicts the national economic interest."[30] Unfortunately, there was no apparent alternative to physical quotas that was not accompanied by a whole host of its own distortions.

The fundamental problem was that there was no elegant way to express product quality in the Plan, because there was no obvious way to measure it. Regulators in capitalist countries tend to use prices and sales volumes as proxies for quality, but in a socialist economy those figures do not convey the same information. Soviet planning grappled with this problem by imposing numerous plan targets; in fact, a typical enterprise was expected to meet more than a hundred separate targets covering all aspects of its operations. Faced with so many priorities, a manager was compelled to devote the most effort to the objectives that were most effectively monitored.[31] The result was that the de facto incentive system failed to provide appropriate incentives to invest in quality control, and quality was crowded out by pressures to increase the level of production. Since, furthermore, the Soviet Union's own criteria for evaluating performance routinely neglected qualitative factors, Soviet negotiators had little determination to win concessions on these issues. As subsequent chapters will demonstrate, Soviet negotiators often defended quantitative targets vigorously but were much more willing to compromise on qualitative issues.

[30]*Pravda*, August. 22, 1974. Quoted in Nove, *The Soviet Economic System*, pp. 97–98. Nove argues that quantitative measures were retained in spite of these distortions because they made it easier for planners to cross-check the values of inputs and outputs, and because they avoided other distortions imposed by employing prices that did not reflect actual scarcities (ibid., pp. 96–102).

[31]Hewett, *Reforming the Soviet Economy*, pp.119–202; Nove, *The Soviet Economic System*, pp. 110–15.

On the other hand, the technology of planning made Soviet negotiators extremely sensitive to time pressure. The Soviet State Plan was a tremendously complex, interlocking set of equations, and the functioning of the whole depended on keeping to timetables. Performance evaluation, consequently, reflected the importance of schedules, and this was the cause of the inefficient practice of "storming" at the end of the month to meet production goals. Similarly, negotiations had to be completed on time so that the Plan could be balanced. This put Soviet negotiators at a distinct disadvantage as deadlines approached, because administrative pressure forced them to make concessions for the sake of agreement. East European negotiators claimed they were able to exploit this weakness by stretching out negotiations until they passed some threshold of Soviet bureaucratic tolerance for delay, at which point the Soviet negotiators gave in.

Credibility. To recapture some of the rents enjoyed by more efficient enterprises, Soviet planning set production quotas high enough to cut off some of the variation at the inefficient end. In other words, quotas were deliberately set at levels that some enterprises would be unable to attain, because that forced other enterprises to cut costs to stay above the threshold. Although it was unlikely that an enterprise would actually be shut down as a result of failure to fulfill the Plan, the consequences could be unpleasant for the manager. The planning system, therefore, was both taut and slack at the same time: efficient enterprises enjoyed a soft budget constraint and felt no incentive to improve or innovate, whereas inefficient ones faced impossible demands. As a result of the mad scramble for inputs at the inefficient end, the Plan became overextended, resources were in chronically short supply, and many industrial managers were compelled to falsify statistics in order to conceal production shortfalls.[32]

The overextension of the planning system created cleavages between levels of the Soviet hierarchy, which undermined the credibility of Soviet commitments. A conflict of interest arose between specialized agencies, responsible for narrowly defined tasks, and generalist agencies, responsible for monitoring the specialized ones. Unable to fulfill all of their obligations to the state, specialized agencies were compelled to shirk selectively, neglecting the tasks that were most difficult to monitor. This became an obstacle to bargaining when the Soviet Union had to make commitments in order to reach agreement, and the commitments depended on cooperation from Soviet branch ministries or enterprises. Soviet trading partners had no confidence that the lower levels of the hierarchy would honor commitments made by central authorities, and they had little incentive therefore to participate in joint efforts. These impressions were reinforced by continuous experience of Soviet policy, as joint projects ran into cost-overruns, chronic delays, and persistent failure to control quality. Consequently, we observe increasing East European cyni-

[32] See Kornai, *The Socialist System,* chaps. 9, 11.

cism, weakening support for bloc-wide objectives, and progressive deterioration of the Soviet Union's ability to coordinate its allies' policies over time. The Soviet Union found it increasingly difficult to convince its allies to take risks or to invest in joint projects.

Linkage. The ratchet effect stifled vertical communication in the Soviet bureaucracy, which hampered Soviet efforts to make strategic linkages between power resources and objectives. Under the ideal policy, planners would make a commitment not to escalate targets for more efficient enterprises, and enterprises would reveal their technology. The central authorities could then use this information about supply and demand to construct an optimal bargaining package with each East European satellite, trading off a sacrifice in one branch of industry for a benefit in another. Since the central authorities were unable to make credible commitments, however, each unit of the bureaucracy guarded its expertise jealously. The result was that the Soviet bureaucracy was extremely compartmentalized, and since information pooled at the lowest levels of the hierarchy, that was where operational decisions had to be made. Consequently, in spite of peak-level negotiations by the central planning commissions, much of the substance of trade negotiations was decentralized, and each organization was left to strike its own best deal. In this context, trade negotiators found it very difficult to make strategic linkages between issues that affected diverse sectors of the economy. As a result, excess bargaining leverage in one issue area was often squandered rather than being applied to disputes in other areas.

The fragmentation of trade issues in the Soviet bureaucracy by branch of industry clearly favored the East Europeans. Since communication frequently broke down in the Soviet bureaucracy, questions involving Czech exports of leather shoes to the Soviet Union, for example, were decided independently of questions involving Soviet exports of iron ore. The Soviets were providing a subsidy by exporting iron ore, but this was not a useful resource during controversies over the number and quality of shoes that Czechoslovakia was supposed to export to the USSR.[33] A Soviet Academy of Sciences report argued that the fragmentation of the bureaucracy dramatically undermined the Soviet bargaining position. "In practical terms," the report claimed, "there is no agency that is responsible for achieving a national economic optimum in the area of foreign ties." The ministries that represented the various branches of industry failed to work together to promote a comprehensive view of national welfare. Instead, each was concerned with the narrow, short-term goals of "importing new equipment and minimizing exports." In short, each agency followed its own organizational priorities, and no agency was charged with safeguarding the long-term Soviet national interest.[34]

[33]Interview with Zdeněk Šedivý, former deputy chairman of the Czechoslovak State Planning Commission, 6.30.1992.

[34]AN SSSR, "Razvitie vneshneekonomicheskikh sviazei Sovetskogo Soiuza do 1990 g.," p. 83. Published 1.2.1973 (ten copies), "Sekretno."

Monitoring. The task of monitoring agreements with the East European satellites was delegated to a variety of Soviet economic organizations that already had full pallets and little incentive to undermine their own plan performance by creating more work for themselves. Monitoring was not a task that was easily accommodated by the vocabulary of planning, so it was difficult to create appropriate incentives. Monitoring, furthermore, is an extremely difficult activity to observe, so when Soviet organizations were ordered to monitor East European behavior, the extent of their diligence remained private information. There was little danger involved in neglecting to report failures, because most of the satellites' indiscretions involved poor quality control, and were therefore unlikely to be picked up in the stream of quantitative indicators that flowed to higher levels. In addition, since the Plan was rigidly chronological, routine activities could never uncover any error that predated the current planning cycle. As a result, it was safe to assume that a shortcoming not reported in the current period would also go unexamined in the future. Much more compelling incentives to concentrate on routine tasks in the Plan crowded out the effort that would otherwise have gone into monitoring the satellites.

The Soviet Union's failure to monitor its satellites' performance is one of the most striking facts to emerge from the former Soviet-bloc archives. Free of Soviet monitoring, the East Europeans ran roughshod over any treaty obligations that they preferred to ignore. The Soviet Union was able to overcome its other institutional shortcomings to some degree, and was consequently able to negotiate agreements with the satellites that seemed to safeguard many of its economic interests. Its failure to enforce these agreements, however, meant that everything that had been laboriously gained was easily lost.

It must be remembered that each of these bargaining failures was generated by Soviet institutions, which had been replicated in detail in each of the East European satellites. Central planning, quantitative quotas, and ratcheting were as typical in Eastern Europe as they were in the land of their birth, although varying degrees of economic reform had made the resulting incentive distortions less severe in some countries. As the following chapters will amply demonstrate, each of the difficulties that the Soviet Union faced in economic management was shared by its trading partners. Because of one key situational variable, however, these shared inefficiencies became East European assets and Soviet liabilities. That variable was the Soviet trade subsidy. Because the subsidy had emerged in the early decades of Soviet domination of Eastern Europe, the status quo point by the 1970s and 1980s was highly favorable to the East Europeans. To reduce the trade subsidy, the Soviet Union had to raise the quality level of East European exports, which involved solving intricate technical and managerial problems. To resist, on the other hand, the East Europeans had only to rely on the natural inertia of their own economies. To move away from the status quo, it was the Soviet Union that had to make credible commitments. The East Europeans, however, had no need to make credible commitments in order to preserve the privileges they already enjoyed. The Soviet Union found its bargaining position weakened because it was unable to forge linkages between trade flows managed by different bureaucratic entities. It enjoyed excess bargaining power as the provider of the subsidy, so the failure of linkage was a disability. The East Europeans faced similar rigidities, albeit on a smaller scale; but there was no loss of bargaining power as a result, because they had no excess bargaining power to squander. Finally, it was the Soviet Union that was compelled to monitor joint undertakings to prevent cheating; the East Europeans had no need to monitor in order to pursue their preferred strategy of evasion. In short, darkness hampers the movements of both the policeman and the thief, but the thief perceives this to be an advantage.

THE PERSISTENCE OF INEFFICIENT INSTITUTIONS

If Soviet institutions created such perverse incentives that Soviet policy-makers failed to achieve their goals over a period of decades, the economies of the Soviet bloc stagnated, and the material underpinnings of the alliance gradually crumbled, why did those institutions persist? How is it that inefficient structures have such staying power in human affairs that whole societies must be reduced to poverty before their premises may be reexamined? This book does not attempt to provide a comprehensive answer. These questions will doubtless provide the subject for the controversies of twenty-first-century historiography, as future generations seek to come to grips with the defining events of the late twentieth century. Just as scholarly works on the French and Russian Revolutions have expanded more rapidly than catalogers can catalog and libraries can shelve, the question of why the Soviet dinosaur failed to reform itself will create its own plethora of speculations.

Focusing on institutional incentive structures, however, makes it possible to identify some of the major obstacles to institutional reform. Soviet reformers faced an inescapable information problem: How were they to identify problems and match them with solutions? The very incentive structure that prevented subordinates from reporting policy failures also kept them from reporting failures of institutional design. The fundamental problem was that institutional reform requires good information about institutional performance, and quality information can only be obtained if the center can make credible commitments to act in good faith. The Soviet leadership could credibly commit to many things, such as to severe punishment, but seventy years of Soviet history made it difficult to make a credible commitment to follow fair procedures.

Soviet officials had no compelling reason to report institutional failures. Managers of less efficient organizations faced overcommitted resources and intense pressure to meet quantitative targets, so any lacuna in the planning system simply offered an opportunity to cut costs. Although it might be collectively rational to fix the information bottlenecks and create a more efficient system, it was individually rational to exploit any margin of error. In order to motivate subordinates to reveal information about institutional failures, therefore, the central authority would have to make a credible commitment that they would at least recoup the rents that they lost because of the tighter monitoring scheme. Managers of more efficient organizations faced a different incentive to suppress information. The more effective the internal Soviet monitoring system, the more information superiors would be able to gather about their subordinates' technological parameters. This information could be used in future periods to design reimbursement schemes that expropriated the more efficient organizations' rents. In order to motivate efficient firms to identify institutional flaws, therefore, the central authority would have to commit to refrain from expropriating those rents. Since the center was unable to make credible procedural commitments, the incentive remained to suppress information that would have underlined the need for systemic reform.

Compounding the incentive to suppress information, there was no guarantee that a whistle-blower would be protected. It was impossible to expose an incentive problem without exposing the behavior induced by it, and anyone close enough to a problem to identify it was probably implicated in the behavior. An observer who was not implicated would nevertheless be subject to the reprisals of those who were. The monitoring system therefore tended to deter revelations rather than reward them. Between any well-informed, low-level official who might be inclined to reveal potentially compromising information and any official who had sufficient seniority not to fear being personally implicated by its exposure, numerous levels of insecure bureaucrats intervened. At each level these officials were better informed than their superiors, so they were better positioned to punish leaks than their superiors were to protect the whistle-blowers. The hierarchy comprised so many levels, and so much misinformation was in circulation, that the information gap between the informed levels and the secure levels was formidable. As a result, it was difficult for senior officials to distinguish quality information from background noise, and also difficult to predict what a senior official might do if confronted with quality information. The benefit of sharing damaging information with high-level officials was dubious, and the more imminent prospect of punishment by the intermediate levels served to deter their exposure. Failing to report institutional failures, on the other hand, was a reliable strategy, because Soviet officials could not expect to be punished for failing to advocate reform. A code of silence, once established, tends to reinforce itself.

Theorists of institutions have gravitated toward this kind of explanation. As Kenneth Shepsle has argued, it is not sufficient to assert that institutions resolve coordination problems by providing equilibrium solutions, because the design of the institutions also represents a coordination problem. The only satisfying answer is that the institutions themselves are equilibrium solutions.[35] Along the same lines, Randall Calvert has argued that institutions tend to persist because they represent stable equilibria; that is, because they reinforce themselves.[36] If true, however, this holds both for efficient and inefficient institutions. Any complex logical problem has multiple equilibrium solutions, and if one represents a stable democracy, another may represent a stable dictatorship. In this sense, a perverse incentive structure can become an institutional performance trap, analogous to quicksand. Facing a code of silence, the dominant strategy for each individual is to suppress information and punish whistle-blowers.

At this point, a reasonable objection would be that the Soviet leadership could have broken the stalemate by initiating reforms that changed the incentives. Why did Soviet leaders fail to adapt? The apparent reason is that the leadership was caught in the feedback from its own institutional arrangements.[37] The leadership had to weigh the costs and benefits of any institutional reform subject to its own informational constraints. In trade with Eastern Europe, as in domestic economic policy and in a variety of other issue areas, the leadership was aware that outcomes were generally unsatisfactory. However, to return to the principal-agent framework discussed above, there were several parameters that the leadership could not have known. If a bad policy has a cost, that cost is composed of two components: a technological parameter representing the best feasible alternative policy, and a moral hazard parameter representing the degree of effort exerted by agents under the existing incentive scheme.

$$C = \beta - E$$

The leadership could only estimate the cost of the policy, and its estimates were always biased downward because agents faced weak incentives to invest in monitoring. In the case of trade relations with Eastern Europe, for example, the leadership often had no grasp of the many ways in which subtle shifts of terminology and slight changes of technical standards undermined the progress that had ostensibly been achieved. The leadership, furthermore, had no

[35]Shepsle, "Studying Institutions."

[36]Calvert, "The Rational Choice Theory of Social Institutions."

[37]Douglass North proposes a feedback mechanism as an explanation for path-dependent institutional development: different institutions motivate different levels and types of investment in knowledge, which in turn lead to different paths of institutional evolution. Some paths, he argues, are more efficient than others in the long run. Left unclear by his analysis, however, is why centralized decision makers would fail to converge on the more efficient institutional arrangements by making a series of random draws from the stock of knowledge. As becomes clear below, I resolve this problem by arguing that institutional arrangements may motivate agents to bias the information that central decision makers receive. Investing in the collection of more biased information does not make the biases go away, so there may be no convergence upon efficient solutions (see North, *Institutions, Institutional Change and Economic Performance*, chap. 11).

way to separate the effects of the technological parameter from the effects of the incentive structure that determined the agents' behavior. Thus the Politburo could not know whether the East European satellites were in fact incapable of producing better products or whether the Soviet negotiators were simply failing to compel them to do so. The Politburo's estimates of the best feasible alternative always had an unfavorable bias, because agents who bargained with the satellites had an incentive to represent the technological frontier as being less favorable than it really was. Consequently, the leadership underestimated the gap between its agents' performance and the opportunities offered by the best feasible alternative institutional arrangement. Believing that the outcome was better than it really was, that the technological frontier was less accommodating than it really was, and that the agents were performing better than they really were, the leadership underestimated the potential benefits of institutional reform, and refused to make the investment. The Soviet leadership was caught in an informational feedback loop. Given an inefficient institutional structure, it received biased information; given the biases, it failed to see the benefits of changing the structure; failing to change the structure, it perpetuated the incentives that created the biases. In the end, the cycle was broken only when a new generation of leaders rose to the top of the structure, a generation that had observed the failures of Soviet institutions from below.

This feedback process is illustrated by the history of the four major Soviet attempts to integrate the bloc. In each case the Soviet leadership recognized that policy outcomes were unsatisfactory, and it sought to revise foreign trade procedures, to create new institutions, and to establish incentive structures that would reward the accomplishment of priority tasks. In each case, however, the Soviet leadership received incomplete information about the causes of performance problems. The experts consistently tailored their advice to fit their superiors' expectations, careful not to advocate the kind of radical reform that they knew was required to change underlying incentives. The poorly informed leadership frequently rejected important elements of expert advice, made arbitrary changes, and rushed the pace of negotiations in ways that frustrated the development and implementation of its policies. Fundamentally, each integration program failed because it left unchanged the incentives that drove Soviet negotiators to sacrifice the long-term national interest to short-term expediency. Incentives to suppress information defeated every attempt to identify the problem and reform the system.

CONCLUSIONS

The Soviet bureaucracy allowed itself to be exploited because of a series of management failures that can be explained in terms of the growing principal-agent literature. Soviet officials were unable to drive hard bargains, to make credible commitments, to forge linkages between issues, and to enforce the agreements that were made. Each of these failures can be traced to perverse incentives imposed by Soviet institutions. Soviet political institutions failed to make credible procedural commitments to officials at lower levels of the hierarchy, so these officials were motivated to suppress information and to act according to planners' expectations rather than according to private knowledge. The same incentives to suppress information defeated attempts to reform the institutions, turning these inefficient arrangements into a self-reinforcing institutional performance trap.

The History of Subsidized Trade

As Soviet forces swept across the plains of northern Europe and into Berlin in May 1945, Stalin apparently had no long-term plans for Eastern Europe. As he faced his uncertain allies across the narrow line of the Elbe, he must have found himself with many more questions than answers. The United States emerged from the war as the world's preeminent military and economic power, and the British Empire still controlled a large portion of the earth's surface. It was surely an accident of history that had brought the Atlantic powers into alliance with the Communist Party of the Soviet Union. Under the circumstances, it was far from a settled question whether Stalin could expect to retain control of the territories he had conquered in the final months of the war.

Stalin's initial policy toward his new subjects was characteristically cautious, but it must have struck them as rather contradictory. On the one hand, he extended an olive branch by inviting all the East European political parties that had opposed the Nazis to join "Popular Front" governments. The offer was warmly welcomed by politicians who had found themselves in the opposition or in prison camps during the war, and it brought liberals, Christian Democrats, Socialists, and Communists together into coalition governments from the Baltic to the Black Sea. The Social Democrats in Germany, in particular, still blamed themselves for failing to form a wide enough coalition to prevent Hitler's rise to power, so the Popular Front approach had a certain appeal. On the other hand, Stalin began the postwar era with a rapacious policy of dismantling East and Central European industry to pay reparations for the war. The Soviet zone of Germany paid the greatest share of the reparations, followed by Hungary and Romania, which had been German allies, but each of the Soviet-occupied territories paid a heavy price. Factories were dismantled in Czechoslovakia, for example, on the grounds that they had belonged to Germans during the war. The Soviet Union also supplied the East European territories with food and other products that were necessary to prevent economic collapse, but for the first few postwar years, the guiding Soviet policy in Eastern Europe was to exact the maximum amount of tribute.

This two-pronged policy was cautious in several senses. If the Soviet Union were eventually compelled to renounce its territorial gains, it would at least have gained something tangible to help in postwar reconstruction. At the same time, dismantling industries in the region would weaken any potential aggressors that might later come to possess them, most notably Russia's traditional adversary, Germany. A cautious policy was also politically astute. In 1945 it was not yet clear how U.S. policy toward the Soviet Union would unfold. Could wartime cooperation continue for a time? Stalin pinned some hopes on an American credit, which he reasoned would help to rebuild the USSR while simultaneously averting a crash of the overheated U.S. economy. Would the United States withdraw from the European continent? That would be a great gain for Soviet security, and both the experience of World War I and Roosevelt's private assurances led Stalin to believe it was possible. Continuing cooperation and a U.S. withdrawal, however, depended on cordial relations and the avoidance of any major diplomatic crisis. In pursuit of these goals, therefore, Stalin allowed a degree of political pluralism to emerge in Eastern Europe, while assuring that his troops were well positioned to control the new territories if the need or opportunity presented itself.

There followed two years of cautious probing by the Soviet Union and gradual disillusionment on the part of the Western allies. The Soviet Union made several conciliatory moves, such as allowing the Austrian Communists to lose a free election and allowing the bourgeois Smallholders' Party to form a government in Hungary in the fall of 1945. Disputes flared, however, over delays in the promised withdrawal of Soviet troops from Iran, Soviet challenges to Turkish sovereignty over the Dardanelles Straits that lead into the Black Sea, and Soviet control of Poland. U.S. policy hardened after George Kennan's famous "Long Telegram," which described Soviet policy as implacably aggressive. Relations gradually worsened throughout 1946, and in the fall, Communists consolidated their control in Bulgaria and Romania. In March 1947 President Truman gave shape to the emerging U.S. policy when he appealed to Congress to provide funds to intervene in a mounting guerrilla war in Greece in language that sounded like a major escalation of the cold war: "It must be the policy of the United States to support free peoples who are resisting attempted subjugation by armed minorities or outside pressures." Historians tend to describe this appeal less as a major foreign policy departure than as a fateful change in public-relations strategy, one that colored U.S. popular perceptions of the unfolding struggle more than it influenced U.S. policy.[1] Nonetheless, the influence on Stalin's calculations was profound, particularly when linked to the Marshall Plan, which was announced in June.

The Soviet response to the new U.S. posture was to draw the dividing line across Europe more starkly. The Cominform, a reincarnation of the Comintern that was intended to coordinate the policies of all Communist Parties, was created in September 1947. This move signaled the end of the Popular Front strategy, and Andrei Zhdanov underlined the point in his opening speech to the conference by arguing that the world was now divided into "two

---

[1]See, for example, Gaddis, *Strategies of Containment*, pp. 22–23.

camps." During the fall Communists seized power in Hungary and Poland, and consolidated power in Bulgaria and Romania by staging show trials, absorbing the former socialist parties, and outlawing all opposition. In February 1948 Communists seized power in Czechoslovakia with the aid of threatening Soviet troop movements. Throughout the year communist consolidation progressed across Eastern Europe, and in January 1949 the Soviet Union, Bulgaria, Hungary, Poland, Romania, and Czechoslovakia formed the Council for Mutual Economic Assistance, or CMEA. The CMEA was an economic organization intended to funnel aid to its members, coordinate their economic policies, and counter the political appeal of the very effective European Recovery Program in Western Europe. It was not endowed with any authority, any significant functions, or any substantial staff, however, so for the first decade of its existence it lived only on paper. It remained for Nikita Khrushchev to attempt to breathe life into the legal structure inherited from Stalin.

The biggest prize to be won in Europe was a unified Germany, but it is unlikely that Stalin ever believed it could be won by the USSR. Early efforts went into establishing the German Communist Party exclusively in the Soviet Occupation Zone, and preparations for the ultimate division of Germany were made immediately by setting up local Party administrations and shadow ministries under German control. Furthermore, the forced merger of the East German Social Democrats with the German Communist Party to form the Socialist Unity Party (SED) in April 1946 so alienated the West German Social Democrats as to make a Popular Front strategy in the West impossible. Stalin apparently did not want the division of Germany to be finalized too soon, however. From his point of view, it was better for Germany to remain poor and poorly organized for as long as possible, particularly if two-thirds of it were to remain in the hands of his political opponents. As long as the prospect of reunification beckoned, Stalin could use his position on the Interallied Control Commission for Germany to obstruct postwar reconstruction and prevent Germany from rearming. Besides, if there were any chance of reunification on Soviet terms, it could only come about through a surprising surge in communist strength in the West, and that seemed most likely if economic conditions remained grim because of heavy reparations payments.

The strategy shifted as the Western powers gradually overcame their differences on German policy and moved toward creation of a true West German state.[2] The first step was the merging of the U.S. and British Occupation Zones at the beginning of 1947. In the months that followed it became clear that meetings of the Inter-allied Control Commission and the Council of For-

---

[2]The most comprehensive discussion of the politics of the division of Germany is in Schwarz, *Vom Reich zur Bundesrepublik*. A very thorough discussion from the point of view of the rearming of West Germany is Wettig, *Entmilitarisierung und Wiederbewaffnung in Deutschland*.

eign Ministers had become locked in stalemate, with the Western powers attempting to cooperate to rebuild Germany and the Soviet Union blocking every proposal and escalating its demands for restitution. To prevent the establishment of a West German state, Stalin was prepared to resort to a desperate gambit. Shortly before the Western allies were to sign the Frankfurt Documents, which committed them to West German autonomy and set them on the road to eventual German statehood, the Soviet Union blockaded all access to the Western sectors of Berlin on 24 June 1948. The Berlin Blockade ultimately failed, however, because of the surprising effectiveness of the Western air convoy. Its most important consequence was the opposite of what Stalin had intended: it galvanized the West's resolve, and led inexorably to the establishment of the Federal Republic of Germany (FRG) in September 1949. The German Democratic Republic (GDR) was proclaimed in East Berlin the next month.

Even so, it was several years before the GDR became a full-fledged member of the communist alliance. It was not admitted to the CMEA until September 1950, and it continued to pay war reparations to the Soviet Union until the beginning of 1954. The turning point was the popular uprising that took place in Berlin and in more than two hundred other cities and towns across the GDR on 17 June 1953. The Community Party leadership was compelled to flee the capital, and order was finally restored only with the intervention of a column of Soviet tanks. Walter Ulbricht, the SED leader, took the opportunity to fly to Moscow and make his case. The Communists would not be able to maintain political stability without improved economic conditions, he argued, and the reparation payments to the Soviet Union were strangling the East German economy. Moreover, the GDR was becoming increasingly essential to Soviet security as West Germany rearmed. He asked for an extensive revision of Soviet–East German trade relations. Reparations were canceled for the following year's plan, and the terms of trade between the GDR and the USSR were substantially revised in East Germany's favor. From that point on, the GDR was treated as the preeminent Soviet ally in Europe.

FROM EXPLOITATION TO SUBSIDIZATION

The precise moment when the Soviet Union ceased exploiting its satellites in Europe and began subsidizing them is difficult to pinpoint, and almost certainly varied from country to country. The Soviet Union did not attempt to keep precise records of the property that was appropriated in the form of reparations, and Soviet trade data were aggregated in a way that makes it difficult to determine exactly which goods were traded in each category and what prices were paid for them. It is clear, however, that the European members of the CMEA were receiving a substantial subsidy by the late 1950s, because they ran a trade surplus with the Soviet Union in the overpriced categories of machinery and equipment, and ran a deficit in the subsidized categories of energy and raw materials. Czechoslovakia probably received the subsidy first, because its highly developed machine industries were least damaged during the war, and consequently were able to supply the whole bloc with a series of profitable export lines. Czechoslovak planners testify that for the first two decades after the CMEA was formed, their bargaining position was very comfortable, because they could essentially sell anything that they desired to produce.[3] The GDR likely received a net subsidy once its reparation payments were canceled in 1954, because it too exported large and rapidly growing quantities of machinery.

The turning point for Poland and Hungary very likely came in the fateful year of 1956. The first decade after the war saw the unfolding of a deadly and covert struggle within the Communist parties of the Soviet bloc between hardline, Stalinist factions and more moderate, reformist ones. As Stalin forsook his Popular Front strategy, the Communist Parties across Eastern Europe purged themselves. Leaders who had spent the war years organizing partisan resistance at home and who held ideas too independent of Moscow, such as Władisław Gomułka in Poland, were gradually removed from positions of influence and were imprisoned. Show trials and widespread executions followed. This "Stalinization" phase ended abruptly, however, when Stalin died in March 1953, the Soviet Politburo arrested his chief of police, Lavrentii Beria, and the new Soviet leader, Georgi Malenkov, announced his reformist "New Course" policy. There followed a period of watchful waiting, as a new power struggle played itself out in Moscow. Nikita Khrushchev, the new Central Committee first secretary, appeared to outmaneuver Malenkov on the left by urging concentration on heavy industry and a more aggressive foreign policy. When he finally consolidated his power, however, he shook the communist establishment by exposing a portion of Stalin's crimes in his famous "Secret Speech" to the Twentieth Party Congress in February 1956.[4] This bold first step was followed by another, as Khrushchev negotiated a warming of relations with Yugoslavia, which Stalin had excommunicated from the bloc because Marshal Tito had been unwilling to follow his lead. A joint Soviet-Yugoslav communiqué in June spoke of a "diversity of socialisms," which opened the door to a substantially greater degree of autonomy in Eastern Europe.

These events seem to have signaled the beginning of a new round of feuding within the East European Communist Parties. The reformist faction had been making steady progress in Poland since Gomułka's release at the end of

[3]Interviews with Vladislav Cihlař, 6.17.1992, and Zdeněk Šedivý, 6.30.1992.

[4]This story has been told elsewhere in much more detail. See, for example, Fainsod, *How Russia Is Ruled*; Shapiro, *The Communist Party of the Soviet Union*; and Heller and Nekrich, *Utopia in Power*.

1954, and in Hungary the reformer Imre Nagy had been stripped of his influential positions in 1955. In the summer of 1956 hard-line Stalinists made dramatic moves in both countries to consolidate their positions. In June Polish members of the hard-line Natolin faction apparently provoked strikes that erupted in a Poznan automobile factory, which were put down with great loss of life, and subsequently used the strikes to appeal to Moscow to intervene in Poland and remove the reformers. In July the Hungarian general secretary, Matyas Rakosi, urged his Central Committee to purge the reformist opposition. This time, it was the reformers who appealed to the Soviet Union for protection, and apparently the request was honored. Soviet Politburo member Anastas Mikoyan arrived in Budapest, and Rakosi was immediately replaced as general secretary by a more moderate politician, Ernö Gerö.

The Soviet Union scrambled to bring stability back to its satellites, but the situation in both countries was rapidly slipping out of control.[5] In Poland a failed hard-line coup in October shook the existing ruling coalition in Warsaw, and the more moderate Władisław Gomułka was able to seal alliances that brought him back to power. Four Soviet Politburo members headed by Khrushchev flew to Poland and Soviet troops advanced on Warsaw, but somehow Gomułka convinced the Soviets that he was the leader who could best guarantee a loyal and stable Poland, and the decision was made not to intervene. Even while the negotiations were going on in Warsaw, however, demonstrations broke out in Budapest, followed by a general uprising that brought Imre Nagy back as premier. The Soviet leadership was apparently troubled not so much by the return of Nagy as by the way it came about, and by the fact that order seemed to be unraveling rapidly in Budapest. The evidence indicates that the Soviet Union decided to intervene in Hungary on October 30; two days later, after becoming aware of Soviet intentions, Nagy withdrew Hungary from the Warsaw Pact and appealed to the West for aid. On the same day, November 1, massed Soviet troops entered Hungary and swiftly crushed the revolt. Any possibility that the West might have interfered was removed by the simultaneous eruption of the Suez crisis, in which Britain, France, and Israel sought to regain control of the Suez Canal from Egypt.

The frightening emergence of instability on the East European frontier reinforced Khrushchev's instinct to transform the bloc into a true alliance of socialist states by extending substantial autonomy to its members. At the same time it underlined the lesson of the 1953 uprising in the GDR: the East European regimes will only be stable so long as they are economically prosperous. The year 1956 was a turning point in Soviet economic policy toward the bloc. The USSR provided substantial aid to Hungary in the wake of the rebellion, which allowed the new Kadar regime to consolidate power without

---

[5]For a more comprehensive discussion of the Polish and Hungarian crises of 1956, see Brzezinski, *The Soviet Bloc.*

alienating the population. It also renegotiated its terms of trade with Poland. Gomułka flew to Moscow late in 1956 with two major demands: an increase in the price of Polish coal and the return of Polish prisoners of war. Both requests were granted. After 1956 the East Europeans were granted an annual subsidy. In the 1950s Soviet planners did not expect to face any restraints on their raw material supply, and they had an almost inexhaustible demand for finished products from industry and the huge Soviet population. Trading raw materials for finished goods therefore seemed initially to be a rather painless way to support socialism abroad.

FROM SUBSIDIZATION TO INTEGRATION

In the 1960s two more factors came to have an important impact on Soviet policy toward Eastern Europe. The first was the rift with China, which began to spread as early as 1957 but shook the socialist world like an earthquake in the early 1960s. The stresses of maintaining relations with the Chinese, despite their extreme ideological formulations and eccentric policy shifts, colored the Soviet Union's relations with each of its satellites. Relations with Yugoslavia were severely damaged, because Khrushchev felt compelled to join the strident Chinese criticisms of the Yugoslav model of communism at a particularly fragile juncture in Sino-Soviet relations, and relations with Albania were severed abruptly when that small country allied itself with the Chinese side in the Sino-Soviet struggle. As the alliance with China became increasingly fragile, the Soviet leadership cast about for ways to compensate for the weakening of the bloc, and found them in Eastern Europe. At the same time a new threat seemed to be emerging from Europe. The Treaty of Rome, signed in 1957, launched the European Economic Community. The Schuman Plan, to link the destinies of West Germany and France by creating an iron and steel consortium, was proving itself to be a brilliant success. NATO had fully integrated the Federal Republic of Germany into the defense of Europe, and it now represented a formidable opponent. The German *Wirtschaftswunder*, or economic miracle, was rapidly turning West Germany into the envy of Europe. This had to be unsettling to Russians, particularly to Russians who had been raised on materialist philosophy. The solution appeared to be to foster East European economic integration in order to balance the economic cooperation emerging in Western Europe.

Khrushchev made the first efforts to promote East European integration with the Soviet Union, and he began by increasing the importance of the CMEA. The first CMEA Branch Commissions were established in 1956 to promote economic cooperation among member countries' ministries responsible for particular branches of industry. In 1958 CMEA meetings were regularized, national representatives were granted more authority, and a long-term goal was set of coordinating capital investment plans. In the next year the CMEA finally adopted a legal charter. In 1962 it resolved that national representatives to the CMEA should hold the rank of deputy premiers, and it adopted the "Basic Principles of the Socialist Division of Labor," which foresaw a gradual integration of the socialist economies based on coordination of short-term and long-term plans. Realist authors have generally framed these changes as part of a struggle between Khrushchev and the satellites over East European economic dependence on the Soviet Union. In this tradition, Zbigniew Brzezinski argues that the degree of economic dependence of each satellite on the Soviet Union was the chief barometer of political loyalty.[6] Consequently, he treated the revitalization of the CMEA under Khrushchev as the beginning of "real efforts for the consolidation of the East European part of the camp."[7]

This interpretation has been furthered by a consistent misinterpretation in Western scholarship of the significance of a proposal made by Khrushchev in 1962 for a dramatic push for East European integration based on joint planning of the whole region by a single Gosplan.[8] Substantial evidence suggests that this was never a serious Soviet proposal. First, the proposal does not appear on the agenda of any CMEA Sessions (annual meetings of the premiers of the CMEA countries), which would have had to discuss it before it could be adopted. Second, East European negotiators who were interviewed did not regard the proposal as serious, and none could remember an incident when it was actually put on the table for formal discussion.[9] Third, Soviet experts did not regard the proposal as practically feasible because of the extreme size and complexity of the task. Soviet Gosplan was not in a position to take over responsibility for Eastern Europe, and no other organization could take over the tasks of Gosplan.[10] Finally, one well-connected Soviet official provided an alternative explanation for the speech. He claimed that the Central Committee had subsequently conducted an internal investigation to determine its origins, and had discovered that the document had been written by a nonspecialist without going through the proper channels. Khrushchev had read it but had not been committed to the idea, and the specialists on Eastern Europe had done their best to bury it.[11]

[6]Ibid., pp. 476–77.

[7]Ibid., p. 456.

[8]See, for example, Kaser, *Comecon*, pp. 93–95. Khrushchev outlined his proposal in Khruschev, "Nasushchnye voprosy," *Kommunist* no. 12 (1962), and in a speech to the CPSU Central Committee on 19 November 1962.

[9]Interviews with Zdeněk Šedivý, 6.30.1992; Istvan Hetenyi, 9.3.1992; and Akos Balassa, 9.9.1992

[10]Interviews with Oleg Rybakov, 3.9.1992; Leonid Krasnov, 2.27.1992.

[11]Interview with Iurii Pekshev, former Head, Group of Economic Consultants, Department for Relations with Socialist Countries, CC CPSU, 3.10.1992.

The greatest mistake of Khrushchev's tenure as first secretary was the failure to recognize the limits of Soviet economic expansion. Khrushchev's guiding assumption was that more was better, and that employing the traditional instruments of Soviet economic planning with greater vigor would lead to ever-increasing rates of economic growth. One of his first policy victories as first secretary was the adoption of the Virgin Lands Resolution, which sought to solve Soviet agricultural problems by expanding the cultivation of marginal land. The predictable result was that yields quickly fell as the soil was depleted by overuse and erosion. Similarly, he emphasized investment in heavy industry and chemical production, but neglected advanced technologies. It was probably these economic mistakes, rather than the public embarrassment of the Cuban Missile Crisis, that galvanized the coalition that removed him from power in a bloodless coup in October 1964. As the 1960s wore on, it became increasingly clear that Soviet and East European industry were falling far behind the West in terms of quality, labor productivity, and efficient utilization of raw materials, and physical resources began to figure as a key constraint in the Soviet economic Plan. Only a shrinking minority of Soviet-bloc products remained competitive on world markets, and most of those were raw materials. Even Soviet military technology, which received the highest priority, rapidly fell behind that of the West.

The new Brezhnev regime sought to correct these problems by redirecting investment into science and technology. "Intensification" became a watchword of the new policy. The goal was to create new potential for intensive growth by improving the quality and technical specifications of products, rather than concentrating on extensive growth or expanding productivity by increasing the volume of raw material inputs. One sign of the new policy line was the creation of a powerful new State Committee for Science and Technology (GKNT), headed by a deputy premier, out of a former division of the State Planning Commission, Gosplan. The Brezhnev leadership became convinced that applying "scientific management" would unlock hidden reserves in the planned economy and allow the socialist countries to overtake the West in the race for advanced technology.[12]

The shift in Soviet domestic priorities led to a reorientation of Soviet policy toward Eastern Europe. This was the era of the great initiatives to integrate the bloc, starting with the Comprehensive Program for Socialist Economic Integration, which was signed in 1971. Authors of a realist persuasion have typically treated the emergence of these programs, and the controversies surrounding them, as evidence of an epic sub-rosa struggle over economic autonomy and domination in the bloc. Raymond Garthoff, for example, ar-

[12]For an excellent discussion of the intellectual roots of scientific management, see Beissinger, *Scientific Management.*

gues that the Comprehensive Program of 1971 was part of an effort to "strengthen the economic, political and military relationships binding the East European countries" together against the double impact of détente with the West and dissension within.[13] Similarly, other authors have treated the emergence of each new document about CMEA integration as evidence of Soviet ambitions to increase East European economic dependence. Helene Carrere d'Encausse views the Joint Plan for Integration Measures, signed in 1975, and the Long-Term Target Programs, signed in 1978 and 1979, as measures aimed at "strengthening Soviet ascendency over its allies."[14] Karen Dawisha describes the 1984 CMEA Summit as a confrontation between Soviet integration goals and East European notions of national self-determination.[15]

The programs did indeed seek to increase the economic integration of the bloc. They were designed to achieve large-scale objectives by pooling resources, and to expand East European trade, which was at a very low level compared to that of West European countries. These objectives, however, were never controversial; in fact, the East Europeans provided most of the pressure for infrastructure investments to facilitate Soviet energy exports and expanded trade in subsidized goods. The controversy over integration, rather, concerned the Soviet Union's attempts to restrict the subsidy by improving its terms of trade.

Gosplan came under new pressure to revise Soviet terms of trade with Eastern Europe in the 1970s as Soviet growth rates slowed, and the cost of raw material production in the Soviet Union steadily climbed. Meanwhile, rising world energy prices caused the subsidy to soar, while East European machinery exports lagged further and further behind world standards. As a result, East European living standards rose much more rapidly than those of the Soviet Union. Confidential reports brought the trade subsidy to the attention of the leadership. A report written by the Institute for the Economy of the World Socialist System as early as 1966 urged a revision of the "unfavorable" structure of Soviet foreign trade, arguing that the prices of finished and primary goods in the CMEA made it unprofitable to export primary goods and import finished goods.[16] Soviet experts argued that comparisons of the relative costs of producing a ruble of machinery exports and a ruble of raw material exports demonstrated conclusively that machinery prices were subsidized. One report estimated that the average investment necessary to produce Soviet exports of raw materials was 3 to 3.5 times greater than that needed to substitute for equivalent Soviet imports of machinery and equipment from Eastern

[13]Garthoff, *Détente and Confrontation*, p. 498.
[14]Helene Carrere d'Encausse, *Big Brother*, p. 260.
[15]Dawisha, *Eastern Europe, Gorbachev and Reform*, pp. 93–94.
[16]IEMSS report, 4.5.1966, IMEPI Archive pp. 2–3, 8.

Europe, and that it took 5 to 8 times more capital investment to earn a ruble by exporting raw materials than by exporting machinery.[17] Another report calculated that it was substantially more expensive to import machinery from Eastern Europe than to produce it domestically: 32 percent more expensive from Czechoslovakia and East Germany, 28 percent more from Hungary, and 20 percent more from Poland.[18] An Academy of Sciences report argued that the Soviet Union faced "heavy losses" because of the mounting expense of producing raw materials for export, citing a Gosplan estimate that the average cost of producing one ruble of exports of finished goods was 60 kopeks, whereas the same figure for raw materials and energy exports was 2.40 rubles.[19] Noting that equipment comprised only 35 percent of Soviet exports, compared to 70 percent of U.S. exports, the Academy of Sciences report concluded that "the commodity structure of USSR trade does not correspond to its scientific and technical potential or to progressive tendencies in the development of world trade."[20]

Subsequent reports argued that the CMEA pricing system failed to account for costs of Soviet raw material exports that were higher than the world average. As the 1960s and 1970s wore on, sources of easily exploitable ores, fuels, and materials were used up, and new, more distant and physically forbidding sources had to be found and developed. The center of gravity of Soviet mining moved east and north, into regions that were either so cold or so hot and dry that special equipment had to be used and special health precautions had to be taken. The cost of transportation rose proportionately. As a result of increased costs and rising East European demand, one IEMSS report estimated, Soviet investments in raw material production would have to rise by 250 to 300 percent between 1970 and 1980, or by approximately 25 to 30 billion rubles.[21] A subsequent position paper, produced by IEMSS in 1973, argued that increasing costs made it imperative to change dramatically the structure of Soviet foreign trade in order to reduce the foreign trade subsidy. Table 2.1, which proposes target proportions for Soviet trade structure to reach by 1990, is taken from the report. Actual 1970 figures are supplied for comparison. These 1990 goals were utopian, even by Soviet standards. A

[17] Bogomolov et al., "O nekotorykh voprosakh povysheniia effektivnosti sotrudnichestva," to Mikhail A. Lesechko, Deputy Chairman for CMEA Issues, Council of Ministers, 2.16.1971, IMEPI Archive, IEMSS report, p. 2.

[18] Bogomolov, "O perspektivakh razvitiia vneshneekonomicheskikh sviazei SSSR," 10.27.1972, IMEPI Archive, IEMSS report, p. 29.

[19] AN SSSR, "Razvitie vneshneekonomicheskikh sviazei Sovetskogo Soiuza do 1990 g.," 1.2.1973 (ten copies), pp. 7, 12. The report was based on a series of drafts by IEMSS.

[20] Ibid., p. 5.

[21] Bogomolov et al., "O nekotorykh voprosakh povysheniia effektivnosti sotrudnichestva," to Mikhail A. Lesechko, Deputy Chairman for CMEA Issues, Council of Ministers, 2.16.1971, IMEPI Archive, IEMSS report, p. 2.

TABLE 2.1
IEMSS Proposed Trade Guidelines (percentage)

	Soviet Export		Soviet Import	
	Total 1970	To CMEA 1990	Total 1970	From CMEA 1990
Machinery and equipment	21.5	67	35.1	14
Raw materials	48.8	5.5	21.9	62
Chemicals	18.6	9.2	8.9	4
Food products	8.4	9.5	15.8	6
Consumer goods	2.7	3.7	18.3	14

Source: V. M. Shastitko, "O perspektivakh razvitiia vneshneekonomicheskikh sviazei SSSR s sotsialisticheskimi stranami v period do 1990 g.," IMEPI Archive, Pervyi otdel, IEMSS report, Table 2, p. 22; 1970 figures are from *Statisticheskii ezhegodnik stran-chlenov Soveta Ekonomicheskoi Vzaimopomoschi, 1971*, and *Narodnoe khoziaistvo SSSR, 1971*.

report by the research institute of the Ministry of Foreign Trade came to substantially the same conclusions about the subsidization of Eastern Europe and the need to reorient Soviet foreign trade, but set a more modest goal of reducing the share of energy and raw materials to 25 percent of Soviet exports to Eastern Europe by 1990.[22]

In the late 1960s Soviet policy began to seek a revision of the prevailing terms of trade. At the level of bilateral trade negotiations, the policy shift was felt in a steady tightening of the Soviet bargaining position. It became increasingly difficult for the East Europeans to obtain additional raw material deliveries, exports came with increasing numbers of conditions attached, and there was increasing pressure on the East Europeans to improve the quality of their exports. At the multilateral level, the new policy meant that the East Europeans were compelled to contribute to Soviet investments in raw-material production, and to join complex specialization schemes intended to increase the proportion of technologically advanced products in their exports.

The East Europeans vigorously opposed integration proposals designed to reduce the subsidy. As chapters 6 through 9 will show, the Soviet negotiators had success in the initial phases of negotiation of each program, but they failed to translate general commitments into concrete undertakings. As the work on each program became more detailed and concrete, the East Europeans were able to whittle down the obligations they had to assume and soften the technical standards they had to meet. Finally, when it was time to implement each program, the satellites found ways to dodge most of the re-

[22]NIKI MVT SSSR, *Doklad o perspektivakh razvitiia vneshnei torgovli SSSR do 1990 g.*, pp. 21–26.

maining conditions that they found onerous. As a result, the Soviet Union did not achieve any of its major goals in economic relations with its satellites from the late 1960s to the collapse of the bloc in 1989. This book argues that the reason for the stunning failure of Soviet policy was that incentive structures in the Soviet bureaucracy were perverse, neither motivating officials to pursue the leadership's objectives nor allowing them to do their own jobs competently.

REFORM AND REVOLUTION

Soviet economic policy toward the satellites remained essentially paralyzed for more than twenty years, unable to achieve its objectives or to provide a flexible response to political crises. Furthermore, the Soviet Union was unable to exploit its trade subsidy as a tool to control the satellites. In the 1970s Soviet influence in Eastern Europe was in a steep decline, just as the Soviet subsidy spiraled upward out of control. The growing rift with China split the international communist movement, and a number of West European Communist Parties began to strike more autonomous poses. Meanwhile, across Eastern Europe, the gap widened between the rising expectations of the captive populations for material well-being and personal freedom, and the stagnating potential of the socialist economic engine.

These pressures ushered in a profound reevaluation of the utility of the socialist model throughout Eastern Europe and the Soviet Union. The slowing of growth rates after the initial burst of industrialization caused the countries of Eastern Europe to take stock of their situations and introduce management changes. The discussions of the Economic Commission of the CMEA were filled with reformist proposals during the 1960s. Reformers like Michał Kalecki and Oscar Lange in Poland, Ota Šik in Czechoslovakia, and Rezsö Nyers in Hungary urged the adoption of market-type reforms and more flexible forms of planning in order to overcome the characteristic failure of Soviet-type economies to innovate. Some of these proposals seemed to strike a responsive chord in the Soviet Union, and in March 1965 the Kosygin reforms took the first hesitant steps in this direction. These moves created an atmosphere that allowed discussion to take place, and the negotiations over the CMEA Comprehensive Program, which began in the spring of 1968, were dominated by the question of how far reform should be allowed to go.

The momentum for reform was abruptly shattered on 21 August 1968, when Warsaw Pact forces from the Soviet Union, Poland, the GDR, Hungary, and Bulgaria invaded Czechoslovakia. Events moved so quickly that most of the world was taken by surprise. Alexander Dubček had come to power in January and quickly initiated widespread changes in top-level personnel, followed by rapid liberalization in the press, and much discussion of economic and political reform. In April the Communist Party published an Action Program for political and economic reform, and in June the censor was abolished. The Czechoslovak press quickly filled the country's neighbors with apprehension because of its radical sentiments, and neighboring leaders Walter Ulbricht and Władisław Gomułka called for Soviet intervention. In August, following several days of intense conversations between the Soviet and Czechoslovak Politburos, the Soviet leadership decided to invade.[23]

This episode set the tone for future discussions of economic reform under Brezhnev. It is likely that the 1968 crisis solidified the coalition that gave Leonid Brezhnev unquestioned sway in Soviet politics, and undermined the position of Aleksei Kosygin along with the reform package that has become associated with his name. Throughout the 1970s the Soviet Union pressed its allies not to deviate too far from the Soviet example. The Hungarian New Economic Mechanism, which was inaugurated in 1968 and took Hungary furthest down the reform path, was subjected to the closest scrutiny. On several occasions Yurii Andropov was dispatched to Budapest to deliver stern warnings that the Soviet Politburo was becoming concerned about the extent of Kadar's reforms. Finally, in 1974, Brezhnev intervened personally and demanded the resignations of four reformist members of the Hungarian Socialist Workers' Party Politburo: Rezsö Nyers, HSWP secretary for economics; Jenö Fock, Hungarian premier; Lajos Feher, deputy premier for agriculture; and Györgi Aczel, HSWP secretary for culture.[24]

There were important limits, however, to the degree of interference that the Soviet Union was willing to impose on its satellites. Yurii Andropov, who had been Central Committee secretary for relations with ruling Communist Parties before he became chairman of the KGB, provided a rationale for the Brezhnev policy. Eastern Europe could best be managed from a distance, he argued, relying on local elites whenever possible and intervening only when absolutely necessary.[25] The degree of East European autonomy was enhanced, furthermore, by important disagreements within the upper-level Soviet leadership. Kosygin remained premier until his death in 1980, and continued to undermine the antireform tendencies in the leadership by making private statements supporting East European reforms. Andropov himself shielded a number of reformist officials, most notably Oleg Bogomolov, who exercised

---

[23]The most thorough treatment of the developments in Czechoslovakia in 1968 is in Skilling, *Czechoslovakia's Interrupted Revolution*.

[24]Interview with Rezsö Nyers, former HSWP Secretary for the Economy, 9.10.1992.

[25]Interview with Rezsö Nyers, 9.10.1992. The Soviet Union did have the capacity to remove recalcitrant leaders in Eastern Europe, as is demonstrated by the case of Walter Ulbricht in the GDR. Resisting the new Soviet policy of détente with West Germany, Ulbricht was publicly criticized in the Soviet press, and was replaced in May 1971 by his heir apparent, Erich Honecker. It is significant that the Soviets did not attempt a full-scale housecleaning, however, but rather relied on the fragile balance of power in the SED to provide an alternative leader (see Childs, *The GDR*, pp. 80–83).

considerable influence as director of the Institute for the Economy of the World Socialist System. Further, the Central Committee bureaucracy was split on the issue of East European reform. The Ideology Department, dominated by Mikhail Suslov, took a strident Stalinist position, whereas the Department for Relations with Ruling Communist Parties, headed by Konstantin Katushev, held a much more moderate view.

The fate of economic reform in Eastern Europe had much more to do with the internal factional politics of each regime than with the sporadic interference of the Soviet Union. The overthrow of Gomułka in Poland in 1970, for example, was an internal affair, precipitated by unforeseen strikes in Gdansk but made possible by the growing political weight of the Silesian faction in the Polish Central Committee. It started a chain of events that moved Poland to the brink of revolution. The new regime of Edward Gierek began an ambitious program of Western-financed investment, which well-placed advisers argue was seen as an alternative to reform.[26] The new Polish premier, Piotr Jaroszewicz, believed that borrowing from the West would allow Poland to simultaneously satisfy the wants of its population and create a modern, new export sector that would pay off the debt. Unfortunately, the regime channeled the lion's share of the new resources into flashy consumption goods and wasteful political patronage. Suppressed inflation undermined the living standards of Polish workers, and in June 1976 attempts to raise food prices led to riots. In the following years the economic vise tightened as Poland's export earnings failed to keep pace with its mounting interest payments. Another attempt to raise prices in July 1980 led to widespread strikes, the founding of the Solidarity movement, and the fall of Gierek. His successor, Stanisław Kania, also was unable to stabilize the situation, and was replaced by General Wojciech Jaruzelski, who quickly moved to impose martial law in December 1981.

The crises in Czechoslovakia and Poland revealed a general malaise within the socialist camp. Political dissidence was on the rise throughout the socialist world, and it had become increasingly articulate and increasingly visible in the West. The debt crisis that gripped Poland was felt with varying degrees of severity throughout Eastern Europe, and was most disastrous in Romania. Central planners across the region found themselves struggling with the rising expectations of their populations, declining potential for economic growth, and an increasingly vicious scramble for scarce resources among politically influential industrial managers. The gap between East and West European living standards became obvious to anyone permitted to travel, and the qualitative advantages of Western products came to be widely appreciated. It is in this context that the origins of Mikhail Gorbachev's policy of perestroika have to be understood.

[26]Interviews with Jozef Pajestka, 5.27.1992; Stanisław Kuziński, 6.3.1992; and Paweł Bożyk, 5.7.1992.

Gorbachev came to power in March 1985, in many respects a typical product of the Soviet bureaucratic milieu. He had served as a local Party first secretary, had become an agricultural specialist with a correspondence degree, and then held a succession of high posts in the Central Committee. He assumed the Party leadership with substantial conservative support, and must have appeared to be a rather unlikely reformer. The times in which he was compelled to take charge of the unwieldy socialist alliance, however, were destined to make unlikely reformers out of many traditional officials. Soviet political institutions created powerful disincentives for low-level officials to share uncomfortable information with their superiors, and as a result, the older generation had been largely shielded from the dawning awareness in officialdom that the socialist model was failing. Younger officials, however, were forced to deal with the reality of these failures as they rose through the hierarchy. The new leadership team that Gorbachev assembled—Ligachev, Ryzhkov, Chebrikov, Shevardnadze, Yakovlev—although they disagreed on many specific policies, and years later became bitter opponents, shared a broad awareness in 1985 that new solutions had to be found.

Gorbachev began with a series of modest steps to strengthen his own political position, to loosen the restraints on public discussion of social and economic problems, and to launch a few moderate reforms. For a time, official opinion teetered between an unfounded optimism that somehow Gorbachev would resolve seventy years of pent-up contradictions and revive a more humane socialism, and a stark pessimism that more sinister forces would inevitably reemerge. Meanwhile, the irrepressible logic of Soviet incentive structures reasserted itself to frustrate partial reforms. Under conditions of uncertainty, and having few protections against offended superiors, mid-level officials sought to paper over problems rather than draw attention to them. Unable to properly identify problems or solutions, the reformers were left like blindfolded dart players, compelled to cast about for targets but afraid to do so. The partial solutions that were advanced collided with underlying incentive structures that had not yet been addressed. Granted the right to elect their managers, workers' collectives asked for whom they were expected to vote. Given new authority to collaborate in setting priorities for planning, managers focused on the indicators that were easy to monitor in order to protect themselves, and continued to produce inefficient assortments of goods and to cut corners on quality. The more management was decentralized, the more the perverse incentives in the system to hoard resources and to hide excess capacity came to the fore.

The agonizing process of domestic reform and the effort to reduce tensions with the United States usurped most high-level attention, but the realization dawned gradually in the Soviet leadership that a crisis was looming in economic relations with Eastern Europe. The debt squeeze was becoming acute, the quality of the region's products had fallen far below world levels, and

Soviet subsidies to the region were becoming an intolerable burden. A report to the Communist Party Central Committee toward the end of Gorbachev's first year in power argues that the East European countries found cooperation with the Soviet Union increasingly unattractive in spite of rising subsidies.

> The countries are becoming increasingly dissatisfied with the state of cooperation and the circumstances under which it is carried out. The other countries of the CMEA face deteriorating terms of trade with our country, which is their basic foreign partner. They are compelled to export ever-increasing volumes of their products in return for a unit of import from the USSR: 28 percent more in 1984 than in 1980. In combination with other factors, in particular the need to repay their debt to Western countries, this has unavoidably impaired the CMEA countries' economic development and slowed their growth (from 4.1 percent in 1976–80 to 3.1 percent in 1981–84), and in a few cases (Hungary, Romania, and to a degree Czechoslovakia) has reduced the living standards of the population.
>
> For its part, the USSR has been compelled to extend credits in order to rectify the balance of payments. Taking this into account in addition to price advantages, the actual subsidization of the European countries of the CMEA by the USSR amounted to approximately 18 billion rubles between 1981 and 1984. This comes as the equivalency of the Soviet Union's trade with the European states is declining, because the share of "hard" goods is 70–80 percent in Soviet exports to those countries, and only 40–50 percent in their exports to the USSR.
>
> In all the countries, the interest in cooperation is falling because of the quality and technical level of the goods being exchanged. The share of our machinery exports to the fraternal countries that is competitive on the world market does not exceed 15 percent, and that in their exports to the USSR is 25 percent (according to Ministry of Foreign Trade figures).[27]

Rising oil prices damaged the East European economies, but since CMEA prices lagged behind world prices, rising world prices pushed the Soviet subsidy up as well. Meanwhile, the quality of machinery available for export in the socialist world had so declined that the East European countries had little incentive to trade with one another. What had been a serious problem in the early 1970s had grown into a crisis of threatening proportions by the mid-1980s.

The Gorbachev regime attempted to solve these problems by reforming economic relations with the East European satellites, but this effort, too, collided with an underlying set of incentives that was more compelling. Most of the details of the Gorbachev proposal, such as price reform, trading in hard currency, and amending national legal codes to allow enterprises to trade with each other directly, were already contained in proposals that Poland, Hungary,

[27]V.M. Shastitko et al., "Tezisy vystupleniia 'O dolgosrochnoi strategii,'" to O. A. Chukanov, CC CPSU, 11.28.1985, IMEPI Archive, IEMSS report, pp. 2–3.

and Czechoslovakia had made to the CMEA in 1968. In a sense, therefore, discussion of reform had come full circle. Nevertheless, by the late 1980s, suspicion overwhelmed optimism in the East European capitals. There was little faith that the Soviet Union could reform its own domestic economy, which was the prerequisite for meaningful reform of Soviet–East European trade. Moreover, the gradual intensification of Soviet efforts to reduce the subsidy during bilateral trade negotiations in the 1980s left the East Europeans suspicious that the true aim of the reform program was to improve Soviet terms of trade. Throughout the process of negotiating the trade plan for 1991 to 1995, the outlines of which were largely complete by the end of 1989, the East Europeans cast aside reformist notions in favor of the traditional counters of unilateral advantage: quantitative quotas for machinery and raw materials. The result was that the reform was superficial. The underlying structure of trade was still determined by illiberal considerations such as distorted prices and relative bargaining power.

The demise of the Soviet bloc came about through a series of events that none of the major players desired or accurately foresaw. Pandora's box opened a crack as Mieczysław Rakowski's government in Poland relaxed the last vestiges of martial law, released key Solidarity activists, and allowed a modicum of union activity to resume. Events moved quickly and soon passed beyond control. Spurred, in part, by March elections in the Soviet Union and in part by the hope that early, controlled elections might dampen public unrest, the Polish United Workers Party consented to compete with Solidarity under a framework that guaranteed the Communists and their allies 65 percent of the seats in the Sejm, or lower house of parliament. As late as the day before the election, the Communists were confidently predicting victory. In a stunning reversal, however, Solidarity won ninety-nine out of a hundred seats in the Senate, and a campaign to vote against unopposed communist candidates in the Sejm defeated thirty-three out of thirty-five, including eight members of the Politburo. The result left the Communists with a working majority, but with the key psychological setback of knowing that they had been firmly rejected by the people. After two months of maneuvering and the splintering of their parliamentary coalition, the Communists finally submitted to the inevitable and allowed Solidarity to form the first noncommunist government in Poland in more than forty years. Gorbachev's spokesman, Evgeny Primakov, declared that this was "entirely a matter to be decided by Poland."[28]

Hungary's leadership had been set on a moderate reformist course since 1988, when Karoly Grosz unseated Janos Kadar as general secretary, and the Hungarian Socialist Workers' Party was likewise negotiating with the opposition in the summer of 1989 over elections the following year. Events in Poland pushed the pace, as the HSWP sought to demonstrate its independence

[28]Gwertzman and Kaufman, eds., *The Collapse of Communism*, p. 132.

from the rest of the bloc. Hungary opened its borders in September, which proved to be the catalyst that spread the Polish infection to the rest of Eastern Europe. East Germans, separated from their own people and in many cases from close friends and family since 1961 by the Berlin Wall, rushed to take advantage of the momentary point of access to the West. When Czechoslovakia, under pressure from the GDR, sought to stem the tide by closing its borders, East Germans flooded Western embassies across Eastern Europe. This visible sign of the weakness of the state, which had seemed monolithic to its citizens for so long, sparked protest demonstrations across East Germany. On October 7 Gorbachev visited Berlin to celebrate the GDR's fortieth anniversary, but significantly neglected to praise its leaders, and warned them privately that Soviet military intervention would not be forthcoming. Ten days later Egon Krenz displaced Erich Honecker as general secretary, but he too failed to stem the tide of popular unrest.

Revolt and capitulation jumped from capital to capital like a conflagration from tree to tree. The pent-up frustrations and discontent of the East European peoples, suppressed for decades by the threat of Soviet intervention, had finally been released. Deterrence fails when the deterring threat loses its credibility, and the collapse of neighboring regimes was the strongest kind of evidence that the Soviet Union would no longer guarantee the solvency of its client states. The collapse of each monolith shook the foundations of the next. On November 9 the Berlin Wall fell, the symbol of the old world order. On November 17 demonstrations broke out in Prague that ushered in the "Velvet Revolution." On December 22 Nikolae Ceauşescu fled Bucharest, and on January 16 round-table discussions began in Sofia. To a remarkable degree, the differences in national style, the varying compositions of the elites, and the varying maturity of the dissident movements in each country were swept aside in an avalanche of identical dominoes. Identical, that is, except in Romania, where the tragic decision of the Ceauşescu regime to fight for survival plunged the country into a bitter, although brief, civil war.

In the weeks and months that followed, each of the East European countries executed a dramatic about-face, creating democratic institutions, launching market-type economic reforms, and forsaking their Soviet orientation for a Western one. For a few months it appeared that something might be retained of the CMEA structure and of traditional economic ties, since the East Europeans had an interest in cushioning their experiments in shock therapy, and the Gorbachev regime had an interest in maintaining the facade of an alliance. In the end, however, as at the beginning, the Soviet trade subsidy was subject to the cold calculation of national interest. The Soviet premier, Nikolai Ryzhkov, had been shocked as late as 1988 by a report that estimated the Soviet subsidy to the East European allies at $17 billion per year. Soviet advisers report that Ryzhkov had mistakenly believed that putting CMEA trade on a world-market basis would bring the Soviet Union an equivalent annual profit from East European trade, and over their objections that it would not be feasible to maintain the existing trade structure at world prices, he had pushed to shift trade with the satellites to world prices.[29] Once the political underpinnings of the alliance had dissolved, there apparently were no countervailing pressures. In June 1990 the Soviet Union announced that the East European countries would no longer receive preferential trade treatment after the first of the new year. The disintegration of the CMEA swiftly followed.

[29]Interviews with Oleg Rybakov, 3.9.1992, and with Aleksandr Nekipelov, 2.21.1992.

Part Two

LINKAGE AND RESOLVE: THE POLITICS OF BILATERAL TRADE

CHAPTER 3

The Politics of Bilateral Trade Negotiations

THIS CHAPTER subjects the arguments laid out in chapter 1 to their first empirical test by comparing their predictions about the patterns of bargaining in bilateral trade negotiations to the historical record. It argues that Soviet-bloc economic cooperation was riven by distributional conflict and fraught with sabotage of joint projects. Disputes raged over Soviet–East European terms of trade, as distorted prices spawned intense maneuvering to export overpriced goods and import subsidized ones. Meanwhile, the central player was paralyzed by perverse bureaucratic incentives that prevented Soviet officials from representing the national interest. The Soviet Union failed to compel its allies to cooperate, and ultimately lost control over the bargaining process, which led to a trade subsidy that spiraled out of control.

MECHANICS

The most important trade decisions in the CMEA were made in the course of bilateral consultations, referred to as *coordination of planning*. The term is misleading, suggesting a rather technical affair involving input-output tables, massive exchange of economic data, and numerous applications of higher mathematics. In fact, however, coordination of planning was a much more mundane process of negotiating quantitative quotas of imports and exports. These negotiations were rendered unusual, however, by the extreme rigidity of the Soviet planning system, which required that every transaction be planned in advance.

The negotiations were carried out by the central planning organs of the countries involved. Each central planning commission had a division assigned to "socialist economic integration," which shouldered the task of preparing negotiating positions and conducting negotiations at the "expert" level. Other departments became involved in working out the detailed trade agreements in particular branches of the economy. A typical negotiating session involved a meeting of the heads of the parallel departments of the two countries, accompanied by a staff of five to ten experts on each side. These bargaining teams prepared protocols, which specified the quantity (or, in some cases, the value) of particular goods or types of goods that each side would export and import, and indicated which issues had not yet been resolved. Once broad agreement was reached, more specialized agencies, such as ministries and enterprises, were brought into the process to finalize the details.

Disputes that could not be settled at the expert level were put on the agenda for a meeting of deputy chairmen of the respective planning commissions, who held ministerial rank; these meetings usually took place five or six times a year. Controversies that remained unresolved were passed on to the chairmen, who were deputy premiers, and generally met biannually, and then to the highest officials of plan coordination, the premiers. In extraordinary cases, unresolved conflicts were raised at meetings of the general secretaries of the Communist Parties. A great deal of the time and energy of top communist government officials—and most of their visits to one another's capitals—were absorbed by this process.

One of the first things to emerge from archival research in the central planning commissions is the continuous nature of socialist trade negotiations. The most important trade decisions were made in the course of coordinating five-year plans, and that process began for the following five-year period during the second or third year of the current plan. It involved meetings at the expert level in various areas—engineering, metallurgy, energy, consumer goods—that more or less overlapped in time. Between meetings, bargaining positions were revised and new proposals were tabled. Meanwhile, each year saw the negotiation of an annual trade protocol for the following year, and toward the end of each five-year period, changes were made in the bilateral Plan to compensate for earlier miscalculations. In addition, long-term agreements were often under discussion in areas such as scientific cooperation, joint resource development, and specialization. In principle, the continuous series of overlapping negotiations provided ample opportunities for the Soviet Union to exercise its strategy of linkage; in fact, however, negotiations on different tracks rarely influenced each other.

ISSUES

The history of bilateral trade negotiations is a record of continuous maneuvering by the East European countries to increase their imports from the Soviet Union of subsidized energy, fuels, and raw materials, and to increase their exports to the Soviet Union in the overpriced categories of machinery and equipment. The most important point was the division of exports and imports into the major categories of (1) energy and raw materials, (2) machinery and equipment, and (3) consumer goods. However, because of the complexity of negotiating international trade flows and the ingenuity of the participants, the fundamental issues quickly became buried in a sea of detail. Within each of the broad categories, there were substantial gains to be made by trading relatively overpriced commodities for relatively underpriced ones. Therefore, for example, the East Europeans preferred to import iron ore rather than pig iron or steel, and raw coal rather than coke; in general, the more finished the product, the less profitable it was to import. Within the category of machinery, each country preferred to export light-weight, relatively simple machinery that did not require substantial investments in new technologies, while seeking to import material- and capital-intensive machinery from its neighbors. It was more profitable to export cheap consumer goods made out of artificial materials than quality goods with expensive raw material inputs. In the food industry, it was more profitable to export canned fruit than fresh fruit.

A new issue was introduced into the mix in the late 1960s, when the Soviet Union began to demand that CMEA countries participate in construction projects on Soviet territory, known as "joint investments," in return for increased Soviet exports of raw materials and energy. The investments were intended to help defray the costs of producing raw materials, and, accordingly, they represented a transfer of resources to the Soviet Union. At first, East European participation came in the form of trade credits, which were a drain on the lending country's economy because they were loans of resources at negative real interest rates. Later, the Soviet Union insisted that participating countries make direct investments in Soviet extraction industries; these direct investments were still more unprofitable because they were subject to the conservative system of Soviet cost accounting, which underestimated the expenditures to be reimbursed.[1] Joint investments could occasionally be so costly that they made it uneconomical to negotiate increased imports of subsidized goods, but in the majority of cases they simply slowed the rate of increase of the Soviet trade subsidy.[2] Beginning in the 1970s terms of trade came to depend increasingly on how much investment the East Europeans were compelled to make in return for incremental imports of raw materials.

The East Europeans naturally resisted participation in joint investments, because it was far more profitable to pay for imports of raw materials with high-priced machinery. Sensing this opposition, the Central Committee of the CPSU distributed a position paper to the Communist Parties of its allies in 1968 that made its view of the matter explicit:

> The majority of the CMEA countries' needs for raw materials are satisfied by exports from the USSR, which allows those countries to economize on convertible currency, and gives them a firm basis to develop their finished industry, which is distinguished by a relatively lower capital cost per unit of production and a high level of profitability.
>
> In addition, it is necessary to keep in mind that the development of the raw-material base in the USSR, which is dictated by the needs of the CMEA countries, involves great capital investments. The cost per unit of capacity is rising

---

[1] Interviews with Janos Czibula, 8.25.1992, and Miroslav Černý, 6.25.1992.
[2] Interview with Zdeněk Šedivý, 6.30.1992.

rapidly as a result of the need to bring into production deposits that are located in the northern and eastern regions of the country, and are distant and difficult to reach. It is sufficient to state that the Soviet Union is investing 3.4 billion rubles in the current five-year plan in order to raise exports of the most important raw materials in 1970 in comparison to 1965, excluding the investments made in order to increase those exports after 1970. This means that the Soviet Union must devote approximately 8–9 percent of the increment in its capital investment in industry for 1966–70 to create additional capacity in raw material branches of the economy to satisfy the rising needs of the CMEA countries. It is still difficult to discuss increases in raw material exports up to 1975; however, according to a preliminary analysis, a far-from-complete satisfaction of the countries' needs for raw materials will require additional capital investment of at least 5 billion rubles. In this connection one must note that the per capita level of capital investments in the USSR is already approximately 30–50 percent higher than in the majority of European CMEA countries.

Further, it is significantly less profitable for the Soviet Union to export the majority of raw materials than to export products of finished industry, which is explained, in particular, by difficult geological and geographical conditions. The profitability of Soviet exports to the CMEA countries of fuels, raw materials, and metals is on average 30–35 percent lower than the profitability of exporting machinery and equipment, whereas the cost of producing the majority of fuels and raw materials exceeds the cost of producing machinery by 2 to 3 times, and in some cases by 5 to 8 times.

Consequently, the problems of satisfying the needs of the CMEA countries in the most important types of raw materials should be solved in the long term, in the opinion of the Soviet Union, by means of uniting the efforts of the interested countries on a mutually advantageous basis.[3]

A rather simple argument was made complex by the Soviet Union's refusal to refer to world prices as an objective standard of equivalent exchange, and by the fact that Soviet accounting did not calculate profitability in terms of cost. Instead, the Soviets calculated the "profitability" of trade, defined as the difference between trade prices and domestic prices, and the "cost per unit of production," defined as the ratio of costs to domestic prices. By either standard, raw material exports were less profitable than machinery exports, so the Soviet Union concluded that it subsidized its trade with Eastern Europe. Consequently, the East Europeans must be prepared to share the costs.

The Soviet position gains circumstantial support from the observation that, among themselves, the East European countries tolerated no terms-of-trade subsidies. A Polish report on the outcome of trade negotiations among the

---

[3]"O sovershenstvovanii sistemy upravleniia i planirovaniia v SSSR (razdel I razvernutogo plana raboty rabochei gruppy I, p. 7)," 3.2.1970, CMEA Archive. The document was prepared by Gosplan USSR for distribution to Working Group I.

CMEA countries exclusive of the Soviet Union for 1986–90 points out that "the balance of exports is the result of the great pressure by all countries, which strove to balance them in the course of plan coordination, not only globally, but *particularly in the group of fuels, raw materials, and [finished] materials.*"[4] An interview with Václav Kotouč, an official responsible for trade with socialist countries in the Czechoslovak State Planning Commission from 1963 to 1980, confirms that this was the rule. He explained that each country attempted to satisfy as many of its raw material needs as possible with Soviet exports, harboring its own potential raw material exports to pay for necessary imports from other socialist countries. When asked whether any country besides the USSR would have been willing to run a surplus in the category of raw materials and fuels, his reply was unmistakably direct: "Of course not. The Soviet Union was the exception. It was the only country willing to tolerate an unbalanced trade structure. All the other countries were careful not to export more than they imported in the crucial categories."[5]

It was clear to the participants in trade negotiations that the primary issue at stake was the size of the Soviet subsidy, although it was often to the advantage of the East Europeans to feign ignorance of this fact and to profess other concerns. This was illustrated by a 1988 meeting between the chairmen of the USSR Gosplan, Iurii Masliukov, and of the Czechoslovak State Planning Commission, Svatopluk Potáč. The Czechoslovak chairman began the discussion by outlining a series of proposed cuts in Czechoslovak exports, including steel and certain consumer goods, which he fully expected the Soviet Union to oppose. He also proposed looking for a new form of joint investments because "under contemporary conditions we are compelled to subsidize 50 percent of the cost of our participation in the construction of integration objects from the state budget."[6] He emphasized that these proposals fit into a Czechoslovak program to reduce the energy-intensity of the economy and restructure industry to make it more efficient during the next five-year plan—all goals that dovetailed with Soviet efforts at *uskorenie*, or economic acceleration, during the early Gorbachev years. This provoked an ironic response from Masliukov, as reported in the Czechoslovak minutes of the meeting:

> Reducing energy- and material-intensity, carrying out significant structural changes, and raising efficiency were also among the basic strategic goals for development of the Soviet economy. He emphasized that the export of a series of other products is unprofitable. For example, the loss owing to exporting personal automobiles amounts to 900–1,000 rubles per car. The foreign trade price covers only 59 percent of the cost of exporting refrigerators, 70 percent for cut lumber, and 58 percent for raw cotton.

[4]Komisja Planowania, "Ocena Realizacji Zadan," January 1988 (emphasis added).
[5]Interview with Václav Kotouč, 7.16.1992.
[6]Ing. Černý, "Výsledky jednání s. Potače se s. Masljukovem," 5.30.1988, SPK Archive, p. 2. The meeting took place on 5.26.1988.

The principles of price formation are deformed. It is necessary to change to world prices. If, however, we raised the price for the work performed by the participating countries on integration objects in the USSR, it would be necessary to raise the price of the products of those objects.[7]

Soviet estimates of foreign trade losses were not particularly precise, since they were based on distorted domestic costs and prices. The essence of Masliukov's argument was correct, however: so long as trade prices were artificial, one side or the other took a loss on every trade transaction. Moreover, Masliukov was telling Potáč that he understood that the Soviet Union subsidized its trade with the East European countries, and that East European participation in investments on Soviet territory simply returned part of the subsidy.

After trade structure and joint investments, the most important issue in bilateral trade negotiations was the balance of payments. Trade surpluses influenced the terms of trade, since they represented temporary transfers of resources at negative real rates of interest, and without a workable international currency, a trade surplus with one country could not be used to pay a deficit with another. Surpluses were often tolerated, however, and in fact they rarely arose unexpectedly. The Soviet Union allowed a number of the East European countries to run deficits following the increase in oil prices in 1975, which dramatically changed the balance of payments in the CMEA. The size of the deficits and the terms of repayment were negotiated in the process of coordination of planning. Certainly, attention was paid to the matter of balancing trade, and the effort to balance the effects of changing world prices sometimes led the surplus country to reduce its exports. However, trade surpluses were usually dealt with as one issue among many on a crowded agenda, and running a trade surplus could be regarded as a suitable concession to gain more favorable treatment on other issues. Substantial gains from trade came from a favorable trade structure, not from running a trade deficit.

Hungary attempted unsuccessfully to use its trade deficit with the Soviet Union, which emerged as a result of the jump in oil prices in 1975, as leverage to extract additional resources. Pointing out that their exports of machinery to the Soviet Union contained hard-currency inputs, Hungarian negotiators argued that it would be impossible to expand production to close the trade gap unless the USSR provided the necessary inputs or other hard-currency goods to compensate.

We proposed it in the mid-1970s, in connection with the oil price shock. They demanded that we export more to the Soviet Union, because they did not want to give us credits. They told us to export soft goods, such as pharmaceuticals. We said, all right, in fact we have the capacity, and the firms want to export. But in

[7]Ibid., p. 4

all of our exports, on average, there were one-third dollar imports, so we proposed that they export one-third of the increase of our exports as raw materials so we could save dollar inputs. So that it would not be an additional burden. We asked for wood, metal—oil was not in question—asbestos. . . .

They said no. Export more, but we cannot increase our exports. We said that under those conditions, we could not increase our exports. So we built up debts between 1975 and 1980.[8]

The Soviet Union rejected the Hungarian argument for additional resources, but finally agreed to give Hungary a 700-million-ruble credit to cover the increased cost of oil imports between 1976 and 1980. The Hungarian experts disputed the Soviet figures, claiming that the impact of the 1975 price changes on Hungarian terms of trade would be 2 billion rubles, but the Soviets refused to compromise further. In the end the Hungarian deficit over five years totaled 675.9 million rubles, just a little under the Soviet offer.

A striking comparison can be made between the situations of Poland and Czechoslovakia at the end of the 1980s. Poland ran a substantial deficit with the Soviet Union, while Czechoslovakia ran a substantial surplus. If willingness to run a trade surplus had represented significant bargaining leverage, we would expect that Czechoslovakia would be able to use this circumstance to advantage in its negotiations with the Soviet Union, securing more favorable treatment than Poland at a time when the Soviets were attempting to improve their trade structure by reducing exports of oil to Eastern Europe and increasing exports of machinery. This did not turn out to be the case, however. The conditions that the Soviet Union offered to Czechoslovakia in the negotiations for the 1991–95 five-year plan were no more favorable than those offered to Poland.

A meeting in October 1987 between the chairmen of the Czechoslovak State Planning Commission and of Soviet Gosplan can be taken as a case in point. The main items on the meeting's agenda were to resolve the problem of the Soviet deficit for 1988–90 that was foreseen because of falling energy prices, and to discuss Czechoslovak requests for an increase in oil and gas imports. The Soviet position coming into the meeting was that only a portion of the deficit could be covered with increased exports, that these increases would all have to be in the area of machinery and equipment, and that the remaining deficit would have to be paid back after 1995.[9] The approach chosen by Potáč, the Czechoslovak chairman, is significant. He did not challenge the Soviet position that trade could not be balanced during 1988–90 and that payments on the debt could not begin until 1995. He argued, however, that although he understood that the increase in Soviet exports would be "primar-

[8]Interview with Istvan Hetenyi, 9.7.1992.
[9]Ing. Černý, "Konzultace o svodných otázkách," to the Chairman, SPK, 9.4.1987, SPK Archive.

ily [in] machinery and equipment," he expected it to include "also other fuels, raw materials, and [finished] materials." He presented a proposed list of Soviet export increases exceeding by 600 million rubles the 1 billion transferable rubles that the Soviets had proposed. He also linked a condition to the Czechoslovak agreement to carry over the deficit: "In connection with the credit being offered, the Czechoslovak side assumes that exports of other fundamental raw materials and fuels from the Soviet Union will be maintained at the level of 1990."[10] The Czechoslovak side regarded the Soviet trade deficit as an appropriate price to pay for secure imports of gas and oil.

Iurii Masliukov, the Soviet chairman, did not agree to the Czechoslovak conditions. According to the protocol, the parties agreed simply to "a state credit by the CSSR [Czechoslovak Socialist Republic] side, offered in case of need, with payment after 1995 on terms that will be further clarified."[11] In the course of the ensuing discussions of exports of gas in 1988, he did show some flexibility. He consented to increase natural gas exports by 360 million m^3 in 1987, part of this coming as an advance on exports planned for 1989, and by 150 million m^3 in 1988.[12] The document, a report for the chairman of the Czechoslovak State Planning Commission, gives no indication that the Soviets regarded the two issues as linked, although they were decided at the same meeting. In any event, the Czechoslovak strategy of trading their trade surplus for Soviet gas did not succeed. Table 3.1 shows that between 1986 and 1989, Czechoslovak gas imports actually fared slightly worse than those of Poland. The conclusion seems to be that the Czechoslovak trade surplus did not have a great deal of bearing on the trade negotiations.

The issue of trade dependence was virtually absent from bilateral negotiations. A few important investment decisions were apparently made in order to avoid excessive dependence on the USSR, such as Gomułka's intensive development of Polish coal production in the 1960s and Romania's extensive industrialization drive.[13] However, in the course of forty-five interviews with East European trade negotiators, no respondent claimed that there was a pattern of East European resistance to Soviet overtures to increase trade. East European trade with the West rose dramatically in the wake of détente. Although official Soviet rhetoric opposed excessive dependence on the West, the Soviets did not apply consistent pressure on their satellites to reorient their trade from West to East. Rather, the evidence from the Polish and Czechoslovak archives is that the East European countries were eager to increase their trade with the Soviet Union, and competed with one another for shares. Stanisław Długosz,

---

[10]Ing. Černý, "Informace o výsledcích jednání," to Husák, Štrougal, Bílak, Jakeš, Adameč, Rohliček, Colotka, Gerle, Urban, Kopecký, 10.19.1987, SPK Archive, p. 3.

[11]Ibid., p. 4.

[12]Ibid., pp. 5–6.

[13]Stanisław Kuziński, Gomułka's top economic adviser, argued that this was a major concern for Gomułka in the 1960s (interview with Kuziński, 6.3.1992).

TABLE 3.1
Soviet Natural Gas Exports to Czechoslovakia and Poland
(million transferable rubles)

	1986	1987	1988	1989	$\frac{1989}{1986}$
Czechoslovakia	1,266	1,176	1,048	1,003	79%
Poland	832	856	734	673	81%

Source: Sovetskaia torgovliia, various volumes.

the chief Polish negotiator with the Soviet Union, argued "there was always a competition to be the first to Moscow, to get the best deal on raw materials. Our partners were open about this: they would sometimes refuse to meet with us because they had not been to Moscow yet."[14] Vladislav Cihlař, who served on Soviet-Czechoslovak trade-negotiating commissions for two decades, put the issue this way:

> Our relations depended more on the USSR than on the CSSR. The Soviet Union's first priority was to fulfill its exports to the West for hard currency, and then the socialist countries got what was left over. Czechoslovakia always wanted to increase its imports from the USSR, but that depended on Soviet capabilities.[15]

Neither official forgot to add, however, that their proposals were always calculated to increase their exports of machinery and increase their imports of raw materials. The most important limiting factor in trade appears to have been the Soviet willingness to expand its exports of primary goods and imports of machinery.

When issues of trade dependence figured in trade negotiations, they played a symbolic role. Czechoslovakia paid lip service to the notion that trade with the Soviet Union should not decline in the late 1980s when falling energy prices created the Czechoslovak trade surplus referred to above. This was an argument for increasing Soviet energy exports to make up part of the difference, disguised as an ideological commitment to socialist integration. Similarly, Poland often resorted to the argument that if the Soviet Union failed to provide it with the raw materials it required, it would be forced to increase its dependence on the capitalist West—something it was loath to do more for economic than for strategic reasons. An excerpt from the protocol of a negotiating session in 1967 shows how this argument was made:

[14]Interview with Stanisław Długosz, 6.8.1992.
[15]Interview with Vladislav Cihlař, 6.17.1992.

The Polish experts particularly call the attention of the Soviet side to the fact that the question of the further increase of exports of raw materials from the USSR to the PRP [People's Republic of Poland] in the period after 1970 is one of vital significance to the Polish economy. If it were impossible to achieve the increase of exports of raw materials after 1970 in the amounts indicated in the Protocol referred to above, this would lead to a slowing of our economic growth, and would force the PRP to carry out a sharp geographical reorientation of our foreign economic ties, with all the undesirable economic and political consequences that this would have for us.[16]

If the Soviet Union had been making a sustained effort to reduce the level of Polish contacts with the West, Poland could not afford to treat the issue in such a cavalier manner. Apparently, the Poles could in fact afford to make a veiled threat of increasing their dependence on trade with the West in order to win concessions about raw material exports.

BARGAINING STRATEGIES

The process of bargaining reveals the significance of the Soviet trade subsidy. It is clear from the reports that East European negotiators wrote for their superiors that the Soviet Union had the upper hand in the negotiating process, although it was not always able to exploit its leverage because of bureaucratic communication failures. Consider this example of Soviet bargaining leverage, when in 1987 the Soviet Union made a serious effort to change the structure of Czechoslovak exports. At the time discussions were under way for a "Conception of economic, scientific, and technical cooperation for fifteen to twenty years," and the balance of trade in machinery and equipment became one of the major issues of dispute. The Czechoslovak delegation put up a brave resistance, but when it was time to report back to the chairman of the State Planning Commission, they simply said that "the Soviet side insists that its proposal for the total level of Czechoslovak exports and imports be taken as the basis for developing the common 'Conception.' "[17] When the Soviet Union insisted that its proposal be taken as the baseline for further discussions, the East Europeans grudgingly acceded to the demand.

The Soviet Union made frequent use of threats and overt linkages in order to achieve its goals, while the East European bargaining position had to rely on much greater use of finesse. The satellites did not follow a strategy of returning tit for tat, as they might have done had they faced a classic collective-action problem. Rather, they covered their noncompliance with a cloud of

---

[16]Komisja Planowania, "Pamiatnaia zapiska [Protocol]," 12.7.1967, CUP Archive, p. 3.
[17]Ing. Prchlík, "Jednání expertů," 10.9.1987, SPK Archive, p. 2. The meeting took place 5–9 October 1987.

extenuating circumstances, and argued from weakness when compelled to discuss specific issues. Ryszard Grabas, a former secretary of the Polish-Soviet Intergovernmental Commission on Economic Cooperation, described the process.

> When we wanted something, we used political arguments, too. We needed the resources because of the unstable internal situation, etc. The question of [Polish] debt often came up, and it was connected to other issues. We responded that we weren't a stable country, a stable people. There are lots of unhappy Poles. These arguments were made at every meeting with the Soviets. . . . Unfortunately, instead of economic criteria, often strength, sympathy, antipathy, the situation— necessary or not—all the more often . . . played a role in decisions.[18]

Similarly, when Czechoslovak planners tried to convince the Soviet Union to accept decreased imports of Czechoslovak steel, which they had determined to be unprofitable to produce for export, they explained that their hands had been tied by the decision of the Czechoslovak Communist Party. In pursuance of the decision of the Seventeenth Congress of the CPC, Czechoslovakia planned to reduce steel production from 14.8 million tons in 1990 to 12.0 million in 2000 and 10.0 million in 2005.[19] Once the Party had spoken, the issue was out of the planners' control; there was no avoiding the fact that less steel would be available for export. Of course, both sides can argue that their backs are against a wall, and the Soviets gradually adopted the same strategy. By the 1980s Soviet negotiators routinely began negotiating sessions by explaining the dire state of the Soviet economy.

Whenever possible, the satellites tried to create the appearance of compliance with Soviet wishes while carefully avoiding the substance. A Czechoslovak briefing paper written in 1988 for the first deputy chairman of the State Planning Commission (SPK) is worth quoting at length as a revealing glimpse into the negotiating process. It was drafted in preparation for a meeting to be held in October, where the Czechoslovaks were attempting to avoid committing themselves to any more investments on Soviet territory, while simultaneously deflecting a Soviet threat to reduce iron ore exports if they refused to participate.

> During the meeting, begin from the principle of maintaining the current level of deliveries of iron ore, 7.19 million tons calculated in terms of metal, for the Long-Term Trade Agreement after 1990.
>
> As an argument for asserting the stated principle, inform [the Soviet side] that the Czechoslovak side counts on maintaining the level of deliveries of rolling equipment to the USSR, even during 1991–95, at more than 100,000 tons. At the same time, we are practically alone in having continuously participated in the

[18]Interview with Ryszard Grabas, 5.26.1992.
[19]Ing. O. Kopečný, "Pamětní zápis," 10.21.1988, SPK Archive, p. 2.

construction of the Krivoi Rog Combine, despite the fact that the conditions of Czechoslovak participation are substantially more costly than was assumed when that bilateral agreement was signed.

Further, the Czechoslovak side delivers a unique contribution of rolling equipment "2500" for the Novolipetsk Metallurgical Combine in the amount of 250 million rubles.

It is advisable to state these facts during the meeting as justifications for the demand that the level of Soviet iron ore shipments to the CSSR be maintained, and as an illustration of the Czechoslovak endeavor to understand the difficult internal Soviet situation regarding the extraction of iron ore.

In case the Soviet side does not agree with the arguments stated above, [the delegation] should be asked to state conditions for maintaining the level of deliveries.

It is to be expected that the Soviet side will propose conditions equivalent to the conditions of Czechoslovak participation in construction of the Krivoi Rog Combine. If a demand for Czechoslovak participation in construction reached a capacity of 1 to 1.8 million tons calculated in pure metal, that would correspond to a value of Czechoslovak participation in the range of 400 to 750 million rubles.

In that case mention the promise that the chairman of USSR Gosplan, Comrade Masliukov, made during a meeting with Secretary of the CC CPC Lenárt in September in Moscow, that deliveries of rolling equipment "2500" for the Novolipetsk Metallurgical Combine can be considered to be a Czechoslovak contribution to the maintenance of deliveries of iron ore from the USSR to the CSSR in the period after 1990.

State further that the Czechoslovak side also intends to use part of the surplus that will appear in the balance of payments between the CSSR and the USSR toward the end of this five-year plan, as a part of the Czechoslovak contribution to participation in developing mining capacity in the USSR.

In case of Soviet proposals to reduce its exports to the CSSR, warn that Czechoslovak exports will also be reduced by a corresponding amount across their whole structure, that is, 60 percent in machinery and equipment, primarily deliveries for the mining and metallurgical industries, and 40 percent in nonengineering goods, particularly steel pipes and consumer goods.[20]

The Czechoslovak side strikes an interesting posture. With no intention of acceding to Soviet demands, the Czechoslovaks nonetheless attempt to create the appearance of cooperating. The Czechoslovaks begin with an effort to show that their proposals are reasonable, demonstrating that they are already making substantial contributions toward meeting Soviet needs. The suggested allusion to current exports does not appear to be a threat to cut them off, but rather an attempt to convince the other side that a good-faith effort is being

[20]Ing. O. Kopečný, "Příprava jednání," 9.20.1988, SPK Archive, pp. 1–2.

made. If this approach fails, the Czechoslovaks move to play a trump card: Masliukov, probably making a strategic blunder, had promised Lenárt that a kind of steel-rolling equipment that Czechoslovakia exported could be considered a form of participation in building metallurgical capacity in the Soviet Union. This card should not be played immediately, the adviser cautions—presumably because the export was considered a valued concession. Next, the Czechoslovak trade surplus is cashed in as an argument: it is a form of credit, the negotiators should argue, and consequently ought to be considered in part as an investment in the Soviet mining industry. Finally, if all else fails, the minister is urged to try a threat. As it turned out, the Soviet side rejected the Czechoslovak arguments, but the Czechoslovak negotiator decided not to make the recommended threat.[21] The question was left unresolved for nine months, and when the Czechoslovaks continued to refuse to participate in the second round of development of the Krivoi Rog complex, the Soviets finally did reduce their planned iron ore exports for 1991–95.[22] The pattern is consistent with the interpretation that the Soviet Union held the upper hand, that the satellites could rarely afford to make direct threats, and that the preferred East European strategy was reassurance, obfuscation, and exploitation of inconsistencies in the Soviet bargaining position.

FAILURES OF SOVIET BARGAINING STRATEGY

It is striking that for most of the CMEA's history the Soviet Union refrained from employing the full array of its bargaining power in negotiations with its East European allies. The Soviet Union not only failed to link economic and security issues, but even failed to make strategic connections between issues within the area of trade. The East Europeans were able to frustrate Soviet efforts at burden sharing, sometimes discretely and at times with open defiance, but the Soviet negotiators did not attempt to hold the trade subsidy hostage to East European cooperation. Instead, for most of the postwar period, they treated "traditional" exports as a given and only increments as negotiable. This was convenient from the point of view of national planning, which puts a premium on predictability. Since the increments were much smaller than the traditional exports in any particular year, however, this practice hobbled the Soviet bargaining position. Istvan Hetenyi, a former first deputy chairman of the Hungarian Planning Commission who had participated in trade negotiations since the late 1950s, divided the evolution of the Soviet bargaining posture into three main stages.

---

[21]Ing. O. Kopečný, "Pamětní zápis," 10.21.1988, SPK Archive.
[22]Kopečný, Prchlík, Marcinov, "Výsledky konzultace," to the Chairman, SPK, 6.30.1989, SPK Archive.

I remember, at the beginning of the 1960s, [the Soviet Union] elaborated twenty-year programs. They never became plans, but they were forecasts. And then they told us, well, in 1965 you will get two million tons of oil, in 1975 six, and in 1980 eight. That we can do for you. And gas, and so on. I think [they decided this] without any economic considerations. And then they knew they would have to import machinery, light industrial and agricultural goods from us. It was all the same, everything was welcome in the deficit economy that they had. So they took all of these articles.

. . . In the 1970s, there were some new phenomena. That was when they decided that they could not export raw materials in large quantities. They could not do it. They could not continue to increase [exports], or only very slowly and in some articles. If you look at the statistics, the main articles of raw materials were held at the level of 1965. . . . For increases in deliveries they wanted special goods, which they called "hard" goods, you know what those are. Yes, we can give you four million tons, but for the fifth and the sixth you have to deliver shoes, and meat. . . .

The third phase, which began in the late 1970s, when they had growing difficulties, was to set an overall balance, not only globally, but also according to hard goods and soft goods. And then they began to ask for hard goods not only for increments of oil and gas, but also for basic deliveries.[23]

Hetenyi described a steady stiffening of the Soviet bargaining position. Key commodities were distributed without conditions in the 1960s, and then conditions were gradually added as the Soviet Union felt an increasing need to restrain the growth of its trade subsidy.

As the Soviet bargaining position hardened, much of the bargaining in the negotiating sessions came to revolve around the question of which issues could be linked. The Soviet position depended on making linkages between issues because the Soviet trade subsidy represented surplus bargaining power that could be used to secure agreements in various areas. Meanwhile, the East Europeans made every effort to prevent linkages between Soviet power resources and issues of contention. In November 1988 a Soviet delegation, led by Deputy Chairman of Gosplan Khomenko, made such a linkage between crucial raw materials and changes it was pursuing in the structure of Polish exports by announcing a new "basket principle." Instead of balancing trade as a whole, a basket of preferred goods would be created and balanced separately—this would allow the Soviet negotiators to directly link quantities of raw material exports that represented political capital to particularly desired imports. The Polish delegation, led by the acting chairman of the Planning Commission, Stanisław Długosz, understandably opposed the innovation.

Rejecting the principle of linkage in the Soviet side's version, Poland represented the position that the entirety of trade flows between the PRP and the USSR

---

[23]Interview with Istvan Hetenyi, 9.3.1992.

has formed historically and has become its own sort of basket, which both sides ought to realize. The fundamental question is not the direct linkage of one good with another, or with several other goods, but the assurance of a full guarantee of receipt of the goods agreed on by the governments of the PRP and the USSR in the course of the coordination of plans.[24]

The Polish negotiators returned to Warsaw without an agreement in this case, but in the end the Soviet "basket principle" prevailed.

East European attempts to avoid linkages of this sort depended on exploiting the compartmentalized process of Soviet decision making. One of the most basic norms governing trade negotiations, for example, was that issues defined as "political" could not be discussed. Soviet central planners did not have the authority to discuss the military ramifications of economic policies or the impact of particular decisions on the cohesion of the socialist camp, and they certainly did not have the authority to make military or political threats.[25] Even discussions of the military-related trade between CMEA countries were carried out by separate and highly secret wings of each country's planning commission, which were staffed by military officers. Trade in military equipment was bilaterally balanced and was never allowed to be offset by trade in other commodities.[26] Thus, at the levels of experts, deputy chairmen, and chairmen of the planning organs, where most trade issues were decided, the whole complex of military issues was quite irrelevant. The consequence was that Soviet and East European trade negotiators met on a much more even field. As deputy chairman of the Polish Planning Commission Stanisław Długosz put it, "At other levels, perhaps there was pressure, but at my level we spoke as equals; either I agreed or I did not. We used economic arguments."[27]

Even within the sphere of economic relations, trade negotiations were fragmented to an extraordinary degree by branch of industry. The process that led to the conclusion of the bilateral Soviet-Czechoslovak long-term treaty on economic and scientific cooperation in the late 1980s will serve as an example. Negotiations proceeded on a number of separate tracks, where portions of the text were written, and then the entire document was pulled together and signed by the premiers of the two countries. The "metallurgical" track discussed only issues related to metallurgy, such as Soviet exports of various ores, Czechoslovak exports of steel, and Czechoslovak participation in ore-development projects in the Soviet Union. Meanwhile, the "machine-

---

[24]Zespół Współpracy z Zagranicą Urzędu Komisji Planowania, "Sprawozdanie z konsultacji," CUP Archive, p. 4. Approved by Stanisław Długosz. The delegations were headed by Długosz, Acting Chairman, Komisja Planowania; J.P. Chomienko [Khomenko], Deputy Chairman, Gosplan.

[25]Interviews with Stanisław Długosz, 6.8.1992, and Zdeněk Šedivý, 6.30.1992.

[26]Interview with Zdeněk Šedivý, 6.30.1992.

[27]Interview with Stanisław Długosz, 5.7.1992.

building" track discussed only issues related to trade in machinery and equipment, and an "energy and raw materials" track discussed only issues related to Czechoslovak imports and participation in energy-production projects. A separate "consumer goods" track discussed refrigerators and leather products, and a "science and technology" track discussed investments in basic research and improving the quality of Czechoslovak exports. The final document did forge a few linkages, such as one between Czechoslovak consumer goods and Soviet exports of energy and raw materials, but the overwhelming effect of the fragmented process of negotiation was to compel the negotiators to resolve the controversies within each branch of industry in isolation.

This was the procedure routinely followed, even though the fragmentation of trade issues did not serve Soviet interests. In fact, it went much further. After a general agreement was reached by the central planning organs, negotiations were farmed out to more than fifty Soviet ministries that managed various branches of industry, and to innumerable foreign trade organizations and enterprises. According to the official rationale, this procedure allowed detailed questions to be decided by industry specialists. The question, however, is why so many specialists were required. In the Soviet bureaucracy, it was disadvantageous to share too much information about an organization's production potential, technology, or input needs, since the State Plan could always be revised to reduce organizational slack. Consequently, the information needed to negotiate the trade plan pooled at the lower levels of the hierarchy, so that was where negotiations had to be conducted. The Soviet trade bureaucracy was effectively subinfeudated into a collection of competing fiefdoms.[28] Czechoslovak trade negotiators spoke of playing the Soviet branch ministries off against the central planners, allowing them to "divide and conquer" in reverse.[29] The fragmentation of the Soviet bureaucracy prevented Soviet negotiators from employing an effective strategy of linkage.

A secret report prepared by the Soviet Academy of Sciences argued that the fragmentation of the Soviet bureaucracy undermined the Soviet bargaining position. The interest of Gosplan and the State Material-Supply Commission (Gossnab) was not to maximize Soviet gains from trade, it claimed, but to "balance materials." The Ministry of Foreign Trade and the Ministry of Finance did not attempt to optimize trade, because their attention was narrowly focused on a "budgetary approach." The branch ministries had no interest in maximizing national welfare; instead, they were concerned with "importing new equipment and minimizing exports." In short, each agency followed its own organizational priorities, and no agency was charged with safeguarding the long-term Soviet national interest. "In practical terms," the report con-

---

[28]Interviews with Oleg Rybakov, 3.9.1992, and Leonid Krasnov, 2.27.1992.
[29]Interview with Zdeněk Šedivý and J. Ružička, 6.30.1992.

cludes, "there is no agency responsible for achieving a national-economic optimum in the area of foreign ties."[30]

The fragmentation of issues in the Soviet bureaucracy was compounded by the failure of specialized agencies to display resolve in bargaining with the allies. The Soviet planning system exerted intense pressure on the managers of industrial ministries, combines, and enterprises to meet quantitative indicators of production, cost savings, wages, and so forth, and left them with little incentive to divert efforts to meeting goals that were monitored less carefully, such as bargaining with their East European partners. This problem tended to intensify in direct proportion to the distance of the negotiator from the center, since more peripheral actors, such as enterprise managers, were far more difficult to monitor than the central actors, such as Gosplan division heads. Since Soviet organizations tended to hoard economic information, however, the practical details of many transactions had to be negotiated by the very specialized agencies that had the least incentive to do a good job.

The most serious problems emerged in the later stages of negotiation, where more specialized organizations were involved. As was demonstrated above, the Soviet Union was capable of using its bargaining leverage to good effect in bilateral negotiations between the central planning agencies. It was able to dictate terms on issues perceived to be particularly important, and when central Soviet negotiators insisted, the East Europeans often acquiesced. In areas of military production and trade, for example, Soviet–East European cooperation was quite extensive. In addition, Soviet negotiators succeeded in wresting agreements from the East Europeans to participate in a number of joint investments in Soviet raw materials. However, because of the size and complexity of the Soviet economy, East European central planners often found themselves negotiating with the representatives of ministries, and industries governed by one East European ministry might be splintered into five or six different ministerial domains in the Soviet Union. This gave the East Europeans a distinct advantage.

The implementation of joint investments is a case in point. Soviet demands for direct investment on Soviet territory opened the door to negotiations about the degree and kind of investments to be made, and under what conditions. When the East Europeans granted trade credits, the quotas to fill the credits had to be negotiated, and the satellites sought to fill them with machinery and consumer goods. Whenever possible, they tried to fill the machinery quotas with large pieces of machinery, such as busses, trucks, and streetcars, that had high value-to-weight ratios and could be produced in large production runs. Each of these details had to be negotiated by the agencies that would actually

---

[30]AN SSSR, "Razvitie vneshneekonomicheskikh sviazei Sovetskogo Soiuza do 1990 g.," 1.2.1973, p. 83.

be involved in carrying out the work. A high-level Hungarian official argued that Hungary's participation in building the Yamburg pipeline, which had generally been believed to be unprofitable, was in fact "one of the best deals for Hungary in forty years."[31] The Soviet ministries were interested in importing machinery, and that was how Hungary paid for most of its investment. According to a Soviet report issued in 1971, the East Europeans apparently played this game with great finesse. Most of their participation in raw material development came in the form of exports that did not in fact contribute to developing raw materials.[32]

The weakness of Soviet resolve was most apparent in the area of quality standards. Among the issues over which the Soviet Union clashed with its allies, quality control was least privileged by the informal incentives in the Soviet planning system. If efforts devoted to negotiating were crowded out by competing pressures, this was even more true of efforts to achieve that most illusive of objectives, quality. Soviet negotiators often stood their ground on quantitative targets, since the failure to meet import targets would upset material balances and compromise the Plan. There were no such compelling incentives to emphasize quality concerns. A close examination of trade documents reveals that quality concerns were systematically deemphasized. Quality was rarely given a prominent place on the agenda of trade negotiations, and was rarely raised in connection with the most important issues. Instead, it was often briefly mentioned as one of many "other issues" that were discussed. I found no documents in the Polish or Czechoslovak planning archives to indicate that the Soviet Union had made a serious effort to improve the quality of its imports from Eastern Europe, although I found many perfunctory references to the issue.

Soviet imports of Czechoslovak shoes present a good example of Soviet unwillingness to sacrifice quantitative indicators in favor of improvements in quality. Zdeněk Šedivý, a former deputy chairman of the Czechoslovak State Planning Commission, recalls that the Soviet negotiators complained that Czechoslovak shoes lagged in quality behind Yugoslavian and Italian shoes. The Czechoslovaks repeatedly offered to improve the quality of their leather shoes, provided the quota for shoe exports could be set in terms of value rather than number of pairs. This would allow them to economize on materials by improving quality, because higher-quality shoes would earn a higher price, and the higher price would reduce the quantity of shoes needed to fill the quota. "But here the system of planning played a negative role. They had a balance, and shoes were a deficit item, and they needed the quantity."[33] The

---

[31]Interview with Joszef Marjai, 9.10.1992.

[32]Bogomolov et al., "O nekotorykh voprosakh povysheniia effektivnosti sotrudnichestva," to M. A. Lesechko, Deputy Chairman for CMEA Affairs, USSR Council of Ministers, 2.16.1971, IMEPI Archive, IEMSS report, pp. 3–4.

[33]Interview with Zdeněk Šedivý, 6.30.1992.

Soviet negotiators were consistently unwilling to trade quantity in return for quality.

Although the East Europeans enjoyed their greatest bargaining advantages at lower levels of the hierarchy, they sometimes found an advantageous tactic in raising issues of contention to higher levels. This was particularly the case if discussions deadlocked between intermediate levels of the central planning commissions. Since Soviet failures of resolve were generally a function of the distance between the negotiator and the center, they were less pronounced in Gosplan than in subsidiary ministries and trade organizations. Consequently, raising issues to higher levels did not cost the East Europeans much of an advantage if negotiations were already proceeding in the central planning commissions. On the other hand, the Soviet bureaucracy was sufficiently rife with failures of communication that it was possible to play off layers of the hierarchy against one another. If the East Europeans found a Soviet proposal unacceptable, therefore, it was frequently possible to obtain a more favorable resolution of the issue at a higher level. Iurii Pekshev, who was close to this process for more than two decades and served as the highest economic adviser in the CPSU Central Committee, recalls that it was often difficult to explain to top leaders the importance of the issues at stake. He and Nikolai Inozemtsev spent hours trying to explain to Aleksei Kosygin, the Soviet premier, why it was necessary to compel the East Europeans to participate in investments on Soviet territory. "He found the argument difficult to follow, and he would not hear it. He simply did not listen to the end." In the end Kosygin was convinced, but that was not always the case. Pekshev reports that Mikhail Lesechko, the deputy premier for CMEA affairs, was singularly unimpressed by Pekshev's explanation of how the East Europeans benefited from CMEA rules for transportation charges. " 'So,' he said, 'what do you think, Bulgaria established the CMEA? Of course we should pay to support their economies.' "[34]

Frequently a position that Soviet experts and deputy chairmen had labored for months to achieve was thrown away by the premier or the general secretary. The result was that threats and linkages made at lower levels of the Soviet hierarchy had no weight. Eva Lašová, who was the chief Czechoslovak price negotiator in the 1970s and 1980s, argued that the East Europeans were much better situated to win disputes than their Soviet counterparts, because their Soviet colleagues were more likely to be overruled at the "political" level (i.e., by their own Politburo).

> There were times when we carried out serious struggles over prices. There was one time that the Soviets threatened to cut off natural gas on January 1 if we didn't agree to their price, and I told them to go ahead, since January 1 was a holiday for us! The agreement would come on the political level, and the side with the better nerves won. We had good nerves, and we achieved a lot. Some-

[34]Interview with Iurii Pekshev, 3.10.1992.

times we had no agreement on the price of oil by April, but the Soviet Union could not very well cut off the supply. We simply did not pay, and we often got them to compromise. The political ties were very close. It was possible to threaten a lot, but it was impossible to carry out the threats.[35]

The result was that the Soviet negotiators were overruled in the interests of fraternal socialist relations. The reverse pattern was also sometimes the case: the top Soviet leaders made such unacceptable compromises in their rush to agree that their lieutenants were sent back to repair the damage afterward. Istvan Hetenyi, a former deputy and first deputy chairman of the Hungarian Planning Commission, remembers this as a "tendency" that became more and more prevalent.

> The situation arose in the 1970s that, for instance, we agreed with Kosygin and Baibakov, but then later the apparatchiks did not respect the agreement that had been reached. They openly said, for example Mr. Vorov, who was head of a department, "Well, the ministers say what they want to, but they do not know the situation, they don't understand the situation. . ." so it was very clear that at times at the top there was a desire to agree, but the demands that the Politburo imposed on Gosplan made these more benevolent agreements unrealistic. They could not make a plan according to the amicable agreement, so they had to come back and say, "A difficult question, a difficult question, unfortunately." Inozemtsev would say, "We tried, but it is impossible," and so on.[36]

This suggests the depth of the gulf between the expert negotiators and the upper-level Soviet politicians. The senior politicians lacked much of the information necessary to make informed choices, and this state of affairs offered numerous opportunities for the East Europeans to exploit.

The negotiations leading to the Soviet-Polish 1986–90 five-year trade plan demonstrate several of these principles. A report by Janusz Brych, Polish acting minister-counsellor, summarizes the Soviet position presented at the latest round of consultations in February 1985. Brych described the new Soviet conditions as unacceptable, and recommended that the Polish government resist them.[37] Stanisław Długosz, deputy chairman of the Polish Planning Commission, shared this view, as is evident from his report of the subsequent meeting on the next higher level in March. The Soviet delegation, led by a deputy chairman of Gosplan, Nikolai Vorov, rejected Polish requests for increased exports of energy and raw materials, and threatened to decrease Soviet exports unless certain conditions were met for Polish exports of similar

---

[35]Interview with Eva Lašová, 6.25.1992.

[36]Interview with Istvan Hetenyi, 9.3.1992.

[37]Janusz Brych, "Zamechaniia k pamiatnoi zapiske," 2.4.1985, CUP Archive. It was apparently a standard procedure to translate certain internal documents into Russian, presumably so they could be referred to during negotiations or distributed to the Soviet side.

materials to the USSR and Polish participation in investments in the Soviet Union.[38]

The Poles appealed to the Soviets to consider the serious consequences that would ensue for the Polish economy. Długosz insisted that increased imports of raw materials and energy from the Soviet Union were essential to the fragile Polish economy, referring to the recent economic crisis and Poland's isolation from sources of Western credit as a result of martial law. In response to demands for participation in further investments on Soviet territory, the Poles argued that the minimum payment on their debt to the West would amount to the equivalent of 10 billion rubles, and the Soviets were essentially demanding another 10 billion. Twenty billion rubles would consume 40 percent of the projected growth of the Polish economy in the coming five-year period. This would be an intolerable burden. These arguments did not convince the Soviets to compromise, but the Polish delegation held its ground. Długosz reports that he returned to Warsaw with no agreement, and recommended that the issue be taken up with the Soviets at a still higher level.[39]

A letter to Wojciech Jaruzelski from Manfred Gorywoda, the chairman of the Polish Planning Commission, referred to the results of the March round of discussions and requested permission to take a hard line with Nikolai Baibakov, chairman of Soviet Gosplan, in their upcoming meeting.[40] Gorywoda explained the reasons for Polish concern, arguing that in the prevailing economic environment it would be very harmful for Poland if Soviet exports failed to keep pace with Poland's needs. Permission was evidently granted, since in a subsequent interview, Długosz said that Gorywoda supported his recommendation and took a very energetic approach to the issue. He successfully resisted a number of Soviet proposals to participate in joint investments, including the mammoth iron-ore development at Krivoi Rog, and he won concessions from the Soviets on certain raw materials.[41] Clearly, Poland benefited by raising trade disputes to high levels of protocol.

This series of events illustrates the potential power of the Soviet bargaining position, as well as the limitations of linkage. In the end the Soviet Union was able to make certain take-it-or-leave-it offers that Poland felt compelled to accept. From 1984 to 1986, Poland had stolidly refused to participate in construction of the Yamburg natural gas pipeline.

> Gorywoda struggled with Baibakov for three years. He supported my recommendation, and we were the last country to sign the Yamburg gas agreement. Their [the Soviet] argument was very simple: all the other countries have signed, and

---

[38]"Rozmowy z ZSRR n. S. koordynacji planów na lata 1986–1990 (25–29 marca 1985 r.)," CUP Archive.

[39]Ibid.

[40]Manfred Gorywoda, letter to Wojciech Jaruzelski, 10 April 1985, CUP Archive: 488/6.

[41]Interviews with Stanisław Długosz, 5.7.1992, and 5.21.1992.

we can't give you special conditions. If you don't want it, don't take it; but you won't receive [more] gas under any other conditions. We decided there was no other option.[42]

The Soviets threatened to withhold increases in natural gas exports, not to cut off exports of gas altogether. Nevertheless, Poland was effectively compelled to accept Soviet conditions for natural gas exports in the Yamburg agreement. An effective linkage had been made between a potent Soviet resource and an important Soviet interest.

What is remarkable, however, is that so few such linkages were made. Exports of natural gas were linked only to the Yamburg agreement, and not, for example, to expanding the iron-ore facility at Krivoi Rog, which Poland, Czechoslovakia, and Hungary each successfully boycotted in the 1980s. The Soviets threatened only to withhold increments of gas, but not to withhold "traditional" deliveries. The Soviet Union employed only a portion of the bargaining leverage at its disposal. Meanwhile, the East Europeans continued to resist important Soviet objectives on a number of fronts.

CONCLUSIONS

The focus of conflict in trade negotiations was the size of the Soviet trade subsidy to each country. The subsidy, in turn, was determined by the gross proportions of finished goods and raw materials, by fine distinctions between more- and less-profitable products in each category, and by participation in investments on Soviet territory. Alternative motivations fail to explain the countries' bargaining positions. The issues typical of collective-action problems were of marginal concern, because each transaction was nested in a continuous series of negotiations and adjustments. Failures to make deliveries or to balance trade did not arouse deep concern and did not become systematic. Trade surpluses arose by agreement, and not because of the failure of one partner to make expected deliveries. Similarly, fear of excessive trade dependency did not play an important role in East European trade politics. It was generally the East Europeans who favored increased trade with the Soviet Union, and the Soviet Union that had to politely decline.

The parties' bargaining strategies were asymmetrical. The Soviet Union enjoyed substantial excess bargaining leverage, since it provided a massive implicit trade subsidy to its allies. Soviet negotiators therefore sought to make linkages between issues explicit, in order to elicit East European cooperation. The East Europeans tried to minimize the Soviet advantage by avoiding linkages between issues. The Soviet Union made frequent use of threats, but the satellites did not practice tit-for-tat retaliation. Their bargaining strategies

[42]Interview with Stanisław Długosz, 5.21.1992.

sought to obscure issues, create the appearance of compliance, and bargain from weakness.

The organizational features of the negotiation process were very important, and when used wisely, they allowed the small countries to outmaneuver the Soviet Union. The Soviet Union was utterly unable to link economic issues to military issues, where it exercised unchallenged dominance, and was often unable to translate subsidies in one area of trade into effective bargaining leverage in another. Obstacles to vertical communication within the Soviet bureaucracy compartmentalized issues and frustrated attempts to link trade subsidies to equivalent East European concessions. Although the Soviet Union had a dominant bargaining position that allowed it to win disputes of great concern, such as East European participation in construction of the Yamburg gas pipeline, it failed to win agreement in many other cases, and it frequently failed to exploit excess bargaining leverage in one issue area to win concessions in others.

In addition, since Soviet policymakers at various levels had very different access to information, it became difficult, if not impossible, to coordinate their bargaining positions. East European negotiators frequently won key concessions simply by raising the level of protocol. In effect, they appealed undesirable conditions to higher levels of the Soviet hierarchy, and often won the appeals. As a result, low-level officials were unable to convincingly represent their superiors' positions. The repeated failures of Soviet officials to make their bargaining positions stick led to a severe erosion of Soviet credibility, and consequently a decline in the usefulness of their threats. Stripped of a crucial line of defense, Soviet interests suffered and the trade subsidy spiraled out of control.

CHAPTER 4

The Costs of Empire?

A REPORT prepared in 1965 by the Soviet Institute for the Economy of the World Socialist System argued that the Soviet leadership should use its economic leverage in a systematic attempt to modify the behavior of its satellites. The report urged the implementation of a "differentiated approach" to the more "nationalistic" socialist countries, specifically designed to reward or punish them for their policies, and criticized existing Soviet policy as "inflexible."[1]

> It would be desirable to develop a flexible, maneuverable tactic with respect to these socialist countries in order not to alienate them, but at the same time in order that they might really feel an economic loss as a result of their nationalistic isolation from the socialist camp; and, in reverse, in order that every step in the direction of unity with the socialist countries gave them perceptible economic benefits. . . . A differentiated approach to the various countries with regard to providing them with deficit fuel, energy, and raw material commodities would be very important in strengthening the cooperation of the other countries of the CMEA with the USSR.[2]

Western observers have long assumed that this was just the sort of policy the Soviet Union pursued toward its socialist allies. Economic largess, they have reasoned, surely does not come without strings attached. Indeed, it has generally been assumed that Soviet economic policy was subordinated to a military-political calculus, and that the East Europeans' economic dependence was an asset shrewdly exploited in Moscow.

A key argument presented in chapter 1 was that this could not be the case, because institutional constraints prevented Soviet negotiators from making effective linkages between issues, and particularly between economic and political issues. Soviet policy was a poor servant of Soviet interests, because an inefficient institutional filter intervened between intention and execution. The subsidy emerged from a negotiation process that the Soviet Union could not control, because Soviet negotiators had weak incentives to represent Soviet national interests.

---

[1]Alampiev et al., "O razvitii i ukreplenii ekonomicheskogo sotrudnichestva," IMEPI Archive, IEMSS report, 6.18.1965, pp. 50, 71–72.

[2]Ibid., pp. 71–72.

This chapter will argue that careful analysis of Soviet–East European trade statistics reveals no evidence to support the common assertion that the volume and distribution of the trade subsidy were linked to the satellites' behavior along political or military dimensions of cooperation. The evidence does not show that the Soviet Union consistently favored some countries over others, although this has been a recurring theme in surveys of the politics of the region. Furthermore, the interpretation of the subsidy as a deliberate policy tool fails to account for its sharp rise in the 1970s and 1980s, buoyed by prices on world markets.

The analysis shows that the most important determinant of variations in subsidization was the recipient country's level of production of key commodities, particularly coal and steel. Although this finding could be interpreted as indicating a Soviet effort to systematically extract the excess rents contained in its subsidy to producers of fuel resources, it more plausibly reflects variations in the East Europeans' bargaining preferences that depended on their ability to find domestic substitutes for Soviet exports. In either case, this finding is inconsistent with the interpretation of Soviet trade policy as driven by, and linked to, political considerations.

VARIATION IN THE SOVIET SUBSIDY AMONG THE CMEA COUNTRIES

"Well," argued one Polish trade negotiator, "if you want to be a hegemon, you should pay for the privilege!"[3] It is a widely held view that the Soviet trade subsidy was indeed just that: a payment for a privilege. This is a common realist argument, which views the Soviet state as a unitary actor and treats its economic policies as instrumental to achieving its security objectives. If this interpretation is correct, we should expect to see some relationship between the level of payments to each country and the privileges that the Soviet Union enjoyed vis-à-vis its various allies. For example, one might argue that, if the Soviet Union used the subsidy to reward or punish its allies for their support or opposition to policy initiatives in various areas, the most loyal countries would enjoy the greatest benefits. Alternatively, if some countries were more independent and more difficult to cajole, they might receive greater benefits, on the principle that the squeaky wheel gets the grease. Either way, the distribution of the subsidy should be correlated with political factors.[4] If such a correlation could be established, it would suggest that Soviet policy had in fact efficiently adapted means to ends, and that the Soviet bureaucracy had therefore behaved as a rational actor.

[3]Interview with Alfred Siennicki, 5.18.1992.

[4]One possible construction of the realist interpretation would not necessarily lead to the expectation of a correlation, but it is an inherently untestable hypothesis. It is as follows: each country has a unique prior level of resistance to Soviet demands, each receives an amount of subsidy

The most detailed study of the Soviet trade subsidy to date, by Michael Marrese and Jan Vanous, concludes that "the size of the implicit Soviet trade subsidy received by a CMEA Six country [Bulgaria, Czecheslovakia, the GDR, Hungary, Poland, or Romania] appears to be related to the amount of nonmarket benefits supplied."[5] In other words, the countries that provided the most political, military, and ideological support received the largest subsidies. To test this claim, Marrese and Vanous created a scale of these "nonmarket benefits" by averaging subjective scores for each country on sixteen different dimensions of loyalty and strategic importance to the Soviet Union, and ranking the countries by their aggregate scores. They then ranked the countries according to the trade subsidies they received from the Soviet Union, and compared the rankings. The rankings corresponded relatively well, so Marrese and Vanous concluded that there was "tentative support for our contention that the Soviet Union has been allocating its trade subsidies in a rational manner."[6] The result of their study is shown in Table 4.1.

These conclusions can be subjected to more rigorous statistical analysis. Consequently, I have run regressions using a variety of dependent and independent variables to verify the Marrese and Vanous conclusions. Rather than aggregate the Soviet trade subsidy, as Marrese and Vanous did, each of the major components of the Soviet trade subsidy is selected as a dependent variable: Soviet exports of oil, gas, coal, and iron ore, and the trade balance in machinery. This approach has the advantage that important variations are not lost in aggregation; moreover, it allows us to investigate whether the subsidy was itself consistent. The assumption is that if Soviet trade subsidization was in fact purposeful, and if the Marrese and Vanous rankings were a fair measure of the Soviet purpose, the rankings should be correlated with each of the major measures of the subsidy. Important Soviet commodity exports and the overall balance in machinery would be the easiest instruments for Soviet policymakers to manipulate, and interviews with trade negotiators confirm that these numbers were closely watched. Finally, the analysis employs an expanded data set. The data used for these regressions cover the period from 1949 to 1989; the Marrese and Vanous analysis was based on data from 1960 to 1978.

---

proportional to deviations from its prior level, and each ends up at a unique level of compliance. In this case, the more resistant and more compliant countries can receive similar amounts of subsidy while still retaining proportionality between the subsidy payment and policy benefits to the Soviet Union. Note that it would be an improbable coincidence for such a procedure not to lead to some correlation between the level of payments and either compliant or noncompliant policies. The more serious problem with this construction, however, is that since prior levels and deviations cannot be observed, the proposition is not testable. I thank Gary King for raising this objection.

[5]Marrese and Vanous, *Soviet Subsidization of Trade*, p. 86.
[6]Ibid., p. 86.

TABLE 4.1

Marrese-Vanous Rankings of CMEA Countries according to Nonmarket Benefits
Provided to the Soviet Union and Three Measures of Implicit Subsidization

Area of Ranking	Ranking of CMEA Six (in descending order of loyalty and importance)					
	Bulgaria	CSSR	GDR	Hungary	Poland	Romania
Nonmarket benefits	3	2	1	4	5	6
Implicit subsidies 1960–1978						
• Dollar value	5	2	1	4	3	6
• Per capita	4	2	1	3	5	6
• Per dollar of USSR Exports	5	3	1	2	4	6
Implicit subsidies 1974–1978						
• Dollar value	4	2	1	5	3	6
• Per capita	1	3	2	4	5	6
• Per dollar of USSR Exports	3	2	1	4	5	6

Source: Marrese and Vanous, 1983, p. 85.

The independent variables simultaneously tested the Marrese and Vanous hypothesis and a logical counterhypothesis: that exports of the commodity in question depended instead on plausible economic criteria. The first set of regressions used a rank ordinal variable coded with the Marrese and Vanous rankings, which tests the hypothesis that two propositions are simultaneously true: (1) the size of the subsidy is correlated with a static measure of political loyalty and importance, and (2) the Marrese-Vanous rankings of the six countries are correct. For the four commodities the independent variables were the rank variable, a lagged variable representing the hypothesis that the observed effects were the result of the multicollinearity typically experienced with time-series data, bilateral trade turnover, and domestic production of the commodity. For the machinery balance the independent variables were the dummy variable, the lagged variable, and trade turnover. Since the Marrese-Vanous ranking runs in descending order (1 is best, 6 is worst), a negative correlation between the ranking and a dependent variable confirms the Marrese-Vanous hypothesis, and a positive correlation or no correlation disconfirms the hypothesis. Table 4.2 summarizes the results of six regression equations.

Three important conclusions can be drawn from Table 4.2. First, the Marrese-Vanous hypothesis does not explain the distribution of the total subsidy as approximated by the total of the four commodities and the balance of machinery. The coefficient for the aggregate subsidy was insignificant. Second, Soviet exports of oil, coal, gas, and iron clearly are not explained by

TABLE 4.2
A Test of the Marrese-Vanous Hypothesis

| Dependent Variable | Independent Variables | | Number of Observations |
	Country Ranking Coefficient	Domestic Production Coefficient	
Aggregate subsidy	7,786	−.21	114
	(10,146)[a]	(.20)	
	.77[b]	−1.0	
Oil exports	1,428	−2.9	180
	(10,223)	(3.4)	
	.14	−.85	
Gas exports	−1,904	−.16	180
	(3,135)	(.06)	
	−.61	−2.9	
Coal exports	−1,548	.04	106
	(1,418)	(.025)	
	−1.1	1.5	
Iron exports	483	−.78	106
	(692)	(.82)	
	.70	−.96	
Machinery balance	−20,409	3.9	194
	(7,657)	(2.5)	
	−2.7	1.6	

Source: Trade statistics were taken from various volumes of *Sovetskaia torgovliia*; national production figures are from various volumes of *Statisticheskii ezhegodnik stran-chlenov Soveta Ekonomicheskoi Vzaimopomoschi*, and from national East European statistical yearbooks. All computations were carried out on SST.

[a]Numbers in parentheses are standard errors for each coefficient.

[b]Numbers in italics are t-statistics. In general, a t-statistic must have an absolute value of approximately 2 or greater for a coefficient to be statistically significant.

the Marrese-Vanous hypothesis. The regressions show that the coefficient of the variable representing the rankings was too small to be statistically significant. The effect of the ranking on the distribution of the subsidy, in other words, is indistinguishable from zero. On the other hand, the negative coefficient of the country ranking when the dependent variable was the machinery balance does support the Marrese-Vanous hypothesis. A better (lower) ranking on the Marrese-Vanous scale is correlated with a larger surplus in the machinery category. These conclusions were found to be robust: the observed effects persisted even when new independent variables were introduced.

Even the success of the Marrese-Vanous hypothesis in explaining machinery balances, however, is subject to several interpretations. When the regression was run again, this time excluding data for East Germany and Czechoslovakia, the observed effect disappeared.[7] This indicates that the observed relationship was really a relationship between East Germany and Czechoslovakia, on the one hand, and the rest of the bloc, on the other; this is not the linear relationship that Marrese and Vanous had hypothesized. Moving down the scale from third place in the Marrese-Vanous ranking did not bring additional deterioration of one's market share for machinery exports. This observation suggests an alternative explanation for the observed effect. The GDR and Czechoslovakia were by far the most industrially advanced countries in Eastern Europe. They produced a much wider variety of machinery than their neighbors, and were not industrializing as quickly, so they had fewer import needs. They produced higher-quality goods than the other socialist states, and in greater quantity and variety, so their total exports of machines were correspondingly greater, both to the East and to the West. This alone may well explain the benefits reaped by East Germany and Czechoslovakia. This is a difficult proposition to test, since no reliable measure of total machinery production or competitiveness exists for all the East European countries, and those that exist for individual countries are not comparable because national currencies are inconvertible. However, this is the interpretation made by Czechoslovak trade officials.[8] Furthermore, this conclusion seems more plausible than the Marrese-Vanous hypothesis, since Marrese and Vanous cannot explain commodity exports, and their hypothesis predicts a distribution of machinery balances among the remaining four countries that did not emerge from the data.

So far, the analysis has proceeded with an ordinal variable because that was the form in which the Marrese-Vanous hypothesis was framed. A more decisive test of the hypothesis, however, employs dummy variables for each of the East European satellites. Unlike using the Marrese-Vanous rankings as a vector, employing separate dummy variables for the countries directly tests the hypothesis that some relationship exists between the subsidy and the identity of the recipient. If such a correlation were found, it would be possible to interpret the findings presented in Table 4.2 as demonstrating simply that Marrese and Vanous had selected the wrong loyalty rankings. The hypothesis that the subsidy was distributed according to political loyalty might not have to be rejected. On the other hand, this is a very forgiving test of the hypothesis, because the dummy variables do not contain any information about political issues. A correlation, therefore, does not prove the hypothesis correct; it merely leaves open the possibility that the hypothesis may not be false. First, I treated the six countries as independent variables explaining the distribution

[7]With 132 observations, the new coefficient for the machinery balance was 22,215, the standard error was 15,835, and the t-statistic was 1.4.

[8]Interview with Vladislav Cihlař, 6.17.1992.

of the subsidy as a whole, represented as the sum of the balance of trade in machinery and Soviet exports of oil, gas, coal, and iron. Although the number coded as "aggregate subsidy" does not represent a ruble value of the subsidy, it is correlated with the most visible measures of the subsidy available to Soviet and East European officials. Additional variables were introduced to represent the volume of each country's trade with the Soviet Union, each country's level of industrial development (represented by steel production figures), and domestic production of the subsidized commodities: oil, gas, and iron ore. Table 4.3 summarizes the results. The results provide mixed evidence. Four of the country variables were indistinguishable from zero, which means that, from the negotiator's point of view, it made no statistically significant difference whether one represented Czechoslovakia, Hungary, Poland, or Romania. This undermines the hypothesis that the distribution depended primarily on politics, since Romania was generally considered the pariah of the bloc, Czechoslovakia (after 1968) was extremely loyal, and Poland was both loyal and in economic crisis for the last two decades of Soviet power. On the other hand, the significant coefficients for Bulgaria and East Germany provide a pattern of distribution that demands an explanation. As we will see, Bulgaria was disfavored and the GDR was favored in the balance of machinery, and this accounts for most of the variation in the total subsidy.[9] If it is true that variations in the machinery balance depend more on the productivity of each country's industry than on political favor, therefore, the same is true of the variations in the total subsidy. The results point to other factors that strongly influenced the distribution of the subsidy: trade volume, domestic steel production, and production of coal and iron were each significantly correlated with the subsidy.

Two questions remain. First, do patterns emerge at the level of individual commodities that are obscured at the aggregate level? The possibility remains that some politically salient portions of the subsidy might be distributed preferentially. Second, are these patterns consistent? If they are, that would lend support to the notion that they are driven by an overarching political calculus. If they are inconsistent, it is much more likely that they are artifacts of other factors working at the micro-level. In order to investigate these questions, regressions were again run using each major component of the subsidy as a dependent variable, and including all the same control variables. Table 4.4 shows the coefficients calculated for each dummy variable and the dependent variable for each regression (the other independent variables are summarized in Table 4.5).

[9]Bulgaria was 1.01 million rubles below the baseline in total subsidized trade, but was 2.04 million rubles below the baseline in machinery alone. The GDR was 4.74 million rubles above the baseline in total trade, but was 1.92 million rubles above in machinery alone. If the coefficients were corrected by those amounts, the Bulgaria variable would reverse its sign, and the GDR variable would no longer be statistically significant.

TABLE 4.3

Statistical Significance of National Variations in the Aggregate Soviet Subsidy
(thousands of rubles of exports/thousands of tons of production)

Independent Variable	Estimated Coefficient	Standard Error	t-Statistic
Trade volume	.16	.02	8.2
Steel production	23	9.2	2.6
Oil production	−12	26	−.47
Coal production	−2.2	.98	−2.3
Iron production	−33	16	−2.0
Bulgaria	−101,529	49,176	−2.1
Czechoslovakia	95,289	79,105	1.2
GDR	473,528	215,712	2.2
Hungary	−7,936	45,939	−.17
Poland	133,343	98,684	1.4
Romania	72,863	304,857	.24

Source: See Table 4.2.
Note: Number of observations: 102.

Several important conclusions emerge from this exercise. First, most of the dummy variables are not statistically significant, which means that the identity of the countries did not make a discernible difference in the distribution of the subsidy—it was distributed according to other factors. Second, when countries are occasionally favored or disfavored, their treatment is not consistent, which means at the very least that the Soviet Union did not distribute its subsidy with a systematic preference for particular countries. Romania was the most favored with respect to natural gas and Poland was most favored with respect to coal, but both were disfavored with respect to machinery.[10] The only country that was treated consistently was Bulgaria, which was disfavored in oil, natural gas, and machinery. Yet this hardly seems to support a political interpretation, since Bulgaria was by all accounts the most pliable of the Soviet allies. Third, the dummy variables were significant in explaining the balance of trade in machinery but had difficulty accounting for commodity exports. It is conceivable that the Soviet Union chose to pursue a linkage strategy that was limited to the balance of machinery, and for some reason chose to forego using commodities strategically. This seems implausible, however, because cutting machinery imports for political purposes would impose costs on Soviet industry, whereas cutting off commodity exports was

[10]Neither was favored in absolute terms; Romania began importing substantial amounts of natural gas only in the late 1970s, and Poland never imported nearly as much coal as the GDR. However, the regression equations show that domestic producers of energy commodities imported less of those commodities than nonproducers. Given their levels of domestic production, Poland and Romania had remarkably high imports of coal and gas, respectively.

TABLE 4.4

National Variations in the Soviet Subsidy by Major Components
(thousands of convertible rubles)

Dependent Variable	Bulgaria	CSSR	GDR	Hungary	Poland	Romania	Number of Observations
Oil exports	-83,481	-34,287	-101,456	-74,571	-42,455	-41,157	180
	(40,903)[a]	(56,946)	(171,719)	(43,204)	(94,422)	(196,016)	
	-2.0[b]	-.60	-.59	-1.7	-.45	-.21	
Coal exports	-4,237	11,159	3,995	-988	2,558	3,902	120
	(5,111)	9,708	(3,113)	(661)	(1,429)	(40,733)	
	-.83	1.15	1.3	-.15	1.79	-.10	
Natural gas exports	-23,785	2,732	74,687	8,825	23,640	187,229	180
	(11,384)	(16,870)	(47,098)	12,135	(27,518	(59,613)	
	-2.1	.16	1.6	.73	.86	3.1	
Iron ore exports	-1,043	5,058	-12,976	2,719	2,169	9,607	106
	(3,405)	(5,492)	(14,492)	(3,253)	(6,945)	(21,515)	
	-.31	.92	-.89	.84	.31	.45	
Machinery balance	-147,718	18,835	68,496	-48,444	-113.724	-73,679	210
	(33,928)	(29,069)	(31,448)	(28,256)	(32,994)	(27,843)	
	-4.4	.65	2.2	-1.7	-3.4	-2.6	

Source: See Table 4.2.

[a]The numbers in parentheses are the standard errors of each coefficient.

[b]The numbers in italics are t-statistics.

TABLE 4.5

Variations in the Soviet Subsidy by Domestic Production
(thousands of rubles of export/thousands of tons of production)

Dependent Variable	Independent Variable					
	Oil	Coal	Iron Ore	Steel	Trade Volume	Number of Observations
Aggregate subsidy	−12.2 (26.1)[a] −.47[b]	−2.23 (.98) −2.3	−32.7 (16.5) −2.0	23.8 (9.19) 2.6	.16 .02 8.2	106
Oil exports	−2.75 (15.7) −.17	.13 (.74) .18	—	−.61 (6.0) −.10	.07 (.01) 5.1	180
Coal exports	−1.21 (3.49) −.35	−.29 (.13) −2.2	3.82 (2.49) 1.5	.63 (1.15) .55	.01 (.002) 6.0	106
Natural gas exports	−17.7 (4.80) −3.69	−.58 (.21) −2.75	—	5.58 (1.60) 3.48	.02 (.003) 6.13	180
Iron ore exports	−.77 (1.84) −.42	.04 (.07) .60	−1.09 (1.14) −.96	2.21 (.85) 2.6	.001 (.001) 1.5	106
Machinery balance	—	—	—	−6.65 (4.42) −1.5	.08 (.01) 9.0	194

Source: See Table 4.2.

[a] The numbers in parentheses are the standard errors of each coefficient.

[b] The numbers in italics are t-statistics.

costless and allowed the Soviet Union to earn valuable foreign exchange by selling those commodities on world markets. If forced to choose, it seems likely that Soviet officials would use commodity exports as a political tool rather than machinery imports. At the same time, discovering no pattern in commodities to match the pattern in trade in machinery is consistent with the interpretation that the pattern in machinery was simply an artifact of differences in the productivity of national machine-building sectors.

A closer look at the results in Table 4.4 reveals another reason to doubt that the Soviet Union pursued a discriminatory policy. If it did so, it applied a very fine touch, since the coefficients are small relative to Soviet–East European trade flows. For example, the big losers in oil, Bulgaria and Hungary, lost 83 million and 74 million rubles worth of Soviet oil exports per year, respectively, which amounted to 8 percent and 10 percent of their imports in 1980. Similarly, the 24 million rubles worth of natural gas that the Soviet Union withheld from Bulgaria was equal to 10 percent of its imports. That was enough to send a signal, but hardly sufficient to bring recalcitrant allies to their knees. If it had launched a policy of economic pressure, why was the Soviet Union so restrained? Only in the area of machinery exports were the variations substantial. Bulgaria lost 148 million rubles of machinery exports per year, and Poland lost 114 million—nearly 20 percent of their respective machinery export surpluses in 1980.

The distribution of the subsidy is more clearly linked to variations in the countries' domestic production. Table 4.5 summarizes the results of a series of regressions using the countries' identities as control variables and using national production of key commodities as independent variables. Each of the variables for domestic production, except oil production, was strongly correlated with the aggregate subsidy. For the most part, domestic production of commodities was correlated with lower imports of those commodities or their substitutes. The weaker results for oil production may occur because in Eastern Europe, only Romania produced significant quantities of oil. Steel production was positively correlated with inputs for steel production: iron ore and natural gas. (Gas was used extensively for smelting.) The volume of trade between each country and the Soviet Union was correlated with every measure of the subsidy except iron ore exports.

These findings lend themselves to two alternative explanations: one that purports to find a purposeful Soviet policy of subsidization, and one that regards the resulting pattern as the result of East European choices of bargaining strategies. The argument for a purposeful Soviet policy goes as follows: the Soviet Union made no effort to link trade to discreet political issues, but rather sought to guarantee the economic viability of the bloc at the lowest possible cost.[11] Consequently, the Soviet Union economized on scarce commodities by compelling its satellites to practice self-reliance. Countries able to produce coal received lower coal exports. In this view, the needs of each country for iron ore, for example, depended on domestic production of steel, and the Soviet Union sought to meet the need. In essence, it faithfully followed the Marxist precept, "From each according to ability, to each according to need." Furthermore, the correlation between bilateral trade volume and various measures of the subsidy can be interpreted as incentives for the East Europeans to intensify their trade with the Soviet Union to the exclusion of other partners.

This interpretation is itself a testable hypothesis. The logical conclusion of

---

[11] Valerie Bunce has argued, along these lines, that the Soviet subsidy was driven by rising consumer expectations in the satellite countries, which caused the price of political stability to rise over time. Thus Bunce does not argue that the Soviet objective was to link the subsidy to satellite behavior, but simply that the Soviet Union was committed to subsidizing the East European countries enough to maintain political stability (Bunce, "The Empire Strikes Back").

this line of argument is that each country should receive a share of the subsidy that is proportional to its potential for instability. If the Soviet Union doled out the subsidy in a deliberate way intended to safeguard political stability, the countries should receive very different amounts of support, since political stability varied substantially from country to country. But there were no patterns of preferential treatment: the dummy variables representing the countries were not statistically significant. I take this to indicate that the Soviet Union was unable to pursue such a deliberate and consistent policy; institutional failures prevented it from doing so.

There are several additional difficulties with this interpretation. If the Soviet Union indeed intended to make its satellites more self-reliant, the way to do so was to offer them incentives to produce commodities, not to punish commodity producers. The optimal policy would be to increase the subsidy for each unit of commodities produced. If the Soviet Union nevertheless desired to recapture some of the excess subsidy to countries capable of producing commodities, the logical approach would be to penalize the potential commodity producers by some fixed sum. The net Soviet subsidy transfer to each country (T) would therefore be composed of a fixed payment (A) that was unique for each country and an incentive payment that was some proportion (B) of each country's commodity production (C). The net transfer is given by the equation, $T = A + B (C)$. This would result in significant variations in the fixed payments (the coefficients of the dummy variables) and *positive* correlations between domestic commodity production and various measures of the subsidy. Instead, we find little significance in the dummy variables for commodities, and negative correlations with domestic commodity production. If the Soviet Union was pursuing a deliberate distributive policy, it was doing so ineptly.

It is difficult to believe, furthermore, that the satellites would have behaved as they did had the Soviet Union chosen to pursue such a ham-fisted policy. For example, if the Soviet Union actually reduced its coal exports by .29 rubles for each ton of coal produced, that tax cost the GDR 72 million rubles worth of coal imports in 1975, or 41 percent of its coal imports from the Soviet Union. Such draconian disincentives would surely impel the East Europeans to cut their domestic coal production. In the most extreme case, if the countries were indeed penalized 32 rubles worth of subsidized trade for every ton of iron ore they produced, why did any of them bother to produce iron ore?[12]

In addition, it is unlikely that the correlations with the trade volume were powerful enough to effectively induce the East Europeans to expand trade. In 1975, for example, approximately 32 percent of GDR-USSR trade was included in one of the five categories identified as subsidized; this, presumably,

---

[12]For purposes of comparison, iron ore was priced at about 8 rubles per ton in the early 1970s.

was approximately the best deal the East German negotiators thought they could achieve. To offer the GDR 16 kopeks of subsidized trade for each additional ruble of trade volume, then, was to offer a deterioration of their terms of trade. The coefficients of the trade volume for each of the components of the trade subsidy were much smaller, suggesting that strategic commodities were not linked to trade volume in any meaningful way. On the other hand, the alternative interpretation is obvious: any increase in trade—in any commodity —increases trade volume. It would be anomalous if there were no correlation. This does not, however, explain the positive correlation between trade volume and the balance of machinery exports. It is not obvious that trade volume should be higher when the East Europeans run a surplus in machinery and lower when the Soviet Union runs a surplus in that category. However, that does not mean we must assume a purposeful Soviet strategy. A more plausible interpretation is that the satellites chose to take advantage of opportunities to widen their machinery surpluses, and increased their trade with the Soviet Union in order to do so. When such opportunities were not available, they chose to concentrate on trade with other partners.

The most plausible interpretation of the correlates of the Soviet subsidy is that the distribution resulted from East European choices, rather than from an overarching Soviet strategy. The satellites bargained with the Soviet Union across a variety of issue areas, and presumably under some set of constraints that forced them to make trade-offs. They were pressed for time, did not want to exhaust the goodwill and patience of their negotiating partners, or were able to exert only some fixed amount of effort; whatever the reason, it is plausible that they did not bargain with the same resolve on every point. Naturally, each country's representatives would have bargained most vigorously for commodities for which the country in question had no accessible domestic substitutes. If a country produced coal and steel, then importing coal was not as high a priority as importing iron ore. As a result, some negative correlation ought to exist between domestic production of a commodity and imports of that commodity, even if domestic consumption is voracious. This tendency also explains the positive correlation between steel production and natural gas and iron exports: producers of steel require more of those inputs, so they will enjoy higher priority. The effect of domestic oil production is not as marked, possibly because only Romania produced oil in any significant quantity, and possibly because the CMEA price of oil was so favorable that importing more for reexport was always advantageous. Oil production had a strong influence on demand for natural gas, however, perhaps because gas is often abundant where oil is found.

The most plausible interpretation of the data leads to the conclusion that the Soviet Union did not use the trade subsidy as part of a strategy of political linkage. There is no demonstrable link between political considerations and the distribution of the subsidy. In fact, no significant pattern of discrimination among the satellites exists. Even the weak form of a linkage argument, which posits that the Soviet Union gave the subsidy and asked for nothing specific in return, fails to account for the pattern of variation according to domestic production. The most plausible construction of the results is that the East Europeans determined the distribution of the subsidy by bargaining most vigorously for the commodities they possessed in least abundance.

VARIATION IN THE SOVIET TRADE SUBSIDY OVER TIME

If the Soviet trade subsidy were a deliberate tool of policy, one would expect to see a pattern of variation over time that reflects the goals of that policy. The share of the subsidy going to each country should vary substantially over time, as the Soviet Union applies rewards and sanctions. Furthermore, the total volume of the subsidy should be closely controlled, assuring a reasonable proportionality between ends and means. If the subsidy was not a conscious tool of policy, on the other hand, the variations in relative subsidization of particular countries should be minimal.

In fact, exports of most key commodities were so predictable in quantitative terms that it is difficult to view them as an active instrument of policy. If the Soviet Union had used oil as a tool to pressure its allies, for example, we would expect to see sharp variations in Soviet oil exports. Soviet trade statistics show, however, that deliveries remained stable in quantitative terms within each five-year plan, although prices varied. Exports of major commodities such as oil, gas, coal, and iron ore were set in long-term agreements, and annual variations from those agreements were slight. Similarly, the ratios of Soviet imports and exports to CMEA countries in broad categories of goods such as fuels, raw materials, and machinery remained stable or changed only gradually. Once a given quantitative plateau had been reached for commodity exports, it was uncommon for deliveries to decline. It seems unlikely, therefore, that commodity exports could have been linked to particular political or economic concessions. The only construction of these trends that is consistent with an interpretation based on strategic linkages is that the Soviet threat to reduce commodity exports was so potent that it never had to be carried out. This seems implausible, however, in view of the increasing tendency in the 1970s and 1980s for certain East European countries to assert their own national priorities in foreign and domestic policy.

Still more telling is that the Soviet leadership did not attempt to regulate the total size of the trade subsidy with any precision, and only made sporadic efforts to control it when it rose rapidly. In the CMEA's first two decades, the Soviet Union rapidly expanded its exports of petroleum, coal, iron ore, and other key commodities in proportion to its increasing domestic production. In its second two decades, increases became much more gradual, as the Soviet economic engine slowed. The increase in the Soviet subsidy after 1970 was caused almost entirely by a factor beyond Soviet control: the rapid rise in world oil prices brought on by the concerted action of the Organization of Petroleum Exporting Countries, which outstripped the CMEA price-adjustment mechanism. Marrese and Vanous estimate that the value of the Soviet subsidy more than doubled in real terms between 1972 and 1973, and rose by nearly three times between 1973 and 1974.[13] The subsidy declined in 1975, when the CMEA adopted a more flexible price system, but increased again following world price trends in 1979, and did not decline again until the mid-1980s.

Throughout this period the Soviets made only one attempt to address the issue of distorted CMEA prices that gave rise to the subsidy. In 1974, when CMEA energy prices had lagged to 41 percent of world levels, Soviet negotiators demanded a revision of CMEA pricing rules.[14] Until this point, prices had remained fixed for many years, and were revised only when they departed substantially from world price levels. Under the new Soviet proposal, prices would be indexed to a running average of the previous five years' price levels, so that they would change annually. Since world prices had risen dramatically in the previous two years, the new formula raised CMEA prices sharply. Czechoslovakia, East Germany, Hungary, and Bulgaria each pressed the Soviet negotiators to ease the transition to higher prices, but they had nothing to offer the Soviets in return.[15] A high-level Soviet negotiating team was dispatched to each of the CMEA capitals, consisting of the chairman of Gosplan, the minister of foreign trade, and the chairman of the State Committee for Economic Cooperation. The Soviets simply announced the new terms, and the East Europeans were compelled to accept them.[16] When it chose to do so, the Soviet leadership was still in a position to dictate terms to its satellites.

What is striking, however, is that the Soviet leadership so rarely chose to exercise its overwhelming bargaining leverage. After 1975 the trade subsidy reverted to a passive instrument, which was allowed to rise and fall with the tides of the international market. The Soviet Union did not again attempt to adjust CMEA oil prices until 1990. If, to paraphrase Clausewitz, the trade subsidy were simply "an extension of policy by other means," then its dimensions should be proportional to the objectives sought. The Soviet Union's renunciation of any ambitions to control the size of the trade subsidy after 1975, allowing it to be determined by the whims of capitalist market forces, indicates that the size of the subsidy was not used as a policy tool. Zbigniew Madej, the Polish deputy premier, noted wryly that this appeared to confirm revisionist Marxism:

> We took the West as our mirror. Kautsky said it clearly, that the socialist countries would have to study the capitalist countries. That is the way it was. We took our

[13]Marrese and Vanous, *Soviet Subsidization of Trade, p. 44.*

[14]Ibid., p. 59.

[15]Interview with Zdeněk Šedivý, former Deputy Chairman, Czechoslovak State Planning Commission, 6.30.1992.

[16]Interview with Istvan Hetenyi, former Deputy and First Deputy Chairman, Hungarian State Planning Commission, 9.7.1992.

prices from the West, and in the end the socialist countries could never separate their economies from capitalism.[17]

Regardless of whether this was a confirmation of Kautsky, world market prices were an ironic standard for socialist fraternalism. Since the Soviets substituted inertia for a policy on CMEA oil prices, we must conclude that the trade subsidy was far from being a deliberate means to a deliberate end.

Instead of targeting the size of the trade subsidy, the Soviet leadership reacted haphazardly to the stresses and strains of the Soviet economy. Although Soviet trade policy went through a gradual evolution, it applied a series of short-term solutions to what was in essence a long-term problem: the deteriorating capacity of the Soviet economy to sustain the far-flung commitments of a world power. In the 1950s and 1960s the Soviet Union set quantitative goals for increasing exports of key raw materials and fuels to its allies, and this was publicly acknowledged as a form of aid. In the mid-1960s Soviet policy-makers concluded that there were limits to extensive growth, and that the Soviet Union would have to put relations with its satellites on a commercial basis. The Soviet Union then began to push for a revision of the terms of trade, demanding that its allies also export surplus raw materials, and urging them to improve the quality of the finished goods they exported. In the late 1960s the Soviet Union began to demand direct investments on Soviet territory in return for incremental commodity exports as a means of defraying the cost of developing raw materials. These demands became more insistent in the 1970s and 1980s. For several decades the Soviet Union sought to scale back its commitments in Eastern Europe and to compel the East Europeans to take more responsibility for their own supplies of raw materials. At the same time, however, the Soviet trade subsidy spiraled out of control.

CONCLUSIONS

This chapter provides evidence that the trade subsidy was not a carefully calibrated instrument of Soviet control over its satellites. The first section challenged the claims of the major study which argued that the subsidy was distributed according to the security and political benefits the Soviet Union received from its various satellites. On closer investigation it was found that the correlation reported by Marrese and Vanous does not hold for major commodity exports. A correlation with the Marrese and Vanous strategic ranking exists for only one element of the trade subsidy: the Soviet deficit in machinery exports. Even this result may be the artifact of the greater productivity of the Czechoslovak and East German machine-building sectors, since the relationship does not hold for the other countries in isolation. Additional tests showed that the identity of particular countries has a statistically insignificant

[17]Interview with Zbigniew Madej, 5.29.1992.

effect on the distribution of major commodities. Consequently, I conclude that there is no evidence to support the realist claim that the Soviet Union discriminated among its allies in distributing the trade subsidy.

The intriguing intepretation that the Soviet Union pursued a deliberately even-handed distributional policy finds some support in the data: domestic production of key commodities is negatively correlated with Soviet exports. One possible interpretation of this evidence is that Soviet exports were based on an estimate of national needs, and that Soviet negotiators sought to compel the relatively raw-material rich satellites to be self-reliant. However, if this were a deliberate policy, it would have created overwhelming incentives for the satellites to cut their production of key commodities, which they did not do. If the Soviet Union was seeking to promote self-reliance among its satellites, it should instead have created positive incentives for the countries to increase their production of key commodities, and tried to recapture their excess rents by using differential fixed payments. Such a policy would have led to a positive correlation between East European commodity production and various measures of the subsidy, and to statistically significant dummy variables for each country identification, neither of which occurred. A more plausible interpretation of the data is that the East Europeans bargained most vigorously for the commodities they needed most, which explains the negative correlation between national production and imports of key commodities. Once again, it is the East Europeans who make the critical decisions that determine the distribution of the subsidy, not a strategist in Moscow.

Finally, this chapter argues that the interpretation of the subsidy as an instrument of political leverage is inconsistent with the pattern of variation in the Soviet trade subsidy observed over time. If the subsidy were in fact instrumental, Soviet exports of major commodities should exhibit sharp fluctuations, indicating that they had been used to punish or reward particular East European countries. Trade in major commodities remained very stable over time in quantitative terms, however, so commodities do not appear to have been used as political instruments. In addition, an instrumental interpretation of the subsidy presupposes some proportionality between means and ends, and consequently between the size of the trade subsidy and the goals to be achieved. This is inconsistent with the subsidy's dramatic growth at a time when Soviet policy sought to reduce it, and with the fact that its volume was determined by forces on the world market rather than by Soviet policy.

The next chapter takes the analysis presented here a step further, arguing that the trade subsidy was not in fact used as a policy tool during the most important political crises of the Brezhnev era: the Warsaw Pact intervention in Czechoslovakia, the Hungarian experiments with reform and overtures to the International Monetary Fund (IMF), and the imposition of martial law in Poland in 1981.

CHAPTER 5

Three Case Studies of Politics and Trade

THE PREVIOUS CHAPTER argued that during ordinary times, no discernible strategy of linkage was in evidence. The Soviet allies in Eastern Europe received a substantial implicit subsidy in the form of distorted prices, and this represented a potential reservoir of Soviet political influence. However, the Soviet Union did not give systematic preference to particular East European satellites, and it allowed the total volume of the subsidy to depend on world market forces beyond Soviet control. This chapter makes a stronger claim. Even during times of extraordinary crisis and strain in the bloc, the Soviet Union typically failed to exploit the bargaining leverage represented by its trade subsidy. This chapter examines three such crisis situations: the Warsaw Pact invasion of Czechoslovakia in 1968, the tensions with Kadar's Hungary in the 1970s and early 1980s, and the imposition of martial law in Poland in 1981.

In each instance the Soviet Union flexed its diplomatic muscles. In the first, it resorted to outright military invasion, and in the third, it mobilized troops on the Polish border. The level of concern in the Soviet leadership warranted forceful action in each case, and in each there is evidence of direct intervention by Soviet Politburo members, which indicates that concern was felt at the highest levels. Nonetheless, the Soviet Union squandered opportunities to use its implicit trade subsidy strategically, that is, to wield it as a threat or a promise.

Furthermore, the Soviet Union failed to use its implicit subsidy to punish Hungary when its policies aroused Soviet displeasure, or to reward the new regimes in Poland and Czechoslovakia for their compliant policies. The distinction between implicit and explicit subsidies is important here; the USSR did offer loans and explicit price subsidies in the wake of serious crises in Eastern Europe, but it did not manipulate the implicit trade subsidy as a means of channeling additional aid. Even in crisis situations, the Soviet Union treated trade politics as business as usual. Linkages were rarely made between trade negotiations and political issues.

CZECHOSLOVAKIA, 1968

The Czechoslovak crisis in 1968 was preceded by a meeting of the two Politburos on the Soviet border, where Soviet concerns about the dangerous course of reform were forcefully expressed. Piotr Shelest, the Party leader of the Ukraine, was reportedly infuriated by articles that had appeared in the Czech newspapers criticizing the Soviet annexation of a portion of Slovakia after World War II, and other Politburo members were deeply concerned by the course the Prague reformers had taken since January.[1] Had there been any doubt of the sincerity of Soviet concern, it was dispelled by the surprise decision to invade in August, supported by all Warsaw Pact countries except Romania. This was a turning point in Soviet-Czechoslovak relations. One would expect the Soviets to employ every possible threat before invading, including economic sanctions. Since the invasion profoundly disrupted the Czechoslovak political system and economy, the Soviets soon found themselves in possession of a conquered nation that had to be rejuvenated. One would expect them to expand the trade subsidy in the years following the invasion, in an effort to reestablish a measure of loyalty in the subject population.

In the months leading up to the Warsaw Pact invasion in August, the Soviet Union gradually escalated a war of nerves with the new regime of Alexander Dubček. The Societ Union demanded that Soviet troops be stationed on the West German border, and unexplained troop maneuvers in Poland and East Germany kept rumors flying in Prague that an invasion was imminent. As a conciliatory gesture, Dubček agreed to host a Warsaw Pact training exercise on Czechoslovak territory. When the exercise was due to end, however, the Soviets extended it on the pretext that Czechoslovak military preparations were not up to standards. Scarcely a week passed without some new overt sign of Soviet displeasure.

It is remarkable, therefore, that Soviet-Czechoslovak trade remained almost undisturbed by the intensifying controversy. Reports surfaced at the end of April that the Soviet Union had stopped shipments to Czechoslovakia of wheat, oil, and cotton, but the Soviet leadership treated this as a momentary embarrassment rather than as a form of political pressure. *Pravda* heatedly denounced the report, and the Soviet Union was evidently embarrassed when Zdeněk Mlynář, a Czechoslovak Central Committee secretary, confirmed that wheat shipments had indeed stopped. The Czechoslovaks made no concessions, but the shipments were hurriedly resumed the following day. If the shipments had been held back to send a signal, the signal was muddied by the hasty retreat. More likely, there was simply a routine supply interruption, as the Soviet side subsequently claimed. In any case, there was no sustained attempt to apply trade sanctions, and no serious economic threats were made. "Certainly the Soviets are nervous," Mlynář said, "but no serious pressure has been put on us."[2]

[1]Skilling, *Czechoslovakia's Interrupted Revolution.*

[2]David Binder, "Soviet Wheat Aid to Czechs Halted," *The New York Times,* April 30, 1968; "Moscow Offering Credit to Prague," *the New York Times,* May 1, 1968, p. 11; "Prague Paraders Acclaim Dubcek," *The New York Times,* May 2, 1968, p. 2.

The one important economic bargaining chip was a proposed $400 million hard-currency loan, which Czechoslovakia wanted the Soviet Union to provide so that it could modernize certain industries. This was an explicit subsidy, so it had to be negotiated outside the ordinary trade channels, and was therefore much more susceptible to Soviet linkage strategies. In the spring, Soviet negotiators encouraged Czechoslovakia to believe that the loan would be made, and Czechoslovakia began compiling a shopping list of licenses and equipment to purchase in the West. A series of tough negotiating sessions followed, however, in which Soviet negotiators apparently attached political conditions and signaled Soviet unease with developments in Czechoslovakia. A high-level Czechoslovak delegation returned from Moscow in early May with no agreement, and the Soviet news agency TASS reported that strong differences had been raised over the course of reforms in Prague. Aleksei Kosygin, the Soviet premier, visited Prague two weeks later, and discussed the loan in connection with assurances that he sought on the continuing leading role of the Community Party in Czechoslovakia. Lubomír Štrougal, the Czechoslovak deputy premier in charge of economic policy, was able to reach agreement in June on routine trade issues such as imports of iron ore and natural gas, but was unable to make progress on the issue of the loan.[3] New, explicit forms of aid were subject to political manipulation, but implicit subsidies remained undisturbed, as invisible as the vast submerged bulk of an iceberg at sea.

At first glance, trade statistics appear to support the hypothesis that trade was linked to Soviet-Czechoslovak political relations; a closer look, however, dispells the illusion. In the years preceding the invasion, the pace of growth of Soviet-Czechoslovak trade slowed. In the 1966–70 Five-Year Plan it expanded by only 24.3 percent (compared to 74.4 percent growth in Czechoslovak trade with the West), and almost all this growth occurred after the invasion. In 1966–68 Soviet-Czechoslovak trade rose by a mere 3.5 percent. Soviet-Czechoslovak trade grew much more slowly than aggregate Soviety–East European trade, which grew 45.2 percent during the same five-year plan, and this followed a healthy growth of 52.7 percent in Soviet-Czechoslovak trade during the 1961–65 period. A confidential Soviet report prepared for the CPSU Central Committee noted these trends with alarm, concluding darkly, "In the past five-year period, negative tendencies are found in CSSR trade with the socialist countries, and particularly with the Soviet Union."[4] Official Soviet trade statistics show that in the years following the invasion, Soviet-Czechoslovak trade rapidly expanded. The same pattern is evident in the balance of trade in machines and in the most important com-

---

[3]*The New York Times*, May 6, 1968, p. 5; May 19, 1968, p. 1; June 14, 1968, p. 4.

[4]Kaie, "K sovremennomu ekonomicheskomu polozheniiu v Chekhoslovakii," IMEPI Archive, IEMSS report, 11.28.1972, addressed to S. I. Kolesnikov, "The Department," CC CPSU, p. 6.

modities: oil, coal, and iron ore. The report goes on to note with satisfaction that the Fourteenth Congress of the Communist Party of Czechoslovakia had decided to give "preferential development" to economic ties with the CMEA, and that in June 1972 the Czechoslovak Council of Ministers had approved "an important document":

> "The Principles of More Effective Engagement of the Czechoslovak Economy in the Development of Socialist Economic Integration." . . . The contents of this document prove that the leadership of the CSSR recognizes the full seriousness for its country of the significance of socialist integration, first of all with the Soviet Union, and is taking steps to accelerate the practical accomplishment of that process.[5]

The author of the report clearly interpreted the 1966–68 trade statistics in political terms, and read the return to rapid growth in Soviet-Czechoslovak trade as a sign of the loyalty of the newly installed Husák regime.

When put in perspective, these numbers lose their apparent political significance. Soviet-Czechoslovak trade fell 7.5 percent in 1966, rose almost to its 1965 level in 1967, rose by a modest 4 percent in 1968, and then climbed rapidly. It is therefore the decrease in 1966 and the increase after 1968 that demand explanation. The drop of 131.8 million rubles in 1966 is attributable to a decrease in Czechoslovak exports of 104.4 million rubles and a decrease in Soviet exports of 27.4 million rubles. The decrease in Soviet exports was caused almost entirely by a decrease in the prices of major commodities introduced in 1965. In fact, exports of oil, the most important commodity, increased steadily throughout the period in physical terms, rising 7.2 percent in 1966. Nor was Czechoslovakia treated worse than the other East European countries in terms of commodity exports. The drop in prices led to a decrease in the total value of Soviet commodity exports to all the East European allies in 1966. The Czechoslovak move to reduce total exports appears to have been a response to the growing Soviet trade deficit, which emerged in the 1960s because of the steady rise of machinery prices. Czechoslovakia ran a trade surplus with the Soviet Union in every year of the 1961–65 Five-Year Plan, and the surplus nearly reached 100 million rubles in 1965. The trade balance improved in 1966, so that the Soviet Union was only 22.9 million rubles in deficit, but almost all the reduction in the Soviet deficit came in the form of decreased Czechoslovak exports of machinery. Czechoslovakia reduced its machinery exports by 73.4 million rubles in order to gain a 77 million ruble improvement in its trade balance.

This seems to have been a common practice. Poland and Romania faced the same difficulty in 1965, and each followed suit by decreasing its exports to the Soviet Union in 1966, primarily in the category of machinery. As the trade

[5]Ibid., pp. 6, 8.

deficits moved into balance, each country expanded its exports, and machinery exports led the pace. This pattern is consistent with evidence presented in the previous chapter (Table 4.5), which shows that East European surpluses in the category of machinery were correlated with increases in aggregate trade volume. This means that when the balance of machinery exports shifted in favor of the Soviet Union, total trade turnover tended to be lower. This is consistent with the interpretation that the East European countries preferred to reduce their surpluses in the category of machines when the Soviet Union ran a trade deficit, rather than extend the Soviets a larger de facto credit. The Soviet Union, for its part, apparently took the logical bargaining position of allowing the East Europeans to reduce their trade surpluses only in the lucrative category of machinery exports.

Soviet-Czechoslovak trade expanded in 1968–70 for two major reasons. First, the Soviet Union finally moved into surplus in 1968, and trade remained very nearly balanced for several years. This provided Czechoslovakia an opportunity to expand its machinery exports by 31 percent over three years. Second, agreements were reached in 1966 to begin joint investments in oil and gas lines, which began to deliver gas and increased quantities of oil to Czechoslovakia beginning in 1968. As a result of these agreements, which predated the crisis in Soviet-Czechoslovak relations and its resolution, oil exports increased by 31 percent over three years, and gas exports increased from zero to 20 million rubles. Together, Czechoslovak machinery exports and Soviet oil and gas exports account for 46 percent of the growth in Soviet-Czechoslovak trade in 1968–70.

Zdeněk Šedivý, who joined the Czechoslovak State Planning Commission in 1965 and served as deputy chairman from July 1968 until his retirement in 1983, insists categorically that the events of 1968 did not affect economic relations with the Soviet Union.

> [The events of] 1968 did not play a role in this. We should say that from the point of view of economic relations, the year 1968 played no role whatsoever. For one thing, most of the reforms had only been begun, and they were never carried out. The basis of these relations remained the same as it had been before 1968. This is to speak objectively. In the macroeconomic sense. The oil shocks played important roles. Hungary continued their reforms after 1968. That played a role only in the internal adaptation of the Hungarian economy. The basis of economic relations remained the same.

When asked specifically whether the crisis in 1968 accounted for the increased level of Soviet-Czechoslovak trade in the aftermath, Šedivý responded negatively.

> No, I would not say that. There were several other reasons that played a role. Already in 1966, we concluded the first agreement with the Soviet Union on

cooperative investments, in oil in this case. This was linked to an increase in oil imports from 9 million tons to 15 million. . . . Our participation in the investments took place from 1966 to 1969, and in 1970 the increases in oil imports took effect. Then, in 1970, we signed a big agreement to build a gas pipeline across Czechoslovakia. This was linked to an increase in imports of gas as payment for transit, which began in 1972 or 1973. This took effect immediately. Then, there was an increase in prices, and of course that magnified the significance of the increase in volume geometrically. Then there was a second agreement in the second half of the 1970s, for a smaller volume.

This was connected with the process of bilateral negotiations, because we, earlier than the other countries—and this is independent of 1968—realized that if we wanted to receive more fuel and raw materials, we should participate in the production of those resources.[6]

Šedivý's testimony is more credible than that of many of the officials appointed after the Soviet invasion, since he was promoted in July and played a role in formulating the Dubček regime's economic reforms. He was one of the few high-level Czechoslovak officials who preserved their positions after 1968, but he did not owe his position to the invasion. Šedivý's claim on this point is strongly supported by Vladislav Cihlař, who was retained as an adviser to the Czechoslovak premier in the 1970s, but who lost all chance of advancement when he was thrown out of the Czechoslovak Communist Party in 1970. When asked whether Czechoslovakia received more favorable treatment in trade negotiations after 1968, Cihlař answered definitely, "No, we did not." Cihlař argued that most of the variations in trade volume depended on changes in prices. Low levels of trade growth in the 1960s, he argued, were largely caused by declining Soviet demand for Czechoslovak machinery and the emphasis on heavy chemicals inaugurated by Khrushchev, which put Czechoslovakia at a disadvantage because of its weak chemical industry. The increases in commodity exports after 1968 were caused by joint investment agreements and price increases.[7]

HUNGARY, 1970–1982

Hungary initiated an economic initiative in 1968 labeled the New Economic Mechanism, a series of reforms intended to introduce market elements into its economy by gradual steps. These reforms continued for several years under the energetic leadership of Rezsö Nyers, the Central Committee economic secretary, who initially enjoyed the full support of the first secretary, Janos

---

[6]Interview with Zdeněk Šedivý, 6.30.1992. Staff member, SPK, 1965–83; Deputy Chairman, SPK, 1968–83.
[7]Interview with Vladislav Cihlař, 6.17.1992.

Kadar. The reforms stalled in 1972. Nothing fundamental was reversed, but the reform policy lost momentum and no new reforms were promulgated. In 1974 Nyers was removed from his most important posts. The natural speculation was that the Soviet Union's more conservative postconsolidation Brezhnev regime had applied pressure on the Budapest leadership, probably by threatening to cut oil supplies. Another significant shake-up in the Hungarian Politburo occurred in 1978, and the reform agenda again moved to the fore. For the next ten years, the Kadar regime pushed ahead with reforms and distanced itself politically from the rest of the bloc. In 1982, over the loud objections of the Soviet Union, Hungary joined the International Monetary Fund. Clearly, important Soviet state interests were being challenged.

Trade statistics provide no compelling evidence to suggest that the Soviet Union used major commodity exports to exert pressure on Hungary, or that trade varied in accordance with changes in the political relations of the two countries. Table 5.1 indicates the quantities of oil exported to Hungary by the Soviet Union for the years for which this data is available.[8] The pattern is one of steady growth. The Soviet Union never reduced its oil exports to Hungary during the period. Oil exports to Hungary grew more slowly in 1971–75 (49 percent) than in 1965–70 (171 percent), but this was true across the bloc. Table 5.2 indicates how Hungarian oil imports from the Soviet Union compared to those of the bloc as a whole in terms of the annual percentage change of their total value. This allows us to factor out changes in prices in order to determine whether there was anything unusual about the variations in the Hungarian oil subsidy.

Table 5.2 suggests two significant points. First, Hungarian oil imports tracked those of the bloc as a whole very closely, which indicates that trends in price and supply outweighed considerations unique to the Soviet-Hungarian relationship in determining the volume of oil Hungary was allowed to import in any particular year. Second, the growth of Hungarian oil imports was consistently higher than that of the bloc as a whole, at least until 1980. This appears to indicate that Hungary was not under any particular pressure during the 1970s. If the Soviet Union had been attempting to compel Hungary to modify its domestic policies by squeezing its oil supplies, one would expect Hungarian imports to increase more slowly than those of the rest of the bloc. The statistics leave open the possibility that Soviet sanctions were applied when more reformist tendencies reemerged after 1978, since Hungarian oil imports exhibited slower-than-average growth after 1980.

High-level Hungarian foreign trade and economic officials, however, are unanimous in arguing that such sanctions were never imposed. Istvan Hetenyi argued that there were good reasons for Hungarian energy imports to be lower

---

[8]After 1975, oil data are published only in terms of the total value of crude oil plus petroleum products, so precise information about the quantity of oil exported is unavailable.

TABLE 5.1
Soviet Oil Exports to Hungary, 1965–1975

	1965	1966	1967	1968	1969	1970
Oil exports (million tons)	2.0	2.5	2.8	3.8	4.3	4.8
Percent change/previous year	16.4	20.9	12.7	35.7	13.3	11.1
	1971	1972	1973	1974	1975	
Oil exports (million tons)	5.1	5.5	6.3	6.7	7.5	
Percent change/previous year	6.2	9.4	13.8	6.9	12.0	

Source: Sovetskaia torgovliia, various volumes.

than those of the other East European countries. Asked whether Soviet oil exports were linked to political issues, such as domestic Hungarian reform, he replied,

> Some said so, and others said that the government was not clever enough to get more oil from the Soviet Union. I do not think that that was the case. Look. Hungary had a much lower demand for energy than the other countries. That was a great advantage, and we in the planning office had the opinion that the cheapest energy is energy that you don't consume! So to pull more cheap oil from the Soviet Union in order to produce something unreasonable, that had no purpose. We never thought so in the planning office, I emphasize. There was an opinion that we should build up our aluminum production, and the Ministry wanted to build a huge factory. We maintained that if this were based on Soviet oil, it too would be unprofitable. One had to base it on hydroelectric power. We also did not want to build up our ferrous metallurgy. We considered it a great advantage that Hungary could develop industries that were not energy-intensive, so that our need for energy was much lower than in Poland or Czechoslovakia.
>
> . . . We imported almost no oil from the West and from other countries. So I can say that we really did not need more. Our imports of 2 million tons were advantageous, and then you add gas, and we did not need any more. Although some said that the Soviet Union should have exported more oil, I find no economic argument there.[9]

Hetenyi believed that economic issues were effectively insulated from political issues in the relations within the Soviet bloc. If Hungary received more or less oil, it was because of the outcome of trade negotiations, in which only economic offers and counteroffers had any significance. Hetenyi was in the best position to know, since it was he who negotiated with the Soviets for oil for more than thirty years, and supervised the departments of the Planning Commission responsible for those negotiations from 1965 to 1983.

[9]Interview with Istvan Hetenyi, 9.7.1992.

TABLE 5.2

Value of Hungarian versus Bloc Oil Imports from the USSR, 1971–1983

	1971	1972	1973	1974	1975	1976	1977
Hungarian oil imports (% change)	8.8	11.5	20.4	24.7	119.3	22.2	33.3
CMEA oil imports (% change)	12.2	11.0	15.1	20.3	101.8	18.5	31.3
	1978	1979	1980	1981	1982	1983	
Hungarian oil imports (% change)	26.5	28.6	−7.7	20.9	22.6	3.3	
CMEA oil imports (% change)	24.9	20.2	17.7	31.2	17.9	15.3	

Source: *Sovetskaia torgovliia*, various volumes.

Matyas Szürös, the ambassador to the Soviet Union from 1978 to 1983, and then foreign affairs secretary for the Hungarian Socialist Workers Party, confirmed that oil exports were never put on the table as an explicit bargaining chip. Asked whether the Soviet Union ever used a direct threat of cutting off or reducing oil supplies to pressure Hungary on issues of domestic or foreign policy, Szürös insisted that although the Soviets had indeed intervened extensively in Hungarian politics, they had never threatened to cut oil exports.

> No, there were mainly political disagreements. You know that the Soviet troops were here, so it was not easy to act. We needed careful negotiations and evidence that we were not going over to the Western side, but were acting in the interests of the socialist camp. For example, in 1968 we began economic reforms, but this process was stopped in the beginning of the 1970s because the Soviet Union considered it to be a revisionist policy. And the other socialist countries reacted with disapproval. The Hungarian government was forced to replace certain personalities in economic policy: Nyers, later Fock, and then Lajos Feher in agriculture. There were constant consultations between the general secretaries. These were general consultations. And then experts criticized [Hungary] in the press, saying that this was actually far from socialism, it was ideologically dangerous, it could lead to a reestablishment of capitalism, and so forth. And it is not to be excluded that the Soviet leadership said concrete names, but that was on the highest level. We did not necessarily know anything about that. But there were concrete names mentioned—against Nyers and Feher—that they took an anti-socialist position. That was the strongest pressure in economic policy. But it also happened in the cultural area. György Aczel, who was the [HSWP] secretary for culture, was also accused of being a revisionist.[10]

These are strong claims. Criticism of Hungarian officials appeared in the Soviet press, and it has been speculated that the Soviet leadership exerted sub-

[10]Interview with Matyas Szürös, 9.3.1992. Szürös was the Hungarian ambassador to the Soviet Union from 1978 to 1983, then the secretary for international affairs of the HSWP Central Committee. He is now vice president of the Hungarian Parliament.

stantial private pressure on Hungary in the 1970s. This could not be proven, however, because the leading figures were not available for interviews before 1989. As is always the case when one relies on interviews, it is important to consider the motivations of the informant. Szürös is a leading socialist politician in Hungary today, so he has an interest in distancing himself from the Soviet Union and his own prominent role as a Communist in the past. This could perhaps lead him to exaggerate the degree of Soviet involvement in unsavory episodes, such as the stagnation of reform after 1972 and the ouster of the reform cabinet in 1974 and 1975. If this is the case, it is particularly interesting that he specifically denies that the Soviets used oil as an explicit threat. If anything, his own personal interests strengthen his claim on that point, because he has no interest in defending the Soviets. In addition, Szürös's testimony closely conforms to that offered by other witnesses.

Rezsö Nyers, who as economic secretary initiated the Hungarian economic reform, confirmed Szürös's account of his ouster in 1974, and identified the same four victims of Soviet intervention: himself, Jenö Fock, the premier; Lajos Feher, the deputy premier for agriculture; and Györgi Aczel, the HSWP secretary for culture. All were Politburo members. In his view, Janos Kadar was compelled to play a delicate balancing act in the 1970s between Soviet pressure on the one hand, which was increasingly turned against the Hungarian reform after the invasion of Czechoslovakia, and a strong, hard-line communist opposition in the Hungarian Politburo, consisting of Zoltan Komocsin, Bela Biszku, and Sandor Gaspar, on the other. At times Kadar was able to resist Soviet pressure and find allies in Moscow, Andropov being the most important. Kadar came under severe pressure in 1972, and Andropov was sent to Budapest to carry the message that changes had to be made in the Hungarian leadership. After a long, intensive conversation, Kadar convinced Andropov to take a compromise back to Moscow: the reforms would stop, but the leadership would remain in place. Nyers argued that Andropov was more receptive to such a compromise than Suslov, Kirilenko, and Ponomarev, because he strongly believed that the indigenous communist leaderships could manage their countries more efficiently than any leaders Moscow could impose. After 1972, Nyers argued, the hard-line group in the Hungarian Politburo was actually weakened, because when the crisis passed, it became clear that the Soviet Union was not ready to support any action against Kadar. Kadar's compromise with the Soviet Union, however, did not last. Increasingly dependent on Soviet support, Kadar was unable to resist the next demand for change, which came in 1974. Nyers argued that, in this instance, Leonid Brezhnev, during his annual meeting with Kadar in the Crimea, personally named the four officials who were deemed unacceptable. He believed there was some flexibility in the Soviet position, however, even in 1974. "I don't know, but I think they demanded that Mr. Feher and I be fired, strongly and certainly, and I think they had a little uncertainty about Fock and Aczel. And they adjusted." Fock was allowed to remain in office for one more year.[11]

Nyers did not believe that the Soviets had ever used oil exports as a direct threat. He made it clear that the Hungarian leadership had always kept its dependence on Soviet oil in the forefront of its attention: "For Hungary, oil imports were a question of life or death." In view of the extremity of this dependence, any suggestion of Soviet dissatisfaction was taken very seriously. Nyers was unable to name a single instance, however, when the Soviets explicitly tied oil exports to any political issue.

> QUESTION: Did the Soviets say openly that they would cut off oil exports if you did not fire particular officials? Did they ever make this linkage directly?
>
> NYERS: Oh, I don't know. But I think it was not direct, it was an indirect connection between these two things.
>
> QUESTION: How did they use the "oil weapon"? Did they refer to it in conversation?
>
> NYERS: Vaguely, vaguely. It was indirect, but very strong pressure. It is an interesting question. Soviet political pressure exerts such a tactic, that they said again and again along the lines of the Party, of the government, in enterprise-level contacts, in trade-union contacts, and in friendship-society contacts—as we say in Hungary—these Soviet elaborations flowed from the tap. From all of the taps. This was the Soviet tactic.[12]

The Soviets apparently relied on tacit signaling to make their wishes known, and avoided making specific threats.

The Soviet position, however, was undermined by its own inconsistency. The Soviet attitude toward reform went through substantial changes in the late 1960s, particularly in the wake of the invasion of Czechoslovakia. Nevertheless, certain Soviet leaders continued to support the reformist tendencies in Eastern Europe. As a result, the messages that East European leaders got "from the tap" in the course of ordinary business and informal conversations with Soviet leaders depended very much on the source. Istvan Hetenyi argued that the Soviet leadership was of two minds on reform:

> I think that in the late 1960s and early 1970s there were two Soviet positions. One was very political, which held that the New Economic Mechanism was very suspicious. The whole thing looked like Czechoslovakia. Kadar was able to keep it in a strictly economic form. Even if some, like Nyers, knew that eventually it had to cause changes in politics, we always said that we had no political intentions. That was not quite true. Otherwise, I don't know whether we could have

---

[11]Interview with Rezsö Nyers, 9.10.1992.
[12]Interview with Rezsö Nyers, 9.10.1992.

survived, not only in the Soviet Union but in our own Central Committee. On the other hand, there were some signs in the Soviet Union that there were people, for example Kosygin, who looked at it [the Hungarian reform] with great interest. As you know, Kosygin started something—or tried to start something, nothing came of it—and he looked at Hungary, and thought, "Let's see what can be done in a small country." They told us that they saw we had done some good things in agriculture and they would like to do the same, but it was impossible. I remember—in 1972 I think, maybe 1973—that Fock [Jenö Fock, Hungarian premier, 1967–75] met Kosygin, and I was present. Some months before, we had raised meat prices. Fock told him that we had done it because it was rational and so on, and Kosygin said, "You are right, but it is impossible for us to do so in the Soviet Union. That is the way that we should follow, but we will never do it!" [13]

Kosygin was clearly out of step with the rest of the Brezhnev Politburo, but this was far from an isolated anecdote. A number of East European negotiators told stories about Soviet officials who encouraged efforts at reform in the 1970s, including several about Kosygin.[14] As premier, Kosygin was the highest Soviet official involved in the coordination of planning, so it was he who had to enforce any political linkage that involved trade.

Hungary's most daring and independent move was to join the International Monetary Fund in 1982. The Soviet leadership bitterly opposed this move, both because it threatened to weaken the solidarity of the bloc by exposing Hungary to more economic pressure from the West, and because it confirmed the superior attraction of Western financial institutions. Hungary made several inquiries about joining the IMF in the late 1970s, but on each occasion the Soviet Union insisted that the matter be dropped. Istvan Hetenyi recalled that in the early 1970s the Soviets had not offered credits or other incentives to prevent Hungary from joining the IMF; they simply regarded the issue as nonnegotiable.

What I remember was that in the first half of the 1970s there was a discussion between Kosygin and Fock; I was present, and Kosygin was very strongly opposed. Later, I listened to Lesechko as well. The Soviet Union was categorically opposed to our joining the IMF, irrespective of such questions as credits. They were in principle, and categorically, opposed.[15]

Given the history and significance of the issue and the vehemence of the Soviet opposition, one would expect to have seen a dramatic response when Hungary finally did join the IMF, and did so without consulting Moscow.

[13]Interview with Istvan Hetenyi, 9.3.1992.
[14]Interviews with J. Pajestka, 5.27.1992; Szita, 9.7.1992; Kuziński, 6.3.1992; Šedivý, 6.30.1992; and Madej, 6.5.1992.
[15]Interview with Istvan Hetenyi, 9.7.1992. Kosygin and Fock were the Soviet and Hungarian premiers, respectively; Mikhail Lesechko was the Soviet deputy premier for CMEA affairs.

Jozsef Marjai, the Hungarian Deputy Premier for foreign and economic affairs, maintained that by the late 1970s "there was a political decision that Hungary no longer had the economic resources to afford to continue putting off IMF membership." He personally urged the policy of joining without consulting the Soviet Union, so that the Soviets would be unable to object in advance. This is a time-tested principle of bargaining: moving first is often the best way to commit oneself to an action that another party is trying to deter. The Soviet Union was informed simultaneously with the official admission of Hungary into the IMF.[16] Matyas Szürös confirmed this account.

> SZÜRÖS: I was ambassador to the Soviet Union for four years, at the end of the 1970s and beginning of the 1980s, and we negotiated for three years over Hungarian membership in the IMF. . . . At the end, I had to present a letter to Tikhonov. He received me for fifteen minutes. I told him that the Hungarian government had decided to take this step. He answered, correctly, but coolly, "That is really your affair. Yours will be the glory and the bankruptcy." If it is successful, it will give you glory, and if not, then bankruptcy.
>
> QUESTION: Did you take that as a threat?
>
> SZÜRÖS: No. No, there was the danger that the Soviet Union would take steps against this, but it did not happen. The Soviet Union was in no position at the time to take any such measures, or they did not want to. They accepted it in the style that I told you. In the Soviet Union, and in the other socialist countries, the opinion of the IMF and the World Bank was that they were tools of imperialism, and that by this means they would gain influence in the internal affairs of the country.[17]

Marjai described the Hungarian decision to join the IMF as "mortally perilous." It was perceived as a great risk, since the Soviet Union could reduce energy and raw material exports to Hungary at any time, and Hungary was in a financial crisis that made it particularly vulnerable to such sanctions. The blow never fell. In the end Tikhonov told Szürös, "That is your affair."

The argument that Marjai presented to his Politburo was that the Soviet Union could not afford another crisis in Eastern Europe in 1982.

> There were so many other problems in Eastern Europe, and the cold war was at a high point. This was the time of Reagan's "Evil Empire" speech. The Soviet Union had increased tensions with China on its flank, and of course there was Poland. The Afghan war had begun. My argument was that the USSR could not afford to impose economic sanctions on Hungary, much less intervene militarily. Because of their international commitments and the deficit on the internal market, they needed every ruble of exports from Eastern Europe—not just consumer goods, but machinery, everything. Furthermore, they would see that imposing

[16]Interview with Jozsef Marjai, 9.10.1992.
[17]Interview with Matyas Szürös, 9.3.1992.

economic sanctions would just push Hungary toward the West, and then the decision would become sharper for them: would they tolerate that, or would they intervene? They could not afford a military intervention. On top of everything else, then they would have to feed the Hungarian people. After all, that is the obligation of the occupying power. In addition, the Hungarians knew that they had political support in Moscow. There were those even then who knew that the current policy was leading to disaster, even without another major war.[18]

It will not escape some readers that Marjai was using a realist argument to explain the Soviet failure to respond: the Soviet Union simply faced too many other commitments and threats, and could not afford to create another crisis. The constraints of bipolarity fell heavily on the leader of the alliance, and the smaller allies were free to maneuver for their own advantage. Perhaps Marjai is correct. If this is the case, however, it is interesting that bipolarity played out to the advantage of the smaller countries, rather than to their disadvantage. One could argue with equal plausibility that the external security threat compels the small countries to cooperate with the Soviet Union, and that the Soviets can force them to bid for favors by playing them off against one another. In the realist schema, the most potent Soviet weapon is the threat to abandon a satellite to the capitalist West. Joanne Gowa has used a similar line of reasoning to explain the cooperative trade policies pursued in Western Europe during the cold war. With the external security threat removed, she argues, interdependence may appear to be a less attractive option.[19] Realism fails to explain why it was so easy for the allies to take the role of free riders, forcing the Soviet Union to pay the costs of their security. For reasons that realist theory cannot illuminate, Soviet threats lacked credibility, and Soviet policies did not concentrate on punishing free riders; linkages across bureaucratic domains remained purely hypothetical.

POLAND, 1981

The case of martial law in Poland is particularly interesting, because in 1981 the Soviet Union compelled its ally to make a dramatic break with the policies of the past, but was not forced to invade the country in order to do so. The cautious Gierek Politburo fell in 1980, along with its promise that Polish soldiers would never again fire on Polish workers. When the Kania regime was unable to make headway in its negotiations with Solidarity in the summer of 1981, it too was replaced, this time by "The General," Wojciech Jaruzelski. It remains unclear whether the Soviet Union played a decisive role in either of

[18]Interview with Jozsef Marjai, 9.10.1992, deputy premier for foreign and economic affairs, 1978–88.
[19]Gowa, "Bipolarity, Multipolarity and Free Trade."

TABLE 5.3
Value of Polish versus Bloc Oil Imports, 1976–1985

	1976	1977	1978	1979	1980	1975–80
Polish oil imports (% change)	12.8	35.6	19.9	15.3	15.2	144
CMEA oil imports (% change)	18.5	31.3	24.9	20.2	17.7	175
	1981	1982	1983	1984	1985	1980–85
Polish oil imports (% change)	26.3	17.1	15.7	15.3	5.3	108
CMEA oil imports (% change)	31.2	17.9	15.3	15.2	5.5	117

these palace coups. Jaruzelski reports in his memoirs, however, that he quickly came under intense Soviet pressure to declare martial law, and in December he complied. This is a case in which the Soviet Union successfully exerted pressure on an ally. However, no threat to withdraw oil supplies was made, and oil exports to Poland after 1981 show no evidence of rewards for compliance. Table 5.3 indicates how trends in the total value of Polish oil imports compare to those of the bloc during the 1976–80 and 1981–85 five-year plans.

If the Soviet Union were pursuing a strategy of linkage, we should observe a drop in relative subsidization in 1980–81, and a rise in relative subsidization beginning in 1982. Polish oil imports did grow more slowly than those of the bloc as a whole in 1980–81, but they in fact grew more slowly than the bloc average throughout the period, so this does not seem to indicate that sanctions were applied in 1980–81. The relatively slow growth of Polish oil imports is consistent with the conclusion reached in the previous chapter, that Poland bargained less vigorously than its neighbors for energy commodities because of its high level of coal production. After 1982, however, Polish oil imports grew nearly as fast as the bloc average. This could be interpreted as evidence that Poland received an economic reward for imposing martial law, or it could be interpreted as a shift in Polish priorities, as the central planners sought to compensate for the drop in coal production brought on by a wave of miners' strikes. Since the growth rates of Polish oil imports continued to hover just below the bloc average, any reward that Poland received for imposing martial law cannot have been very handsome.

As will be shown below, this interpretation is broadly consistent with those offered by Polish trade officials. No sanctions were in fact applied, and no threats were made that linked oil imports to martial law. The Soviet Union extended credits after 1981, and granted explicit price concessions in an attempt to rescue the Polish economy from the disruption caused by the Solidarity strikes. Polish officials insisted, however, that the ordinary negotiations over the proportions of trade were not affected; trade politics remained business as usual.

A portion of Wojciech Jaruzelski's memoirs deserves to be quoted at some length, since it attempts to build the opposite case. Jaruzelski claims that the Soviet Union imposed drastic economic pressure on Poland, beginning in August 1981, with the clear objective of compelling Jaruzelski to suppress Solidarity.

The first serious signal arrived on August 20. A delegation from our Planning Commission led by Director Alfred Siennicki was visiting Soviet Gosplan. A member of the Collegium of that institution, Nikolai Vorov, declared that Poland would receive 4 million tons less oil in 1982. Exports of cotton would also be reduced. "The Soviet side," said Vorov, "cannot take on any multiyear obligations, since as a result of the unstable political situation there is no certainty concerning the fulfillment of the obligations assumed by Poland."

Shortly thereafter, on August 9, the consecutive negotiations on the subject of Polish-Soviet trade exchange for the year 1982 began in Moscow. Stanisław Długosz led our delegation—an experienced diplomat and economist, and the deputy chairman of the Planning Commission. The Soviet side declared: since Poland has a passive trade balance with the USSR, trade can only take place in 1982 on the basis of full balancing of payments, including repayment of the deficit for the previous year. This indicated a drastic reduction of imports, going much further than the offer of August 20. Now this without a doubt was the consequence of the first activity of the "Solidarity" union. This was the offer:

	Proposal of the Polish Side for 1982	USSR Response 9.9.1981
Crude oil (million ton)	13.1	4.1
Gasoline (thousand ton)	600	—
Airplane fuel and kerosine (thousand ton)	180	—
Motor oil (thousand ton)	1800	—
Natural gas (billion m³)	5.3	2.8
Raw Phosphorus P_2O_5 (thousand ton)	250	100
Nickel (thousand ton)	6.8	3
Aluminum (thousand ton)	53	18
Cellulose connected with Ust'-Ilimsk (thousand ton)	137	82
Paper (thousand ton)	45	20
Cotton (thousand ton)	105	70
Tea (thousand ton)	3	—
Cheese (ton)	750	—
Canned fish (million cans)	3	—
Refrigerators (thousand)	200	—
Black-and-white televisions (thousand)	50	—
Color televisions (thousand)	50	—
T25A tractors (thousand)	10	—

This time it was declared even more distinctly than on August 20 that not only the failure of Poland to fulfill the agreed-on exports had decisive influence on this position, but also the growing anti-Soviet campaign.

It had become clear. This was not the individual initiative of officials of Soviet Gosplan. This was a decision by the highest leadership of the USSR. An ultimatum of this type was a declaration of an economic blockade. We knew that if the intended radical [trade] restriction were carried out, the economy of Poland would be completely paralyzed. That would be a catastrophe. It was possible to overthrow the state by that means, without employing a single tank, and without firing a shot. A saying reached me at that time: "Tanks are unnecessary; banks suffice."

. . . I telephoned Premier Tikhonov. He spoke with me politely, as usual, but coldly. He did not say that this was punishment for our sins, for such things in general are not said directly. Instead, "we ourselves have so many difficulties, and you are not giving us this, you are not sending us that. We have to take care of our society." I requested a visit from the deputy premier, chairman of the State Planning Commission of the USSR, Baibakov.

Before his meeting with me, Baibakov had several conversations in Silesia and in Belchatów. He shared the opinion that the state of our economy was dramatic. He told about his visit to Czechoslovakia in 1968 and to Cuba in the difficult year of 1970. Poland's situation was worse, however, without comparison. Production had fallen significantly, among other reasons because of the shortfall of energy. That had a particularly distinct impact on metallurgy, the chemical industry, and construction. This, in turn, disorganized the whole economy. "So what if we give you raw materials," he said, "because of the deficit of coal and energy, that will not do any good anyway." The decline of mining had a significant influence on exports. At one time 26 million, and now only 8 million tons of coal. That, in turn, had repercussions for imports. They expected, therefore, that we would fulfill our obligations to export coal and sulfur. They had difficulties. There had been a poor harvest, and they had to buy millions of tons of wheat.

. . . In each of these conversations, an unchanged note appeared: if there is no peace and discipline, if the political situation is unstable, the economy will not move. I knew that well enough without him. I raised the key topic for us: the imports for 1982. Baibakov ducked the subject. I felt that a political decision was lacking. There was no reason to count on a change of position. This, after all, was pressure, the condition that was supposed to incline us to more decisive actions. . . . Today's critics of the state of martial law, who are not concerned with this, in the best case commit the sin of naivete.[20]

According to Jaruzelski's account, the Soviet Union was making demands that Poland could not possibly meet. These demands became more unreasonable as time went on, rather than less, which reinforced the impression that they were meant as political signals. Soviet officials, and particularly Nikolai Bai-

---

[20]Wojciech Jaruzelski, *Stan wojenny dlaczego . . .* , pp. 248–51.

bakov, were quite aware of the gravity of the Polish economic crisis. Instead of taking this as an argument for flexibility, however, they insisted that it made Poland an untrustworthy trade partner, and drove a still harder bargain. Throughout this process, the Soviets never stated their intentions openly. They relied instead on hints about Poland's political instability and economic decline, and Jaruzelski assumes that his partners expected him to read between the lines. Instead of making a clear linkage between Soviet resources and objectives, the Soviet negotiators made excuses for reducing their exports: Poland had a trade deficit, Poland had not fulfilled its export obligations, and the Soviet Union had suffered from a poor harvest.

High-level trade officials confirmed many of the details of Jaruzelski's account in independent interviews, but they disputed his interpretation that the Soviet Union was trying to send signals about Polish domestic politics through trade bargaining. Instead, the Soviet position was seen as a typical example of posturing to secure better terms of trade. Stanisław Długosz, who received the ultimatum in September 1981 that Jaruzelski recalls as being so disturbing, did not view it as a form of political pressure, and specifically did not view it as linked to the rise of Solidarity.

> In September 1981 I led a group of experts to Moscow, including Trze-ciakowski and Płowiec, who were in Solidarity, to show the Soviets that Solidarity was already in power! They explained the reform, begun in 1980 by the Baka Commission, and the Soviets were very satisfied. In my experience, they criticized, but they never pressured. How could they, at my level? I was just in charge of foreign trade. I was not at the political level. They may have used pressure at that level.[21]

In another interview, Długosz emphasized that his response to the Soviet position in September 1981 was to treat it as a bluff. The Soviet Union was interested in liquidating the Polish trade debt, and in order to convince the Poles to cooperate, the Soviet negotiators outlined an extreme response. The threat was that if Poland refused to balance its trade, the USSR could balance it unilaterally by reducing exports of key commodities. The Soviet negotiators made a strategic error, however, in staking out such an extreme position. It was clear to Długosz that the Soviet Union could not cut its exports to Poland in the drastic way that its negotiators had outlined, because the Polish economy was so weak that it might collapse under the strain. In Długosz's view, he had successfully called the Soviet bluff.

> Jaruzelski writes about me in his book. He writes that on September 9, 1981, I was in Moscow and sent back in code what was practically an ultimatum from the Soviet Union, that in 1982 they would not make certain deliveries of raw materials and other goods. I wrote once in a newspaper that this is true, but it's not the whole truth. I was there in Moscow, and they told me this, but I told them that I

---

[21]Interview with Stanisław Długosz, 6.8.1992.

not only did not take this under consideration, but I was not even listening, and got up and walked out. The next day I was invited to see Baibakov, and [his deputy], Vorov, told Baibakov that I had not only rejected their position, but I refused to listen, and he left. Baibakov smiled and said, "Listen, you fool, last night they sent everything that you [*ty*] said to Warsaw!" That's exactly how it was. Baibakov asked why I had reacted that way. I said, "Well, how is this possible? You yourself understand that if you do this, everything will collapse in Poland. If you want that, that's your affair, but as an expert at this level, I cannot carry on negotiations with you. This is a political question. I am supposed to agree on how much oil we will import, how many refrigerators, and so on. I will return to Warsaw, report to my government, and it will make a decision as it sees fit." He replied, "Well, I cannot tell you anything else, but I agree with you, that one cannot speak to you this way." He meant, not to Długosz, but to Poland. . . . This was a case of pressure, but it came in such a form that I could immediately reject it—it was nonsense. . . . They said we should pay off our debt for 1981 and achieve balanced trade for 1982. It was utterly impossible. I told them, it would have meant cutting our imports of raw materials, therefore a reduction of our production, consequently a reduction of our exports to them, and therefore a further reduction of their exports, and so on until we got to null!

Długosz smiled and added ironically, "At the time I didn't think it was such an important set of negotiations that I was carrying on; only now, when so many highly-placed people are writing about it."[22] His implication was that the incident was not nearly as significant as Jaruzelski would like to maintain.

Zbigniew Madej, who was chairman of the Polish Planning Commission at the time, was well positioned to know about any Soviet economic threats. He insisted that none were made.

The economic representatives of the Soviet Union did not make big maneuvers before the state of martial law, nor did they help much after it was introduced. Of course, they expressed concern, both from an ideological and a practical point of view. Ideologically, they were concerned by our disorders, but they were calm people; they were not the ones standing with a pistol and saying, "Introduce order or else!" The military did that. Our discussions took place under a state of some tension, but there were no threats. In practical terms, they were concerned that strikes might paralyze our exports. They said things like, "Well, the situation in Poland is uncertain. We don't know with whom we will have to negotiate," and they used these arguments tactically in discussions about trade, just as political arguments were always used; but there was no sense that their policies were really affected by the rise of Solidarity in 1980 and 1981. Baibakov and Ryzhkov did not make use of Soviet economic influence to force decisions on us in this question.[23]

[22]Interview with Stanisław Długosz, 5.21.1992.
[23]Interview with Zbigniew Madej, 5.29.1992.

As far as Madej was concerned, economics and politics were insulated realms. The Soviet Union applied plenty of pressure on Poland for a firm response to Solidarity in 1981, for the most part through the military; but economic levers were not used.

When asked about Baibakov's visit to Warsaw in December, Madej made it clear that he did not believe Baibakov was sent to deliver an ultimatum, or that the conversations with Baibakov had been a factor in Jaruzelski's decision to impose martial law.

> That was a conciliatory gesture, not a threat. First, Jaruzelski invited Baibakov. He wanted to gauge Soviet economic intentions before introducing martial law; he wanted to be sure that the Soviets would maintain the economic obligations that they had already assumed. Baibakov assured him that they would, though I do not know whether Jaruzelski told him that he was going to introduce a state of martial law. I participated in some discussions, but the subject was strictly economic; I don't know what was said between four eyes. I was not a party to Jaruzelski's plans; that was literally kept between a few people— Jaruzelski, Kiszczak, and the head of the armed forces.
>
> Baibakov was a very sympathetic figure. It was easy to discuss things with him. He did not become nervous, and he had a calming influence. The Soviets knew this, and they always sent him when there was a tough situation. They sent him to Czechoslovakia in 1968, too. He had good sense. He would not have been the one the Soviets would send with a threat.[24]

Taken together, the testimonies of Stanisław Długosz and Zbigniew Madej throw substantial doubt on Jaruzelski's account of the fall of 1981. The officials closest to the events he describes did not believe that Soviet actions in the economic arena were intended as threats or signals. In addition, there is substantial evidence that the Soviet Union was indeed concerned about CMEA trade debts in 1981, and that the policy of putting new emphasis on compelling the countries to balance their trade was carried out toward all the countries, not just toward Poland.[25] Jaruzelski himself, furthermore, does not claim that any direct linkage was made between trade and domestic politics; he argues simply that Soviet negotiating maneuvers were signals he was expected to understand. The credibility of Jaruzelski's own interpretation, meanwhile, is undermined by the polemical purpose of his memoirs, which is to cast the responsibility for martial law on the Soviet Union. One is forced to conclude, therefore, that the Soviet Union did not in fact use its economic leverage to compel Poland to declare martial law.

Furthermore, Zbigniew Madej claimed that trade politics was unaffected by martial law. The Soviet Union gave Poland significant explicit aid by consent-

[24]Interview with Zbigniew Madej, 5.29.1992.
[25]Interview with Zdeněk Šedivý, 6.30.1992.

ing to run a trade surplus, by reducing the prices of key exports (including oil), and by making hard-currency loans. However, the new situation did not substantially change the climate of ordinary trade negotiations. According to Madej,

> Economics was generally more important than politics. After martial law was introduced, I began the most intensive attempts to get aid from the other socialist countries. I was in at least two foreign capitals every week. We did not get what we expected. During the blockade from the West, the socialist countries all made token contributions to Poland, but compared to our trade balance, they were insignificant. Planned economies are very inelastic. The agreements that had already been negotiated went ahead, but getting increased imports above that was very difficult; we practically had no success. . . . After martial law was introduced, there were lots of words of support, but no concrete results. Look at our trade statistics.[26]

The five-year plan for Soviet-Polish trade was abandoned in 1982 because the economic crisis made it impossible for Poland to meet its export targets, and certain prices were revised.[27] Poland was allowed to reduce its coal exports, was granted credits that allowed it to continue to run a trade deficit, and was extended loans in hard currency.[28] Even after 1982, however, the Soviet attitude toward Poland can hardly be regarded as solicitous. The following exchange of letters between Jaruzelski and Andropov is very revealing.

> 4.18.1983.
>
> Most Honorable Comrade Andropov!
>
> Allow me to express to you personally, and to the leadership of the party and government of the Union of Soviet Socialist Republics, sincere thanks for your many forms of aid and support, and in particular for making available to Poland 300,000 tons of grain in the current year. This has made it possible for us to maintain the continuous sale of bread and flour products for the population.
>
> However, in spite of your aid, as well as additional purchases in Romania and Hungary, and also for convertible currency in the capitalist countries, the deficit of grain in the second quarter will amount to another 500,000 tons. We do not possess the means that would allow us to purchase this grain in the capitalist countries. Meanwhile, we are unable to obtain exports on a credit basis even from such traditional exporters as Canada and France.
>
> In reference to our telephone conversation on 4.13.1983, I ask you once again, Honorable Comrade Andropov, to sell to our country an additional 500,000 tons of grain, with delivery in the second quarter of this year, which would be calcu-

[26]Interview with Zbigniew Madej, 5.29.1992.

[27]Interview with Stanisław Długosz, 5.7.1992.

[28]For estimates of the explicit subsidies extended to Poland, see Bunce, "The Empire Strikes Back," pp. 17–21.

lated within the framework of the trade protocol for mutual exchange of goods for 1983. This will allow us to assure the provision of bread until the next harvest, and thereby prevent a deterioration of the social and political atmosphere in the PRP [People's Republic of Poland].

. . . In light of the above, I turn to you with a request to sell to Poland in 1983 200,000 tons of Al-93 gasoline.

. . . In the course of [earlier] discussions Poland appealed, among other things, for an increase in exports to the PRP of long-fiber cotton in 1983 of 10,000 tons. The Soviet side informed us of the impossibility of carrying out such exports.

In connection with the above, I appeal to you to reconsider this request, so that these exports could be replaced from the next harvest, in the second half of this year.

. . . In this connection, we would like to begin the construction of an additional gas line with 3–4 billion cubic meter capacity on the line from Kobryn-Warsaw without delay. In this situation, we appeal once again for the connection of the segment of the gas line from Kobryn to Brest to the area of work foreseen to be carried out by Polish organizations in the years 1983–85, so that an increased quantity of gas could flow to the PRP beginning in 1986.

I wish to inform you, Honorable Comrade Andropov, that the matters raised in this letter have already been raised at the government level by Deputy Premier J. Obodowski in conversations with Deputy Chairman of the Council of Ministers of the USSR N. K. Baibakov.

I remain in the hope that you will consider our request, as always, with fraternal goodwill.

I beg you to accept expressions of deep respect and the most sincere good wishes.

Wojciech Jaruzelski

April 29, 1983

Honorable Comrade Jaruzelski,

The Politburo of the CC CPSU has examined with understanding the request contained in your letter of April 18 of this year.

Considering the difficulties that the PRP has in providing its population with bread and food products, the Soviet side has sought out means of making additional exports to Poland in the second quarter of 1983 of 350,000 tons of consumption-grade wheat in the form of a credit to be offered to the PRP in connection with the participation of Soviet organizations in the completion of construction in Poland of enterprises in ferrous metallurgy, and 20,000 tons of salted sardines with payment by the Polish side in additional exports to the USSR in 1983 of goods necessary to the national economy of the USSR.

With the goal of improving the provision of the light industry of the PRP with raw materials from the USSR, an additional 3,400 tons of wool, 200 tons of cotton, 1,000 tons of flax fiber and 340 tons of polyester fiber will be exported according to conditions agreed on by specialists of the USSR and the PRP in negotiations in Warsaw in April of this year. The question of the possibility of an additional export to the PRP of 10,000 tons of long-fiber cotton from the 1983 harvest will be examined later, after the results of the cotton harvest in the USSR in the current year.

Concerning the question of expanding the gas-transportation system between the USSR and the PRP, including the construction of a gas line between Kobryn and Brest, It is considered expedient by the competent Soviet organizations to consider this in the course of the upcoming work on the coordination of national economic plans of our countries for 1986–90, simultaneously with the decision of the question of the level and conditions of exports of natural gas to the PRP after 1985.

With a communist greeting,

Iu. Andropov[29]

Poland was in the depths of economic crisis in April 1983, and Jaruzelski's letter to Andropov took a pleading tone. "Allow me to express to you personally, and to the leadership of the party and government of the Union of Soviet Socialist Republics, sincere thanks for your many forms of aid and support," he wrote. "I ask you once again, Honorable Comrade Andropov, to sell to our country an additional 500,000 tons of grain." The list of requests included gasoline, cotton, and the extension of the Kobryn-Brest natural gas pipeline. Andropov responded coolly, promising 350,000 instead of the requested 500,000 tons of wheat, failing to acknowledge the request for gasoline, and reaffirming the agreement reached earlier in April to substitute a meager increase in assorted fibers for Poland's request for 10,000 tons of cotton. The letter reaffirmed that the issue of the gas pipeline would have to be dealt with through the appropriate channels. Whereas the Jaruzelski letter ended extravagantly, "I beg you to accept expressions of deep respect and the most sincere good wishes," Andropov signed his simply, "With a communist greeting." Even in the wake of the economic crisis that engulfed Poland with the Solidarity strike, the declaration of martial law, and the isolation from trade with the West brought about by the Western boycott on new lending and much trade that followed, the Soviet Union continued to treat trade negotiations with Poland as business as usual. Poland was given substantial explicit aid, but any attempt to renegotiate the terms of the implicit trade subsidy met with great skepticism. This is consistent with the analysis of Soviet oil exports to Poland, above, which concluded that Poland's share of the oil subsidy slightly increased after 1981, but that the improvement was not substantial.

[29]Jaruzelski, "Notatki w sprawach gospodarczych Polski z Związkiem radzieckim (Pisma na najwyzszjem szczeblu)," Letter to Iu. Andropov, Polish, 4.18.1983. Reply by Iurii Andropov, Russian, 29 April 1983. CUP Archive.

CONCLUSIONS

This chapter has shown that there is no compelling evidence that the Soviet Union ever used its trade subsidy as leverage to force the East Europeans to make domestic political changes. This is not to say that the Soviet Union did not intervene in the domestic affairs of its allies, since it obviously did. It invaded Czechoslovakia, compelled Janos Kadar to fire his four closest allies in the Hungarian Politburo, and threatened to invade Poland. Yet despite the lengths to which Soviet policy was willing to go, the threat to withdraw the trade subsidy was never brought into play. Nor is there evidence that the subsidy was used in a calculated attempt to reward obedient allies and punish disobedient ones. Poland received some explicit subsidies after 1981, but politics did not decisively influence the bargaining over implicit subsidies. Hungary, furthermore, does not seem to have suffered after joining the IMF in 1982.

The Soviet Union failed to link the subsidy to political issues, even in crisis situations, and even when its vital interests were at stake. When a potent power resource is not used in time of need, one has to ask whether it is in fact usable. The most plausible explanation for the Soviet failure to pressure, reward, or punish with the subsidy seems to be the one repeatedly offered by East European negotiators: politics and economics were simply different realms, staffed by different cadres, and expected to fulfill different functions. In other words, the Soviet bureaucracy was so rigidly compartmentalized that it was effectively unable to make linkages between economic power resources and political objectives.

Part Three

MONITORING AND CREDIBILITY:
THE POLITICS OF MULTILATERAL
INTEGRATION

CHAPTER 6

The Comprehensive Program

THE COMPREHENSIVE PROGRAM was adopted in 1971 after two years of controversy and the most wrenching self-examination that the socialist world had ever allowed itself. It was billed as a document that would raise socialist economic integration to a "qualitatively new level," through joint planning, industrial specialization, and cooperation in science, technology, and production. It promised innovations in the financial sphere and the completion of an array of new investment projects in the energy and raw material sectors.

From the outset, the Comprehensive Program was buffeted by conflicts at two levels. The first was the level of general principles: the basic tendency of reform, the fundamental arrangements for cooperation, and the mechanism of foreign trade. There was a sharp clash of perspectives on these issues, with Poland, Czechoslovakia, and Hungary arrayed on the side of moderate market-type reforms, and the other countries favoring centralization or the status quo. The Soviet Union ultimately prevailed on these issues and imposed its own blueprints. Conflict also existed at the level of material interests: which concrete projects would the countries undertake, and how would they adjust their trade flows. Material interests became engaged when the countries moved from negotiating the general principles of cooperation to designing concrete programs of industrial specialization, cooperation, and joint investments. The details of these agreements would determine the profitability of foreign trade, and it was at this level that Soviet objectives were consistently frustrated. Even here, the program could boast of several significant, large-scale successes; but wherever the complexity of the issues or the vagueness of the criteria of success permitted, the smaller countries reneged on their agreements in order to improve their own trade profiles.

It would be a mistake to argue that Soviet policy failed to achieve its objectives with the Comprehensive Program because the basic principles of economic reform were compromised. A close examination of Soviet objectives shows that the Soviet Union achieved everything it sought to achieve at the level of principle; the Soviet leadership did not desire market-type reform, and that is why it did not occur. Nonetheless the program failed in Soviet terms, because the Soviets were unable to control the program's implementation phase.

A LETTER FROM GOMUŁKA

The Comprehensive Program was probably the only significant departure in CMEA politics that did not begin as a Soviet initiative. It began with a Polish proposal, which was distributed in 1968 by the Central Committee of the Polish United Workers' Party (PUWP) to the other Communist Parties.

Władisław Gomułka, the PUWP first secretary, was no particular friend of economic reform. He tolerated economic reformers, and brought Władimierz Brus and Oskar Lange back to esteemed positions in Poland after 1956, but when the Polish economy began to stagnate in 1961, he reversed the economic experiments that they had begun. He did not restrain conservative elements in the academic community from launching a vicious anti-Semitic attack in 1968 against Michał Kalecki, the foremost Polish economist and proponent of "market socialism." What applied to domestic experiments, however, did not necessarily apply to international economic arrangements. A fervent Polish nationalist, Gomułka was suspicious of Soviet ambitions to expand control over the East European economies; a committed Communist, he regarded economic integration as the wave of the future. For Gomułka, economic integration through market liberalization of CMEA trade seemed a progressive undertaking that would both benefit the economies of the region and weaken the Soviet grasp. Polish trade officials date the end of Soviet economic exploitation of Poland to 1956, when in one of his first acts as the new first secretary, Gomułka used the unstable situation in Poland to renegotiate the price of Polish coal. Still, with no personal experience in foreign trade, Gomułka was more keenly aware of the disadvantages facing the small East European countries than of their advantages in bilateral negotiations with the Soviet Union. Gomułka believed that the regularized, rational interactions of the market would tend to dilute Soviet bargaining power.[1]

Gomułka delegated the construction of the Polish position on CMEA reform to a commission headed by Stanisław Kuziński, the head of the Economic Department of the PUWP. Kuziński was a long-time ally. Like Gomułka, he had achieved prominence in the Polish resistance, rather than in exile in the Soviet Union. He had played a key role in the unrest that brought Gomułka back to power in 1956 by using his position in the Warsaw party organization to help paralyze the capital. Unlike Gomułka, however, Kuziński was committed to market reform. He describes himself as deeply influenced by the work of Michał Kalecki and Oskar Lange. He was regarded by the leading Polish economists of the time as a well-educated, qualified economist who consistently promoted the cause of economic reform. Kuziński

---

[1]Interviews with Stanisław Kuziński, 6.3.1992; Jozef Soldaczuk, 5.26.1992; and Jozef Pajestka, 6.3.1992.

surrounded himself with like-minded economists, such as Jozef Soldaczuk, Witold Trzeciakowski, and Jozef Pajestka.

The result was a Polish position paper that was startlingly critical of the existing foreign trade regime in the CMEA. It argued that the ideological verities of central planning were historically limited:

> The present cooperation among the member countries of the CMEA is based on methods of economic management whose historical roots are in the period when there existed only one socialist state, which carried on only limited exchange of goods with foreign countries because of the discriminatory policies of the capitalist environment, and which was compelled to depend on its own forces to build the foundations of a new order.
>
> . . . On a higher level of development of industry, the methods of planning applied so far have not been capable of securing the necessary growth of labor productivity, technical progress, and efficient capital investment.[2]

The report argued that the fundamental obstacle to socialist integration was that the countries had incompatible price systems. Each country had its own price system; the CMEA had another, independent system of calculating foreign trade prices; the rest of the world used yet another system that only influenced the first two indirectly. It was impossible to compare the prices of individual goods in different countries, because the currencies of the member countries were not convertible in any meaningful sense. Each country used a variety of exchange rates to calculate the economic effects of trade, and insulated its enterprises from the effects of foreign trade prices by putting them on the state budget or employing an array of taxes and subsidies.

> Under these circumstances, the enterprises and higher economic organizations that determine whether to import or export lack a correct orientation regarding the future trends of economic development. The enterprises are not interested in expanding the turnover of foreign trade, since they perceive no economic benefit in doing so.
>
> The divergence in methods of price formation makes productive costs and benefits incomparable, which seriously hampers the development of economic relations among the socialist countries.[3]

The report offered solutions along four major lines. First, the CMEA countries should establish a system of "real exchange rates," which would be established by the International Bank for Economic Cooperation (IBEC) as parities with a new international currency. This new currency would be used

[2]"Napravleniia i metody integratsii stran-chlenov SEV," March 1968, CMEA Archive, pp. 2–3.
[3]Ibid., p. 4.

to settle accounts in international trade, and each country's subscription would be backed by stocks of "first-priority goods," or basic raw materials. The new currency should allow trade to clear multilaterally by presenting an incentive to pay off trade debts. Second, the Poles urged the CMEA countries to unify the principles that they used to set domestic prices and to revise their price structures to make them gradually converge. An index of domestic prices would be used to set exchange rates, so the convergence of domestic price structures should gradually bridge the gap between domestic and foreign trade prices. The existing procedure for determining trade prices would be maintained for a transition period, but by the late 1970s domestic prices should become comparable, and should then replace world prices as the basis for foreign trade prices. Third, coordination of planning should be made much more flexible. "Hard" quotas expressed in physical terms, with prices set in long-term agreements, would be retained only for the most essential raw materials, basic food exports, and important machinery. For other goods, more general quotas would be used that expressed only the type of good concerned and the total value of exports and imports; the specific quantities and models would be negotiated by the enterprises concerned. Finally, a gradually expanding list of consumer goods would be "liberalized," which meant that imports and exports would be put on a cash-and-carry basis, with no quotas. The countries would be required to create reserves of the goods they proposed to list for sale, and to sell to the first customer. Prices, still, would be fixed in long-term agreements. The Poles hoped that the listed goods would grow from a proposed 10 percent of all consumer goods exported in 1970 to 50 percent by 1975, and include almost all consumer goods by the end of the decade.

The Polish proposal was a half-hearted reform. If adopted, it would not have overcome the basic obstacle to efficient economic decisions in the CMEA, which was irrational pricing. CMEA prices would continue to be based on formulas rather than on supply and demand, and therefore would fail to reflect real scarcities. This is all the more true because the proposed formula followed CMEA practice in including only supply factors in calculating prices, excluding demand factors, and further excluding certain supply factors, such as rents, that were not deemed politically acceptable.[4] Nonetheless the document was remarkably liberal for its time. Private reports show that the Polish economists understood that efficient allocation of resources and efficient international cooperation were possible only if prices conveyed information about supply and demand.[5] However, they were realistic enough not to expect the CMEA to transform itself instantaneously into its ideological oppo-

[4]Ibid., pp. 25–26.
[5]See, for example, Mycielski and Trzeciakowski, "Kurs złotego a rachunek efektywności handlu zagranicznego oraz system finansowy w gospodarce narodowej i w skali międzynarodowej;" Paweł Bożyk, "Teoreticheskie problemy torgovli mezhdu stranami-chlenami SEV."

site. Consequently, they proposed a series of measures that would gradually introduce market incentives into the CMEA. They proposed a gradual transition to convertible currencies, calculated to help overcome the structural bilateralism of CMEA trade without producing extreme dislocations. Centralized bargaining over plan coordination would continue, but enterprises would gradually be granted greater rights to expand their contacts with foreign partners. The sphere of "liberalized" trade would expand step by step. There was already a small margin in the annual trade protocols for "other goods," which were agreed on in the course of the year to overcome temporary shortages or to provide room for exports that were too insignificant to warrant inclusion in the Plan. Under the Polish proposal, this category would gradually expand.

The Polish proposal was naive in its expectation that the other CMEA countries could be persuaded to grant a great deal of power to supranational structures. The International Bank would have become a potent force under the reform blueprint, charged with recommending and approving changes in national exchange rates, issuing international currency, and imposing penalties for failure to meet debt repayment obligations. The Bank was even expected to negotiate debt rescheduling in return for financial adjustment programs— the central function of the International Monetary Fund. Poland proposed to introduce sanctions to enforce specialization agreements: nonspecializing countries that developed parallel capacity for a product included in such an agreement would not be allowed to export it to other CMEA countries. The proposal also advanced a new level of intervention in domestic planning. CMEA countries would be required to create reserve funds of goods intended for liberalized trade, so that supply would be available to meet unforeseen demand. They would be expected to revise their internal legal codes to permit enterprises and institutes to carry on a wide range of relations with foreign organizations that had hitherto been the province of ministries and central planning commissions.

Some of the Polish proposals aroused vigorous opposition even within the reformist camp. The proposal went further than any previous CMEA discussion in terms of regulating the domestic price systems of the member countries, something that the Poles must have expected Hungary to oppose, since it was in the midst of developing its New Economic Mechanism. Hungary fired back:

> Unification of the internal economic mechanisms of the member countries is not a condition for the beginning of integration. Such a task, to build integration on analogous national economic mechanisms, or indeed to demand a radical change of the present national mechanisms, cannot be realistic. It is necessary to retain the autonomy and sovereignty of the national states in the economic sphere, which means that the process of integration will take place along with the maintenance of autonomous national currency policies, budget policies, and price poli-

cies, and policies in the areas of planning and capital investments. However, it is clearly necessary to create, by means of mutual agreements, a new and effective international mechanism to stimulate integration by economic means. The new international mechanism can be founded on the basis of the existing national mechanisms that vary among themselves.[6]

Most of the countries shared the Hungarian view, which ultimately prevailed. In the final text of the program, one can find numerous applications of the qualification, "in accordance with each country's form of planning and management of the national economy."

If naive in certain respects, the Polish proposal was nonetheless canny in measuring the costs and benefits of reform to the Polish economy. The Poles proposed that trade prices be based on regional costs rather than on modified world prices, which was the existing practice. This would tend to lock in, and even increase, the Soviet subsidy to Eastern Europe, because East European costs were higher than the world average, whereas the quality of their exports was significantly lower. In addition, since CMEA pricing rules did not include rents, a price system based on regional costs would substantially understate the value of Soviet exports of petroleum and natural gas. Even before the explosion of petroleum prices in the 1970s, the cost of producing oil and gas was only a fraction of its value, and the rest of the price was rent. Basing trade prices on cost, meanwhile, would be beneficial to Poland because it was a major exporter of coal. The cost of producing coal was higher per unit of value than that of other forms of energy, and Poland balanced oil imports with coal exports. Basing prices on costs would improve the price ratio.

The Polish proposal was further calculated to uncouple Soviet raw material resources from disputes over machinery and consumer goods by relaxing the system of quotas for all goods except raw materials.[7] Raw material exports would continue to be guaranteed in long-term contracts that specified the quantity of each good to be exported, whereas most other categories of exports would be fixed in more general terms, with the details left to be determined in subsequent negotiations. This would allow the East Europeans to bargain in order to improve their trade profiles after they received assurances that their most important import needs would be met. If the long-term agreement specified that Poland export a certain value of agricultural machinery to the Soviet Union, for example, Poland could seek to export more tractors and fewer combines, or more complete tractors and fewer spare parts. Soviet bar-

---

[6]"Soobrazheniia Vengerskoi Sotsialisticheskoi Rabochei Partii po ekonomicheskoi integratsii sotsialisticheskikh stran," circulated by Apro Antal to N. V. Faddeev, 18 July 1968, CMEA Archive, p. 6.

[7]Interviews with Jozef Soldaczuk, 5.21.1992, and Alfred Siennicki, 5.6.1992. Soldaczuk was a professor at the Instytut Koniunktur i Cen, and played a major role in writing the Polish position. Siennicki was an official in the Polish Central Planning Commission and later served as head of the Department for Foreign Economic Cooperation.

gaining power on these issues would be substantially diluted, because the Soviet negotiators would find it more difficult to link oil exports to their preferred ratio of Polish machinery exports. In addition, the Poles proposed to begin liberalizing trade in consumer goods. The East Europeans ran surpluses with the Soviet Union in consumer goods, and liberalization could be expected to expand those surpluses. Since most consumer goods were relatively profitable exports, it would be beneficial to expand the proportion of consumer goods in exports to the USSR. Moreover, the East Europeans could benefit by altering the mix of consumer goods that they exported: manufactured cloth, for example, was a more profitable export than shoes. If sales were made directly by enterprises, the enterprises could offer only the most profitable exports, and Soviet organizations would presumably accept whatever was offered because of the severe deficits on the domestic market. Gosplan would be unable to influence trade in consumer goods by linking its preferences to raw material exports.

INTERNATIONAL POLITICS, PHASE 1: THE POSITIONS OF THE COUNTRIES

The Polish letter provoked a flurry of activity in the CMEA. The Soviet side decided to use the opportunity to advance integration and to conduct an overhaul of CMEA trade practices. The CPSU requested responses to the Polish proposal from each of the CMEA countries, and directed Gosplan to use the responses to formulate a Soviet proposal. The Soviets then called the Twenty-third CMEA Session for April 1969, to set the guidelines for developing a "Comprehensive Program for Socialist Economic Integration."

The Poles were not alone in promoting a conception of liberalized trade in the CMEA. Since the early 1960s the Czechoslovaks and Hungarians had been moving in the same direction, and the three countries even cooperated to press the case for liberalization on a few occasions. In the early 1960s, for example, they presented a joint proposal to liberalize visa regulations in the CMEA.[8] Beginning in 1968 the three countries held a series of strategy sessions on trade policy, and although they did not dare to present a joint position, since this would seem to divide the bloc, they did coordinate their positions and attempt to support one another in the CMEA working groups that hammered out the text of the program.[9] The Czechoslovaks ceased taking an active part in these strategy sessions after the Warsaw Pact invasion in August 1968, but their official position on reform in the CMEA did not

[8]Interview with Janos Szita, 9.7.1992.

[9]Interviews with František Stranský, 7.23.1992, and Janos Szita, 9.7.1992. Stranský and Szita were the heads of the departments of foreign economic affairs of the Council of Ministers for Czechoslovakia and Hungary, respectively.

change. The Czechoslovak position paper had been drafted before the invasion, and it was never retracted. Although most of the key players on the Czechoslovak side were replaced, several reformers remained in their positions, such as Zdeněk Šedivý, who served as deputy chairman of the State Planning Commission for CMEA affairs from May 1968 until 1980, and conducted the negotiations on the Comprehensive Program. There is no evidence of a connection between the Czechoslovak position on CMEA reform and the Warsaw Pact intervention, and Czechoslovak officials who participated in the negotiations before and after August vigorously resist the suggestion that the Soviets used the opportunities the invasion presented to influence the Czechoslovak position in discussions taking place in the CMEA.[10] The Czechoslovak delegates, however, were much more cautious after August, and Czechoslovakia did reverse itself on some liberal innovations that it had proposed to Hungary on a bilateral basis.[11]

The East Germans, Bulgarians, and Romanians opposed liberal reforms to varying degrees. Their opposition had both practical and ideological aspects. Pragmatically, the three agreed on the importance of stable prices and long-term agreements for the most important industrial inputs, which reflected the strict, quantitative planning that these countries practiced. They opposed any deliberate program to loosen the obligations assumed during plan coordination, and they argued that liberal objectives such as convertibility would have to wait until traditional planning had had time to eliminate the deficits on the CMEA market. Of the three, the Bulgarian position was the most flexible, maintaining the high ground of Marxist-Leninist rhetoric while supporting Polish proposals on a number of particular details. The Bulgarians wrote, for example: "We are opposed to liberalization carried out on the model of the capitalist states. The transition to that kind of liberalization will have an unfavorable influence on the development of our economies."[12] On the previous page, however, the Bulgarians endorsed the very proposal that the Poles had described as "liberalization," coining the less objectionable term *nonquota trade*, which came to be the official CMEA designation for trade carried on by ad hoc agreements outside the realm of plan coordination.

> At the same time, it is appropriate to begin using new forms in foreign trade. In the treaties and protocols, for example, along with goods designated in quotas, it

[10]Interviews with Zdeněk Šedivý, 6.30.1992; Vladislav Cihlař, 6.17.1992; and František Stranský, 7.23.1992.

[11]Interviews with Istvan Hetenyi, 9.3.1992; Akos Balassa, 9.9.1992; and Janos Szita, 9.7.1992.

[12]"Kontseptsiia Tsentral'nogo Komiteta Bolgarskoi Kommunisticheskoi Partii i Pravitel'stva Narodnoi Respubliki Bolgarii sotrudnichestva dlia predstoiashchego Soveshchaniia na vysokom urovne," circulated by T. Tsolov, Deputy Chairman of the Council of Ministers, Permanent Representative of Bulgaria to the CMEA, to N. V. Faddeev, Secretary of the CMEA, 31 January 1969, CMEA Archive, p. 30.

is possible to determine a nomenclature of goods for which trade will take place without cost—or other quotas. *It would be possible to make a gradual transition to nonquota trade in the sphere of manufactured consumer goods.* As a result, with the accumulation of a certain experience, that circle might widen to include other groups of goods in which the countries indicate an interest.[13]

Bulgaria also supported the Polish proposals for domestic price reform to cause prices to converge in the CMEA countries, for strengthening the role of the transferable ruble, and for expanding the use of commercial credit in CMEA trade, all steps that could be characterized as moving the CMEA in the direction of a market.

The German position was the most doctrinaire. The planned economy, the Germans argued, which focuses resources with precision on the most important objectives, is best able to take advantage of opportunities for scientific and technical development. Market reform, on the other hand, weakens the economy, the state, and the socialist commonwealth.

> The differences among the socialist countries are expressed in the varied development and implementation of the economic system of socialism, depending on the specific conditions of each country's development. The differences in the economic system of socialism are reflected in the level of the system of planning, the level of labor productivity, and the cost-efficiency of production. . . . Cooperation between the various socialist countries develops most effectively when the long-term plan and the fundamental questions of structural development are decided most precisely by adherence to prognoses.
>
> The workers' and peasants' power in the peoples' democracies has by its very nature long been burdened with the remnants of bourgeois economic theories, and also with the difficult task of gradually attracting various classes and strata of the populations to socialism with measures for social and economic development. The complexity of this task is intensified by the continuous influence of bourgeois ideology, and in particular by the conduct of an ideological war by the imperialistic powers.[14]

The GDR called on the other countries to forsake general statements of principles (such as monetary and foreign trade reform) and to make concrete proposals for cooperation: that is, to propose specific projects that could be negotiated and carried out by the countries' central planning organs. These should concentrate on technological development in strategic sectors, such as computers and engineering.

[13]Ibid., pp. 29–30.
[14]"Memorandum Politbiuro TsK SEPG i Prezidiuma Soveta Ministrov Germanskoi Demokraticheskoi Respubliki po voprosu o razvitii sotsialisticheskogo ekonomicheskogo soobshchestva Soveta Ekonomicheskoi Vzaimopomoshchi," circulated by G. Weiss to N. V. Faddeev, 4 October 1968, CMEA Archive, p. 6.

The Soviet position paper attempted to reconcile the opposing East European views. According to Oleg Rybakov, who was a member of the Gosplan team that wrote the document, and Iurii Pekshev, who supervised the process for the Central Committee, the Soviets consciously tried to assimilate as many of the conflicting East European viewpoints as possible.[15] Consequently, although the Soviets used much of the East European vocabulary, the same words took on very different meanings. Elements of liberal reform were endorsed, such as realistic exchange rates, gradual progress toward convertibility, direct ties between enterprises and expanding "nonquota" trade. These reforms, however, were hedged in with caveats. For example, although the Soviets agreed with the Poles that direct links between enterprises should expand across national boundaries, they stipulated that they should expand first in the areas covered by long-term trade agreements, and that the planning organs of each country should decide which enterprises formed such ties.[16] The Soviets affirmed the gradual development of trade without quotas, but also endorsed the German condition that it could only expand if the countries first took administrative measures to increase the availability of consumer goods for export.[17] The Soviets agreed to convertibility and "real" exchange rates, but without recommending steps to back up the collective currency with goods. They insisted that such a currency remain an accounting unit of the International Bank and not be issued as a true currency. They refused, furthermore, to agree to a unified exchange rate for all types of payments, preferring a system of discounts and surcharges.[18] With all the caveats in place, the Soviets could safely agree to many of the Polish proposals without opening the door to substantial change.

The apparently liberal elements in the Soviet position have to be interpreted in light of the limited ambitions of the Kosygin reforms. The Soviet conception of reform differed markedly from that promoted by the East Europeans. A report prepared by Soviet Gosplan for the working group on planning, "On the Improvement of the System of Management and Planning in the USSR," spelled out the limits of the Kosygin reforms. The primary objectives were to: (1) increase the importance of the five-year plan (over the annual plan); (2) increase the powers and responsibilities of branch ministries (vis-à-vis the center and the enterprise); and (3) improve the incentives for fulfilling the major plan objectives by reducing their number and introducing more financial accounting. This was not a program for market-style reform, but for incremental tinkering with the accepted system of planning to make it more

---

[15]Interviews with Oleg Rybakov, 3.9.1992, and Iurii Pekshev, 3.10.1992.

[16]"O problemakh ekonomicheskogo sotrudnichestva stran-chlenov Soveta Ekonomicheskoi Vzaimopomoshchi (Pledlozheniia Sovetskogo Soiuza)," circulated by M. Lesechko to N. V. Faddeev, 12.31.1968, CMEA Archive, p. 15.

[17]Ibid., pp. 38–39.

[18]Ibid., pp. 44–45.

effective. The report claimed that the experience of 1966–69 demonstrated that "the new system of planning and economic stimulation makes it possible to strengthen centralized planning while simultaneously expanding commercialization [*tovarno-denezhnye otnosheniia*] by means of further development of financial accountability [*khoziaistvennogo rascheta*]."[19] This was exactly the position that the Soviet Union took on reform in the CMEA. It argued that it was possible to combine increased centralization with increased decentralization, and that the resulting hybrid would not only be viable, but more efficient.

The Soviet position paper embedded these tentative reformist tendencies in proposals for a much more centralized trade regime, to be based on "joint planning." The Soviets proposed to deepen the coordination of planning substantially, to take in all stages of planning rather than trade alone. It was to embrace "joint long-term and current planning of a series of products and some branches of industry." It was hoped that joint planning would reduce deficits on the CMEA market. This meant, however, that it would call upon the countries to create the capacity to export goods that none of them wanted to export, in many cases because of their unfavorable prices. It was intended to create joint gains for the countries by "exploiting existing capacity rationally on the basis of international specialization and cooperation." In many cases, however, existing capacity was underutilized for a perfectly rational reason: distorted CMEA prices made it hard to justify additional production of many deficit goods for export. Finally, it was hoped that specialization agreements would make it possible to invest in "new, optimal enterprises with modern technology, or modernizing existing enterprises" by pooling resources and sharing costs.[20] This hope clashed, however, with incentives for the satellites to avoid technological innovation. The Soviet proposal was designed to overcome a collective-action problem, but it clashed with underlying incentives that impelled the satellites to exploit the provider of the subsidy.

The paper went on to say that "compiling joint plans, of course, should not impair the sovereign rights of each country to plan its own economy."[21] Nevertheless, the Soviet position could only be interpreted as a call for much closer coordination of national investment policies, and for extensive changes. The proposal suggested how large a scale joint planning was expected to take by proposing four branches as a "pilot program": radio-electronics and computers, shipbuilding, machine-tool building, and ferrous

---

[19]Gosplan USSR, "O sovershenstvovanii sistemy upravleniia i planirovaniia v SSSR (razdel I razvernutogo plana raboty rabochei gruppy I, p. 7)," to Working Group I, 3.2.1970, CMEA Archive, p. 5.

[20]"O problemakh ekonomicheskogo sotrudnichestva stran-chlenov Soveta Ekonomicheskoi Vzaimopomoshchi (Pledlozheniia Sovetskogo Soiuza)," circulated by M. Lesechko to N. V. Faddeev, 12.31.1968, CMEA Archive, pp. 12–13.

[21]Ibid., pp. 12–13.

metallurgy.[22] If the pilot program took in such important and extensive areas of the economy, one could expect the ultimate Soviet ambitions to be very far-reaching. The paper proposed a method of arriving at joint plans:

> The transition to joint long-term and current planning could be carried out, in our opinion, approximately according to the following schema. The branch ministries of the interested countries will specify the demand of each of the socialist countries for the corresponding types of products, taking into account likely exports to third countries. On the basis of existing capacity and resources, and of the resources made available for capital construction, the ministries will agree on a program to satisfy social needs, both by better utilizing existing productive capacity, and by expanding it.
>
> . . . The proposals of the branch ministries (or associations) of the interested countries will be conveyed to the planning organs, which will coordinate these proposals with the other sections of the national economic plans. Final agreement will then be reached on a single plan of development of the given branch or type of production.
>
> The plans for production and specialization, once accepted by the governments of the interested countries, will be legally registered in multilateral or bilateral treaties, which will form the basis for concluding foreign trade contracts. In this connection, along with the questions of foreign trade, the aforementioned treaties should foresee mutual obligations for capital construction, the introduction of new products, the solution of important scientific and technical problems, etc.[23]

The significance of this proposal was that coordination was meant to precede national planning, rather than follow it. Traditionally, the CMEA countries had compiled their plans and then negotiated with each other bilaterally about how to relieve their deficits. The range of possible agreements was limited by the maximum surplus of the weaker partner in each pair. Instead, the Soviets proposed that the countries first determine their import needs in a particular branch, and compile an international plan that balanced supply and demand. Then, they should adjust their national plans to the requirements of the international agreement. The new procedure should dramatically expand the set of possible bargains, and increase regional trade flows accordingly.

Joint planning called for three different kinds of agreements: (1) joint investment projects, (2) specialization agreements, and (3) cooperation agreements. Joint investment projects were intended to build factories or mining complexes to produce scarce raw materials, and the investing countries would be repaid in the corresponding type of raw material. Since joint investments were effectively limited to the raw material and energy branches of the economy, other approaches were needed to integrate manufacturing and to im-

[22]Ibid., p. 18.
[23]Ibid., pp. 19–20.

prove the quality of CMEA machinery exports. Specialization agreements committed the exporter to supply unspecified quantities of a particular type of product, and obliged other countries to import that product rather than producing it themselves. The objective was to coordinate investment policies over a long period, so that countries would not duplicate each other's productive capacity. This should save investment funds, provide large enough export markets to make the introduction of new technologies feasible, and expand the opportunities for trade. Cooperation agreements took specialization to a greater level of detail. The cooperating countries agreed to supply the specializing country with intermediate goods that were required to produce some final product, such as the Hungarian Icarus bus. Hungary, in this case, agreed to export busses in return for front axles, rear axles, cushions, and air-conditioning systems. The goal was to increase the possible gains from trade by trading in goods needed at all stages of production, rather than simply trading in finished products.

The Soviet Union proposed to expand dramatically the practice of specialization and cooperation, arguing, for example, that "it is expedient to assume that productive cooperation and specialization shall become the basis for exchange of machines and equipment among the CMEA countries."[24] The USSR hoped to introduce specialization and cooperation in leading sectors, areas that could be expected to increase substantially the productivity and technological sophistication of the CMEA economies. A particular area of concentration was to be the computer industry, which the CMEA countries were just beginning to construct.[25] Specialization would guarantee external markets, allowing small countries to make investments in technology and development that could not be justified by the scale of their own economies. Cooperation would divide up complex tasks, bringing them within the reach of limited national resources. Above all, these agreements were to be a mechanism for pushing up the level of quality standards for CMEA products. Each agreement would set technical standards and require the countries to invest in new types of products.

> The most important condition for integrating the CMEA countries' industrial production is raising the technical level and quality of their products. . . . To this end, it would be appropriate in the first place to correct national standards so that the production of the socialist countries not only corresponds to the best foreign designs, but itself determines the world level of technological development.[26]

This was an objective as utopian as any the Poles had advanced, but again, it was grounded in a firm sense of the Soviet national interest. If the quality of

[24]Ibid., p. 29.
[25]Ibid., p. 27.
[26]Ibid., p. 29.

East European machinery could be substantially improved, the Soviet Union would be a major beneficiary, and the implicit Soviet trade subsidy would be reduced.

The Soviet proposals to stimulate greater technological progress in the bloc provide a glimpse of how the specialists at Gosplan expected decentralization of some functions at the national level to fit into a strategy of centralizing CMEA planning at the international level:

> The further development and deepening of socialist integration in the area of science and technology should, in our opinion, be carried out in the following ways:
>
> • Concentration of the scientific potential of the interested countries upon the resolution of concrete tasks of scientific and technical progress in the most important branches of the economy;
>
> • Development and improvement of the effectiveness of the coordination of national plans for science and technology, and the strengthening on that basis of the control of planning in scientific and technical cooperation;
>
> • Introduction of the principles of financial accountability [khoziaistvennyi raschet] in the area of scientific and technical cooperation, and expanding the practice of contractual ties;
>
> • Tight linkage between scientific and technical cooperation and specialization, industrial cooperation, and foreign trade;
>
> • Granting greater autonomy to the cooperating scientific-research and design and construction organizations in carrying out the measures that have been agreed on on a bilateral or multilateral basis.[27]

The Soviet proposal was a union of opposites: more autonomy combined with more control; more initiative from the periphery joined with more coherent focus of resources on priorities set by the center. There is no paradox, however. Financial accounting [Khozraschet] was not seen as a step toward the market, but rather as one of the tools in the arsenal of centralized planning, which could stimulate enterprises to follow central priorities with greater precision than could be achieved with traditional quantitative indicators. Soviet calls for direct ties were calls for more cooperation agreements, which would establish links between enterprises by administrative fiat.

The announcement of a Soviet position, which judiciously weighed the contributions of the various countries and wove them into an authoritative pronouncement, set the possible boundaries in CMEA reform. At the Twenty-third CMEA Session in 1969, the countries unanimously agreed to accept the Soviet proposal as the basis for discussion; any proposals they wished to introduce thereafter had to be amendments to the Soviet draft. The countries offered numerous such amendments, many of which contradicted each other

[27]Ibid., p. 32.

either in substance or in grammar, so the resulting negotiations became very complex. Almost all the amendments, however, amounted to marginal changes of language. The discussion dragged on, for example, with a dispute between the Czechoslovaks and the Bulgarians about whether the Executive Committee should be directed to work out the "principles, procedure, and *economic, organizational, and legal* preconditions" for expanding direct ties between national enterprises, or simply to direct it to decide on the "principles, procedure, and *necessary* preconditions."[28] The difference was simply a matter of emphasis, with no legally binding consequences. There was somewhat more substance to the Polish objection to the Soviet wording that direct ties should develop "*planomerno*," which means "systematically" but also "according to plan." However, it is not clear that anything was gained for reform by the Soviet agreement to drop the offensive word.[29] In the end the Soviet point of view prevailed. According to the IEMSS resumé of the Twenty-third Session:

> It is a very significant fact that in the preparation for the Session and in the process of its work, a conception of integration prevailed whose central link is the planned organization of industrial cooperation, including joint planning of the leading branches of industry, and that the conception of primarily market-type integration was rejected.[30]

The Soviet proposal came through the process intact, with no substantive changes, owing in large part to the dogged persistence of the new CPSU secretary for relations with socialist countries, Konstantin Katushev, who chaired the editing commission straight through the night.[31]

The only "objection of principle" was raised by the Romanian delegation, which objected to the title of the proposed program, arguing that "integration" was an imperialist concept, and as such was not a proper goal for socialist

[28]Stenogramma zasedaniia redaktsionnoi komissii XXIII Sessii SEV, 4.23, 1969, CMEA Archive, pp. 158–71; ibid., 24 April 1969, pp. 1–5 (emphasis added).

[29]Stenogramma zasedaniia redaktsionnoi komissii XXIII Sessii SEV, 4.23, 1969, CMEA Archive, pp. 155–57.

[30]Dudinskii et al., "Razvitie mirovoi sotsialisticheskoi sistemy v period posle XXIII S'ezda KPSS," 6.25.1970, IMEPI Archive, IEMSS report, p. 21.

[31]The transcript indicates that the commission met during the day of April 23, took a break, and then continued from 8:00 P.M. to 11:00 A.M. the next morning, with Katushev presiding. "Stenogramma zasedaniia redaktsionnoi komissii XXIII Sessii SEV," 23 April 1989, CMEA Archive. Several Soviet officials pointed out that this was very unusual, since the duty of chair would normally have fallen to Mikhail Lesechko, the Soviet deputy premier for CMEA affairs. The older Lesechko, however, was physically unable to take the strain, and fell asleep during the proceedings. Katushev, his superior, was determined to achieve results in his first major international appearance. Katushev's Soviet colleagues were very impressed with the former Gorky First Secretary's performance. It has been suggested that Katushev was ineffective and that this may explain his sudden demotion in 1977, but the evidence contradicts this view (interviews with Krasnov, 2.27.1992; Pekshev, 3.10.1992; and Rybakov, 3.9.1992).

nations. Gogu Radulescu, the Romanian delegate, stated the objection forcefully:

> In the first place, Comrade Chairman, I would like to ask you to allow me to make a more general comment, so there will be no need to repeat myself later. We cannot consent to any formulation which might contain the word *integration.* We cannot agree to that. I request that this be taken as a general comment from our side, so that even if I fail to make this comment about some particular text, I ask you to consider that this is simply an omission on my part.[32]

Even the strident Romanian opposition, however, was rather superficial. A close examination of the Romanian position paper shows that the Romanians proposed a number of practical measures to increase the interdependence of the bloc. The Romanians had been reluctant at first to join the International Bank for Economic Cooperation, but by 1969 they favored expanding its functions by granting it the right to make long-term loans and to borrow hard currency from the West. Although Romania eventually refused to join the International Investment Bank because of a dispute over voting rules, it was Romania that first proposed its creation. The Romanians viewed most other proposals to create new international organizations with suspicion, but they were not at all opposed to expanding international trade. In fact, after the Soviet Union, it was the Romanians who made concrete proposals to expand CMEA cooperation in the largest number of industries.[33] Romania raised a number of objections during the discussion at the Twenty-third Session, but none of its proposals would have weakened the program significantly.

This is a conclusion of some significance, because the realist critique of the CMEA that became widespread in the West was based largely on the evidence of Romanian opposition to Soviet overtures that spilled out into the socialist press or crept into allusions by communist leaders. It was assumed that these hints revealed a deep-seated opposition to economic integration per se, and the frequent Romanian references to national sovereignty supplied support for the realist view: Romania opposed economic integration because it would undermine the country's hard-won independence. The Romanians never did accept the word *integration,* and finally omitted it from the Romanian-language version of the text. This resistance, however, was purely symbolic; the Romanians accepted all the Soviet proposals that were supposed to add up to integration, and rejected only the label.

[32]"Stenogramma zasedaniia redaktsionnoi komissii XXIII Sessii SEV," 23 April 1969, CMEA Archive, pp. 22–24.

[33]"Soobrazheniia Tsentral'nogo Komiteta Rumynskoi Kommunisticheskoi Partii i Soveta Ministrov Sotsialisticheskoi Respubliki Rumynii po voprosu o sovershenstvovanii ekonomicheskogo i nauchno-tekhnicheskogo sotrudnichestva stran-chlenov SEV," circulated by V. Bukur, Deputy Permanent SRR Representative to CMEA, to N. V. Faddeev, Secretary, CMEA, 28 February 1969, CMEA Archive, pp. 15, 17, 23.

INTERNATIONAL POLITICS, PHASE 2: THE WORKING GROUP
FOR PLANNING

The Twenty-third Session set out only the program's basic objectives, so a great number of critical details remained to be negotiated. The Session established seven working groups, which developed proposals over the next two years for cooperation in planning, regulation of foreign trade and exchange rates, scientific and technical cooperation, and legal reform. These proposals were reviewed at the Twenty-fourth Session in 1970, and the program was adopted at the Twenty-fifth Session in 1971.

The delegates to the working groups were high-level officials. The delegates to the First Working Group, for coordination of planning, were the chairmen of the countries' central planning commissions, who held the rank of deputy premier. When the group met, each chairman was accompanied by a team of six to ten "experts," which included deputy chairmen of the planning commissions, advisers for foreign affairs to the countries' premiers, and representatives of various ministries. The delegates sat at a separate table, and the meeting took place in an auditorium. The discussions in this format were rather stiff and formal. The delegates delivered prepared statements, usually in Russian. According to the minutes, almost all the attention of the meetings was devoted to editing documents, such as reports on various aspects of cooperation and draft sections of the text of the final program. Before any document reached this stage, it had to be discussed by the Bureau of the First Working Group, which consisted of deputy chairmen of the countries' planning commissions and corresponding delegations of slightly lower rank. The Bureau, in turn, received its initial material from the CMEA Secretariat, which generally passed on Soviet proposals.

The Soviet delegation thus controlled the agenda, both formally and informally. The chairman of the First Working Group was the chairman of Soviet Gosplan, Nikolai Baibakov; the chairman of the Bureau was his deputy, Mikhail Misnik. The secretary of the CMEA was an undistinguished Soviet official, Nikolai Fadeev, and the Secretariat acted almost as an arm of the Soviet government. The Soviets were usually able to assure that only documents that met with their approval came before the working group. The Soviet delegation went to great lengths to avoid embarrassing confrontations in the plenary sessions, so compromises were often reached before the meetings began. This does not mean, however, that the working group was a rubber stamp. The minutes show that the countries did not hesitate to object when they felt that their interests or their proposals were being treated lightly. Under CMEA rules, any country could introduce a section of text to any document as its own "particular opinion," and those sections could not be eliminated by majority vote. Every document, consequently, began as a mass of particular opinions and went through numerous iterations as the chair tried to forge consensus around a single text.

The Romanian delegation expressed the largest number of "particular opinions," and frequently insisted on frivolous points. The Romanians often objected to the title of a document or its preamble, for example, without making substantive criticisms of its contents. Many arguments revolved around the choice of words, rather than the real intent of the text. The Romanian delegation usually came to meetings bearing a prepared text to be inserted into the minutes, or into a document under discussion, which concerned general principles. The Romanian text was often redundant, as in the following example from the working group's report on the creation of new international organizations. The following is the original Soviet text:

> The cooperation that is carried out by means of international economic organizations should be built on the general principles of economic cooperation of the socialist countries: socialist internationalism, free choice, respect for sovereignty and national interests, full equality of rights, comradely mutual aid, mutual gain, and mutual responsibility. The international economic organizations that are formed should not have the character of supranational organs.[34]

Whether this language would have been a sufficient guarantee is open to dispute, but its defects would not seem to be addressed by more language to the same effect. Nevertheless, the protocol goes on to read, "The SRR experts propose to add at the end of this text the following words: 'and shall not interfere with the sovereign rights of the countries in the areas of planning, management of the economy, or in other areas.' " The Romanian delegations repeatedly claimed that they were not authorized to compromise; they had been ordered to present the Romanian position and to insert it into the text if possible, or to leave it on the table as the opinion of the Romanian side if no other course were available. Soviet officials regarded the Romanian delegates as almost comical in their pedantic fidelity to cumbersome formulations. On several occasions, the Romanians insisted on their wording even though it was phrased in ungrammatical Russian, because their superiors would be infuriated if they permitted any changes in the Romanian translation of the text.[35] These tactics could occasionally provide cover for the other small countries, and even some Soviet negotiators have credited the Romanians with preventing the CMEA from making mistakes by slowing down the process; for the most part, however, the Romanian positions simply infuriated all the other parties. Still, since the Romanian delegation generally staked out its positions on symbolic grounds, it rarely kept the Soviets from achieving what they set out to do.

---

[34]"O printsipakh, poriadke," 12–15 January 1970, CMEA Archive.
[35]Interviews with Leonid Krasnov, 2.27.1992, and Oleg Rybakov, 3.9.1992.

Perhaps the best illustration of the process followed in these discussions is an anecdote about an occasion when the Soviet delegate failed to follow the proper procedure. Istvan Hetenyi, who was deputy chairman of the Hungarian Planning Commission and led most of the Hungarian delegations, remembers that a Soviet official who was not experienced in CMEA work once stood in for the chair, and had to be corrected by the other delegates.

I think [the chairman] was Baibakov, and Misnik was not around, so his first deputy came. I don't know who it was, but it was someone who had never been involved in international affairs, and didn't know anything about what we were discussing. He took the document, and there were the points and the comments of the countries. "First page, O.K.; next page—comment by Hungary"— or Romania; we made the most comments. "What is this?" He was reading the text for the first time. "Who is in favor of this comment? Bulgaria?" No. "Hungary?—Oh, this is your comment—GDR?" No, no, no. "Very well— rejected. We shall go on." We had to tell him, "Those are the positions of the countries. You can't reject them!" That was a Soviet type. He thought he was at home. But by page twenty he knew what he was supposed to say.[36]

The rules of procedure were clear, and the transcripts and protocols indicate that they were followed. Dozens of participants in the negotiations confirm that the Soviets did not use any overt pressure to push through their own proposals. Intimidation, in any case, was not available as an option to the chairman of Soviet Gosplan. Baibakov was not a Politburo member, and many of his East European counterparts were. If intimidation had been the order of the day, it could only have taken place at a higher level.

Nevertheless, through a combination of persuasion, manipulation of the agenda, and playing the countries off against one another, the Soviet delegations were able to control the outcome of the discussions fairly closely. It was the Soviet conception of integration that prevailed. Table 6.1 indicates which countries supported particular reform proposals in their position papers, and which proposals ended up in the adopted version of the Comprehensive Program. No significant reform proposal made its way into the final draft without Soviet support. Only one major point that the Soviet Union supported failed to be adopted, which was a proposal to increase interest rates on trade deficits to spur the countries to repay their debts. This was a proposal that enjoyed broad support, but the various countries had differing ideas about how far interest rates should rise. The vague compromise that was finally reached was that "credits and interest rates should more actively contribute to the development of the foreign trade turnover of the countries and the execution of their respective responsibilities."[37] This seems to have satisfied the Soviet delegation,

[36]Interview with Istvan Hetenyi, 9.8.1992.

[37]Sovet Ekonomicheskoi Vzaimopomoshchi, Sekretariat, *Osnovnye dokumenty Soveta Ekonomicheskoi Vzaimopomoshchi*, 4th ed., vol. 1, p. 73.

TABLE 6.1

Major Reform Objectives

	Hungary	GDR	Bulgaria	Poland	Romania	USSR	CSSR	Final
Nonquota trade	•	•	•	•		•	•	•
Reduce quota trade	•		•	•			•	
Reform exchange rates	•		•	•		•	•	•
Convertibility of TR*	•		•	•		•		•
National convertibility				•	•		•	
Single-exchange rate				•			•	
Dual-exchange rate	•	•	•			•		•
Equalize prices			•	•			•	
Raise interest rates	•		•	•	•	•	•	
Expand direct ties	•	•	•	•		•	•	•
Regulate direct ties			•		•	•		•
Contract inviolability	•			•			•	

Source: Compiled by the author from the original position papers of the countries in the CMEA Archive, TsGANKh, Fond 561, Opis 53s, Delo 5, No. pp. 6.

*transferable ruble.

which in any case did not expect financial instruments to play a very major role in CMEA trade policy.

The Soviet delegations never pressed actively for market-type reforms, even when such proposals were contained in the Soviet proposal. Many of these proposals had been incorporated simply in order to smooth over relations with the more reform-minded governments. In retrospect, one Soviet specialist argued that the Soviet delegates had "started from the point of view of what was realistic." Poland, in particular, pushed for much more far-reaching proposals, but the group around Mikhail Misnik and Nikolai Inozemtsev at Gosplan thought that the Polish ideas were "pure fantasy."[38]

Leonid Krasnov, who was a consultant in the CPSU Central Committee, later recalled that "the weakness of the [Polish and Hungarian] proposals was that they were distant from economic reality. We had a particular economic system, based on centralized commands. It would not have worked to make piecemeal changes, while leaving the rest of the system as it was." He argued that the proposals for nonquota trade, in particular, reflected the East Europeans' commercial interests rather than their market convictions.

> The centerpiece of their proposals was nonquota trade, but they were not prepared to make the change to pure market pricing. Instead, they wanted to maintain a tight quota system for certain "strategic goods"—energy and raw

[38]Interview with Oleg Rybakov, 3.9.1992. At this point, Misnik was the deputy chairman of Gosplan responsible for relations with socialist countries, and Inozemtsev was the director of the Department for Relations with Socialist Countries.

materials, or in other words, Soviet exports—while allowing other goods to be sold at contract prices—manufactured goods, or in other words, Soviet imports. . . .

Kosygin caught them on this point at the Twenty-fourth Session in 1970, in Warsaw. A draft of the Comprehensive Program was ready for discussion. When the Poles and Hungarians brought up the subject of nonquota trade, he asked, "So why don't we make all of our trade nonquota?" He suggested using contract prices for Soviet oil and raw materials as well as for imports of machinery. The Polish representative was [Bolesław] Jaszczyk; I don't remember who the Hungarian was. Silence descended upon the hall. The GDR delegation looked over at their Polish and Hungarian comrades with evident satisfaction, and some of them even laughed out loud.[39]

The Soviet opposition to nonquota trade could not have been made more clear.

The Poles, Hungarians, and Czechoslovaks of course understood the Soviet point of view on reform, but they hoped to embed a few reformist ideas in the program that could later be used as precedents. They did not believe that the CMEA could be reformed dramatically in the short term.

Formally you can find [direct ties] in the document, and formally you can find in the document the basis for nonquota trade. At the meetings the Soviets were against them, because they could not fit them into their planning system. One partner, Nikolai Vorov, said, "Well, if you force it, we can write it, but I can tell you that there will be only two articles that will be without quotas: roses," and I don't remember the other one, fresh flowers or something. . . . We knew, and the Soviets told us, that even if we had direct ties between enterprises, under their internal mechanism, the enterprises would only sign agreements that Gosplan gave them permission to sign. It was not our business how they regulated things within their country. We knew at the time that those sentences had no meaning. But who knows? Maybe in ten years, fifteen years, perhaps not in the Soviet Union or the GDR, but in Czechoslovakia or Poland or Bulgaria, they would introduce an economic system like in Hungary, and in that case, there might be some possibilities for decentralization in foreign trade. . . . It was best to put it in, in any case.[40]

The discussions of the role of "direct ties" between CMEA enterprises illustrates the degree to which Soviet views prevailed in matters of principle. All sides affirmed the importance of such links, but they understood their place in the overall scheme of economic integration in significantly different ways. For the reformers, "direct ties" meant the liberation of smaller economic units from crushing micromanagement by the planning commissions and ministries of foreign trade, and it was the first legal prerequisite for any meaningful

[39]Interview with Leonid Krasnov, 2.27.1992.
[40]Interview with Istvan Hetenyi, 9.3.1992.

economic reform. First, they reasoned, enterprises, institutes, associations, and other economic units should be given the full range of legal rights to establish relationships with partners in other CMEA countries; then they should be placed in an institutional context that fosters those relationships. That would mean gradual liberalization of international trade and finance. The symbolic affirmation of "direct ties" by the CMEA would be a first step.

The Soviet delegation used the term *direct ties* to mean operational connections between enterprises that were created by administrative fiat. "Of course," Oleg Rybakov reported, "we understood 'direct ties' in the spirit of the times. This was not a radical market proposal. The idea was that the strategic decisions would be taken by Gosplan and the ministries, and the enterprises would become involved at the implementation phase. Most of these ties would not be trade ties, but just exchange of information in the area of scientific-technical progress, and so forth."[41] This does not mean that the Soviets did not take direct ties seriously, but rather that they used the same term to mean something quite different. "Direct ties" were a means of deepening integration by increasing the complexity of the Plan. Coordination of planning, they reasoned, had hitherto led to poor results because it was too superficial. It embraced only the end products of industry, a situation the Soviets described as relations of "mere trade." The Plan could become much more effective, they reasoned, if integration led to contacts between enterprises rather than simply between central planning agencies. This would make it possible to plan cooperation in research, development, production, and service.

It was the Soviet perspective that prevailed. According to the document on direct ties adopted by the Working Group on Planning, the central planning commissions would determine which organizations could participate in direct ties:

> The competent organs of the CMEA member countries, on the basis of the tasks and conditions of internal economic development and international economic, scientific, and technical cooperation, will assign the ministries, departments, other state organs, and economic organizations that have the right to establish direct ties. Depending upon conditions, their number might expand.
>
> It will be necessary to organize a regular [exchange of] information between the CMEA member countries regarding which ministries, departments, other state organs, and economic organizations have the right to establish direct ties and to conclude the corresponding contracts.[42]

The document goes on to limit the functions that these organizations are expected to fulfill, and trade clearly did not fall within the sphere of competence

[41]Interview with Oleg Rybakov, 3.9.1992.

[42]"O printsipakh, poriadke," 12–15 January 1970, CMEA Archive.

of enterprises. Enterprises that were permitted to engage in direct ties could "develop proposals" and "participate" in the process of coordination of plans, but they were not empowered to make decisions about imports and exports on their own authority. Their most important role was to implement the decisions made at a higher level during the coordination of plans. Furthermore, most of the functions delegated to them were the invisible activities that were understood to improve productivity, but that were too diffuse to be assigned a monetary value in socialist planning: "exchange of experience," "technical aid," "service," and "exchange of scientific and technical documentation."[43]

The Soviet delegation saved its passion for a series of procedural changes that were intended to improve the coordination of central planning. Table 6.2 indicates which countries' position papers supported which proposals, and which were endorsed by the program as it was finally adopted. All the major Soviet proposals were adopted. Some of the Soviet proposals were popular, and these passed without particular difficulty. All the countries, for example, were in favor of strengthening the International Bank for Economic Cooperation. All but Hungary supported a comprehensive CMEA science and technology policy; five countries proposed creating new international research and development centers, and five proposed to cooperate in buying patents and licenses on world markets. On the other hand, the countries accepted proposals such as joint investment projects only as inevitable concessions to Soviet demands. The Soviet Union had made it clear during the trade negotiations in 1968 that, in the future, increases in raw material exports would have to be accompanied by East European investments on Soviet territory. The Czechoslovaks and Bulgarians conceded more cheerfully, the Hungarians and Poles more ruefully, but none of the countries were eager to see joint investments become a quid pro quo for imports of raw materials. The Soviet proposal to subject whole industries to joint planning was eyed suspiciously by all the countries. Akos Balassa, who was then head of the subdepartment of the Hungarian Planning Commission most closely involved in the negotiations, later recounted how the Hungarian negotiators had made every possible attempt to dilute the proposal for joint planning, and had succeeded in hedging it in with caveats and escape clauses.[44] Nevertheless, the proposal remained in the final text that was adopted in 1971. The Soviet specialists were satisfied that they had achieved everything they had set out to achieve up to this point.[45]

---

[43]Ibid., pp. 6–7.

[44]Interview with Akos Balassa, 9.9.1992.

[45]Interviews with Leonid Krasnov, 2.27.1992, and Iurii Pekshev, 3.10.1992. Both were consultants in the CPSU Central Committee apparatus, and each took an active role in negotiating the Comprehensive Program.

TABLE 6.2
Major Soviet Objectives

	Hungary	GDR	Bulgaria	Poland	Romania	USSR	CSSR	Final
Long-term specialization and cooperation	•	•			•	•	•	•
Coordinated investment	•	•	•			•		•
Joint investments		•			•	•	•	•
Joint branch planning						•		•
Higher standards		•	•			•		•
Joint prognoses					•	•	•	•
Science policy		•	•	•	•	•	•	•
Stronger IBEC	•	•	•	•	•	•	•	•

Source: See Table 6.1.

IMPLEMENTATION: THE JOINT PLAN IN PRACTICE

The test of the new planning mechanism was the Joint Plan for Integration Measures (*Sovmestnyi plan integratsionnykh meropriiatii,* or SPIM). Work began on the Joint Plan in 1973, and it took effect for the 1976–80 five-year plan. In theory, this was to be the first time the CMEA countries based their relations with each other on a single plan. Bilateral "coordination of plans" had simply been a process of negotiating balances of exports and imports, with each country's bargaining position depending on its own scarcities and its own plans. Disconnected, short-term plans determined the range of possible agreements. In contrast, the Joint Plan was intended to establish common objectives before the countries developed their own plans, so that each country could accommodate its investments to the others' long-term needs. The Joint Plan was to be drawn up by the new CMEA Committee for Planning, and each country would include the projects contained in the Joint Plan in a special section of its own State Plan. The Joint Plan would include joint investments in raw materials and energy, and agreements for specialization and cooperation.

In practice, however, work on the Joint Plan proceeded in much the same way as trade negotiations had in the past, and recapitulated many of the same shortcomings. In the first stage, the countries submitted proposals for imports and exports, which were compiled by the CMEA Department for Integrated Economic Work. In principle, these proposals should have been based on technical information, such as the projected supply and demand for particular goods, which was known only to the national planners. If the planners provided accurate information, it would be possible to design an international plan that balanced supply and demand. This would allow the countries to capture the gains from returns to large-scale production and divide up expensive investments in raw materials and technology. The problem was that the planners had no incentive to provide accurate information, and ample reasons to deceive each other.

Since CMEA prices differed from world prices, any particular good was either overpriced or underpriced in the CMEA relative to world markets. If a good was overpriced, all the countries sought to export it, or, if that were impossible, to import it from a supplier outside the CMEA. This was the case with most machinery and consumer goods. If a good was underpriced, all the countries sought to import it, or to export it to a buyer outside the CMEA. This was true of raw materials, energy, and most agricultural products. Each planner, therefore, had incentives to distort the national demand and supply of particular goods in order to make imports and exports coincide with the categories that were most profitable. A Hungarian veteran of these discussions recalled how prognoses were used tactically in the bargaining over coordination of plans.

> So what did the Hungarian colleagues sit down with? They came with prognoses prepared by the Department for Prognosis about Hungarian needs for oil: how much they had to get from their pleasant friends. Of course, they said in the beginning twice as much, that is to be understood; but on the other side, they said only half as much as their real capabilities.[46]

The result, when all the bluffs and counterbluffs were tallied, was a plan that could not possibly balance. The national planning commissions resisted any adjustments that would move supply and demand into equilibrium. Any new proposals they might make followed the same logic as their previous proposals, and proposals that had already been rejected were frequently recycled.

The specialization and cooperation agreements were the least effective element of joint planning. First, the countries faced strong incentives to specialize in goods they were already producing, both because their current exports were already calculated to maximize their profits from the distorted CMEA prices, and because it was more costly to tool up to produce something new. As was demonstrated so often in the CMEA, the most painless way to resolve conflict was to paper it over. Consequently, many of the specialization agreements were filled with traditional exports, which turned the new procedure into a hollow ritual.[47] Second, since all the countries sought to specialize in

[46]Interview with Andras Zsolnai, 9.1.1992.
[47]Interview with Istvan Hetenyi, 9.3.1992.

the same goods, it was difficult to persuade anyone to cede market share in profitable categories. In many cases, therefore, several countries "specialized" in the same good, so that the agreement did not involve any real specialization. Third, when the specialized exports turned out to be unprofitable, the agreements were generally abrogated by the exporters. In a few important cases, specializing countries reneged on their agreements to export goods that were in deficit throughout the bloc, particularly consumer durables such as motorcycles and automobiles.[48]

To save time the specialization programs were developed in parallel with the Comprehensive Program. As early as 1971 Soviet observers could tell that the programs were being prepared poorly, and were subject to the same distortions as traditional trade negotiations. A draft speech prepared by the Institute for the Economy of the World Socialist System for the Twenty-fifth Session took an unusually critical tone.

> The development of new, comprehensive forms of cooperation is for the most part running up against the same obstacles as in past years: imperfection of the systems of prices and accounting for mutual trade, [and] insufficient material interest and responsibility of the sides for the obligations they assume and for the quality of the traded products. . . . This particularly impairs multilateral cooperation, and especially multilateral treaties for specialization and cooperation in the production of machinery. . . . Unfortunately, these questions have fallen out of the field of vision of the working groups that have been developing the Comprehensive Program.[49]

Because CMEA prices were distorted, the countries felt no material interest in implementing a rational specialization program, in fulfilling their commitments, or in raising the quality of their products.

Although the purpose of specialization agreements was to promote technological advances, the agreements failed to incorporate any incentives for continuous technical improvement, and usually did not in fact raise products' technical parameters. In the fall of 1974, a confidential Soviet report for Gosplan and the CPSU Central Committee identified a series of "essential failures" that characterized the specialization and cooperation agreements being drawn up:

> The CMEA countries:
> • Have not perceived the advantages of real specialization and cooperation in production. They receive, for the most part, commercial advantages, which orients their attention not to the restructuring of physical production, and to concrete

---

[48]Interviews with Alfred Siennicki, 5.18.1992, and Janos Czibula, 8.25.1992.

[49]Bogomolov, "Materialy k XXV Sessiia SEV," to Iu. S. Firsov, USSR Council of Ministers, 7.16.1971, IMEPI Archive, IEMSS report, pp. 6–8. The speech was apparently intended to be delivered by the Soviet premier, Aleksei Kosygin.

enterprises in order to improve efficiency, but to the effort to receive high prices; not to long-term, but to immediate advantages; not to the international interest, but, in the first instance, to national advantages.

• So far have not taken measures toward a serious structural transformation of their machine-building industries, and toward raising the technical and economic level of production, which is reflected in their increasing imports of contemporary technology from the capitalist countries.

• Are not intensively developing among themselves the most progressive forms of specialization and cooperation by components and assemblies (especially on an international basis); they have had great successes with capitalist firms.

• . . . Although there is a relatively small demand for a number of types of machinery and equipment, for example for agricultural machines, continue to expand their production according to considerations of prestige, which is aroused by the potential to export, in spite of high production costs, because of their high foreign trade prices.

• . . . Employ interministry treaties that foresee, as a rule, production of machines and equipment that have already been brought into production, and that have traditionally been exported in the framework of foreign trade. The content of these treaties is in fact reduced for the most part to a list of goods and services that are objects of mutual trade in accordance with the ordinary norms of the practice of foreign trade; that is, they simply duplicate the [existing] foreign trade treaties.[50]

The East European countries did not perceive specialization and cooperation to be in their interests, they did not invest in improving the quality of their products, and they preferred to cooperate with Western firms rather than with one another. CMEA prices continued to create incentives for the countries to distort their trade profiles, turning inefficient products into profitable exports. Facing these incentives, the countries filled the specialization and cooperation agreements with "traditional" exports, and turned the agreements into mere formalities. Coming as it did toward the end of 1974, when work on the Joint Plan had almost been completed, this report repudiates official CMEA claims of the same period that the new methods of Joint Planning had produced a "qualitative improvement" in specialization and cooperation.

Several reports written by the Institute for the Economy of the World Socialist System show that the Soviet ministries charged with negotiating many of the agreements displayed a lack of interest in their outcomes, delayed the

[50]Kormnov and Leznik, "Analiz prichin voznikaiushchikh trudnostei," to N. N. Sliun'kov, deputy Chairman, USSR Gosplan, O. A. Chukanov, CC CPSU, 9.2.1974, IMEPI Archive, IEMSS report, pp. 8–11. It is interesting to compare this with Kormnov's much more optimistic published opinions (see Kormnov, *Mezhdunarodnaia sotsialisticheskaia spetsializatsiia i kooperatsiia*).

process, and failed to raise the issues of specialization and cooperation.[51] According to one report, the Soviet negotiators were poorly prepared for the discussions of specialization and cooperation that arose during the coordination of plans for 1976–80. During the first stage of negotiations, representatives of branch ministries met with their foreign counterparts to discuss specialization and cooperation. However, with two exceptions (Minneftekhimprom, the Ministry for the Petrochemical Industry, and Minstankoprom, the Ministry for the Machine-tool Industry), the ministries had no proposals for specialization and cooperation to present during the negotiations. Operating without a long-term plan for the development of their industries, Minkhimprom (the Ministry for the Chemical Industry) and Minlegprom (the Ministry for Light Industry) were unable even to respond to the East European proposals.

> When negotiations began for the coordination of economic plans for 1976–80, the ministries did not have a scientifically based conception of cooperation at the branch level. No proposals had been developed to promote stable industrial specialization and cooperation, to avert the expansion of parallel productive capacities in the socialist countries, or to relieve the pressure on capital investments to develop the corresponding products in the USSR.
>
> In the absence of a conception of branch-level cooperation, the selection of areas for cooperation and the details of implementation were principally shaped not by the Soviet side, but by our partners. The absence of precise conceptions of branch-level cooperation, and of initiative from Soviet ministries and organs, makes it impossible to carry out the cooperation plans with the maximum economic benefit for the USSR.[52]

The report goes on to argue that even when the Soviet negotiators did raise the issues of specialization and cooperation, they failed to pursue the negotiations with sufficient diligence to achieve results, sometimes treating them as mere formalities. They avoided pressing their East European partners about the quality of their exports, and failed to forge links between discussions of trade and issues such as specialization and technical standards.

> The great majority of the branch ministries did not focus on specialization and cooperation as first-priority issues during the negotiations. This particularly applies to industrial cooperation, about which the protocols and notes of the ministries contain only a few individual proposals, without sufficient technical and

---

[51]Dudinskii, ed., "Razvitie mirovoi sotsialisticheskoi sistemy v period posle XXIII S'iezda KPSS," IMEPI Archive, IEMSS report, 6.25.1970, p. 92; Shiriaev, "V komissiiu Prezidiuma soveta ministrov SSSR po voprosam Soveta Ekonomicheskoi Vzaimopomoshchi," 4.14.1972, IMEPI Archive, IEMSS report, pp. 1–5.

[52]Bautina et al., "Ob itogakh pervogo etapa koordinatsii," to Nikolai N. Vorov, Head of Department for the Development of Economic Cooperation with Socialist Countries, Gosplan, 3.9.1974, IMEPI Archive, IEMSS report, p. 4.

economic justification. In the cases where specialization and cooperation were discussed, the work was not completed, frequently took on a purely formalistic character, and in practical terms did not differ from the discussion of foreign trade quotas. For example, in the negotiations between the representatives of the Ministry of Tractor- and Agricultural Engineering and the corresponding Polish and Czechoslovak representatives, the issue of specialization was usurped by the issue of exports of spare parts; that is, in essence it was a matter of [negotiating] the foreign trade quota for spare parts.

. . . The majority of the machinery and equipment traded does not correspond to the contemporary demands of world technological progress. Nevertheless, the branch ministries rarely raised the issue of organizing the technical cooperation necessary to develop advanced machinery and to modernize the machinery in the existing quotas. Proposals for joint development of new types of products . . . were almost never discussed.[53]

These omissions doomed the Soviet strategy for expanding CMEA trade on the basis of specialization and cooperation. The East European countries achieved the initiative, and filled the specialization programs with the most advantageous exports: traditional, low-quality, primitive machines and equipment. The technical standards for exports remained low or were simply not enforced.

In the end even the fundamental principle that the Joint Plan should precede national planning was itself sacrificed to expediency. The CMEA compiled the Joint Plan by simply adding up the treaties that were in progress or that had already been signed. Andras Zsolnai, who supervised the CMEA department that compiled the Joint Plan, explained that it contained literally nothing new. Every project or item had already been agreed on in greater detail in several other documents: in bilateral or multilateral treaties, five-year agreements for coordination of plans, annual trade protocols signed by the ministers of foreign trade, and contracts between foreign trade associations or enterprises.[54] The Joint Plan became a compendium of existing cooperation projects, rather than an engine producing new ones. Oleg Rybakov, who was a principle advocate of the Joint Plan within the Soviet bureaucracy, admits that this blunted any cutting edge the Plan might have had.

The biggest failure was that the idea that the SPIM would drive joint projects was disrupted. In fact, the projects were developed alongside or prior to the SPIM and were included in it as it arose, so it had a rather limited impact on the level of cooperation. To view it cynically . . . the SPIM played only an informational role in the end. It compiled all the joint projects. However, the process of working out the Plan and going through multilateral discussions got people talk-

---

[53]Ibid., pp. 6–8.
[54]Interview with Andras Zsolnai, 9.1.1992.

ing to one another, and certain obstacles were overcome that could not be overcome at the bilateral level.[55]

Rybakov acknowledged that an "informational role" was a far cry from the ambitious transformation of CMEA trade practices which had been intended.

Zsolnai went on to argue that the Joint Plan could not even have had informational value. It could not guarantee that the projects it contained would be carried out, nor could it prevent duplication of efforts or even catalog the cooperation projects, because it was a secret document.

> I just want to say one thing. That document, SPIM, was a secret document, so practically speaking, no one could use it or even see it except for the people who put it together. It was the greatest—I beg your pardon—stupidity, one of the most useless pieces of paper that was ever put together in the history of the CMEA. I can say that with complete responsibility. It is really probably difficult for you to understand that a great number of useless, bureaucratic, administrative, needed-by-no-one documents were created by this system. It is not a law, it did not have to be that way. It was possible to reduce the quantity of paper at times. But the basic instinct of a planning system—as you probably know, the bureaucracy in the centrally planned countries was very swollen—was to write in order to justify one's existence. We have two documents, from them we will make a third. From that one we will make the next. . . .
>
> [I]n a meeting of the Economic Commission for Europe of the UN in Geneva . . . the Soviet delegate reported on the huge work under way on the [Ust'-Ilimsk] cellulose factory. The American delegate commented that it would be more expedient and economical not to cut down ever more forests, but instead to reduce the quantity of poorly used and ruined paper in the form of all the bureaucratic and administrative calculations and other documents. . . . I remember because I was completely in agreement with him on that point. I recommend that you forget that Joint Plan.[56]

Joint planning had not been attempted. The Joint Plan became a redundant document, filled with specialization and cooperation agreements which themselves did little more than ratify the status quo. It was so thoroughly discredited that even the people who compiled it believed it to be worthless.

The Comprehensive Program had concrete accomplishments, but it is fair to conclude that they were limited to a few large joint-investment projects to develop raw materials and energy resources, which were proposed by the Soviet Union and carried out on Soviet territory. Some of these projects were

---

[55]Interview with Oleg Rybakov, 3.9.1992. Rybakov wrote the first report that suggested compiling a Joint Plan while he was still in the Department for the Development of Economic Cooperation with Socialist Countries, Gosplan, where he worked from 1964 to 1974. He continued to pursue the project when he became a consultant in the CPSU Central Committee.

[56]Ibid.

very substantial, such as the Orenburg natural gas pipeline, which made a significant impact on the East European economies. Most were much less ambitious, such as an asbestos factory in Kiembaevo and a cellulose plant in Ust'-Ilimsk, each with a 500,000-ton capacity. A number of these projects were proposed by the Soviet Union, and those that aroused sufficient interest among the East Europeans were written into the text of the Comprehensive Program in general terms. They were then fixed in multilateral treaties, which in turn were included in the Joint Plan. The treaties committed the countries to make certain "target exports," a form of credit, and to send construction crews to participate directly in the construction. The credits were paid off in kind over twelve years, and thereafter the investors could exercise a right to import the same quantities of the product on a commercial basis for an additional twenty years. All the projects that reached the point of being codified in international treaties were completed. There were only minor delays, and although disputes arose over which goods could fulfill the countries' obligations for target exports, Soviet officials considered the projects to be successful.

The secret to the success of joint investments, while the other instruments of joint planning failed, was that the East Europeans' receipt of raw materials and energy was directly linked to their performance of the obligations they incurred in the treaty. The Soviet negotiators did not compel any of the East Europeans to participate, but they did the next best thing: they made a clear commitment to repay the investments by increasing raw material exports in the corresponding categories. At the same time they stated forcefully that countries that failed to participate would not receive additional supplies in the corresponding categories. East European negotiators found these commitments to be credible for two reasons: the Soviet Union had consistently fulfilled its export quotas, and they believed that the increasing costs of producing raw materials would prevent the USSR from being as generous in the future as it had been in the past.[57] No such commitments were made regarding specialization, cooperation, or technical standards, although those initiatives were far more central to the Soviet strategy of joint planning, and their success would have clearly been much more beneficial to Soviet terms of trade.

CONCLUSIONS

The Comprehensive Program for Socialist Economic Integration failed in its own terms. The most important Soviet objective was to inaugurate a new method of coordinating the various State Plans of the CMEA countries in order to replace bilateral trade negotiations with multilateral joint planning.

[57]Interview with Istvan Hetenyi, 9.8.1992.

Although this included a number of joint investments on Soviet territory, which were eventually carried out, the centerpiece of joint planning consisted of a new schema for promoting specialization and cooperation. It was the long-term specialization and cooperation agreements that were designed to expand the set of possible trade agreements, to deepen integration in order to encompass all phases of production, and to assure the steady improvement of technical parameters. When specialization and cooperation turned out to be no more than the latest Soviet slogan, the Comprehensive Program became a paper tiger.

The first two sections of this chapter demonstrate that it would be a mistake to view the lack of market-type reform in the CMEA as evidence of the Comprehensive Program's failure. The program, as designed by the officials of Soviet Gosplan, was never intended to produce market-type reforms. Insofar as the published version of the program contained references to such reforms, these were concessions to East European governments, and were never taken seriously by Soviet officialdom. One need look no further than this to explain the disjuncture between the tone of the program and subsequent Soviet behavior.

The third section shows that when the Soviet leadership concentrated its efforts, it was able to achieve its preferred outcomes on issues of principle, even over significant East European objections. The Soviets were able to block any reform proposal to which they strenuously objected, and were able to pass all the key elements of their own program. They were compelled to compromise frequently on language, but not on substance. In addition, it is important to recognize the type of resistance the Soviets faced from their East European allies. None of the allies objected to increased trade flows, and each of them made significant proposals that would increase the interdependence of the bloc. Most of the disputes revolved around the question of whether to introduce liberal reforms or maintain socialist orthodoxy, but even ideological disputes were heavily loaded with economic calculus. Each country advanced proposals that were calculated to improve its own trade profile. The only direct objection to integration came from Romania, and as we have seen, that objection was purely symbolic. Finally, none of these disputes derailed the Comprehensive Program. The Soviet Union prevailed on every issue of principle, and the program still failed.

The final section shows where the program failed: at the implementation phase. By that time, all disputes over economic reforms had been set aside, and the countries acted uniformly to advance their own commercial interests. In the process they trampled over the interests of the Soviet state, whose guardians were nowhere to be found. The Soviet bargaining position—impenetrable on matters of principle—was dramatically weakened when the discussions turned to concrete details. The lower-level agencies and officials charged with carrying out the program's design had no incentive to struggle with the East Europeans, and the attention of high-level officials could not be everywhere at once. The Soviet bureaucracy proved itself incapable of maintaining a constant purpose and executing such a complex task.

CHAPTER 7

The Long-Term Target Programs

THE LONG-TERM Target Programs (DTsPS), launched in 1978 and 1979, were an ambitious attempt to advance CMEA economic integration along a series of fronts. They attempted to expand trade between the member countries by coordinating their five-year plans around long-term investment programs, totaling an estimated nine billion transferable rubles, in five key sectors of the economy: energy, machine building, consumer goods, agriculture, and transportation.[1] These sectors were regarded as necessary for the transition from extensive to intensive growth, and had been neglected in the 1960s during the rush to develop metallurgy, chemicals, and military industries. The objective was to create a new generation of products through joint efforts, which would revitalize the economies of the region by energizing trade.

THE ORIGIN OF THE TARGET PROGRAMS

The initiative for the Target Programs came from experts in the Institute for the Economy of the World Socialist System of the Soviet Academy of Sciences, who had close working contacts with consultants in the Central Committee apparatus of the CPSU. The IEMSS experts had reached the conclusion that one of the greatest obstacles to technological development in planned economies is the very routine that makes planning possible. The Soviet State Plan was so complex that it could only be comprehended in small segments, and the segments could only be revised and implemented by specialized agencies. One might call the process of developing the State Plan "organizational planning": the planner began with the existing organizational chart and list of resources and tasks, and extrapolated them into the future. Each organization was incorporated into the Plan and was provided with resources and tasks appropriate to the sort of organization it was, subject to the constraint that total inputs and outputs had to balance. Coordinating the activities of all these organizations was difficult, because the weight of precedent was so heavy in the planning process. In the absence of appropriate incentives, it was hard to transfer technology from one sector of the economy to another, or to pool the

---

[1] Nine billion transferable rubles is the figure commonly used in Soviet publications. Of course such estimates could only be approximate and were subject to all the familiar distortions imposed by socialist accounting systems.

resources of enterprises that were subordinated to different ministries to solve joint problems. The obstacles at the national level were compounded and multiplied on the international scene. For this purpose, the experts argued, it was necessary to break the routine by introducing a method they dubbed "target planning": priority goals were to be established first, and the Plan would then be developed backward from those goals. The steps necessary to achieve the targets would be divided according to a rational plan, and these tasks would be introduced into the Plan with priority over all the routine tasks that organizations ordinarily performed. The Plan would become an active agent of industrial policy, rather than a passive accumulation of incremental decisions made by disconnected agencies.[2]

Beginning in 1974 IEMSS prepared a series of reports for the Department for Relations with Socialist Countries of the CC CPSU that outlined the rationale for the Target Programs. The IEMSS proposal represented a substantial reshuffling of the traditional priorities of the socialist countries. Iurii Kormnov, the head of the IEMSS General Economic Department and the guiding hand behind the development of the Target Programs, explained that the programs initially represented an attempt to shift resources into the agriculture and consumer goods sectors of the economy in order to improve living standards.[3] The Target Programs were constructed as a pyramid, with the programs for agriculture and consumer goods at the apex; programs to develop the energy, transportation, and machine-building sectors were designed to feed inputs into the first two. The IEMSS specialists identified underinvestment as the major problem in the CMEA agriculture and consumer goods industries. Writing of agriculture, an IEMSS report observed that, "on a per capita basis, the countries of the CMEA lag behind France, the FRG, and the United States. . . . Our underdevelopment is connected with the fact that, in spite of successes in developing the productive forces of agriculture, its material and technical basis in the CMEA countries still has not achieved an optimal level."[4] The report went on to discuss the much greater mechanization of Western agriculture and the superior productivity of agricultural laborers in Europe and North America. The conclusion was that in order to solve the CMEA agricultural deficit, it was necessary to increase the capital- and energy-intensivity of agriculture, which in turn entailed investments in the energy and machine-building sectors. The program for energy and raw materials was considered necessary in order to satisfy the increased demand for fuels and materials that would be produced by expanding production of food and consumer goods. The program

[2]Interviews with Iurii Kormnov, former Deputy Director, IEMSS, 2.5.1992, and Dr. Ruben Evstigneev, Deputy Director, IMEPI, 12.20.1991.

[3]Interview with Iurii Kormnov, 2.5.1992.

[4]Kormnov, Shintiapin, and Frumkin, "Vozmozhnye puti resheniia prodovol'stvennoi problemy," to O. A. Chukanov, Iu. A. Pekshev, B. I. Gostev, CC CPSU, 8.14.1974, IMEPI Archive, IEMSS report, p. 1.

for transportation was introduced later, because transportation became a bottleneck that prevented the expansion of trade in raw materials. The program in machine building consisted of five major subprograms, which were dedicated to providing machinery for each of the other programs, and to improving the technological standards of the machine-building industry itself.

The IEMSS specialists launched a barrage of proposals for economic reforms. IEMSS reports argued that the international economic organizations (MKhO) created under the Comprehensive Program were inadequate to the task of creating direct links between CMEA enterprises because the basic financial incentives to form such ties had not been established. In effect, IEMSS was approaching the reformist position of the Hungarians and Poles.[5] Kormnov argued that the same failure to reform the basis of CMEA pricing rendered specialization agreements ineffective and formalistic, and urged that an elite commission be formed to draft a "Statute on Cooperative Ties," which he envisioned as a reform of "planning, management, prices, currency, credits, direct ties of cooperating parties, and so forth."[6] Although none of these more far-reaching proposals were included in the Target Programs, the specialists at IEMSS were given a leading role in drafting the Soviet proposal. One of the drafts that IEMSS proposed included a long list of measures to ensure the completion of the projects. The countries were to agree in advance on imports and exports of particular goods, contribute to funds of goods and hard currency to finance projects, and create an array of international firms capable of operating on the territory of all the CMEA countries and establishing direct relationships with national enterprises.[7]

The organizational measures favored by IEMSS did not become part of the final Soviet proposal. A number of other organizations were involved in the process of drafting the proposals, including the Central Committee apparatus, Gosplan, the Ministry of Foreign Trade and the office of the Soviet Permanent Representative to the CMEA, and the proposals were changed and rewritten so many times that authorship is now impossible to establish.[8] Several of these organizations specifically opposed the IEMSS proposals. The Ministry of Foreign Trade opposed measures that eroded its control over foreign trade

[5]Kormnov and Leznik, "Obespecheniie uslovii," to O. A. Chukanov, Iu. A. Pekshev, CC CPSU; M. A. Lesechko, CMEA, 8.15.1974 , IMEPI Archive, IEMSS report.

[6]Kormnov, "Nekotorye voprosy razvitiia kooperatsii," to Iu. A. Pekshev, CC CPSU, 5.20.1974, IMEPI Archive, IEMSS report, p. 6.

[7]Kormnov, Zubkov, and Frumkin, "Skhema mezhdunarodnoi dolgosrochnoi tselevoi programmy sotrudnichestva," to Iu. V. Firsov, USSR Council of Ministers; O. A. Chukanov, Iu. A. Pekshev, and O. K. Rybakov, CC CPSU; M. A. Lesechko, V. S. Shapovalov, and N. A. Shevandik, CMEA; N. K. Baibakov, A. M. Lalaiants, P. A. Paskar', N. N. Inozemtsev, N. N. Sliunkov, V. P. Vorob'ev, and N. N. Vorov, Gosplan, 7.23.1976, IMEPI Archive, IEMSS Report, pp. 26–28.

[8]Interviews with Oleg Rybakov, former Deputy Head, CC CPSU Department for Relations with Socialist Countries, 3.9.1992; Leonid Krasnov, former Deputy in the office of the Permanent USSR Representative to CMEA, former Consultant, CC CPSU Department for Relations with Socialist Countries, 2.27.1992.

organizations. Gossnab and divisions of Gosplan opposed joint funds, and the experience of the Joint Plan (see the previous chapter) had convinced some Central Committee officials that joint funding was not technically feasible.[9] Probably most important was that the support for the IEMSS position in the Central Committee was soft. Iurii Pekshev, the head of the Group of Economic Consultants in the Department for Relations with Socialist Countries of the CC CPSU, was Kormnov's close friend, and each reports that they generally agreed on issues concerning the Target Programs. It was Pekshev's support, and that of his patron Katushev, that initially launched the programs.[10] Still, Pekshev was not personally committed to the organizational innovations that IEMSS proposed. He regarded the Target Programs primarily as an investment initiative, and more as a way of attracting East European resources to defray the costs of raw material investments than as an effort to privilege the agriculture and consumer-goods sectors.[11] The package of organizational measures was eliminated from the Soviet proposal before it was shared with the other CMEA countries. Interviews with the East European delegates to the first negotiating sessions on the Target Programs confirm that the proposals for joint funding and new international firms were never on the table.[12]

The Soviet Union was in firm control of the Twenty-ninth CMEA Session in 1975. It presented the proposal to develop the Target Programs without any prior warning to the East European delegates, which was very unusual, but provoked only expressions of mild surprise. The proposals were adopted without great opposition. When the Romanian delegate attempted to modify the proposal by creating an additional program to equalize levels of economic development in the CMEA, however, his proposal was rejected unceremoniously.[13] At the level of symbolism and general initiatives, there were no serious challenges to Soviet leadership.

NEGOTIATION PHASE

The 1975 CMEA Session left most of the details of the Target Programs to be worked out by groups of specialists, and a sharp conflict emerged between the Soviet Union and the East Europeans in the ensuing negotiations. The East

[9]Interview with Oleg Rybakov, 3.9.1992.

[10]Interviews with Kormnov, 2.5.1992, and Iurii Pekshev, former Head, Group of Economic Consultants, Department for Relations with Socialist Countries, CC CPSU, 3.10.1992.

[11]Interview with Iurii Pekshev, 3.10.1992.

[12]Interviews with Akos Balassa, former Deputy General Manager, Hungarian Planning Commission, 9.9.1992; Alfred Siennicki, former Director of Department for Socialist Countries, Polish Planning Commission, 5.18.1992; and Andras Zsolnai, former Head, Department for Integrated Economic Work, CMEA, 9.1.1992. The officials stated that they would have opposed the formation of joint funds had that been one of the Soviet proposals, but that they did not have to do so.

[13]Stenogramma zasedaniia XXIX sessii Soveta Ekonomicheskoi Vzaimopomoshchi, 24 June 1975, CMEA Archive, pp. 169–77.

Europeans were primarily interested in the Target Programs as a means to increase their imports of fuels and raw materials and to optimize their machinery exports, whereas the Soviet negotiators were basically interested in increasing East European investments on Soviet territory and improving the quality of East European machinery exports. During the negotiations, consequently, the East Europeans made every effort to minimize their investments on Soviet territory and in their own export industries, while pushing the Soviets to increase their exports.

The clash of perspectives quickly focused on the Target Program for energy and raw materials. The Soviet objectives in proposing a programmatic approach to energy and raw material supplies were primarily to impose upper limits on East European demands for additional supplies, and secondarily to compel the East Europeans to contribute to the costs of production and transportation. Consequently, the program title that the Soviet Union proposed to the Twenty-ninth CMEA Session in 1975 was "Long-term Target Program for Cooperation to Assure Satisfaction of the Rational Needs of the Member Countries of the CMEA for Fundamental Types of Energy, Fuel, and Raw Materials." The phrase "rational needs" immediately excited the disapproval of the Romanian deputy premier, Marinescu:

> COMRADE MARINESCU: I ask that the word *rational* be deleted, and to leave simply *needs*.
>
> COMRADE LESECHKO [USSR]: I consent only to replace that word with *justified*.
>
> COMRADE MARINESCU: Instead of the word *rational*, perhaps, to find another word, which would precisely and correctly express and define this understanding, in order to regulate this situation, because each country determines rational needs in accordance with its needs. . . .
>
> COMRADE LESECHKO: As for the word *rational*, it will be necessary to replace it with the words *economically justified*—this is an appropriate recommendation by Comrade Zarev.[14]

This sort of symbolic bickering over the titles of documents was typical of the CMEA, but in this case it represented a serious conflict of objectives. Just how serious the conflict was became clear during the negotiations in the working group for energy.

The Soviet experts believed it was essential to base the programs on the real needs of the East European countries in order to assure that the countries felt an interest in carrying them out. Consequently, the first step in the development of the program was for the countries to propose areas for cooperation and to predict their import needs and export potentials in basic sources of

[14]"Rabochaia zapis' zasedaniia redaktsionnoi komissii 25 iiunia 1975 [29th Session of the CMEA, 6.25.1975]," CMEA Archive, pp. 36–37. Lesechko was the USSR deputy premier in charge of relations with the CMEA.

energy and raw materials. The hope was that the countries could help one another to develop their own raw material supplies and expand trade. Poland, for example, could trade copper for Hungarian aluminum and coal for Romanian oil, so that the Soviet Union could reduce its exports of copper, aluminum, coal, and oil.[15] The results, which were collated by the CMEA and appended to the minutes of a working group of the Committee for Cooperation in Planning (KSOPD), were very disappointing. There was a great deal of disagreement. As a rule the countries were not interested in including the raw materials that they exported in the Target Program, because they would then be expected to increase those exports. The Soviet Union did not offer to cooperate in oil or gas; Poland withdrew its cooperation in coal and copper; Czechoslovakia showed no interest in collaborating in steel, steel bars, or steel pipe. The countries that did wish to cooperate in particular raw materials were importers or had deficits in the materials in question. The GDR and Hungary were most interested in cooperation in ferrous metallurgy, for example, and all the East European countries were interested in oil, gas, electric energy, and iron ore.[16]

Since each country withheld its potential raw material exports from consideration and demanded additional imports, there was no way to balance supply and demand, and the Soviet attempt to devise a "rational" division of labor failed from the outset.[17] Rather than increase their own exports to make up the difference, the Soviet negotiators abandoned the attempt at multilateral plan balancing; instead, they introduced proposals to reduce East European demand for petroleum and natural gas. These proposals consisted of three main points: (1) international cooperation to construct nuclear power plants to replace oil-fired plants throughout Eastern Europe; (2) joint investments in two new nuclear power plants in the Soviet Union and two new high-voltage lines to convey power to the East European power grid; and (3) petroleum conservation measures, such as improving refining techniques and expanding the use of coal to generate electricity.[18] The Romanian delegation briefly resisted this tactical change, arguing that it would be a waste of effort to abandon all the work that had been done in coordinating the countries' energy needs:

> Having examined the documents prepared by the Secretariat, you become increasingly convinced of the inexpediency of developing more and more new

---

[15]One of the most important sponsors of the Target Programs, Iurii Pekshev, made a point years later of arguing that the East Europeans had substantial deposits of raw materials, and that a central objective of the DTsPS was to bring those resources into CMEA trade. Poland was repeatedly singled out in this respect (Pekshev, *Dolgosrochnye tselevye programmy sotrudnichestva stran-chlenov SEV*, pp.73, 80–81).

[16]"Protokol zasedaniia rabochei gruppy," Prilozheniia 4, 12.16–18.1975, CMEA Archive, pp. 1–3.

[17]Interview with Leonid Krasnov, 2.27.1992.

[18]"Pamiatnaia zapiska soveshchaniia ekspertov," 7.18–22.1977, CMEA Archive.

documents. . . . If there are no new resources, what do we need new subprograms for? We will use what we have. . . . The most proper approach would be as follows: we have proposals submitted by the countries last year, we have a list of topics, and it is necessary to get to work. What we should be concerned with is how to carry out this cooperation.[19]

The Romanian delegate argued that it would be more "expedient" to concentrate on fulfilling the countries' demands than to create a mountain of paper, but of course the effect of using the countries' existing proposals as the basis for developing the program would be to increase the pressure on the Soviet Union to expand fuel deliveries to Eastern Europe. Nikolai Vorov, the Soviet delegate, called him on this point:

You say that we have dealt with these problems many times before. Yes, we have dealt with them, and we have carried out the first step in our work, which is the preliminary list of topics for the fuel and materials program. There is a list of goods of the corresponding types. In connection with this, we received from all the countries, as they promised, materials, let us say, concerning oil. All the countries wrote how much oil they needed to receive. There are no proposals to export oil, only to import. It is obvious that we have to examine the situation that has emerged and choose a realistic solution. This is what we have attempted to do, and all that is proposed here are serious problems, which, from our point of view, have to be solved.[20]

The Soviet proposal was accepted as the framework for discussion, but this was only the beginning of East European opposition to Soviet attempts to reduce the cost of its subsidy.

A major Soviet objective in this program was to reduce East European demand for oil by increasing the countries' reliance on their own coal resources. An IEMSS report urged that Poland, the GDR, and Czechoslovakia be encouraged to develop their local coal supplies to generate electricity and produce synthetic fuel.[21] One of the Soviet proposals along these lines was to increase the use of Polish coal for generating electricity by expanding joint investments in coal development on Polish soil. Czechoslovakia and East Germany had been investing in the Polish coal industry since the 1960s. The Poles, however, reacted to this proposal cautiously. They had no inclination to increase their exports of coal, so at the first meeting of the working group to

[19]"Rabochaia zapis' soveshchaniia ekspertov," 7.18.1977, CMEA Archive, pp. 28–30.
[20]Ibid., p. 30.
[21]Kormnov, Kozlov, and Yakushin, "Poiasnitel'naia problemnaia report k MDTsP 'Toplivo-energiia,'" to O. A. Chukanov, Iu. A. Pekshev, O. K. Rybakov, CC CPSU; Iu. V. Firsov, SovMin USSR; M. A. Lesechko, A. N. Zademidko, V. S. Shapovalov, CMEA; and N. K. Baibakov, A. M. Lalaiants, N. N. Inozemtsev, Gosplan, 8.23.1976, IMEPI Archive, IEMSS report 14306/665, pp. 2–3.

develop the "basic principles" for the program, they set extremely costly conditions for participation:

> The Polish experts announce that the creation of productive capacity for coal mining may be conducted by receipt of credit from the interested member countries of the CMEA, which should be fulfilled with exports of oil and refined oil products, partially refined chemicals and grain. Exports of coal or electricity above the credit received should be balanced with energy resources.[22]

These were costly conditions because the standard practice was to incorporate credits into the trade balance of the two countries, and to negotiate the list of goods to fill the quota bilaterally. These credits would ordinarily consist of machinery for the appropriate branch of mining or other goods that the two sides agreed on, but never such valuable assets as fuels and grain. Since practically no interest was charged on CMEA credits, granting them could only be advantageous if the creditor were allowed to export goods of lesser "hardness" than the goods used to pay the debt. Czechoslovakia, which had been involved in joint investments in the Polish coal industry since the 1960s, protested the Polish position at the second meeting of the working group:

> The CSSR proposes that fuel and energy projects be developed on the territory of the PRP in the way that corresponds to the principles and forms of cooperation of the member countries of the CMEA existing in this area up to the present time. The concrete conditions would be agreed upon on a bilateral basis.[23]

This impasse was never resolved, and the end result was that the Target Program failed to stimulate any further investments in coal production in Poland.

The centerpiece of the Target Program in machine building was an ambitious program to expand construction of nuclear power plants in Eastern Europe, which in turn was to fulfill the major objective of the program for energy. The target was to build plants with VVER-440 and VVER-1000 (pressurized-water, shell-type) reactors with a total capacity of 37 million kilowatts in six

---

[22]"Osnovnye printsipial'nye polozheniia Dolgosrochnoi tselevoi programmy sotrudnichestva po obestpecheniiu ekonomicheski obosnovannykh potrebnostei stran-chlenov SEV v toplive i energii," Prilozhenie 3 k pamiatnoi zapiske soveshchaniia ekspertov stran-chlenov SEV po podgotovke materialov dlia Rabochei gruppy po razrabotke DTsPS v oblasti topliva, energii i syr'ia i Biuro Komiteta SEV po sotrudnichestvu v oblasti planovoi deiatel'nosti, 7.18–22.1977, CMEA Archive, TsGANKh, Fond 561, Opis 21c/pp, Delo 50, p. 6.

[23]"Osnovnye printsipial'nye polozheniia Dolgosrochnoi tselevoi programmy sotrudnichestva po obespecheniiu ekonomicheski obosnovannykh potrebnostei stran-chlenov SEV v toplive i energii," Prilozhenie 2 k protokolu vtorogo zasedaniia Rabochei gruppy Komiteta SEV po sotrudnichestvu v oblasti planovoi deiatel'nosti po razrabotke proekta Dolgosrochnoi tselevoi programmy sotrudnichestva po obespecheniiu ekonomicheski obosnovannykh potrebnostei stran-chlenov SEV v osnovnykh vidakh energii, topliva i syr'ia, 8.30–9.1.1977, CMEA Archive, TsGANKh, Fond 561, Opis 21c/pp, Delo 51, p. 4.

East European countries and Cuba, which would increase the generating capacity of these countries by 39 percent from 1980 to 1990.[24] Perhaps more ambitious than the immense scale of the undertaking was the Soviet determination that the East Europeans themselves should produce most of the specialized equipment for the power plants. The Soviet Union already planned to expand the use of nuclear power on its own territory, building a projected 25-million-kilowatt capacity in 1981–85, and this program was severely hampered by shortages of equipment and materials, particularly special alloys.[25] The Soviets were unable to carry out both programs simultaneously without substantial contributions from the East Europeans. It seemed reasonable to expect that the satellites would be willing to contribute resources to the effort, since they had expressed an enthusiastic interest in obtaining nuclear power plants.[26]

At this point the Soviets ran into one of the fundamental obstacles to CMEA trade in machinery and equipment. Although it is true that exports of machinery were generally profitable under CMEA pricing principles, some types of machinery were much more profitable to export than others. Just as there was an annual struggle over the gross proportions of machinery and raw materials, so too was there a struggle—more fine-gauged, but no less crucial—to determine the internal structure of trade in machinery. The most profitable exports were older models, which did not require additional investments or improvements; light machinery, with a higher "kilogram value," which contained less valuable raw material imports; and relatively primitive devices, which contained little or no investment of hard-currency resources.[27]

[24]Pekshev, *Dolgosrochnye tselevye programmy*, p. 67, for the Target Program goal; Sovet Ekonomicheskoi Vzaimopomoshchi, Sekretariat, Statisticheskii ezhegodnik stran-chlenov soveta ekonomicheskoi vzaimopomoshchi (Moscow: Finansy i statistika, 1989), p. 138, for CMEA electrical generating capacity.

[25]*Pravda*, 4 June 1981. The plan to expand nuclear generating capacity was an important part of the Soviet 1981–85 plan, which had been drawn up by 1978, so the decision must have been made well before the Soviets began promoting nuclear energy as a key component of the Target Programs.

[26]All the countries declared their interest in cooperation in this area in the earliest stage of the Target Program's development, and without exception they requested greater or more rapid deliveries than the Soviet Union proposed. For the initial expressions of interest, "Predlozheniia ekspertov stran-chlenov SEV po krugu voprosov dlia razrabotki dolgosrochnoi tselevoi programmy sotrudnichestva po obespecheniiu soglasovannogo na dvustoronnei i mnogostoronnei osnove razvitiia mashinostroeniia na baze glubokoi spetsializatsii i kooperirovaniia proizvodstva," Prilozhenie No. 5 k protokolu zasedaniia rabochei gruppy Biuro Komiteta SEV po sotrudnichestvu v oblasti planovoi deiatel'nosti, 16–18.1975, CMEA Archive, Fond 561, Opis 15 pp, No. pp. 61, Delo 40–36, p. 3; For the countries' concrete proposals, "Prilozhenie k protokolu shestogo zasedaniia Rabochei gruppy po mashinostroeniiu Komiteta SEV po sotrudnichestvu v oblasti planovoi deiatel'nosti," 12–15.1978, CMEA Archive, TsGANKh, Fond 561, Opis 18s/pp, No. pp. 64, Delo 232, p. 2.

[27]Interviews with Ryszard Ziółkowski, former Director, Department for Cooperation with Socialist Countries, Polish Ministry of Industry and Metallurgy, 5.27.1992; Janos Czibula, former department director, Hungarian Ministry of Foreign Trade, 8.25.1992.

Consequently, although the East Europeans viewed the plants as an important part of the solution to their growing energy needs, none of them had an interest in producing and exporting the machinery that was needed to bring the plants into operation.[28] This was highly specialized equipment, which would have no other market than the CMEA, and required substantial investments in scarce materials and technology. Under CMEA pricing principles, it was unlikely to prove a profitable investment.[29]

The East Europeans presented a united front, demanding that the Soviet Union adopt the role of "general supplier" of nuclear power plants. The countries sought to delete every obligation to engage in specialization and cooperation from the text of the "Treaty on Multilateral International Specialization and Cooperation in Production and Mutual Delivery of Equipment for Atomic Electric Stations for the Period 1981–90." In place of the language that the countries would "order equipment and other services from *the countries that specialize* in the production of equipment according to the present Treaty," the East Europeans proposed that the countries should "order equipment and other services from *the USSR* according to the appropriate schedule, including nonspecialized equipment necessary for the complete construction of the AES [nuclear power plants]."[30] Five countries went on to attempt to shift all the responsibility to the Soviet Union:

> The Soviet side takes upon itself the responsibility of general designer of the AES and will fulfill the function of general supplier of equipment and services in connection with the construction of AES, with the exception of equipment that is produced in the country on whose territory the AES is being built and services performed by that country.[31]

This would practically obligate the USSR to perform all but the most basic construction work, making it impossible to shift the burden of producing the

[28]Interviews with Istvan Hetenyi, former Deputy Chairman for the Department for Relations with Socialist Countries, First Deputy Chairman, Hungarian Planning Commission; former Minister of Finance, 9.8.1992, and Siennicki, 5.6.1992.

[29]Direct evidence indicates that the East Europeans did not expect the export prices for nuclear technology to keep up with its costs. There was substantial controversy about whether to apply standard CMEA price principles. The decision was made to place a cap on the total cost of the components equal to the world market price of a complete power plant. This decision was persistently opposed by Czechoslovakia, which the Soviet Union had assigned to produce the most expensive components. "Soglashenie o mnogostoronei mezhdunarodnoi spetsializatsii i kooperirovanii proizvodstva i vzaimnykh postavkakh oborudovaniia dlia atomnykh elektrostantsii na period 1981–1990 gg.," Protocols of the Ninth and Tenth meetings of the working group for machine-building of the CMEA Committee for cooperation in planning (KSOPD), 5.14.1979 and 6.7.1979, CMEA Archive, TsGANKh, Fond 561, Opis 18s/pp. No. pp. 67, Delo 232, p. 7; No. pp. 68, Delo 232, p. 8.

[30]"Soglashenie o mnogostoronnei mezhdunarodnoi spetsializatsii," 9.12–15.1978, CMEA Archive, p. 2 (emphasis added).

[31]Ibid., p. 3.

machinery to the East Europeans. The Soviet Union baulked at the prospect of providing all the CMEA countries with finished power plants, and insisted that the East Europeans participate in producing the parts. The Soviet Union inserted the following text into the preliminary version of the treaty:

> The representative of the USSR in the Working Group, in connection with the countries' proposals concerning the Soviet Union fulfilling the function of general supplier, declared that the Soviet Union is unable to accept the functions of general supplier of equipment.[32]

Finally, in bilateral negotiations, the Soviet Union required each country to produce certain parts in return for delivery of the critical elements that only the USSR could provide. When the GDR refused to specialize in the production of carbon-steel armature, the Soviet experts replied that, in that case, the Soviet Union would not be able to provide the GDR with the types of armature in which it had specialized. Poland complained that its limited production capacity made it impossible to export carbon- and stainless-steel regulating valves, but the Soviet experts declared these objections groundless. Czechoslovakia declared that it was unable to produce several types of pumps for export, but the Soviet Union insisted that Czechoslovakia produce exactly the types of pumps it had recommended, in the quantities and within the schedule that had been laid down in Moscow.[33]

The struggle over specialization dragged on from 1977 to the middle of 1979, and the Soviets were forced to make a number of concessions. The countries refused to export many of the products they agreed to produce. With persistence, the USSR achieved a degree of burden sharing, but it was forced to bear the lion's share itself. The Soviet Union exported two-thirds of the major types of equipment coordinated under the agreement. Table 7.1 shows the number of types of equipment (of a total of fifty-nine types specified in the specialization agreement) that each country produced, and the proportion of those types that it was willing to export. The most important share of the work done in Eastern Europe was borne by Czechoslovakia, Hungary, and Poland; only Czechoslovakia and the Soviet Union developed the capability to produce nuclear reactors. Yet these countries, which produced the most important and sophisticated components, were precisely the ones that most resisted exporting their equipment to other CMEA countries. The GDR, Bulgaria, and Romania, which exported a larger proportion of the goods they agreed to produce, specialized disproportionately in popular goods, such as cranes and transportation equipment. These goods were more profitable for export because the countries already produced them, and they required no new investments. Since the most important East European partners refused to export the

[32]Ibid.
[33]"Protokol soveshchaniia ekspertov planovykh organov," 1.4–5.1979, CMEA Archive, pp. 4–6.

TABLE 7.1

Specialization in Equipment for Nuclear Power Plants

	Number of types of equipment in which country specializes	Percentage available for export
USSR	38	100
Czechoslovakia	30	63
Hungary	11	64
Poland	17	65
Romania	7	86
GDR	5	80
Bulgaria	7	100
Yugoslavia	8	100

Source: "Spetsializatsiia stran-chlenov SEV i SFRlu v proizvodstve oborudovaniia dlia AES," Prilozhenia 3 k protokolu 10 zasedaniia Rabochei gruppy po mashinostroeniiu Komiteta SEV po sotrudnichestvu v oblasti planovoi deiatel'nosti, 9.12–15.1978, CMEA Archive, TsGANKh, Fond 561, Opis 18s/pp, No. pp 68, Delo 232.

most expensive components, the Soviet Union was compelled to serve as the sole exporter in 20 percent of the categories of equipment covered in the agreement, and the East Europeans were forced to develop parallel productive capacities for a number of the goods they were unwilling to export to each other.

Just as the incentive to optimize machinery exports led the satellites to oppose Soviet plans for specialization in expensive nuclear-power technology, it also drove them to fill the remainder of the Target Program for machine building with standard, light-weight, low-technology products. Since the East Europeans exported much more machinery than they imported, they naturally approached the Target Program for machinery from the perspective of exporters: their primary objective was to secure markets. They expected that products included in the Target Programs would ultimately be easier to export to the Soviet Union, because the East European negotiators would be able to claim that these were products of international cooperation, and the Soviets would be compelled to accept them.

The result was that the Target Programs gradually expanded. The lists of exports that the countries proposed to include in the program for machine building fill dozens of tomes in the CMEA Archive. Andras Zsolnai, who supervised the compilation of the Target Programs as director of the CMEA Department for Integrated Economic Work, explained that each country tried to fit as many of its current exports into the program for machine building as possible.

Under the price relations that had existed for twenty years, and while the Target Programs were under development, it was profitable for every exporter to export machinery. There was, naturally, a striving by each country, and within each country by major enterprises, to get their production included in the Target Programs, and [a hope] that in the optimal case they would be able to export it. . . . There is nothing better than to have an order for ten, fifteen, or twenty years into the future! [These orders came] with established characteristics and the conviction that the particular product was under a certain kind of protection. Various improvements were made, but a certain rent, or profit, was guaranteed to the government. . . . [We] exported finished goods that we could produce on a huge scale, in the first place to the Soviet Union, such as tractors, and in return we could get oil and electric energy, and, for the countries that didn't have sufficient results in agriculture, agricultural products. It is always cheaper, if you already have productive capacity—Icarus [the Hungarian bus company], for example—to develop that [product], even with Western credits, than to begin with some kind of completely new product. That is where the interest came from for each country to maintain the export structure that had developed, without any changes. This was one of the most serious problems. . . . Certain improvements did take place, but without fundamental changes, without changing to production of something new.[34]

Consequently, aside from the agreement on nuclear power plants, the Target Program in engineering contained very little that was original. The lists of products in the Target Program came to resemble more and more closely the lists of products in the annual trade protocols.

The East European export orientation tended to undermine the cooperative, multilateral aspect of the program. Of the initial proposals the countries made for areas of cooperation, more than a third were of interest to only one country. Although some of these were proposals to import specialized equipment, such as high-voltage cable that Romania wished to obtain, most were for exports that the countries particularly wanted to promote. For example, Bulgaria pressed its case to include construction equipment and computers, which were of notoriously poor quality, and Hungary promoted its Icarus busses, which were of good quality for Eastern Europe but were extremely profitable to export because their price was nearly that of a Mercedes.[35] There was no clear procedure for determining which topics were germane to a particular program, so the programs tended to grow.

The mushrooming of the topics under development had two major negative consequences. First, when the East Europeans made their proposals for the inclusion of certain products in the Target Programs, numerous products were included that had little or no relation to the programs' goals. In so far as the

[34]Interview with Andras Zsolnai, former Head, Integrated Economic Department, CMEA, and Director, Department for CMEA Affairs, Hungarian Planning Commission, 9.1.1992.

[35]"Protokol zasedaniia rabochei gruppy," Prilozheniia [appendix] 5, 16–18.1975, CMEA Archive, pp. 1–8.

Target Programs were intended to correct the deficiencies of incremental, overspecialized, and localized planning procedures, they failed because these procedures were inserted into the Target Programs themselves. It was the existing practice of negotiating plan coordination that determined the structure of the Target Programs, rather than the Target Programs themselves setting new priorities for the next round of coordination. Second, the programs expanded to the point that practically every area of foreign trade was affected, so it was no longer possible to speak of concentrating resources on a few priority projects. The most commonly heard criticism of the Target Programs was their failure to set a few, clearly defined goals. This created a sense of unreality about the whole undertaking, which in turn undermined any commitment the countries might feel to carrying out the programs once they had been drawn up.

IMPLEMENTATION PHASE

The partial and unsatisfactory implementation of the Target Programs was punctuated by struggles over investment in the Soviet Union, which had already become a focal point of bilateral trade negotiations, and by the failure of East European governments to invest the resources necessary to fulfill their commitments. The pattern of implementation of the programs was marked by struggle over the commodity composition of Soviet–East European trade: there were much more satisfactory results in the sectors of energy, raw materials, and transportation than in machine building, consumer goods, and agriculture.[36] Achievement of the programs' goals was more clearly linked to benefits to the East Europeans when the programs concerned the production and transportation of energy and raw materials than when they involved improvements in finished goods and agriculture.

A prerequisite for the success of the Target Programs was that their projects have priority over the routine tasks that the member countries included in their five-year plans. This was essential because planning in CMEA countries was taut, rather than flexible: resources were routinely overcommitted. Organizations routinely hoarded resources in order to assure themselves of reserves, which made it easier to fulfill the Plan. In order to squeeze the hoarded resources out of enterprises and ministries, central planning agencies set goals that were not strictly attainable, given the resources available on paper. Consequently, many more investments were planned than could actually be completed on schedule, which meant that new investments had to compete for overcommitted funds. To complicate the picture further, political authorities

[36]Interviews with Anatol Dikij, 5.26.1992; Zdeněk Šedivý, 6.30.1992; Alfred Siennicki, 5.18.1992; and Andras Zsolnai, 9.1.1992.

lobbied the central planners and party officials on behalf of projects located in their regions or in their sectors of the economy.[37] Thus the most accurate picture of the planning process is one of a hierarchy of official and unofficial priorities, rather than one of mechanistic and precise accounting. If the Target Program projects became relegated to the status of routine tasks, therefore, they would never be implemented. To fulfill the objectives of the programs, they had to be given real political priority over routine tasks.

The situation in Poland serves as an extreme illustration. The overambitious investment plan of the Gierek regime, combined with the failed innovation of concentrating economic activity in huge industrial combines (WOGs) in the early 1970s and the surge in world price levels and interest rates after 1973, led to severe imbalances in the Plan. Productivity did not rise fast enough to pay for the planned investments, investments did not keep up with development plans for particular branches of the economy, and the production of several major industries did not keep up with the needs of others, so that choke points emerged in production, and capacity was underutilized. Under these circumstances, the usual competition for investment funds was dramatically intensified. Andrzej Karpinski, who was a deputy chairman of the Planning Commission at the time, writes that severe political pressures led the Politburo to raise the investment expenditures that the Planning Commission had proposed for the 1976–80 Five-Year Plan.

> The cause of the increase in the investment program was the strong pressure from the ministries, at a time when the discrepancy between the estimate of possible investments by the Planning Commission and the demands of the ministries was particularly great. The demands of the ministries exceeded the level adopted in the Instructions [from the Politburo] by several tens of billions of złotys. Despite long negotiations and resistance by the Planning Commission, a level of investment was finally adopted that was 17 billion złotys higher than the original level.[38]

The result was a plan that was unachievable. Of the twenty main plan indicators, the only goals reached were those for real wages and employment. The goal for gross domestic product was met by only 75.8 percent, investment expenditures by 76.9 percent, industrial labor productivity by 76.8 percent, and exports by 69.5 percent.[39] Poland slipped into an economic crisis in 1980, which led to the emergence of Solidarity, the collapse of two Polish governments, and the introduction of martial law in 1981. The first priority for the

---

[37]Interview with Stanisław Długosz, 5.21.1992; Jan Mazur, 5.7.1992; Siennicki, 5.18.1992; Šedivý, 6.30.1992; and Miroslav Černý, 6.25.1992.

[38]Karpinski, *40 lat planowania w Polsce*, pp. 233–34.

[39]Ibid., p. 235. Karpinski's source for the plan targets is "Załącznik nr 1 do uchwały nr 224 Rady Ministrów z 22 listopada 1976 r. o pięcioletnim narodowym planie spoleczno-gospodarczym na lata 1976–1980." The levels of the various indicators achieved are published in *Rocznik Statystyczny*, the main publication of the Polish Main Statistical Office (GUS).

1981–85 period was to scale back investment commitments in order to reduce the bottlenecks that were paralyzing industry. Planned investment was 9.2 percent lower in 1982 than in 1981, and actual investment was 12.2 percent lower.[40] The scramble for investment funds intensified. The Polish plan contained a number of "operational programs," which were special projects with priority funding, and the ministries and enterprises saw these projects as a chance to avoid the general credit crunch. Under "enormous pressure," the number and character of these programs was broadened to the point that in 1982 they embraced over 55 percent of material supply in the Plan, which of course meant they could no longer serve as effective priorities.[41] In an interview Karpinski argued that the erosion of the Planning Commission's ability to set priorities was the primary reason that Polish obligations under the Target Programs were not fulfilled.

> Every ministry, every factory director had an interest in being included in the Target Programs, because this was a way of ensuring priority in the Plan, which meant imports and licenses and access to investments and resources. The Plan was a hierarchy of priorities. At one point we had 163 priority plans! Those could not be priorities. Every industry had a priority. Anything that was not included in a priority was a third-category project. We called [the Plan] a Christmas tree.[42]

Although the Polish situation at the turn of the decade was extreme, the problem of severe competition and political conflict over investment resources was general.[43] A Czech researcher who studied investment patterns for three decades was unable to find any correlation between completed investments and the economic criteria ostensibly being used to allocate investment funds, leading him to the conclusion that investment was thoroughly politicized.[44] This conclusion was supported by interviews with planning officials.[45]

The problems of cost overruns and failure to complete joint integration projects in Czechoslovakia had become so severe by the late 1980s that they provoked a study of several notable cases by the Peoples' Control Commission (VLK, or Výbor lidové kontroly). In the controversy that followed, the State Planning Commission produced a mea culpa, which by implication blamed the outgoing government for widespread abuse, and recommended adoption of a

[40]Karpinski, *40 lat planowania w Polsce*, p. 256.

[41]Ibid., p. 259.

[42]Interview with Andrzej Karpinski, former Deputy Chairman, Polish Planning Commission, 6.10.1992.

[43]Interviews with Černý, 6.25.1992; Długosz, 5.21.1992; Karpinski, 6.20.1992; Šedivý, 6.30.1992; and Zsolnai, 9.1.1992.

[44]Interview with Dr. Miroslav Kolanda, 7.14.1992. His results are in Kolanda and Kubišta, "Náklady, výkony a chování podniků."

[45]Interviews with Mazur, 5.7.1992; Siennicki, 5.18.1992; Długosz, 5.21.1992; Karpinski, 6.10.1992; Šedivý, 6.30.1992; and Černý, 6.25.1992.

set of "Principles for the Central Planning Organs for the Future Guaranteeing of Czechoslovak Participation in the Preparation and Execution of Integration Projects in CMEA Member Countries." After detailing the problems created by the Soviet side, the SPK report describes a series of problems on the Czechoslovak side which clearly indicate that the situation in Czechoslovakia was similar to that in Poland.

> The second set of problems touches on the internal Czechoslovak safeguards for Foreign Integration Projects (VIAs), and they can be described as the traditional problems of Czechoslovak construction investment. In particular, the quality of management is uneven along the whole organizational structure of the productive sphere. Further, problems arose in relations between suppliers and consumers. Not in the last place, the responsibility for adhering to the interests of the whole society during the expenditure of significant financial resources . . . was splintered in the central administration.
>
> . . . [L]egal management by the ministries' instructions, although responding in principle to the main directives governing central organs and Czechoslovak producer organizations, was unable to react to changing circumstances that could only be ascertained in the course of construction. Since coordinated management of this area practically did not exist, the most important consideration became ministerial and enterprise interests, which is one of the main reasons for the deficiencies that have emerged in VIAs. Excessive numbers of workers and machines appear in the construction areas, unjustified imports of machinery and equipment from nonsocialist countries, and so on.
>
> . . . It is necessary to acknowledge that the effort to give VIAs a special place in the system of state planning has not achieved the expected results. Certainly the VIAs are listed separately from other exports in the State Plan, but since they do not have the character of enumerated tasks, they are not regarded as a component of export. This has [negative] consequences, because the Ministry of Foreign Trade and Czechoslovak supply organizations are already fully occupied with tasks for execution.[46]

The report makes three major observations. First, the system of central management of integration projects was weak, and responsibility was "splintered" among a variety of organizations. Second, the interests of the ministries and enterprises conflicted with the technical priorities of integration, which led to cost overruns and failure to complete tasks on schedule. Finally, although the integration projects were formally included in the Plan, they were not "enumerated tasks," which meant that no organization had final responsibility for assuring that they were carried out. Since the Ministry of Foreign Trade and

[46]Dr. Nad', "Navŕh Zásad," 5.18.1988, SPK Archive, pp. 3–4. The report was approved by Ing. Pavel Svoboda, Director, Department for Socialist Economic Integration, and was distributed within SPK, the Office of the Council of Ministers, the Committee for Science and Technology, the Ministry of Foreign Trade, and several other state organs.

the supply organizations were already stretched to the limit to fulfill their parts of the Plan, they could not afford to devote scarce resources to integration projects. As a result, the integration projects were executed poorly and behind schedule, if at all.

The observation that investment funds were tight and that many planned investments were never completed, however, does not lead automatically to the conclusion that the countries would not fulfill their obligations under the Target Programs. The Target Programs could have received the priority that had been intended had the political leadership chosen to make the proper trade-offs. Alternatively, internal pressure on behalf of other priorities could have been overruled by external pressure had the Soviet Union chosen to exert such pressure on behalf of its own priorities. Two questions arise: Why were the East European governments not motivated to give the Target Programs priority, and why did the Soviet Union fail to enforce compliance with the obligations the East Europeans had assumed.

Part of the answer to the first question is that the Target Programs became embedded in a continuing struggle over investments on Soviet territory. Since the negotiations over the 1971–75 Five-Year Plan, which began in 1968, the Soviet Union had refused to expand exports of critical raw materials and energy sources to East European countries without corresponding increases in East European investments on Soviet territory to develop raw materials and transportation facilities. Under the Target Programs, the Soviets offered to increase exports of particular goods in return for investments in a variety of major and minor projects. The East Europeans fell back on their previous bargaining positions, attempting to reduce their participation, bargaining over its terms, and seeking to adjust the accounting methods to make it more profitable. They viewed joint investments as an undesirable concession from the outset, which was only justified as a means to secure additional deliveries of strategic goods.[47]

If the East Europeans had failed to implement the Target Programs simply because of the general shortage of investment funds, one would expect to find a roughly even distribution of successes and failures across the programs. In fact, however, the successful projects were heavily concentrated in the energy and extractive industries, and there was very limited success in the other areas. The Soviet Union was able to secure fairly full East European compliance in projects dedicated to the production and transportation of energy and raw materials, since each country had a powerful interest in obtaining the final products of their cooperation: subsidized raw materials. Failure to complete discrete cooperation projects would automatically reduce Soviet raw material exports. The Khmelnitskaia and Iuzhno-Ukrainskaia nuclear power plants

[47]Interviews with Dikij, 6.2.1992; Hetenyi, 9.7.1992; Marjai, 9.10.1992; and Siennicki, 5.18.1992.

were finally built on Soviet territory, though not without delays and some controversy, as were the high-voltage lines from Khmelnitskii to Rzeszów, Poland, and from Odessa to Dobrudzha, Bulgaria.[48] This permitted the Soviet Union to nearly double its exports of electricity between 1980 and 1988.[49]

The situation in machine building and consumer goods was more grim. The East Europeans had no real economic incentive to improve the quality of their exports. Although the official Soviet position was to press the East Europeans to improve the quality of their products, Soviet negotiators were unable to apply consistent pressure on the East Europeans to carry out their commitments to produce new kinds of machinery. In part, this was because the demand in the Soviet Union for East European products was so great that Gosplan had little bargaining leverage. The Soviet bargaining position seemed to be fractionalized according to branches of industry, and the East Europeans came to understand that they could take advantage of these divisions. An example is provided by exports of the Tatra heavy truck. The Czechoslovaks exported Tatras with no significant design changes from 1975 to 1985, and the Soviet mining industries annually clamored for more imports.[50] Consequently, the Czechoslovaks knew that they would be able to fill their quotas of machinery without investing in advanced technologies and new products. In fact, Soviet branch ministries often opposed proposals to modernize the design of East European products, because design changes would lead to price increases that would in turn allow the East Europeans to export fewer units to fill the existing quota.

> Practically, there was no competition, so there was no pressure for technical advance. If some producer increased his technical level, this automatically pushed the price up, which made a problem for the ministries. . . . There were times when the buyers—mainly in the Soviet Union—said, "We don't need improvements. We are very satisfied with this product. We know it is twenty years behind the current world technical level, but we don't need any development."[51]

Soviet negotiators faced weak incentives to insist on quality improvements, because efforts devoted to quality control throughout the Soviet economy were crowded out by competing priorities. This was particularly the case in the specialized agencies charged with monitoring East European progress on particular projects.

The fate of the cooperation agreements for nuclear power plants is indicative of the general failure to carry out agreements in machine building. Many of the East European countries, which had reluctantly agreed to cooperate in the project in the first place, and had done so only after insistent Soviet prod-

---

[48]The irregularities at the Khmelnitskaia plant were sufficiently egregious for criminal charges to be brought (*Pravda*, 26 October 1984, p. 2).

[49]Sovet Ekonomicheskoi Vzaimopomoshchi, Statisticheskii ezhegodnik, p. 387. Electricity exports rose from 19.9 to 38.9 million kilowatts between 1980 and 1988.

[50]Interviews with Mindoš and Fábik, 7.3.1992, and Šedivý, 6.30.1992.

[51]Interview with Janos Czibula, 8.25.1992.

ding, never allocated sufficient resources to meet their obligations. A number of countries were delinquent in making deliveries of key parts, so construction timetables had to be revised repeatedly, and the final deliveries were substantially delayed or cut back.[52] Under CMEA rules, the penalties for late deliveries were insignificant. The cost to the importer could be tremendous, on the other hand, particularly if the lack of key components meant delaying operation of a power plant. In the end the nuclear power plants planned for Poland were never completed, although construction began at Żarnowiec in northern Poland, and the Target Program included deliveries to Poland of two VVER-440 and five VVER-1000 reactors between 1983 and 1990.[53]

The nuclear power plant project was plagued by cost overruns and poor-quality equipment. Polish and Hungarian experts complained that countries that were monopoly suppliers of particular components exploited the situation to raise their prices. The first deputy chairman of the Hungarian Planning Commission argued that a particularly egregious offender was Czechoslovakia, which was responsible for supplying the reactors for Eastern Europe. Hungary planned to build a second nuclear power plant but scaled back its nuclear program, in part because the Czechoslovaks demanded that payment be made in hard currency.[54] The Czechoslovaks, for their part, argued that their prices had risen because of inflation on the world market and rising costs. The quality of parts prepared for the plants suffered as well, which led the countries to practice import substitution on a large scale. There was substantial concern that the substandard equipment exported by the CMEA countries would make the plants unsafe, so the countries produced their own. As a result, the share of "specialized" production in the construction of the nuclear plants declined sharply.[55]

The Soviet Union made no extended effort to monitor or enforce the extent to which the East Europeans fulfilled their obligations under the Target Programs. Instead, the programs were used as one argument among many in the continuing struggle over direct investment and trade structure during the negotiations over plan coordination, and they were gradually eclipsed by more pressing short-term objectives. In the negotiations over the 1981–85 Five-Year Plan, a primary Soviet objective was to liquidate the debt that many East European countries had accumulated in the 1970s because of the increases in Soviet oil and gas prices, and which had emerged as a substantial factor in the trade subsidy.[56] As events unfolded, however, the Soviets were forced by circumstances to make further concessions. The strikes that broke out in Po-

---

[52]Interviews with Mindoš and Fábik, 7.3.1992; Siennicki, 5.6.1992; and Zsolnai, 9.1.1992.

[53]"Prilozhenie 3.2 k protokolu vos'mogo zasedaniia Rabochei gruppy," 1.9–11.1979, CMEA Archive, p. 54.

[54]Interviews with Hetenyi, 9.7.1992; and Siennicki, 5.6.1992.

[55]Interview with Zsolnai, 9.1.1992.

[56]Interviews with Czibula, 8.25.1992; Długosz, 5.7.1992; Grabas, 5.26.1992; and Šedivý, 6.30.1992.

land in 1981 and the international repercussions of the declaration of martial law forced the Soviets to renegotiate the entire five-year plan with Poland, allowing a substantial Polish debt to accrue. Under these circumstances, it was difficult to press the Poles to meet their obligations under the Target Programs. As this crisis was subsiding, Gosplan began a campaign to enlist East European aid in the construction of a new iron-ore mining and purifying complex at Krivoi Rog and a new gas pipeline from Yamburg to the western border of the USSR. The controversy that swirled around these projects became the major subject of discussion in the coordination of plans, preempting attention from the Target Programs.[57]

The Target Programs were not systematically included in the next round of CMEA activity. A report prepared for the CPSU Central Committee apparatus by the International Management Institute (known by its Russian acronym, MNIIPU) criticized the Target Programs for their uneven development and implementation, and urged that they be revised and included in the successor program, the Comprehensive Program for Scientific and Technical Progress (KP NTP), which is described in the next chapter.[58] The response from the Party apparat was indicative of the degree of attention that the central leadership paid to detail. The Target Programs were a "spent wave," MNIIPU experts were told. Their value lay not in the particular projects they contained, but in the degree of momentum they were able to generate behind economic integration on an international scale. It was impossible to create enthusiasm about two major undertakings simultaneously, and the Target Programs were already considered a failure.[59] All reference to the Target Programs was removed from the proposals for the KP NTP on the orders of the CPSU Central Committee bureaucracy. This served as a clear signal, if one were needed, that the Target Programs were no longer a Soviet priority. As one jaded observer noted,

> The DTsPS were practically forgotten after five years, which was typical for the CMEA and the thinking of these countries, and particularly of the Soviet Union. There was never a time when a conception that had been agreed on was actually implemented; and if the implementation was not working, [there was no attempt] to study the causes and try to remove them. There was never an adequate answer. Instead, they always looked for a new conception, a new program. Because if you just look at the Comprehensive Program, after about three years the question was raised, because many things were not being carried out as had been expected—of course, the Comprehensive Program remains in force—let's develop Target Programs. They are developed for two or three years, and the propaganda is that they

[57]Interviews with Długosz, 5.21.1992, and Marjai, 9.1.1992.

[58]MNIIPU, "Kompleksnaia programma nauchno-tekhnicheskogo progressa stran-chlenov SEV: Osnovnye polozheniia kontseptsii. Struktura, poriadok i sroki razrabotki," Moscow, 1984, p. 8.

[59]Interview with Akademik Boris Chumachenko, General Director, MNIIPU, 2.18.1992.

will be the answer to all our problems! The whole structure remains the same in the countries, and in the commonwealth—and then the next one is thought up.[60]

References to the Long-Term Target Programs gradually dwindled in the Soviet press and in academic writings, supplanted by references to the earlier Comprehensive Program. Finally, no effort was made to consider the continuing implementation of the Target Programs in the 1986–90 Five-Year Plan. Some of the projects continued, but the Target Programs as such had ceased to exist.

A confidential IEMSS report written in 1988 refers to the Target Programs as an example of the sort of glaring failure that can be expected if Soviet policy fails to take account of East European interests.

> The almost forty-year practice of cooperation by the member countries of the CMEA shows that success can be assured only to those steps and concrete undertakings in whose completion the countries have a real economic interest, and for whose implementation the economic preconditions have matured. The construction of logical and theoretically competent blueprints is doomed to fail, if these are not founded on concrete economic calculations that indicate that the results will have utility for all. It is enough to cite the example of the Long-Term Target Programs, which are now almost forgotten.[61]

Given the extraordinary weakness of the Soviet bureaucracy, it is perhaps a fair conclusion that nothing could be achieved that violated the interests of the Soviet satellites. The truly remarkable conclusion, however, is that such dramatic examples of failure as the Long-Term Target Programs could be so quickly and thoroughly expunged from organizational memory.

CONCLUSIONS

The Target Programs were not without concrete results, as many critics claim; they did achieve results in the areas of nuclear energy and strengthening links between Eastern Europe and the Soviet power grid. Developing extensive reliance on nuclear energy in Eastern Europe was profoundly misguided; this, however, does not detract from Soviet successes in achieving cooperation in that area. Still, the Target Programs did not achieve their primary objectives, which were to produce a substantial increase in intrabloc trade, to improve the quality of East European exports, and to introduce a long-term economic calculus into the planning of the member countries. These objectives were hampered by the satellites' efforts to optimize the structure of their exports and to

---

[60]Interview with Andras Zsolnai, 9.1.1992.

[61]Shastitko and Nekipelov, "Pervoocherednye zadachi formirovaniia ob'edinennogo rynka SEV," IMEPI Archive, IEMSS report, 1988, pp. 8–9.

avoid costly investments in efforts that were perceived as primarily serving Soviet interests. In the negotiation phase, the East Europeans refused to increase their exports of raw materials and sought to avoid investments in costly new technologies and products, meanwhile attempting to fill the Target Programs with exports of standardized, low-technology goods. In the implementation phase, the East Europeans were very selective about performing their obligations. Investments were made when Soviet policy made explicit linkages between investments and raw material exports, and rarely in other cases. Consequently, the positive results in the Target Programs were concentrated in the programs for energy and raw materials and for transportation; the objectives for machine building, agriculture, and consumer goods were generally not met.

Soviet policy failed every test of consistency. During the negotiation phase, the USSR failed to defend its own interests. When the Soviets insisted, and linked exports of subsidized commodities to East European participation, as in the specialization agreements for machinery for nuclear power plants, they could compel the East Europeans to compromise. The Soviet Union was unable to hold a firm bargaining position across the entire spectrum of issues, however, and the machine-building program quickly deteriorated. Nor was the Soviet Union able to maintain its bargaining positions over time. In the implementation phase, long-term Soviet policies were derailed by short-term priorities. Even the compromise the Soviets had achieved on nuclear power plants did not hold. There was no consistent effort to monitor East European performance in the Target Programs, so the satellites were able to fulfill their agreements selectively, and they chose to fulfill only those agreements that promised to improve their trade profiles. Most damning of all was the failure to incorporate the satellites' remaining obligations from the Target Programs into the next round of integration programs (the KP NTP), and to connect the Target Programs with the Soviet bargaining strategy for the 1986–90 Five-Year Plan. Those decisions lifted all incentives for the East Europeans to implement the program, and they severely undermined Soviet credibility in future rounds of negotiations.

CHAPTER 8

The Comprehensive Program for Scientific and Technical Progress

WHEN THE Comprehensive Program for Scientific and Technical Progress (KP NTP) was unveiled at the Forty-first Session of the CMEA in December 1985, it was greeted as Mikhail Gorbachev's first major foray into the international politics of socialism. The program's preamble declared it "the fundamental document of socialist economic integration," or no less than a revision of the rules that governed East European trade politics. It was intended to set the investment priorities for the 1986–90 Five-Year Plan and beyond, and to concentrate the resources of the CMEA in order to overtake and surpass the West in five priority areas: computers, robotics, new materials, nuclear energy, and biotechnology. These five areas of scientific research were relied on to provide a generation of technological advances in order to rejuvenate the lagging economies of the Soviet bloc.

ORIGINS OF THE KP NTP

The idea of a comprehensive program for scientific and technical progress, according to one of its principle authors, had been "hanging in the air" for some time before it began to be spoken of officially.[1] Scientific and technical progress had been one of the principle goals of East European integration since it came to be recognized in the 1960s as essential to economic growth and international competitiveness. The Comprehensive Program, signed in 1971, contained a substantial section on scientific and technical cooperation, and the Twenty-eighth Council Session in 1974 established a Committee on Scientific and Technical Cooperation (KNTS) to oversee this growing area of CMEA activity. The Long-Term Target Programs, too, were intended to introduce leading-edge technologies into production, which was expected to increase productivity, improve the quality of products, and lead to more efficient use of energy and raw materials. The 1970s saw the development of a Comprehensive Program for Scientific and Technical Progress in the Soviet Union, and it seemed a natural extension of that initiative to launch such a program on an international scale.

[1] Interview with Vladimir Yezerov, MNIIPU, 12.4.1991.

A series of classified reports produced by the Institute for the Economy of the World Socialist System for the CPSU Central Committee in the 1970s and 1980s urged substantial changes in the management of East European relations in the field of science and technology.[2] A typical example is a report prepared in 1974, which argued that, "in the context of the prevailing revolution in science and technology, the most important and most dynamic direction of development for socialist economic integration is integration in the area of science and technology."[3] The report goes on to criticize current CMEA practice in science and technology:

> The Comprehensive Program [of 1971] provides for consultations on questions of science and technology policy. In practice, however, these are limited to an exchange of experience and agreement on the basic directions of scientific-technical cooperation. Of course, this leads to a certain mutual accommodation of the scientific and technological development of the CMEA countries and the elimination of parallelism, but it still does not lead to the development of a policy that would be obligatory for the countries in this area. Under the conditions of a rapid expansion of scientific potential . . . this kind of indirect accommodation is insufficient, and does not achieve the goals of socialist integration. The time has become ripe for the CMEA countries to reach agreement on the most important parameters and conceptions of scientific and technological development, which form the basis for a coordinated policy in this area. The most important element in such a policy is a program to develop the scientific and technical cooperation of the CMEA countries. It should include fundamental integration objectives, a rational scheme of international scientific-technical centers and organizations, joint institutes dedicated to basic research, and international scientific-productive associations for applied research and the implementation of its results in practice.[4]

This could serve as a concise formulation of the goals and instruments of the Comprehensive Program for Scientific and Technical Progress as proposed ten years later.

The first official statement proposing a Comprehensive Program for the CMEA in the area of science and technology was an article that appeared in *Kommunist* in November 1982, signed by Olimp Chukanov.[5] As head of the Group of Economic Consultants in the Central Committee Department for

---

[2]O.T. Bogomolov, I.I. Orlik, A. N. Bykov, "Sotsialisticheskaia ekonomicheskaia integratsiia i ee mezhdunarodnoe znachenie," to G. E. Tsukanov, CC CPSU, 1.10.1974, IMEPI Archive, IEMSS report, pp. 4–7; Shiriaev et al., "Materialy po vneshneekonomicheskim aspektam," to AN SSSR, 5.2.1976, IMEPI Archive, IEMSS report 14206/112; Bykov, ed., "Integratsiia stran SEV v oblasti nauki i tekhniki," 1980, IMEPI Archive, IEMSS report, pp. 143–44.

[3]Bykov, "K voprosu o soglasovannoi nauchno-tekhnicheskoi politike stran SEV," to Comrade D. I. Sedov, The Department, CC CPSU, 8.29.1974, IMEPI Archive, IEMSS report, p. 1. Bykov was Chief of the Sector for Scientific-Technical Progress and Cooperation, IEMSS AN SSSR.

[4]Ibid., pp. 2–3.

[5]Chukanov, "Integratsiia kak faktor intensifikatsii ekonomiki stran SEV."

Socialist Countries, Chukanov had powerful influence over Soviet integration policy, so the appearance of the article was a signal that the other CMEA countries could not ignore. The article was probably written by Chukanov's deputy for Science and Technology, Ladygin, since Chukanov's personal involvement in the development of the KP NTP was superficial.[6]

The initiative for the Comprehensive Program for Scientific and Technical Progress came from the midlevel staff of the CPSU Central Committee Department for Socialist Countries. Boris Chumachenko, general director of the International Institute for Problems of Management (MNIIPU), recalls that, on a Friday evening in early March 1984, he and Stanislav Iemel'ianov, the director of MNIIPU, were called to the Central Committee headquarters on Old Square for a meeting that lasted approximately two hours.[7] They were met by a large group of consultants led by Chukanov, and were told that the decision had been made to design a Comprehensive Program for Scientific and Technical Progress. They were instructed to prepare a proposal for its basic priorities, along with a timetable and a mechanism to implement them, by the following Friday. They were instructed to pare the seventy-three priority areas listed in the Soviet Program for Scientific and Technical Progress to no more than seven.

Chumachenko recalls that the poor academics protested. First, a week is not nearly long enough to carry out such an important piece of preparatory work; second, it was practically impossible to reduce the range of essential research and development projects to seven priorities; third, by carrying out a piece of work like this without the usual process of consulting with the other "interested" institutes, they would ruin their relations with the Soviet Academy of Sciences. They were made to understand that failure to comply would be punished by loss of Party membership. MNIIPU produced a proposal within the required time frame, as did several other institutes, and the MNIIPU proposal was accepted.[8]

From this point forward, MNIIPU exercised substantial influence over the development of the KP NTP. The proposal presented by Chumachenko included seven priority areas. A space program and a priority for consumer goods were rejected by the Central Committee, but the other five priorities framed by the MNIIPU proposal were retained: computerization, robotics, atomic energy, new materials, and biotechnology. A brief process of discussion within the Soviet government and Academy of Sciences followed, and Chumachenko reports that he was able to rely on support from the Central Committee, and was thus able to prevent any further substantial changes from being made to the proposal.

The Soviet proposal to develop a KP NTP and a general description of the

[6]Interview with Boris Chumachenko, 2.18.1992.
[7]Ibid.
[8]Ibid.

five priority areas were circulated to the CMEA countries in the beginning of April along Party channels, and preparations began for ratification on the Conference on the Highest Level (a conference of Communist Party first secretaries) approaching in June 1984. The process of international discussion was completed in a month, and the protocol of the coming meeting was prepared on schedule in the middle of May. No substantial changes were made in the proposal, according to its drafters. It was adopted, and the Fortieth CMEA Council Session was set as the forum for adoption of the completed KP NTP. Work now commenced in parallel on the five substantive Priority Programs, and on the reform package intended to make their achievement possible. International working groups were formed to organize the work on each of the subprograms, which in turn were broken down into ninety-three problem areas comprising more than three thousand specific projects. The work on the reform package remained de jure in the competence of the CMEA Committee on Scientific and Technical Cooperation, but de facto in the hands of MNIIPU, over the course of the next year.[9]

The first stage of development of the KP NTP illustrates the dramatic ability of the CPSU Central Committee apparatus to achieve simple results. It was Chukanov who summoned leading experts in March, and his department that chose which proposals to pursue. Little was changed in hasty internal consultations in April, or in international consultations in May. The proposals were adopted and favorably reviewed in all the speeches at the Conference on the Highest Level in 1984. However, the proposals adopted in June 1984 represented the bare skeleton of what was to become a sweeping reform package and a massive organizational undertaking. It was too early for serious opposition to emerge, and the details would determine the ultimate significance of the undertaking.

DEVELOPMENT PHASE: MNIIPU REFORM PACKAGE, 1984–1985

The International Management Institute was formally an international body, but that did not prevent MNIIPU from acting as the principal articulator and defender of the Soviet conception of the KP NTP. MNIIPU was staffed by cyberneticists and management scientists, who shared the enthusiasm of the late-Brezhnev and early-Gorbachev years for scientific management. They consciously patterned their approach on Western models. Chumachenko described the KP NTP as an attempt to apply the experience of the United States with the PPBS—Prognosis, Program, Budgeting System—introduced in the Pentagon under the Kennedy administration. Vladimir Ezerov, a principal author of many of the MNIIPU position papers, explained that it was inspired in

[9]Interviews with Vladimir Ezerov and Vladimir Korsun, 12.9.1991.

part by the Eureka program to develop competitive technologies in Europe. MNIIPU researchers claim, in retrospect, to have believed that market-type reform was essential in order for the program to reach its full potential, but the proposals they submitted for the KP NTP did not envisage dramatic liberalization. Rather, they sought to use the techniques of management science to unlock productive possibilities they believed to be hidden in the centrally planned economy. They later defended this approach as a pragmatic adaptation to the political realities that prevailed at the time.[10]

MNIIPU researchers argued that achieving the ambitious goals of the program would require more than a list of investment projects. "The KP NTP," they wrote, "should become the central link of a concentrated system of joint planning and management of scientific and technical cooperation."[11] MNIIPU identified three major obstacles to technological development in the CMEA. First, the organizations charged with basic research and development of new technologies were isolated from the industrial giants that were required to introduce innovations into production. No adequate mechanism existed to incorporate new techniques, and enterprises felt no incentive to do so unless they received direct instructions from the State Planning Commission. Second, organizations active in different branches of the economy were administratively isolated from one another, since each branch was the domain of its own specialized industrial ministry. Modern technological innovation, however, often involves spin-offs of processes developed in one industry to solve problems that emerge in another. Third, the central planning system isolated organizations working on the same sets of problems in different CMEA countries, so they were unable to pool their resources, share experiences, and specialize in order to divide up complex projects. The reform program was meant to overcome these obstacles by reorganizing institutions to cross traditional lines of command, focusing them on interdisciplinary tasks.[12]

In December 1984 the Soviet delegation to the Thirty-first Session of the CMEA Committee for Scientific and Technical Cooperation presented a proposal prepared by MNIIPU, which embodied these principles in a dramatic

[10]Ibid.

[11]"Kompleksnaia programma nauchno-tekhnicheskogo progressa stran chlenov SEV: Osnovnye polozheniia kontseptsii. Struktura, poriadok i sroki razrabotki," MNIIPU Archive, February 1984, p. 3. This document, prepared by MNIIPU as a continuation of its series of reports to the CPSU Central Committee on the KP NTP, became the basis for the document that was presented as a Soviet proposal to KNTS in December 1984 (interview with Ezerov, 12.9.1991).

[12]Interview with Ezerov and Korsun, 12.9.1991. The authors also describe their approach in an early article (Leont'ev et al., "Kompleksnaia programma nauchno-tekhnicheskogo progressa stran-chlenov SEV," in Problemy Teorii i Praktiki Upravleniia, MNIIPU, March 1983). A fuller exposition is contained in Chumachenko, Ezerov, and Korsun, Problemy organizatsii upravleniia realizatsiei i obnovleniem Kompleksnoi Programmy Nauchno-Tekhnicheskogo Progressa stran-chlenov SEV (Moscow: MNIIPU, 1989).

reform of the CMEA foreign trade system.[13] The proposal stated that the KP NTP would be the basis for a "consultative, and in some cases unified, science and technology policy." It mandated strict inclusion of KP NTP projects in the five-year plans of the CMEA countries, and a system of bilateral treaties covering the whole program to be signed by the CMEA premiers. It introduced extensive organizational reforms. Five new CMEA committees were to be created to supervise the five priority areas, each with a council of experts empowered to make operational decisions, and a potent, new Scientific and Technical Center to monitor progress. There was to be an international research center to oversee the KP NTP as a whole and to propose modifications to the program over time. The KP NTP was intended to spin off numerous international research centers and joint-stock companies to bridge the gaps between the national economies.

It quickly became apparent that views diverged sharply between the Soviet Union and its satellites regarding the package of reforms that should accompany the KP NTP. Since the proposal came with the sponsorship of the Soviet State Committee for Science and Technology (GKNT), it is significant that the document was not accepted, but merely "taken into consideration." More significant is that two countries, the GDR and Romania, refused to agree even to this neutral step, and rejected the proposal outright.[14] There was clear opposition to some aspects of the draft, and the subsequent development of the proposal indicates the areas of disagreement.

There ensued a year-long process of negotiation. A close comparison of eight successive draft versions, including the adopted version, shows a steady deterioration of the proposals. As Table 8.1 indicates, most of the reforms were eliminated from successive drafts.

The first and second drafts were substantially the same. Each envisioned a substantial reshuffling of the organs and responsibilities of the CMEA to create a hierarchy of organizations dedicated only to carrying out the KP NTP:

> The CMEA member countries assign decisive significance to the organization and management of the process of implementing the Comprehensive Program. In so far as the Priority Programs for cooperation will be the fundamental form of implementation of the Comprehensive Program, the CMEA member countries consider it expedient to create a central organ for joint management for each Priority Program in the form of an Intergovernmental Commission to solve strategic problems concerning its implementation.

[13]MNIIPU, GKNT SSSR, Sekretariat, SEV, "Predlozheniia po sisteme upravleniia realizatsiei Kompleksnoi Programmy Nauchno-Tekhnicheskogo Progressa stran-chlenov SEV" (Moscow: SEV, 1984). The supervising editors were B. A. Chumachenko (MNIIPU), V. A. Koniushko (GKNT), and V. A. Prokudin (SEV); the managing editors were V. B. Ezerov, E. P. Vlasov, and V. S. Korsun (MNIIPU).

[14]"Protokol, 31. Zasedaniia Komiteta po Nauchno-Tekhnicheskomu Sotrudnichestvu," 12.6–7.1984, MNIIPU Collection, p. 9.

TABLE 8.1

Eight Draft Versions of the Comprehensive Program
for Scientific and Technical Progress

	Drafts							
Organizational reforms	1	2	3	4	5	6	7	8
Five new committees	•	•						
Five councils of experts for priority areas	•	•	•	•	•	•	•	
Five scientific centers for priority areas	•	•						
KP NTP Scientific and Methodological Center	•	•						
Coordinating Council for the KP NTP			•	•	•			
Research centers and joint firms for important projects			•	•	•	•	•	•
Automated international information system					•	•		

Source: Compiled by the author from original drafts held in the MNIIPU Archive.
Note: A bullet indicates that an organizational reform, listed at the left, was present in the draft represented by a particular column.

Program Councils that comprise leading scientists and specialists of the CMEA member countries will be formed under the central organs as consultative bodies, to solve scientific, technical, and industrial problems connected with the implementation of the Priority Programs.

Leading Organizations (or agencies) will be charged with the operational tasks of supervising and managing each Priority Program. The functions of Leading Organizations may be delegated to international scientific and technical centers or important scientific-industrial combines, with flexible forms of cooperation among the national scientific and industrial organizations.[15]

What had been foreseen was a three-tiered structure. At the top were five Intergovernmental Commissions, which in CMEA parlance meant international commissions whose members were deputy premiers. This implied that the CMEA countries would have to delegate deputy premiers to sit on each commission, and to add the KP NTP Priority Programs to their duties. This was an ambitious change in the CMEA structure, since only three of the existing

[15]Sovet Ekonomicheskoi Vzaimopomoshchi, "Kompleksnaia Programma Nauchno-Tekhnicheskogo Progressa stran-chlenov SEV, Osnovnye polozheniia (Predvaritel'nyi proekt)," 1984, MNIIPU Archive, pp. 12–13. The first document, "Predlozheniia po sisteme upravleniia realizatsiei Kompleksnoi Programmy Nauchno-Tekhnicheskogo Progressa stran-chlenov SEV," MNIIPU Collection, pp. 9–10, contains the same language in slightly different redaction.

standing committees were staffed at that level.[16] MNIIPU experts regarded this proposal as particularly important, because they blamed the "branch" structure of the CMEA and the national governments for obstructing technology transfers from one branch to another. To overcome this bias in the bureaucracy, they believed it was necessary to create structures that were responsible for comprehensive final results, rather than for particular branches.[17]

The second tier was to consist of five Program Councils of scientists and specialists, who in CMEA practice would be drawn from the national central planning agencies and ministries of science and technology. Finally, each of the five priority areas in the KP NTP was to become the charge of a Leading Organization or a Scientific and Technical Center. Vladimir Leont'ev, the deputy chairman of the Soviet State Committee for Science and Technology who presided over many of the crucial negotiations, explained that these centers were the key link in the Soviet strategy to break through the isolation of the national economies of the CMEA. Each was to be governed by a Council of Representatives, whose members would be empowered to make commitments on behalf of their countries. Otherwise, the centers would be paralyzed by the CMEA practice of endless, multilevel negotiation.[18]

In addition, the first and second drafts proposed creation of an International Scientific and Methodological Center for the Comprehensive Program, which was intended to perform the following functions:

- Preparation of proposals . . . for a unified methodological approach to the development and implementation of the Comprehensive Program. This will include determination of the Comprehensive Program's goals, structure, and content, and the procedure for organizing work for its formation, implementation, and further development.
- Expert guidance and approval of proposed versions of Priority Programs of the Comprehensive Program based on the following considerations: their correspondence with a unified science and technology policy; with the final goals, the general structure, and the confirmed order of organization of work on the Comprehensive Program; and with the deadlines for its implementation.
- Development of a structure for an international system of programmatic target planning and management of the implementation of the Comprehensive Pro-

[16]The CMEA Executive Committee (Ispolkom) consisted of the Permanent Representatives of the countries to the CMEA, who under the CMEA Charter must be deputy premiers; the Committee for Cooperation in the Area of Planning (KSOPD) consisted of the chairmen of the national planning commissions, who generally held the rank of deputy premier; the Committee for Scientific and Technical Cooperation consisted of the deputy premiers charged with science and technology policy.

[17]Interviews with Chumachenko, 2.18.1992, and Ezerov, 12.9.1991.

[18]Interview with Vladimir Leont'ev, former Head of the division of the Soviet State Committee for Science and Technology (GKNT) that supervised development of the KP NTP, 2.21.1992.

gram. This will assure the systematic planning of cooperation in the CMEA for the entire cycle from science and technology to production.[19]

This Center, in short, was to oversee the entire process of development and implementation of the KP NTP, to ensure the logical connection of topics of research and the fulfillment of international obligations. Past experience had shown that these were terribly important functions, since the first Comprehensive Program and the Long-Term Target Programs had gradually lost their coherence in the process of negotiation and had been incompletely implemented by the countries.[20]

The third draft text eliminated all reference to the creation of a new international center to monitor the KP NTP, and it abandoned the commitment to create five centers to supervise the priority areas. The East European negotiators opposed the creation of international centers because they expected them to be expensive and intrusive, and ultimately to serve Soviet interests rather than their own.[21] Instead of creating five new CMEA commissions, the third draft adopted a compromise that MNIIPU specialists had opposed, and still regretted years later: the task of managing the Priority Programs was simply added to the responsibilities of existing CMEA commissions, and some priority areas were divided up among two or three such organs.[22] In place of the rejected mechanism for carrying out the program, however, the new draft proposed different innovations. First, a Coordinating Council for the KP NTP, sometimes referred to as a "Conference of Plenipotentiary Representatives," would be created with a broad mandate:

> To produce effective cooperation among the CMEA Committees in resolving general difficulties in coordinating efforts to implement the Comprehensive Program and analyze the progress toward its fulfillment, and to prepare comprehensive proposals for the periodic correction and extension of the Comprehensive Program for the following long-term period.[23]

[19]Sovet Ekonomicheskoi Vzaimopomoshchi, "Kompleksnaia Programma Nauchno-Tekhnicheskogo Progressa stran-chlenov SEV, Osnovnye polozheniia (Predvaritel'nyi proekt)," 1984, MNIIPU Archive [second draft], pp. 13–14; also contained in the first draft, "Predlozheniia po sisteme upravleniia realizatsiei Kompleksnoi Programmy Nauchno-Tekhnicheskogo Progressa stran-chlenov SEV," MNIIPU Archive, p. 10.

[20]Interview with Vladimir Ezerov, 12.4.1991.

[21]Interviews with Dr. Wiesław Grudzewski, former Deputy Minister, Polish Office for Progress in Science, Technology, and Development (UPNTiW), 5.19.1992, and Tamas Szabo, Deputy General Director, Hungarian National Committee for Technical Development, 8.26.1992.

[22]For the content of the third proposed version, see Sovet Ekonomicheskoi Vzaimopomoshchi, "Kompleksnaia Programma Nauchno-Tekhnicheskogo Progressa stran-chlenov SEV, Osnovnye polozheniia (Proekt)" (Moscow, 1985), MNIIPU Archive, pp. 16–17. MNIIPU views based on interviews with Ezerov and Korsun, 12.9.1991.

[23]Sovet Ekonomicheskoi Vzaimopomoshchi, "Kompleksnaia Programma Nauchno-Tekhnicheskogo Progressa stran-chlenov SEV, Osnovnye polozheniia (Proekt)" [third draft] (Moscow, 1985), p. 19.

The Council would be composed of representatives of ministerial rank rather than deputy premiers, however, which would give it less authority than the organs proposed in the previous drafts.

The third draft sought to resurrect international technological centers, but in a less intrusive form. Gone was the commitment to create five such centers immediately and to delegate extensive powers to implement the KP NTP.

> For the joint solution of the most important problems of scientific and technical progress, the member countries of the CMEA will, when necessary, create international scientific-technical centers for the development and introduction of progressive technologies and joint scientific-industrial combines formed by national scientific and industrial organizations with flexible forms of cooperation . . . particularly in areas in which a high level of cooperation is achieved.[24]

This language survived the editing process and remained in the final version of the KP NTP, but in practice it was very rare indeed that it proved "necessary" to create such organizations.[25]

The new draft relied more heavily on the Councils of Experts for the five priority areas, renaming them Priority Program Councils and raising their profile by incorporating representatives of the central planning organs into their membership. It broadened their mandate to take on the functions of monitoring, analyzing, and adjusting the KP NTP that had previously been assigned to the Scientific and Methodological Center for the Comprehensive Program. In addition, they were assigned the important political tasks of reaching a "judgment of the results achieved from the point of view of their correspondence with the final goals of the Priority Programs and the concerted science and technology policy" and "developing a future science and technology policy for the member countries of the CMEA for the priority areas of scientific and technological progress."[26] In effect, the third draft sought to re-create the structures that had been rejected, but on a lower level of the government hierarchy. One of the Soviet negotiators recalled that numerous attempts had been made to find a mechanism that would be acceptable to the East Europeans, but that all had assumed the same basic objectives: breaking the national ties of the cooperating organizations, incorporating them into an international system of management, and creating a structure of accountability that could monitor progress.[27]

[24]Ibid., p. 20.

[25]One of the few examples of such centers was INTEREVM, a complex built outside Moscow to develop computer technology. Itself a classic example of the East Europeans' ability to whittle down Soviet proposals, INTEREVM was initially planned as a development on the scale of Silicon Valley, but ended up as a very modest complex funded almost exclusively by the Soviet Union (interview with Laszlo Pal, 9.3.1992).

[26]Sovet Ekonomicheskoi Vzaimopomoshchi, "Kompleksnaia Programma Nauchno-Tekhnicheskogo Progressa stran-chlenov SEV, Osnovnye polozheniia, (Proekt)" [third draft], (Moscow, 1985), p. 17.

[27]Interview with Leont'ev, 2.21.1992.

Negotiating sessions over subsequent drafts eliminated most of the remaining infrastructure of the KP NTP. The proposed Coordinating Council for the KP NTP was eliminated from the sixth draft, and it did not reappear. The Priority Program Councils were edited out of existence in the fall of 1985, and failed to appear in the final draft. A short-lived proposal for an "automated international information system," dedicated to monitoring the progress of the KP NTP and replacing some of the functions of the previously eliminated Scientific and Methodological Center, made its appearance in the fifth draft and vanished quietly in the seventh. All that remained in the final version of the KP NTP of the once ambitious package of reforms was a single sentence:

> The priority problems are developed under the organizational control and coordination of Leading Organizations, which are responsible for quality and a high technical level, for the completion of the projects by the established deadlines, and for the development of draft agreements, treaties, and other cooperation proposals for consideration by the participating sides according to the established procedure.[28]

The KP NTP assigned Leading Organizations, which were Soviet institutes and enterprises, to each of the ninety-three problem areas covered in the five Priority Programs, but the precise definition of the category of "Leading Organization" remained to be negotiated after the KP NTP had been signed in December 1985.

The objective of the Soviet negotiators was to reintroduce an element of accountability into the KP NTP mechanism by charging the Leading Organizations with responsibility for achieving the goals set forth in the program, and delegating to them enough authority to compel the cooperation of organizations from the other countries. The Leading Organizations were to take the role of the "customer" of scientific and technological advances, which they would commission from the CMEA countries, combine, and translate into industrial advances.[29] In the absence of other coordinating organs, the Leading Organizations were responsible for the whole process of technological progress, from conception to final production. Unfortunately, they were not entrusted with the resources and authority necessary to carry out such a broad mandate.[30]

Stenographic records of a conference of ministers and deputy ministers of

---

[28]"Kompleksnaia Programma Nauchno-Tekhnicheskogo Progressa stran-chlenov SEV do 2000 goda, Osnovnye polozheniia," *Problemy Teorii*, p. 106.

[29]Interviews with Vladimir Ezerov, Vladimir Korsun, Konstantin Lavrov, Boris Chumachenko, 2.18.1992, and Vladimir Leont'ev, 2.21.1992.

[30]"Predlozheniia o zadachakh, pravakh i obiazannostiakh golovnoi organizatsii-koordinatora rabot po probleme Kompleksnoi Programmy Nauchno-Tekhnicheskogo Progressa stran-chlenov SEV do 2000 goda," published in Sovet Ekonomicheskoi Vzaimopomoshchi, *Dokumenty SEV*, 1986.

science and technology, which had been called to compose a document to define the rights and obligations of Leading Organizations in February 1986, show that each of the East European countries took steps to weaken the Leading Organizations, with the exception of Czechoslovakia. Romania took the most extreme position, making numerous proposals that, if accepted, would have bound the Leading Organizations hand and foot with red tape.[31] It was the East Germans, however, who were most direct. In his speech to the plenary session, the German delegate made it quite clear that his government's position was that cooperation should continue on the existing legal footing, and that the GDR would oppose any attempts to turn the Leading Organizations into an authoritative superstructure.

> We believe that the basis for all our work should be contracts between the Leading Organizations and the executors of projects, and among the executors. The way in which the work needs to be organized should determine how we prepare and seal concrete contracts.
>
> In this connection, some of the rights of Leading Organizations contained in the proposal of the Soviet side assume that, for example, the Leading Organizations will distribute projects to the executors. This procedure of distributing concrete projects to the executors is outside the competence of the Leading Organizations, however, and is rather the result of the conduct of concrete negotiations and the signing of contracts. For example, in the GDR we assume that, if our participation is needed to solve a concrete problem, then we should carry it to production and export. . . . This means that we should organize the work of distributing obligations to the particular participants and determine this concretely in contracts, for only a contract can be an obligatory document, on the basis of which work can be carried out.
>
> . . . This means that, if the Zeissov combine has an order from the Soviet Union to develop a particular new kind of equipment for microelectronics, we will be the executor and in the end also the consumer of scientific research, since the Soviet Union wants to receive from us equipment, and not a scientific result.[32]

We see here a clear conflict between the commercial interests of the East European countries and the technical requirements of international cooperation. As the German delegate made clear, the GDR preferred to contract for complete projects, which would result in exports of machinery, rather than for scientific research, which in the end would increase the productivity of the industries of other socialist countries. The Polish delegate expressed the same

[31]The changes proposed by the Romanian side emphasized that the role of the Leading Organizations was a purely coordinating one, and eliminated their involvement in auditing the work of lower-level subcontractors, adjusting the detailed cooperation programs as circumstances changed, and signing contracts on their own authority. See "Protokol soveshchaniia polnomochnykh predstavitelei," 2.4–5.1986, CMEA Archive, pp. 1, 5–8.

[32]"Stenogramma soveshchaniia predstavitelei," 2.4–5.1986, CMEA Archive, pp. 12–14.

preference.[33] The East Europeans were quite correct to argue that for that purpose, the existing legal structure was adequate. The design of the KP NTP, however, presupposed a deeper degree of technical cooperation among the CMEA countries, in which scientific resources would be pooled. Such deeper cooperation would require some mechanism to break through the institutionalized isolation of the centrally planned economies.

In order to serve the function of "consumer" of scientific research, as the Soviet Union proposed, the Leading Organizations would need to have disposal of some form of resources—financial or otherwise—that were valuable to the organizations with which they were intended to establish cooperation. A consumer is a consumer by right of the ability to pay for results. This was an objection that the Soviet negotiators of course understood, and attempts were made to create a system of joint funding of KP NTP projects. These efforts, however, met a united front of resistance from the East Europeans. A protocol from an early meeting on the subject shows that the Soviet Union attempted to establish the principle that research would be funded by equal shares paid by each participating country, while Bulgaria, Hungary, the GDR, Cuba, Poland, Romania, and Czechoslovakia insisted that contributions be based on "the level of exploitation of the results in the economies of the countries"—essentially, on the principle that the producer of finished goods internalizes the costs of research and development.[34] This was the principle that ultimately prevailed.[35]

The adopted version of the KP NTP provided for the creation of joint funds, but left the decision of whether to create funds for particular projects up to the parties to the agreement:

> The financing of adopted cooperation measures for the implementation of the program will take place on the basis of the exploitation of national means, credits from the International Investment Bank, the International Bank for Economic Cooperation, and also joint funds, which will be created for financing isolated and particularly important undertakings, which will be selected by agreements and contracts.[36]

This formulation left the issue of how to finance the KP NTP to be determined in the next phase, during the development of the detailed cooperation programs. A speech delivered by Guryi Marchuk, the Soviet deputy premier for Science and Technology, to the Council of Ministers in June 1985 left no doubt that conflict over the issue was expected to continue:

[33]Ibid., pp. 41–42.

[34]"Protokol soveshchaniia ekspertov zainteresovannykh stran-chlenov SEV," 8.7–9.1984, CMEA Archive, p. 9.

[35]Sovet Ekonomicheskoi Vzaimopomoshchi, Sekretariat, *Dokumenty SEV*, pp. 38–39, 55.

[36]"Kompleksnaia Programma Nauchno-Tekhnicheskogo Progressa stran-chlenov SEV do 2000 goda, Osnovnye polozheniia," *Problemy Teorii*, p. 106.

It is difficult to assess the concrete contribution of each member country of the CMEA to the realization of the KP NTP at the present time. This will be determined by the system of contracts and treaties that will establish the fundamental conditions of cooperation and the obligations of the sides for each problem area. However, we should expect that the countries will strive to delegate to the Soviet Union the greater part of the effort and expense, particularly in the area of fundamental research. We understand this, and we are prepared to conduct our work with the countries in such a way as to protect the interests of our country, to raise the efficiency of cooperation, and to fulfill the principle of mutual advantage with greater consequence in the new contracts and treaties.[37]

When it came to the stage of signing these contracts, the East European countries uniformly resisted the creation of joint funds, and in fact no such funds were ever created. Interviews with Polish, Czechoslovak, and Hungarian trade officials who participated in these negotiations leave no doubt that the East Europeans felt that the funds, if created, would serve Soviet interests, and would bring no substantial benefits to the contributing countries.[38]

It is ironic that a confidential Polish report, written several years later, argued that in light of the failure of the KP NTP to achieve its objectives, its "mechanism of implementation" should be reexamined. As particularly promising "new mechanisms," the report listed "joint funds, the creation of consortia of enterprises and [other] organizations of the participating nations, [and] the creation of international centers." In addition, it proposed that "the KP NTP should be 'managed' by a Program Council, which should be composed of representatives of the ministries of the countries participating in the program and eminent scientists representing the various countries."[39] All these proposals, of course, had been contained in the MNIIPU proposals, and had been bitterly opposed by the East European negotiators. As technocratic solutions go, these proposals were quite logical. They clashed, however, with the underlying conflict of interest that motivated all discussions of trade in the Soviet bloc.

In the absence of any agreements on the amount of resources that each country was to provide, or of any procedure for determining those amounts, the commitment that was undertaken in signing the KP NTP was rather abstract. The countries agreed to carry out the obligations they assumed, but

[37]Guryi Marchuk, Speech to the Council of Ministers of the USSR, draft version, 6.4.1985, MNIIPU Archive, pp. 12–13. The speech was written by Chumachenko's department at MNIIPU.

[38]Interviews with Dr. Wiesław Grudzewski, 5.19.1992; Dr. Jerzy Rutkowski, 5.4.1992; Tamas Szabo, 8.26.1992; Andras Zsolnai, 9.1.1992; and Laszlo Pal, 9.3.1992.

[39]Urząd Postępu Naukowo-Technicznego i Wdrożeń, "Ocena realizacji Kompleksowego Programu Postępu Naukowo-Technicznego krajów członkowskich RWPG," KBN Archive, March 1990, pp. 5, 10.

retained discretion as to which obligations to undertake. The national shares of participation in various projects were to be decided in the next phase.

THE DETAILED COOPERATION PROGRAMS

The economic summit in 1984 had spelled out the purpose of each program only in general terms, and a great deal of technical work remained to determine the scope and specific focus of each priority area. For each of the five priority areas, a working group was formed within the CMEA. Each country was represented by six to ten experts (members of its Academy of Sciences, directors of factories, and so on) headed by a minister, for a total membership in each group of seventy to a hundred individuals. Each group met several times inside the CMEA building on Prospekt Kalinina, and each meeting lasted about three days.[40] The five priority areas were subdivided into ninety-three problem areas, which in turn consisted of several thousand projects. The working groups determined which countries were interested in participation in each project, which organizations would represent each country, the technical specifications of the work, and the deadlines for its completion. Subsequently, Leading Organizations from the Soviet Union took responsibility for each of the ninety-three problem areas, and coordinated the negotiation of a series of contracts among organizations from various CMEA countries that determined the precise obligations of each party.

In order to carry out the intent of the programs, it was essential that the detailed projects add up to a coherent whole and fit together according to a rational pattern. According to MNIIPU experts, the development of the KP NTP was intended to be an exercise in "programmatic planning": goals are set, the steps needed to realize the goals are broken down into achievable tasks, and the tasks are farmed out to competent organizations. If the program is properly designed, fulfillment of the tasks should contribute to achievement of the final goals.[41] According to a subsequent MNIIPU analysis, however, the design was lost in the process of negotiation.

> During the development of the detailed programs of cooperation, as a result of serious management failures, one of the most important principles of programmatic planning was violated: the principle of programmatic focus [*tselevaia napravlennost'*]. The Leading Organizations took the path of least resistance: the basis for formulating the detailed programs was not achievement of the indicated goals for the particular problems (the cutting edge [of technology]), but the minimization of effort and risk. In effect, the Leading Organizations applied the tradi-

[40]Interview with Chumachenko, 2.18.1992.
[41]Interview with Ezerov, 12.9.1991.

tional principle of planning "from what has been achieved," and included in the detailed programs the work they were already carrying out even before the development of the Comprehensive Program. Consequently, it turned out that the work planned for one-third of the problems did not correspond to international quality standards.

As a result, the Priority Programs, which had already decomposed at the moment of their formation into ninety-three problems that were weakly connected even within a single priority area, ceased to exist at all as a single whole. They disintegrated into approximately three thousand separate tasks, the majority of which not only did not correspond to the international level expected for the year 2000, but did not even meet contemporary international standards and the demands of the world market.[42]

An independent Polish analysis, conducted by the Office for Progress in Science, Technology, and Development (UPNTiW), came to substantially the same conclusions:

An analysis of the implementation of the KP NTP indicates that, although the tasks posed in the program were intended to liquidate backwardness relative to the advanced industrial countries in the priority areas of scientific and technical progress, work to date has not been sufficiently advanced, and no significant results have been achieved in the most important areas of scientific and technical development. Fundamental errors were made in the division of problem areas into projects, and therefore during the development of the detailed programs of cooperation. Those programs expanded excessively, with no comprehensive connection of projects in a full cycle [from R&D to production], and without their completion being divided among the cooperating countries. In many cases, projects were formulated in a way that was not concrete, which led to a significant diffusion of topics and their repetition under [the headings of] various problem areas.[43]

Why were the detailed cooperation programs plagued by such incompetence?
The process of filling out the details of the programs became the focus of frenetic international bargaining and maneuvering. Numerous East European participants and observers testify that their commercial interests in trade conflicted with the rational, technical objectives of the program for science and technology. Since it was not from the CMEA that the East Europeans expected to receive new transfers of technology, but from the West, they did not regard achievement of the goals of the KP NTP as necessary for their eco-

---

[42]Vladimir Ezerov, "O perestroike struktury i mekhanizma upravleniia KP NTP SEV," MNIIPU Archive, date unknown, pp. 1–2.

[43]Urząd Postępu Naukowo-Technicznego i Wdrożeń, "Ocena realizacji Kompleksowego Programu Postępu Naukowo-Technicznego krajów członkowskich RWPG," KBN Archive, March 1990, pp. 5, 10.

nomic development. As one Hungarian specialist on international science and technology policy explained the situation,

> The point is that we [East European countries] did not import technology from one another, because it was inferior to Western technical levels. The Soviet Union, as a huge market and country, even more cut off from the West, had a demand for technology that was better than its own. It was able to get it from us, because we traded on the gap between the Western level and the Soviet level. We imported technology from the West, produced goods, and exported them to the Soviet Union. We made our profit on that gap. The Soviet Union could not buy personal computers in the West, but we copied them, made them on the basis of Western parts, and exported them to the Soviet Union. We bought little technology from one another, because [CMEA technology] was no advance over our own. If we had done that, we would not have advanced, but would have fallen further behind, and would have lost the Soviet market as well.[44]

The conclusion drawn was that the KP NTP was primarily in the Soviet interest; it was directed toward liquidating the technology gap between East and West, which was the basis of the East European export strategy. This conclusion was reinforced by the Soviet policy of withholding from the program its own most advanced technology, most of which had military applications. It became a widely held view in Eastern Europe that the KP NTP represented in fact a one-way flow of technology to the Soviet Union.[45]

As countries that bought most of their technology from the West, but that sold large quantities of machinery to the Soviet Union, the East European countries regarded their primary interest in the KP NTP as that of producers, and not that of consumers. East European trade negotiators sought to maximize their exports of machinery to the Soviet Union. It comes as no surprise, therefore, that East Europeans who negotiated the details of the KP NTP Priority Programs and their superiors testify that their primary objective was to assure their countries the greatest possible share of machinery exports to the Soviet Union.[46]

The most visible consequence of the East European orientation toward exporting machinery, as we saw in the previous chapter on the Target Programs, was that the national delegations included a great number of projects in the proposed programs that had no direct bearing on their goals. Like an appro-

[44]Interview with Szabo, 8.26.1992.

[45]Interviews with Zbigniew Machula, 5.20.1992; Tamas Szabo, 8.26.1992; Konrad Tott, 6.8.1992; and Andras Zsolnai, 9.1.1992.

[46]Interviews with Janos Czibula, 8.25.1992; Anatol Dikij, 6.2.1992; Ryszard Grabas, 5.26.1992; Dr. Wiesław Grudzewski, 5.19.1992; Joszef Marjai, 9.10.1992; Ladislav Mindoš and Anton Fábik, 7.3.1992; Piotr Pajestka and Ryszard Ziółkowski, 6.3.1992; Zdeněk Šedivý and Dr. J. Ružička, 6.30.1992; Tamas Szabo, 8.26.1992; Matyas Szürös, 9.3.1992; and Ewa Wacowska, 5.25.1992.

priations bill in the U.S. Congress, the programs swelled to match the ambitions of their sponsors. The negotiators hoped that by including a particular product in the KP NTP, they would improve their prospects for exporting that product during the forthcoming round of plan coordination. By 1984, when work began on the detailed cooperation programs, the Soviet Union had begun to impose a series of more stringent conditions on East European manufactured goods, which disqualified some exports that had traditionally been used to balance Soviet exports of raw materials and energy. The East Europeans, consequently, were eager to replace these exports with something that the Soviets would regard as an acceptable substitute, and expected that products included in the KP NTP would be accepted. In addition, it was particularly beneficial for the East Europeans to increase the share of their exports that consisted of goods that formally belonged to the category of "high technology"; such goods generally commanded higher prices than other sorts of machinery and equipment, which were regarded as "traditional" exports.[47] Consequently, the East European strategy was to include as many potential exports as possible in the list of KP NTP projects—quite apart from whether these projects were technologically advanced.[48] The Polish Minister for Science and Technology at the time, Konrad Tott, testifies that,

> The basic problem, as I said before, was that the program was flawed from the outset. Most of the projects that we introduced into the KP NTP, to be honest, did not belong there. There were no criteria to determine what could and could not be included, only political considerations. The sole criterion was, the more the better. So each country proposed whatever was convenient and close at hand. The result was a horror: much too much was included in the program.[49]

In fact, any sense of the program as a coherent whole was destroyed, and it became increasingly unclear whether carrying out the individual projects would actually bring the countries significantly closer to their ultimate goals.

The East European strategy of export promotion also led to a systematic attack on the norms and standards that were set for new products under the KP NTP. The East European countries, as the potential exporters, had an interest in keeping the KP NTP standards low in order to reduce development costs. They knew that in the vast majority of cases, their real technical advances would never accrue to their benefit.[50] The avowed priorities of the integration program, to concentrate on advances in technology, simply conflicted with the

---

[47]Interviews with Dikij, 6.2.1992; Grudzewski, 5.19.1992; Eva Lašová, 6.25.1992; and P. Pajestka and Ziółkowski, 6.3.1992.

[48]Interviews with Mindoš and Fábik, 7.3.1992; P. Pajestka and Ziółkowski, 6.2.1992; Szabo, 8.26.1992; Tott, 6.8.1992; and Wacowska, 5.25.1992.

[49]Interview with Konrad Tott, former Minister, UPNTiW, 6.8.1992.

[50]Interviews with P. Pajestka and Ziółkowski, 6.3.1992; Zsolnai, 9.1.1992; and Szabo, 8.26.1992.

real Soviet priorities as expressed in the negotiations over plan coordination, where very clumsy indicators of technical performance were employed. Meanwhile, the Soviet Leading Organizations that coordinated the work on the detailed cooperation programs also had an interest in keeping the KP NTP standards relatively low, since they were responsible for the completion of the projects under Soviet law. As a result, they failed to conduct the negotiations over product specifications with the diligence needed to overcome East European resistance. A Hungarian expert with long experience dealing with the Soviet Union, who worked directly with dozens of Soviet Leading Organizations, offered this judgment:

> Soviet politics manifested itself here unmistakably. . . . The government *chinovnik* [bureaucrat] knew perfectly well the situation in his area of the economy, and the world scientific level. He knew what could be done, and what had to be done. But if he set high standards, because of the needs of the state, and the enterprises and institutes could not fulfill them, it could later "turn out" that it was because he had done a bad job of planning. The state official had an interest in setting the kind of plan that would be fulfilled. . . . The high party leadership could safely be led by the nose.[51]

The Soviet bureaucracy, once again, had created a set of incentives that defeated its own objectives. Because the criteria for judging success were so inflexible, and the sanctions for failure were so high, the practical matters of satisfying the Plan, and even of drawing up the Plan, were subordinated to the need to avoid blame. Consequently, Soviet negotiators had no interest in representing true state interests; indeed, they dared not attempt to do so. East European trade negotiators, well acquainted with this state of affairs, could rely on the discretion of Soviet officials to avoid pushing too hard to raise quality standards. In the end many observers were left believing that the KP NTP did not achieve anything concrete, because the standards that it set did not require the countries to make substantial improvements in their exports.[52]

Another serious consequence of the need to promote machinery exports was that the East Europeans expressed a decided preference for bilateral cooperation with the Soviet Union over multilateral cooperation. As has been discussed above, this preference led East Germany and Poland to oppose delegating the kinds of powers to the Leading Organizations that would have allowed them to organize multilateral cooperation, with a deep international division of tasks. In the detailed cooperation programs, this expressed itself in what the Polish deputy minister for science and technology, Wiesław Grudzewski, referred to as a "struggle for work-intensivity [*pracochłonność*]."

---

[51]Interview with Szabo, 8.26.1992.

[52]Interviews with Stanisław Długosz, 5.7.1992; Szabo, 8.26.1992; Tott, 6.8.1992; Wacowska, 5.25.1992; and Zsolnai, 9.1.1992.

Each country sought to dominate those projects in which it participated, so that it would be the exporter of the machines and equipment that comprised the final product. The Polish objective was to achieve at least 50 percent participation, although in some cases Poland consented to participate in projects where it had no more than 20 to 25 percent participation.[53] Since the strongest partners—GDR, Poland, and Czechoslovakia—struggled to monopolize the projects in which they participated, and preferred to cooperate directly with the Soviet Union, the KP NTP gradually turned into a series of bilateral Soviet–East European agreements.[54]

The consequence of these incentives was that, instead of following the normative KP NTP procedure of agreeing on a structure of projects and then inserting them into their national plans, the East Europeans followed the reverse policy. Each country had a program for science and technology that predated the KP NTP, and each country strove to insert as many projects as possible from its existing program into the CMEA program. Rather than overtly resist onerous Soviet integration policies, the reorientation of their internal plans, and the accompanying investment outlays, the East Europeans transformed the KP NTP into the mirror image of its original design. In so doing, they believed they were guaranteeing themselves an export market. Since this meant little more than the continuation of the existing science and technology policy, it is not surprising that technical parameters and standards did not change dramatically. Since the existing projects were generally oriented toward export to the Soviet Union, the preference for bilateral cooperation was preserved.

To the annoyance of the Soviets, the East Germans proclaimed this policy openly from the outset.[55] At an early CMEA conference on the KP NTP, the GDR delegate made the following announcement:

> In the GDR, a Proclamation of the Central Committee and the Government has been prepared that assigns concrete tasks to ministries, associations, and the Academy of Sciences for the implementation of GDR obligations in the framework of the Comprehensive Program.
>
> In this regard, we have assumed that all work should be directed toward the achievement of the highest world level and economic efficiency, and toward the expansion of our exports, with consideration of the needs of the USSR and other socialist countries. The draft of the State Plan for the Development of Science and Technology for 1986 contains more than seven hundred concrete tasks that correspond to the priorities and goals of the Comprehensive Program and which

---

[53]Interview with Dr. Wiesław Grudzewski, 5.19.1992.

[54]Interviews with Czibula, 8.25.1992; Grabas, 5.26.1992; Grudzewski, 5.19.1992; Mindoš and Fábik, 7.3.1992; P. Pajestka and Ziółkowski, 6.3.1992; Szürös, 9.3.1992; and Wacowska, 5.25.1992.

[55]Interviews with Grudzewski, 5.19.1992; Leonid Krasnov, 2.27.1992; Marjai, 9.10.1992; and Tott, 6.8.1992.

correspond to the treaties that exist with the Soviet Union and the other countries for this period.[56]

This statement must have galled the Soviets, since on the day it was made, 4 February 1986, no firm contracts had yet been drawn up to determine any country's degree of participation in the KP NTP. Nonetheless, the German delegate could already declare exactly which projects the GDR would carry out, because the GDR intended to follow its existing Plan. The overlap between the GDR Plan and the KP NTP was so great, after the detailed programs had been negotiated, that the GDR participated in 40 percent of the KP NTP projects.[57]

The Polish policy was more subtle, but achieved the same result. Polish negotiators found that there was enough overlap in subject areas between the existing Polish Central Plan for Research and Development (CPBR) and the KP NTP that as many as three-quarters of the CPBR projects could be inserted into the new program.[58] It proved possible to incorporate 80 percent of the previously negotiated bilateral Polish-Soviet program for scientific and technical cooperation into the KP NTP, which indicates how successful the Poles were at limiting their participation to bilateral cooperation with the Soviet Union.[59] "We did what we intended to do all along," explained Minister Tott, "and we called it KP NTP in order to please the Russians. There was never any combination of efforts to gain greater results than we could gain on our own, but we could never say that openly."[60]

The Hungarian position, again, was slightly different, but had very similar results. The Hungarians insisted throughout the negotiations that Hungarian enterprises would participate in the KP NTP on their own initiative, at their own risk, and using their own funds. Under the Hungarian economic reforms, enterprises had substantial freedom to conclude their own contracts, and were expected to make their own investment decisions based on their own balance sheets. The Hungarian government did not enter into any binding commitments regarding the KP NTP, nor did it provide any special funding to finance it. As a result, Hungarian participation in the program was minimal, and was limited for the most part to those areas where Hungarian enterprises already exported technology-intensive goods to the CMEA countries and desired to maintain their markets. The enterprises made successful efforts to include these products in the KP NTP, and did not substantially change their production profiles.[61]

[56]"Stenogramma soveshchaniia predstavitelei stran-chlenov SEV po konkretizatsii prav i obiazannostei golovnykh organizatsii," 2.4–5.1986, CMEA Archive, p. 10.

[57]Interview with Krasnov, 2.27.1992.

[58]Interview with Konrad Tott, 6.8.1992.

[59]Interview with P. Pajestka and R. Ziółkowski, 6.3.1992.

[60]Interview with Konrad Tott, 6.8.1992.

[61]Interviews with Krasnov, 2.27.1992; Marjai, 9.10.1992; Szabo, 8.26.1992; Zsolnai, 9.1.1992; and Pal, 9.3.1992.

IMPLEMENTATION PHASE

After the program had been framed and broken down into a series of concrete projects, it remained to be implemented by the CMEA countries. Since the decision had been made to finance each country's contribution directly from its national budget, this meant that each country had to allot resources for this purpose and include the necessary tasks in the State Plan. Although each country did this in formal terms, implementation was highly selective. In many cases, the promised resources were never provided. In others, projects were funded through the stages of research and development, but the investments needed to bring new products into production were never allocated. In some cases, national authorities decided to terminate projects because they were judged not to be cost-effective, months or years after the contracts had been signed. According to interviews conducted in Poland and Hungary, very little was actually done within the KP NTP that had not in fact been planned before the program was designed.[62] New projects simply received no funding.

A report written by the Institute for the Economy of the World Socialist System in 1988 explains the satellites' lack of interest in carrying out the program.

> Their experience of relations with us proves that they cannot resolve the problems of modernizing and raising the technical level of their products by means of imports from the USSR: we export to them (as, incidentally, they to us) for the most part the technology of yesterday. (It is well known that the share of our machinery exports that is competitive on the world market is approximately 15 percent.) It is impossible to break into the world market with this kind of technological base. Consequently, they are attempting to modernize their production and increase the competitiveness of their exports by means of contacts with the developed countries of the West, even at the price of excessive debts and various concessions.
>
> All the countries signed the Comprehensive Program for Scientific and Technical Progress to the Year 2000 of the Member Countries of the CMEA, but they are not demonstrating great zeal in carrying it out. This is because of errors in the development of the program itself, and also because of the urgency of its mechanism of realization. Disbelief in the program is intensified by the organizational confusion and helplessness of the Soviet Leading Organizations, which were intended to be leaders in its fulfillment.
>
> The lack of clarity about its results (not so much scientific and technological as economic) does not stimulate the foreign participants to invest resources in the research and development of the topics foreseen in the program. The inter-industry

[62]Interviews with Grudzewski, 5.19.1992; Pal, 9.3.1992; Szabo, 8.26.1992; and Tott, 6.8.1992.

character of many of the projects creates additional difficulties that are connected with the subordination of the Leading Organizations in the USSR to [branch] agencies.

As a result, the KP NTP of the CMEA did not exert any noticeable influence on production, especially on cooperation within the CMEA framework, and consequently did not contribute to improving the structure of trade on the socialist market.

An analysis of the practice of cooperation, and of the positions of the CMEA countries in bilateral and multilateral discussions, suggests the conclusion that [the countries] see no potential for a radical improvement of affairs in the development of scientific and technical progress within the socialist commonwealth or for saturation of the market for mutual trade with quality goods in the foreseeable future. The countries have doubts that the Soviet Union, as the main link of the commonwealth, on whom solution of the issues of scientific and technical progress in general depends, will be able to overcome the negative tendencies in its own economic development and carry out a transformation in the process of integration. Therefore, preserving the existing conditions of cooperation, which provide certain advantages to our partners and allow for at least the minimum necessary stability of economic development, has become the point of departure for the majority of them in their economic relations with the USSR, and determines their position in the CMEA. In other words, the countries are acting on the principle, "better a titmouse in the hand than a crane in the sky."[63]

The KP NTP was not implemented, fundamentally, because the CMEA countries did not perceive any interest in carrying it out. By the late 1980s the Soviet Union could no longer promise to modernize East European industry, because only 15 percent of its own products met international quality standards. Cooperating with Western multinational corporations, on the other hand, offered the prospect of real technological advances. Meanwhile, the most profitable arrangement that could be made with the Soviet Union was the one that the East Europeans already had: importing subsidized raw materials and exporting poor-quality machinery. Investing in joint research and development with the Soviet Union would simply undermine these advantageous terms of trade. Perhaps there would indeed have been joint gains if all the countries could have been counted on to contribute, but either they did not believe this was the case or they expected these gains to be smaller than their profits from continuing to exploit the Soviet Union. The prospect of joint gains was further undermined by the program's poor development and the inability of the Soviet bureaucracies to pursue a coordinated policy. As a result, the countries preferred to pursue relatively certain private gains from their advantageous trade structures rather than highly uncertain, long-term

[63]Shastitko and Nekipelov, "Pervoocherednye zadachi formirovaniia ob'edinennogo rynka SEV," IMEPI Archive, IEMSS report 14306/640, 1988.

joint gains by investing in the future of the bloc. "A bird in the hand is worth two in the bush."

These conclusions can be verified for the Polish case because of the existence of a series of files held by the Polish Committee for Scientific Research, which is the successor to the Office for Progress in Science, Technology, and Development, which managed Polish participation in the KP NTP. Whereas the official analysis of the program by the Polish UPNTiW, quoted in the previous section, explains its unsatisfactory results in terms of "errors" made during the design of the detailed cooperation programs, an external audit performed by Poland's Highest Bureau of Control (NIK) identified an important factor that UPNTiW had neglected to discuss.

> Proclamation 48/86 of the Council of Ministers required the chairman of the Committee for Science and Technical Progress . . . to ensure the priority of KP NTP projects. In reality, these principles of financing and implementing the KP NTP projects were not upheld.
>
> . . . The audited organizations explained that only those projects of the program were carried out that had previously been included in the implementation plans of national programs, or that were undertaken on the orders of economic organizations. Other obligations were not fulfilled, if their potential executors did not wish, or were unable, to cover the investments with their own resources. This was equivalent to nonrecognition of the priority of KP NTP projects in the formulation of national programs and the rejection of the order of procedure enjoined by the Proclamation.[64]

In bureaucratic politics, this is the equivalent of a smoking gun. The Council of Ministers had directed the relevant authorities to finance all the projects of the KP NTP, and they had failed to do so, financing instead only their preexisting research program. The audit goes on to accuse UPNTiW, the deputy premier for science and technology, and a series of other organizations of malfeasance:

> The system of supervision and coordination of the KP NTP set forth in Proclamation Nr. 48/86 of the Council of Ministers . . . proved ineffective in practice, primarily because the obligations arising from that Proclamation were not fulfilled. Both the chairman of the Committee for Science and Technical Progress and the directors of the ministries and central organs named in the Proclamation showed insufficient interest and engagement in the implementation of the program, and failed to carry out their obligations in this area.[65]

This would have been a highly charged political accusation were it not for the fact that when the charges were made, Deputy Premier Szałajda, Minister

---

[64]Konarzewski, "Informacja o wynikach kontroli," 9.11.1989, KBN Archive, pp. 15–16. Accepted by Stanisław Mach, Wiceprezes NIK.

[65]Ibid., p. 17.

Tott, and Deputy Minister Grudzewski had all been swept out of office by the new Rakowski government.

The official UPNTiW response to the audit by the Highest Bureau of Control is revealing. The new chairman of UPNTiW, Jan Janowski, rebutted the charges in a letter to the president of the auditing organization, Tadeusz Hupalowski. UPNTiW did not, however, deny the charge that financing had been provided only to projects that predated the KP NTP; rather, Janowski argued that it was a "one-sided approach" to hold Poland to its international commitments.

> The process of implementing the Comprehensive Program for Scientific and Technical Progress to the Year 2000 of the CMEA was influenced by the wider political conditions that accompanied its genesis, and particularly by the domination of the goals and needs of the Soviet partner, according to which Soviet institutions were given a monopoly on fulfilling the function of Leading Organization at the CMEA level. In that context, putting emphasis on the formalistic and legal side, and particularly on the conclusion and implementation of agreements, without the required consideration of their consequences—immediate and potential—is a one-sided approach. . . . The criteria of profitability did not always recommend adherence to, or continuing cooperation in, the framework of the Comprehensive Program.[66]

The argument is that, in fact, it would not have been profitable for Poland to carry out all its commitments under the KP NTP, and that consequently financing was not provided for projects that were deemed to serve Soviet, rather than Polish, interests.

A letter from Marek Bogucki, the deputy chairman of UPNTiW, to Stanisław Mach, the deputy president of the Highest Bureau of Control, laid out the UPNTiW position more explicitly. First, Bogucki argued that the fact that financing under Proclamation 48/86 flowed through "traditional channels," which meant that it came from sources other than UPNTiW, was not technically a breach of the procedure laid down by the Proclamation. He did not claim that all the projects were financed in the end, but rather that one could interpret the Proclamation as upholding the UPNTiW policy of requiring ministries and other economic organizations to fund the majority of KP NTP projects from their own resources.

> The projects arising from the Comprehensive Program were financed according to the framework of central and ministerial research programs. The directors of those programs determined the quantity of necessary funds consistent with their needs and resources, and with their specialized knowledge about the implementa-

---

[66]Jan Janowski, Wiceprezes Rady Ministrów, Minister-Kierownik Urzędu Postępu Naukowo-Technicznego i Wdrożeń, letter to Prezes Najwyzszej Izby Kontroli, Tadeusz Hupalowski, 10.21.1989, KBN Archive, p. 1.

tion of the projects. Pages 15 and 16 [of the Highest Bureau of Control assessment] speak of the assurance of the priority of KP NTP projects by Council of Ministers Proclamation 48/86. However, Article 6, Point 2, of the Proclamation declares that "the general executors of central research and development programs or the coordinators of central programs of basic research shall assure the priority implementation of projects arising from these programs, in correspondence with their research programs."[67]

Under the Polish economic reforms introduced in the 1980s, many economic organizations were permitted to retain a portion of their earnings, and there were overlapping funds of resources, some controlled by the Central Planning Office directly but many disposed of by ministries or by UPNTiW. The passage that Bogucki quotes seems to spread the responsibility for funding the KP NTP to other "central research and development programs or . . . central programs of basic research," which were controlled by other ministries and organizations.

The Polish Highest Bureau of Control, however, had a strong counterargument. According to Proclamation 48/86, "the chairman of the Committee for Science and Technical Progress of the Council of Ministers shall assure that financial resources allocated for the implementation of projects and topics . . . are included in the annual plans of the Central Fund for Research and Development Works [CPBR]."[68] The CPBR was the fund administered by UPNTiW to carry out the preexisting Polish program for science and technology, and the Committee was the organ that directly supervised UPNTiW, so this was equivalent to a direct order to UPNTiW to fund the program. The Proclamation does not specifically state, however, that only UPNTiW funds are to be used, or that UPNTiW was obligated to use its own resources to fund all the projects. This was the interpretation, at any rate, made by UPNTiW. Instructions issued in August 1986 by Minister Konrad Tott, who directed UPNTiW, declare that the financing of KP NTP projects is to come from "resources of the enterprises themselves, bank credits, and subsidies from budget resources . . . obtained with the aid of the Planning Commission of the Council of Ministers, the Ministry of Finance, and UPNTiW."[69] Interviews confirmed that UPNTiW practiced selective financing of KP NTP projects. Only those that predated the program in fact received central funding; others had to be funded by the enterprises themselves or by some other source.[70]

[67]Marek Bogucki, Podsekretarz Stanu, UPNTiW, letter to Stanisław Mach, Wiceprezes Najwyzszej Izby Kontroli, 8.2.1989, KBN Archive, p. 1. The quote from the Proclamation is correct, but comes from article 8, point 2, not from article 6 ("Uchwała Nr 48/86 Rady Ministrów, z dnia 7 kwietnia 1986 r.," KBN Archive, p. 6).

[68]"Uchwała Nr. 48/86 Rady Ministrów z dnia 7 kwietnia 1986 r.," KBN Archive, Article 9.

[69]Konrad Tott, "Instrukcja w sprawie trybu i zasad współpracy," 10.1. 1986, KBN Archive, part 2, point 2.

[70]Interview with P. Pajestka, 6.9.1992, Tott, 6.8.1992.

According to the minutes of a meeting of the Polish Coordinating Council for Implementation of the KP NTP in October 1989, Bogucki continued to defend the UPNTiW policy:

Minister M. Bogucki emphasized in his speech that financing of projects arising from the KP NTP followed the framework of the central and ministerial research programs. There were, however, certain projects that were financed by scientific and research agencies with their own resources. If we had created sources of financing other than the central system, we would have had a situation that was still more complex.[71]

In his letter to Stanisław Mach, cited above, Bogucki goes on to justify the UPNTiW policy of selective financing by arguing that UPNTiW was expected to exercise a degree of discretion in implementing the KP NTP:

The selection of problem areas and projects was governed by the needs of the country as set forth in the preamble to Proclamation 48/86: intensification of the economy, structural transformation, export development, increasing labor productivity, and decreasing consumption of raw materials and energy.

In some cases it was possible to practice complete discrimination at the level of negotiation with our partners from other CMEA countries regarding the detailed programs of cooperation. There were also cases of concessions, which it would be difficult to regard as unjustified. The Polish side undertakes international cooperation when it sees opportunities and interests (which is the cause of the changes discussed on pages 8 and 11 of the draft "Information" [the Highest Bureau of Control assessment]).[72]

In simpler language, Bogucki is saying that while the detailed cooperation programs were being negotiated, Poland had been compelled to participate in some projects that UPNTiW did not consider to be in the Polish interest—projects that failed to promote exports, reduce consumption of raw materials and energy, and improve the efficiency of the Polish economy. These are the same formulas that Polish trade negotiators used to justify to the Soviet Union their disinclination to continue exports that were unprofitable because of the artificial terms of trade established by CMEA pricing rules. The "changes" that were subsequently made, Bogucki argues, were a legitimate exercise of discretion by UPNTiW: projects that were not in the Polish interest were not funded.

This account was confirmed in an interview with Konrad Tott, the minister

[71]"Notatka z 3 posiedzenia Rady Koordynacyjnej," 10.5.1989, KBN Archive. The Council had been formed by Proclamation Nr. 48/86 to implement and monitor the KP NTP, and consisted of representatives of ministerial rank from UPNTiW, the Central Planning Office, and a number of other agencies involved in implementing the program.

[72]Marek Bogucki, Podsekretarz Stanu, UPNTiW, letter to Stanisław Mach, Wiceprezes Najwyzszej Izby Kontroli, 8.2.1989, KBN Archive, p. 1.

of UPNTiW from 1985 to 1988. Tott explained that he was personally convinced from the outset that the KP NTP would not yield any substantial benefits for Poland. It was too hastily designed, too poorly organized, and above all, too thoroughly subordinated to Soviet priorities. Poland, he explained, preferred to continue to finance its preexisting programs for science and technology, which it believed to be more firmly grounded in experience.

> If there had been a real partnership in the KP NTP, we would have taken several times more initiative. We could have agreed with the Planning Commission, with the ministries, and overcome the obstacles. But if the specialists in UPNTiW had so much aversion to the KP NTP, no one else was inclined to make the effort. It was a poor plan that could yield nothing, so we did what was necessary so that there would be no conflict. We did not want to be accused later of being inactive, or give the deputy premiers difficulties when they went to Moscow because we were being recalcitrant, so we formally fulfilled all the requirements of the KP NTP. Actually, it was a bluff, because what we were really implementing was simply our own program.[73]

Given the difficulties of securing funding in a shortage economy, any "priority" not backed up by a strong lobby was likely to be overlooked. But since UPNTiW was convinced that carrying out the KP NTP to the letter would not be in the Polish interest, it never came to a conflict. Tott's understanding was that Proclamation 48/86 was never meant to be implemented: "The Proclamation was a bluff. We could afford to issue ten of them a day, because they cost nothing."

THE FAILURE OF OVERSIGHT

None of the Soviet officials or experts interviewed could identify any Soviet organization that opposed the implementation of the KP NTP, or that had any institutional interest that conflicted with it. Nonetheless, the Soviet government acquiesced in a situation in which its objectives were obstructed, its efforts were frustrated, and a major Soviet foreign policy initiative was reduced to slogans.

During the negotiations over the organizational reforms to accompany the KP NTP, Soviet negotiators acceded to compromises that led to the successive degeneration of the reform package, in spite of expert advice that such compromises would imperil the program. In the judgment of Vladimir Leont'ev, the head of the division of the Soviet State Committee for Science and Technology that supervised the program's development,

> Unfortunately, there were two aspects to the KP NTP that were poorly connected. The political aspect took priority: unity, cooperation, integration. The scientific-

[73]Interview with Tott, 6.8.1992.

technical and organizational aspect took second place, and consequently many basic questions were never resolved. . . . One of the basic obstacles to overcome was that our leadership did not understand what was at stake in designing the organizational details of the KP NTP. Just like a child who is told not to touch a hot stove, they did not understand, and reached out to touch.[74]

Leont'ev described a complicated process of international negotiation, in which numerous committees and subcommittees had to pass judgment on each detail, and where the Soviet proposals could be altered beyond recognition at any stage in the process. Since the officials who led the negotiations often had little appreciation for the subtleties of the issues at stake, irreparable damage could be done. Of course, they had expert advice to guide them; but they did not always follow it, and the experts were not always present when the higher officials met behind closed doors. For his part, Leont'ev found it almost impossible to determine where the opposition was coming from. As he expressed it, "It was a blow from the shadows."

Boris Chumachenko, whose department at MNIIPU authored most of the Soviet proposals, found the process of negotiation similarly frustrating. He insisted that although Olimp Chukanov, the head of the Group of Economic Consultants in the Central Committee, was sufficiently committed to the KP NTP to be willing to make enemies in order to see the program adopted, he had no particular interest in the details. When the experts attempted to explain their organizational proposals, he waved his hands disapprovingly and muttered, "mathematics." Similarly, Guryi Marchuk, the deputy premier for science and technology, and Nikolai Baibakov, the chairman of Gosplan, were generally supportive but did not delve into the details. Chumachenko reserves his most bitter criticism for Nikolai Talyzin who, as deputy premier for CMEA affairs and then chairman of Gosplan, presided over the weakening of several of the MNIIPU proposals.[75]

There is general agreement that the preparation of the KP NTP suffered immensely from the feverish pace set by the Soviet political leadership. Frustrated by the slow progress of the negotiations, and eager to sign the agreements before the 1986–90 Five-Year Plan commenced, the Party leadership overruled MNIIPU estimates of the time needed to consult with the East European countries.[76] During the summer and fall of 1985, Gorbachev and

[74]Interview with Vladimir Leont'ev, former Nachal'nik Upravlenia, Chlen Komiteta, GKNT, 2.21.1992

[75]Interview with Boris Chumachenko, 2.18.1992.

[76]In a memo to the Central Committee dated January 1984, Chumachenko and Ezerov argued that it was possible to finish the "Conceptual Section," or the package of reforms, in time to ratify them at the 1986 Council Session, and that the "detailed cooperation programs" could be developed in 1986–87. This would mean they would be ready in time to become the basis for the coordination of plans for 1991–95, which was scheduled to begin in 1988 (Chumachenko and Ezerov, "Nekotorye soobrazheniia," January 1984, MNIIPU Archive, p. 10). The Central Committee apparatus insisted that the whole process be completed in time to implement the program in

Ryzhkov each personally intervened to urge the negotiators to complete a settlement before the end of the year.[77] Faced with a hard deadline, and intransigent opposition on a series of organizational points from their East European partners, the Soviet negotiators had little option but to compromise.[78] The result, as described above, was that the document had been sanitized by the time it was adopted.

In the negotiations over the detailed cooperation programs, the Soviet negotiators permitted the other countries to include numerous projects that were not germaine, and allowed them to soften the technical standards that embodied their commitment to technological improvement. Instead of collaborating, the countries divided up the projects and carried them out with their own resources according to their preexisting plans. The result was that the programs were thoroughly subverted before they began. East European observers were convinced that the political pressure to complete the program on time destroyed its coherence, and several claimed that this pressure increased the effectiveness of their delaying tactics. Simply by threatening to delay agreement, the East Europeans could compel the Soviets to compromise.[79]

In the implementation phase, Soviet officials stood by as East European governments financed their projects selectively. If the case of Soviet-Czech trade negotiations is representative, the Soviets made no serious attempt to link completion of the KP NTP projects to negotiations about plan coordination, which was the one way that the USSR could have exerted pressure on the East Europeans to fulfill their obligations. Searching the Czechoslovak records of trade negotiations from 1987 to 1990 revealed no instances where performance of KP NTP obligations was put on the agenda for substantive discussion. The subject did not arise in any of the meetings in which the all-important proportions of raw material and machinery exports were negotiated.[80]

The only Soviet-Czech trade document from this period in which the KP NTP is frequently mentioned is the Conception for the Economic, Scientific, and Technical Cooperation of the CSSR and USSR for 15 to 20 Years, which was signed by premiers Ryzhkov and Adamec in February 1989. This document set forth a long-term strategy for economic cooperation, including bilateral specialization in particular kinds of machinery. The Soviets used the negotiations as an opportunity to revise their terms of trade with Czechoslova-

---

1986–90, so the development of the reform package and the detailed programs took place simultaneously and at a frenetic pace (interview with Vladimir Ezerov, 12.9.1991).

[77] Interviews with Krasnov, 2.27.1992, and Ezerov and Korsun, 12.9.1991.

[78] Interview with Szabo, 8.26.1992.

[79] Interviews with Pal, 9.3.1992; Szabo, 8.26.1992; Tott, 6.8.1992; and Zsolnai, 9.1.1992.

[80] I had unrestricted access to the documents preserved in the Archive of the Czechoslovak Ministry of the Economy, the successor to the State Planning Commission (SPK), in the summer of 1992. The officials of the SPK conducted all the substantive negotiations of bilateral coordination of plans, and substantial, though not complete, documentation is preserved.

kia. The KP NTP was frequently referred to, but no specific measures were agreed on. Instead, the Soviet negotiators settled for vague assurances that the "techical level" of Czechoslovak machines and equipment would be raised. There were no numbers or concrete obligations connected to the specialization agreements in machinery; the agreements simply listed types of machines that each country agreed to produce for export. One might be inclined to conclude that the Conception was meant for propaganda purposes, but drafts of the agreement and internal Czechoslovak reports show that many of its details were clearly subject to intense negotiation.[81] Furthermore, the Conception did spell out a number of quantitative agreements regarding the levels of exports of important raw materials and consumer goods for the next five years. The only remaining conclusion is that by 1989, the KP NTP occupied a low position in Soviet priorities, and that the negotiators did not make a serious effort to link performance of obligations assumed under the KP NTP to Soviet bargaining leverage in other areas.[82]

According to Leonid Krasnov, the KP NTP fell victim to a general crisis of faith in socialist integration, a crisis so profound that the Soviet officials charged with implementing the agreement stopped making the effort.

> There was a lack of interest in integration, a lack of stimulus. We felt it physically at every level, from intergovernmental negotiations down to bargaining between enterprises. Gradually, the psychology changed. If in the early 1970s there was a certain optimism about the potential benefits of integration, by the late 1970s an ideology of apathy had set in. One began to hear new phrases: "it's not worth a lightbulb," and, "I spit on it." We lost the belief that by our efforts we could really change things. Everyone was aware of the level of corruption and abuse of privilege in every one of the East European countries, and that led to cynicism.
>
> . . . No ideal models would work here—neither those of MNIIPU, nor of any other origin. By the time of the 116th Session [1985] of the Ispolkom [CMEA Executive Committee], all work on the KP NTP had taken on a formal character. No one really believed in it anymore. Hungary openly declared that it expected nothing to come of the undertaking but was complying with Soviet pressure. The GDR took an even more unconstructive position.[83]

It was not that Soviet officials were unaware of the East European opposition; they simply came to the conclusion that they could do nothing about it.

[81]Prchlík, "Jednání expertů," to the Chairman, SPK, 9.10.1987, SPK Archive. The meeting took place 10.5–9.1987; Ing. Prchlík, "Jednání ustředních plaňovacích orgánů," to the Chairman, SPK, 11. 25.1987, SPK Archive; Dr. Nad', "Informace pro náměstka předsedy," 4.14.1988, SPK Archive; "Sprava o výsledcích první etapy koordinace," to the Chairman, SPK, B. Urban, 6.9.1989, SPK Archive.

[82]"Koncepce hospodářské a vědeckotechnické spolupráce ČSSR a SSSR na příštích 15–20 let," Signed 1.17.1989 by L. Adamec and N. Ryzhkov, Moscow. SPK Archive.

[83]Interview with Leonid Krasnov, 2.27.1992.

CONCLUSIONS

On one level, the Comprehensive Program for Scientific and Technical Progress failed because of the incentives created by artificial trade prices in the Soviet bloc. The East European negotiators opposed Soviet proposals for the organization, design, and implementation of the program, and their preferences prevailed, ultimately frustrating Soviet integration goals. The East Europeans did not oppose integration per se, however, and none of the trade officials interviewed suggested that they were motivated by anything other than commercial interests. Rather, the preexisting pattern of trade negotiations created a set of incentives that compelled the East Europeans to sabotage integration in order to achieve the most advantageous terms of trade possible with the Soviet Union. This is the most compelling explanation for the pattern of events. The KP NTP was not deliberately sabotaged by the Soviet bureaucracy; it was not until the Soviet proposals met East European opposition that they began to erode. The implementation of the KP NTP was not blocked by interest groups or factions in the East European countries; the strategic elites in Eastern Europe held a consensus that opposed allocating additional resources to finance it.

On a deeper level, the case of the KP NTP demonstrates the degree to which institutional failures crippled the performance of Soviet foreign economic policy. Soviet negotiators bargained away the entire structure of organizational reforms that was intended to ensure the implementation of the program. Next, Soviet experts allowed the East European negotiators to wreak havoc on the technical details of the program, bloating the problem areas with incompatible projects and driving technical standards down to the lowest common level of mediocrity. Finally, Soviet trade negotiators made no effort to enforce East European obligations, so the satellites could freely renege on any agreements that turned out to be unprofitable. During three different phases of negotiation, in three different bureaucratic contexts, and on a staggering multitude of concrete issues, Soviet officials compromised principle to preserve form.

There was a remarkable failure of communication in the Soviet hierarchy. Upper-level Soviet policymakers were poorly informed about the policy decisions they had to make. Lower-level officials tailored their advice to their superiors' naive expectations, however, because they feared the consequences of excessive candor. Numerous low-level officials watched as the entire undertaking gradually unraveled, but found it more advantageous to allow the policy to go awry than to communicate their concerns to their superiors. Even the program's designers, the experts from MNIIPU, failed to advocate the kind of sweeping changes of incentive structures they knew were essential in order to overcome the barriers to technology transfer in the planned economy. Instead, they proposed a series of organizational adjustments that they knew would be inadequate to the task.

Meanwhile, the incentives imposed by the central planning system pushed Soviet negotiators to undermine the program. The Soviet Leading Organizations had no incentive to uphold the highest technical standards during the negotiations that developed the detailed cooperation programs, since those standards would simply complicate their efforts to fulfill their plan quotas. Knowing the biases of central planning, furthermore, they knew that they could lower technical standards without being exposed. In addition, Soviet negotiators were hampered at each phase of the program's development by the fact that their superiors pushed them to meet unrealistic deadlines. Over expert objections, the detailed cooperation programs were negotiated in tandem with the package of organizational reforms. Finally, the negotiators were pushed to complete the program in time for the beginning of the 1986–90 Five-Year Plan. Faced with a hard deadline and implacable East European opposition, the Soviet negotiators sacrificed the program's organizational details and seriously compromised the program's technical integrity. By no intentional design, the Soviet bureaucracy put a higher value on deadlines than on the quality of its proposals.

The most disastrous institutional failure was neglecting to enforce East European obligations. No organization was obligated to defend a comprehensive view of the Soviet national interest, and no official had an incentive to dredge up past controversies. Foreign trade negotiators developed no routine for evaluating East European progress toward achieving KP NTP objectives, and were never evaluated according to their ability to monitor the satellites. Consequently, the whole complex of issues was ignored in bilateral trade negotiations. The result was that all the hard-won compromises contained in the program unraveled, and the East Europeans turned it into a smorgasbord: they took what they wanted and left the rest on the table. The weakness of the Soviet bureaucracy allowed the satellites to impose their own preferences.

CHAPTER 9

Perestroika and the Unified Socialist Market

MIKHAIL GORBACHEV surprised his country, his East European allies, and the Soviet Union's traditional opponents by launching a reform program of unprecedented breadth and significance, which transformed every aspect of Soviet life, and which in 1991 finally toppled the system he was trying to reform. He has since stated repeatedly that his goal was to reform socialism, not to destroy it; in that sense at least, the experiment of perestroika has to be considered a failure. Perestroika, however, was a multifaceted enterprise, and one could measure its success on many dimensions. This chapter is limited to the sphere of Soviet–East European trade relations and a brief time period. To what extent did the Soviet Union achieve the short-term goals it had set forth in reforming its foreign economic relations before the collapse of the Soviet bloc in 1989–90? I will argue that the most ambitious Soviet attempt to re-form the CMEA had apparently already failed before the dramatic political events of 1989 swept it away.

This chapter has four sections. The first seeks to define the mature Soviet conception of perestroika in foreign economic relations, which represented the optimal program of the Gorbachev leadership. The second describes the positions the various countries took in the negotiations on CMEA reform, arguing that many of the East European objections can be traced to attempts to protect the countries' privileged terms of trade with the Soviet Union. The third section shows how the principles of the Soviet reform program were blunted in the course of negotiations in the CMEA. The fourth argues that the reforms that were adopted in principle were frustrated in the key phase of implementation, the negotiation of the trade plan for 1991–95. Since these negotiations were largely completed before the collapse of the CMEA, one can draw tentative conclusions about the limits reform would have faced if not for the political upheaval of 1989.

SOVIET CONCEPTIONS OF PERESTROIKA

The Gorbachev period was a time of flux in Soviet domestic politics and foreign policy, and Soviet trade relations with Eastern Europe were inevitably caught up in the ebb and flow of reform's fortunes in Moscow. Mikhail Gorbachev became general secretary without a clear mandate or constituency for change, but amid widespread expectations that changes would be made because they were so manifestly needed. His first three years were largely occupied with the business of palace politics and courting important constituencies; it was not until 1988 that his appointees controlled the Politburo, Central Committee, Red Army high command, and KGB. Meanwhile, important policy decisions were being made, which opened up Soviet politics, society, and economic life—but always cautiously, in a stepwise fashion, and after many compromises and all due burcaucratic process. Most of the concrete implications of the changing policies in the Kremlin were worked out by old hands, officials who had seen general secretaries come and go, and who must have felt uncertain about the staying power of the current reformist course. The process of ruling often overwhelmed policy-making. The strategic vision of the leadership was unclear, and the hand on the rudder was unsteady.

The Soviet leadership felt impelled to act in the mid-1980s by a growing sense of crisis within the community of economic experts. Confidential reports from the Institute for the Economy of the World Socialist System presented a picture of a Soviet economy unable to maintain its international commitments and a socialist commonwealth in stagnation and under siege from the superior attractive power of the West. The following excerpt is from a briefing paper for the Central Committee written in November 1985:

> The "structural barrier" has become an increasingly serious obstacle to expanding cooperation, because the potential to increase exports of fuel and raw materials from the USSR to the CMEA countries is rapidly narrowing. In 1981–84, production of the most important export commodities has held even (crude oil, black coal, iron, and manganese ores), while production of other commodities has declined every year (sawn lumber, cotton fiber, brown coal). Meanwhile, although machinery and equipment production has increased (26 percent in 1981–84), it has not been possible to use [machinery] exports to compensate for the slowing growth of fuel and raw material exports. In fact, the physical level of machinery exports to the European CMEA countries has dropped 13–15 percent during this period.
>
> . . . The situation that has emerged impels the CMEA countries, on the one hand, to strengthen cooperation among themselves excluding the USSR and, on the other, to develop economic ties outside the boundaries of the socialist commonwealth.
>
> . . . Therefore, the present model of cooperation in fact has no future. Moreover, maintaining this model is fraught with serious economic and political consequences: the development of tendencies toward disintegration, and the weakening of the leading position of the USSR in the commonwealth.[1]

[1]Shastitko et al., "Tezisy vystuplenniia 'O dolgosrochnoi strategii razvitiia vneshneeknomicheskikh sviazei SSSR so stranami SEV,'" to Olimp Chukanov, Head of the Group of Economic Experts in the Department for Socialist Countries, CC CPSU, 11.28.1985, IMEPI Archive, IEMSS report, pp. 1–4.

The extensive model of growth, which had led to the rapid industrialization of the Soviet Union and Eastern Europe, had been based upon ever-increasing exports of Soviet raw materials and energy. The Soviet Union, however, could no longer afford to expand its exports of these commodities. Seeing no prospect of solving their problems in cooperation with the Soviet Union, the East Europeans turned increasingly to the West. Poland became heavily indebted to Western Europe. Hungary joined the IMF. Soviet observers felt their grip on Eastern Europe weakening, and the IEMSS urged sweeping reform to create a new interest in integration.

Aleksandr Nekipelov argues that the IEMSS analysis was very influential, but the bottom line that convinced the Central Committee bureaucracy "more than the usual tinkering" was required to pull the CMEA out of crisis was the sharp decline in the real volume of CMEA trade.[2] Nekipelov was a coauthor of most of the IEMSS reports on CMEA affairs in the mid- to late 1980s, and as deputy director he played an important role in the later negotiations over the course of reform. The first stage in the development of the Soviet position was the preparation for the Conference at the Highest Level in November 1986, which the Communist Party of the Soviet Union called to give a new impulse to CMEA integration. The declaration adopted in November, however, was very general, simply reaffirming traditional solutions to traditional problems: joint planning, specialization, scientific and technical cooperation, and a litany of already-adopted, long-term agreements.[3] The Party turned to IEMSS again once the conference was over.

> Once the decision had been made, it needed to be carried out, so once again the Central Committee apparatus turned to our institute: what needs to be done? The institute had been preparing for this eventuality, so we presented a series of recommendations. The Central Committee apparatus was shocked by the far-ranging nature of the proposals, which entailed a gradual transition to market mechanisms in CMEA trade and within the CMEA countries. A series of discussions followed, some of them not very pleasant, with Central Committee officials who urged more moderate reform proposals. We wrote various versions, and gradually our position was adopted.[4]

The Soviet negotiating position gradually evolved, but it is accurate to say that all the major points of the mature version circulated in 1989 were present in IEMSS drafts written as early as 1987.[5] Even the phrase that became the

---

[2]Interview with Aleksandr Nekipelov, 2.21.1992.

[3]"Zaiavleniie ob osnovnykh napravleniiakh dal'neishego razvitiia i uglubleniia ekonomicheskogo i nauchno-tekhnicheskogo sotrudnichestva stran-chlenov SEV," Reshenie ekonomicheskogo soveshchaniia stran-chlenov SEV na vyshem urovne, 11.10–11.1986, CMEA Archive.

[4]Interview with Aleksandr Nekipelov, 2.21.1992.

[5]Compare "Soobrazheniia o perestroike mekhanizma ekonomicheskoi integratsii stran-chlenov SEV," 12.1987, a document prepared by IEMSS that became the official "Proposal of the Soviet

watchword of perestroika in the CMEA, the goal of forming a "Unified So-cialist Market," was coined by an IEMSS deputy director, Vadim Shastitko. Shastitko was unexpectedly asked to address the gathered deputy premiers of the CMEA countries in 1987. A fine extemporaneous speaker, he gave an enthusiastic pitch for radical reform, surprising the East Europeans by daring to call the transferable ruble a "shadow dollar," and in the spirit of the moment he called for formation of a "unified socialist market." His superiors appar-ently liked the phrase, and it stuck.[6]

In all fairness, one must acknowledge that the reforms of the CMEA pro-posed by IEMSS and promoted by the Soviet Union were limited and unorigi-nal. They were limited in that they presupposed that the end point of reform was a socialist economy along the lines of the Hungarian model, rather than a capitalist market economy. They were unoriginal because in almost every case, they recycled proposals that had been made twenty years before in the Polish, Hungarian, and Czechoslovak position papers for the Comprehensive Program. The Soviet proposals outlined reforms in four major areas: coor-dination of planning, foreign trade prices, domestic legal codes, and national exchange rates.

In the area of plan coordination, the Soviet goal was to convert the annual cycles of meetings from trade negotiations into consultations on long-term economic policy. This would increase their significance in some respects and decrease it in others. The meetings would become forums for discussing the course of reform in the various countries, and as more domestic reforms were introduced, the areas for coordination would proliferate: monetary policy, tax policy, tariff policy, and so on. Meanwhile, intergovernmental bargaining over concrete trade flows would gradually be phased out in favor of enterprise initiative. In the short term, which covered the cycle of coordination of plan-ning for 1991–95, the countries should narrow the range of goods covered by physical quotas, expand the use of more flexible "value" quotas, and intro-duce nonquota trade on a large scale. The volume of planned trade should be reduced, allowing the enterprises room to forge their own trade agreements.

Experts" with only minor changes to its title, and A. D. Nekipelov et al., "Predlozheniia Sovet-skoi storony k Tselostnoi kontseptsii perestroiki mekhanizma mnogostoronnego sotrudnichestva i sotsialisticheskoi ekonomicheskoi integratsii i deiatel'nosti SEV," 3.31.1989, IMEPI Archive, IEMSS report 14306/402. The two versions contain the same concrete proposals. Successive drafts of the latter document in the IMEPI Archive show that the institute had an essential role in editing the final version: IEMSS reports 14306/1417 (1988), 14306/279 (1989), and 14306/382 (1989).

[6]Shastitko's account of the event is secondhand, from an interview with Aleksandr Nekipelov, 2.21.1992. Stanisław Długosz, deputy chairman of the Polish Planning Commission, was present at the meeting, and years later recalled his surprise at Shastitko's words (interview, 6.8.1992). The text of Shastitko's presentation is in "Stenogramma vstrechi postoiannykh predstavitelei stran v SEV," 6.5.1987, CMEA Archive, pp. 48–53.

In order to foster this development, the Soviet Union proposed that the next round of trade coordination be negotiated in three phases: at the intergovernmental phase, the ministry phase, and the enterprise phase. The agreements reached should take on increasing degrees of specificity as they incorporated increasing degrees of initiative by economic units.[7]

In the area of foreign trade prices, the ultimate Soviet goal was a convergence of CMEA prices and world prices. For 1991–95, however, it was assumed that only a moderate price reform was feasible. The Soviets proposed that the current CMEA pricing practice be retained for goods traded in quotas. The CMEA used a complex formula to calculate what were known as "contractual" trade prices based on a running average of world market prices, which in effect guaranteed that price distortions would persist. For goods that were traded in nonquota trade, however, the Soviet Union proposed that the enterprises making an exchange be allowed to negotiate the price of the product and all the conditions of trade, such as financing and service. Price distortions would persist as long as the countries had domestic price structures that did not reflect global conditions of supply and demand, and as long as they had inconvertible currencies with artificial exchange rates; but "negotiated" prices should be less distorted than the existing contractual prices, and they should become less and less distorted as the countries carried out domestic reforms. The following is an excerpt from a briefing paper sent by IEMSS to the deputy chairman of the Council of Ministers for CMEA affairs, Nikolai Talyzin, in 1988:

> Under conditions where the core of the mechanism of cooperation remains bilateral coordination of plans exclusively in the form of regulating physical quantities of exports, the formation of contractual prices on the basis of world prices remains not only the most expedient, but also the *single possible* solution.
>
> In the portion [of trade] in which quota trade is maintained, the application of world prices is necessary as a contractual basis. If the structure of trade is assigned from above, then prices are necessary only for accounting, in order to assure *mutually profitable* exchange. The single objective criterion for determining their proportions is *world prices*.
>
> . . . As far as negotiated price formation is concerned, that is, the redistribution of authority to set prices to the advantage of the immediate economic subjects, it becomes necessary only once nonquota trade is introduced. In this connection, the important consequence of negotiated price formation is not that it moves away from consideration of world prices, but rather [that it accomplishes] the transition to a system in which the price begins to play the structure-determining role that is presently lacking, and in which price formation ceases to be carried out according to an inflexible schema. Only within the framework of

[7]Nekipelov et al., "Predlozheniia Sovetskoi storony k Tselostnoi kontseptsii perestroiki," 3.31.1989, IMEPI Archive, IEMSS report pp. 22–23.

nonquota trade can the negotiated price fulfill the function of an economic catalyst of real specialization and cooperation. The fundamental prerequisite for
introducing negotiated price formation is the introduction of (initially limited)
convertibility of national currencies according to more or less (initially calculated) realistic exchange rates.[8]

This was the view that was ultimately adopted. The Soviet decision to allow
the introduction of equivalency in trade in effect to await the gradual expansion of nonquota trade was a fateful one. It had three important consequences.
First, it avoided the danger that the CMEA countries would immediately drop
out of the Soviet orbit, as they might if they no longer received a trade subsidy. Second, it slowed the course of reform, because without meaningful
foreign-trade prices, enterprises had no solid basis to be interested in international cooperation. Third, it gave the East European countries a strong
incentive to prevent the expansion of nonquota trade, since it would be accompanied by the end of their lucrative contract prices.

In the area of domestic legal reform, the goal was to transform the enterprise from a link in the bureaucratic chain of command into an economic
subject that, although owned by the state, was still capable of maximizing its
profits. The Soviet Union proposed a long-term convergence of the legal systems of all the CMEA countries in order to allow enterprises to exercise the
same rights and have the same access to markets in all the countries. Ultimately, this should lead to a "Unified Socialist Market" patterned on the
"Single Market" of the European Community: a tariff union, with free movement of goods, services, people, and capital. For 1991–95, however, the
objectives were to liberalize the trade regulations of the CMEA countries to
allow enterprises to participate in direct ties, to import and export goods, and
to negotiate prices. Each enterprise was to exercise the right to choose its own
partners. In addition, the countries were to establish internal markets for
wholesale goods, which would gradually allow foreign enterprises to buy and
sell competitively. The countries would experiment with a wide variety of
forms of direct ties, including auctions and joint firms. National trade regulations were gradually to be replaced by financial instruments, such as tariffs,
subsidies, and excise taxes.[9]

In the monetary sphere, the ultimate Soviet objective was to make all the
CMEA currencies convertible, and to make the transition from bilateral clearing to multilateral hard-currency trade. For 1991–95, however, the goals were
more modest. The countries were encouraged to expand operations in con-

---

[8]Shastitko et al., "Materialy po osnovnym problemam razvitiia integratsionnogo sotrudnichestva," to N. V. Talyzin, Deputy Chairman of the USSR Council of Ministers for CMEA Affairs,
10.25.1988, IMEPI Archive, IEMSS report, pp. 13–15.

[9]Nekipelov et al., "Predlozheniia Sovetskoi storony k Tselostnoi kontseptsii perestroiki,"
3.31.1989, IMEPI Archive, IEMSS report, pp. 4–6.

vertible currency, to introduce the use of national currencies gradually in accounting for direct ties between enterprises, and to take the first steps toward convertibility. According to the March 1989 version of the Soviet position, by 1995 the countries should:

- Introduce and gradually expand the practice of accounting for intergovernmental trade in convertible currency, including in the form of clearing;
- Gradually introduce various forms of convertibility among the national currencies;
- Expand the use of national currencies, above all of the Soviet ruble, in accounting for direct ties and other forms of economic cooperation by interested countries;
- Form an appropriate financial infrastructure (monetary auctions, commodity markets, chains of banks and their branches, and systems of communications) to provide operational service and credit for direct ties and other new forms of cooperation between the enterprises and organizations of the CMEA countries.[10]

This was far from full convertibility, but these were important steps in that direction. For the transitional period, the countries were to calculate rates of exchange for their currencies based on wholesale buying-power parities, and introduce convertibility of CMEA currencies to one another on that basis. Once domestic markets formed, it was hoped that exchange rates could be set by supply and demand.[11]

These were limited reforms. It should be clear that a huge leap of faith separated the concrete, market-oriented reforms proposed for 1991–95 from the postulated end point of a unified market. There can be no doubt that these limited measures, even if fully implemented, would not themselves have solved most of the region's economic problems. A further liability was that the postulated reforms depended significantly on one another. A failure to progress toward freeing the enterprise to conduct foreign trade, for example, would nullify any progress made toward convertibility. In addition, certain very important reforms were not proposed. The Soviet Union did not propose to move rapidly to introduce hard-currency trading, which was the one step that could quickly establish equivalency in CMEA trade prices. Nevertheless, the Soviet proposals contained concrete steps that could have substantially improved economic cooperation among centrally planned, socialist economies.

THE INTERESTS OF THE COUNTRIES

The Soviet proposals for perestroika met more open and determined opposition than had any previous Soviet initiative in the CMEA. As in the case of the

[10]Ibid., p. 24.
[11]Ibid., p. 26.

Comprehensive Program, objections to the Soviet conception of a unified market emerged on two levels: that of general principles, and that of particular interests. On the level of general principles, the countries' positions diverged according to their domestic reform policies: the most advanced reformers (the Hungarians) criticized the Soviet reform for falling short, whereas the most conservative proponents of central planning (the Romanians and East Germans) lambasted it for undermining the infrastructure of socialism. The disputes on this level were genuine, and one cannot reduce all of them to reflections of the on-going struggle over terms of trade. The majority of the positions the countries took, however, citing "political" considerations, were actually motivated by material interests. Meanwhile, the East European satellites devised a variety of proposals designed to defend their privileged terms of trade with the Soviet Union. In the end, even the most reform-minded countries shied away from particular reform proposals when they perceived a threat to their material interests.

At the most general level, the East Europeans were content to follow the Soviet lead. Wide consensus was reached as early as 1986 that dramatic changes were required in order to put the CMEA economies on a par with those of the capitalist West. It was not long, however, before the diversity of views in the socialist camp sprang into bold relief. Stanisław Długosz, a former deputy chairman of the Polish Planning Commission described the situation:

> The period of rather monolithic Soviet control ended in 1984 or 1985, and the CMEA countries formed several camps. At first it was just Poland and Hungary—I should say, Hungary and then Poland—in favor of reform, with the USSR, CSSR, and GDR opposed. Romania always took its own, special position. Then Bulgaria joined our group, then the CSSR.[12]

At the end of 1986 the Soviet Union joined the reform camp by extending its commitment to perestroika to the realm of international affairs. It was far from clear in 1986 that Gorbachev's program would entail radical reform of the Soviet economy, however, so the countries' consent to abstract commitments to reform was easily obtained. After the Conference on the Highest Level in November, when the countries' negotiators sat down to the work of turning these general intentions into a reform program, a great number of controversies arose. According to a report prepared by IEMSS,

> The line for a radical perestroika of the economic cooperation of the CMEA member countries and of the activity of the Council, which the CPSU proposed during the working meeting in Moscow in 1986, was supported by the majority of the fraternal parties.
> However, in the course of designing the concrete means to promote integration during the preparation of the decisions of the Forty-third Session of the CMEA,

[12]Interview with Długosz, 6.8.1992.

fundamental differences regarding the direction, magnitude, and depth of the proposed transformation still appeared in the positions of particular countries.[13]

"A group of countries," the report continued, "in the first place Romania and the GDR, and also Cuba, in fact do not accept the conception of perestroika of the mechanism of cooperation suggested by the Soviet Union, although they have not announced this openly."[14] The Soviet negotiators had become accustomed to Romanian opposition, indeed to the extent that Nikolae and Elena Ceauşescu had become a favorite subject of jokes in the halls of the CMEA building in Moscow. As was noted in chapter 6, most of the Romanian objections were superficial, touching on the putative autonomy of the satellites rather than on the essential issues of contention in the bloc, so the objections could be easily ignored by the Soviet delegations. Because Romania had a small share in CMEA trade, it was not essential in many cases to secure Romanian agreement in order to move forward. In the negotiations on perestroika in the CMEA, Romania confirmed these conclusions by objecting to the titles of documents and introducing motions to reexamine and implement vague, outdated documents on specialization.[15]

East Germany, however, was an entirely different case. The GDR was the largest Soviet trading partner. The Germans rarely opposed the Soviet Union in the CMEA, and when they chose to do so, they usually won their point. When the GDR took an adamantly obstructive position, Soviet negotiators became concerned.[16] The German delegate to the 123d meeting of the Ispol-

---

[13]Shastitko and Nekipelov, "Pervoocherednye zadachi formirovaniia ob'edinennogo rynka SEV," 1988, IMEPI Archive, IEMSS report p. 1.

[14]Ibid., p. 3.

[15]"Stenogramma vstrechi postoiannykh predstavitelei stran v SEV," 10.12.1987, CMEA Archive, pp. 3, 16–26, 27–33.

[16]The following excerpt from a 1987 letter from Oleg Bogomolov to Deputy USSR Permanent Representative to the CMEA, Aleksandr Rusanov (personal files, IMEPI) underlines the seriousness of the conflict with the GDR over perestroika.

In accordance with your request, I am sending the observations of the Institute about the material received from the GDR regarding the preliminary draft declaration of the Forty-third CMEA Session, "On Perestroika of the Mechanism of Socialist Economic Integration and the Activity of the Council for Mutual Economic Assistance."

This material, in our opinion, is impossible to assess other than as a revision by the GDR of the consensus reached at the November 1986 working meeting of the leaders of the Communist and Workers' Parties of the CMEA member countries on issues of perestroika of the activity of the Council and raising the cooperative integration of the fraternal countries to a new level. Making such a sharp assessment, we proceed from the fact that the basic leitmotif of the document presented is to confirm the adequacy of the existing forms and methods of cooperation for meeting tasks in the sphere of mutual economic relations of the CMEA member countries. The GDR not only did not introduce a single concrete proposal to improve cooperation, but in fact introduced no arguments against the proposals contained in the preliminary draft declaration of the Forty-third CMEA Session.

In our view, these circumstances will make the upcoming bilateral consultations most

kom in June 1987, Guenther Kleiber, made it quite clear that he regarded any reform of the system of coordinating plans as incompatible with the East German economy.

> Comrades, if trade is to be coordinated only for the basic types of goods in the future, along with the strategic areas for cooperation, the question inevitably arises (and I beg your indulgence for raising yet another question), which goods are included in the category of "basic goods," and which in the category of "less important goods." Opinions diverge radically, depending on who is an exporter and who is an importer. In this connection, we should be aware that for objective reasons the structure of trade has been different for each country, and remains different, particularly in trade with the Soviet Union. Therefore we regard the coordination of mutual exports according to concrete products, on the basis of a nomenclature determined bilaterally, to be an important achievement, which makes it possible to carry out a more planlike development of our economies. We regard demands for the creation of conditions for the free exchange of goods, services, and other factors of production among the CMEA member countries as incompatible with the necessity of strengthening the planlike cooperation of our countries.[17]

Kleiber went on to argue that the CMEA had an adequate conception of how to develop trade between its members, namely, the KP NTP, and the CMEA countries would be better advised to get to work carrying it out than to devise dubious improvements to the existing system. As far as East Germany was concerned, the existing system of price formation was preferable to one that might more closely emulate the world market. Furthermore, Kleiber argued, the existing transferable ruble provided all the support that was needed for effective economic and technological exchange. Using national currencies instead would simply be a regressive development, and creating a tariff union would simply retard CMEA ties with developing countries. In short, the GDR rebuffed all the Soviet proposals.[18]

An IEMSS report from the summer of 1987 went so far as to claim that compromise was impossible with some of the CMEA countries, because the points of dispute were the fundamental principles of reform.

> The disagreements with some of the countries have a principled character, and in fact exclude the possibility of any convergence of opinions. This particularly applies to the GDR and Romania, which in essence reject the conception of

---

difficult for the Soviet side, since in fact two contradictory approaches to the future of improving the economic mechanism of socialist integration will clash.

[17]"Stenogramma 123 zasedaniia Ispolnitel'nogo Komiteta Soveta Ekonomicheskoi Vzaimopomoshchi, Plenarnoe zasedanie," 6.4.1987, CMEA Archive, p. 31.

[18]Ibid., pp. 28a–30, 32, 33.

radical perestroika of the system of cooperation, and speak in favor of the preservation of the existing forms and methods of work. Objectively, they are repudiating the conclusions of the Conference on the Highest Level, which took place in November 1986 in Moscow.[19]

The transcripts of CMEA meetings demonstrate that East European countries also exerted very strong pressure on behalf of perestroika. At the 123d Ispolkom Session in June, Jozsef Marjai, the Hungarian representative, insisted that international economic cooperation could not be improved without a radical reform of its financial instruments.

> We consider the integral condition for raising socialist international coopera-
> tion to a higher level to be the adjustment of the economic mechanism of that
> cooperation to the new demands of systematically developing commercialization
> [*tovarno-denezhnye otnosheniia*]. Without this, autonomy cannot be achieved for
> economic organizations or their direct ties, or only in part, and with very poor
> results, since at present the necessary conditions have not been satisfied to any
> significant degree. The greatest backwardness is observed namely in this area.[20]

In an unrehearsed exchange of views that followed the Ispolkom meeting, Marjai made his point more forcefully, setting himself in direct opposition to the GDR delegate.

> You have to look at the data, which our institutes sum up so beautifully, which
> demonstrate the stagnation of trade in the CMEA, even in the key industries, and
> the reductions, which show that socialist integration, and its individual countries
> taken together and individually, are losing their position in the world. I beg your
> pardon, but the fact that this happens to refer in the least degree to the GDR
> makes no difference. I think that Comrade Shastitko correctly characterized the
> essence of this whole issue, when he saw the key question in relation to the role
> of economic organizations in the most recent period. . . .
>
> I think that, in the way Comrade Kleiber has formulated the issue, there is
> barely a subject for discussion between us.[21]

The Polish delegate, Władysław Gwiazda, took a similar position, arguing that there could be no compromise with the hard-line opposition threatening to enervate attempts at reform.

> Our apprehension concerns the possibility of achieving essential progress in
> the area of integration and the development of cooperation. [It] arises from the

---

[19]Nekipelov, "O khode i perspektivakh sovmestnoi rabote stran-chlenov SEV po perestroike integratsionnogo sotrudnichestva," to the CPSU Sekretariat, 1987, IMEPI Archive, IEMSS report, pp. 1–2.

[20]"Stenogramma 123 zasedaniia Ispolnitel'nogo Komiteta Soveta Ekonomicheskoi Vzaimo-pomoshchi, Plenarnoe zasedanie," 6.4.1987, CMEA Archive, p. 20.

[21]"Stenogramma vstrechi postoiannykh predstavitelei stran v SEV," 6.5.1987, CMEA Archive, pp. 59–61.

completely different approach that some countries take to analyzing the cooperation that has existed in the CMEA to this point, and the urgent necessity to move that cooperation in new directions. . . . The development of an integrated, long-term conception to change the economic, organizational, and legal mechanism, and carrying it to completion, demands a different approach from all the CMEA member countries. The absence of such unity means in practice that it will be necessary to find compromise decisions, to limit ourselves to half-measures, and to narrow the dimensions of perestroika. We cannot resolve a single one of the mature issues that are hampering the growth of cooperation in this way, for example, such issues as currency convertibility and multilateral trade balancing. Under such circumstances, we should seriously consider introducing the principle of developing several proposals that concern changes in the mechanism of cooperation by those countries that are prepared to agree to them, leaving the possibility for other countries to join this resolution later.

We are deeply convinced that compromise decisions on the most essential issues will not allow us to achieve the goals that our leaders have set.[22]

The reformist camp was just as adamant as its opponents; compromise was out of the question.

The positions the countries took roughly corresponded to the degree of economic reform that they were pursuing domestically. The Hungarian and Polish delegations began distributing a common position paper in mid-1987, and thereafter took essentially the same positions on a variety of issues, from joint planning to price reform to currency reform. The Polish reforms of the mid-1980s brought the Polish economy much closer to the Hungarian model, although the reforms were not systematically implemented. The GDR and Romania did not tinker with their domestic economic systems, and both remained solidly opposed to change in the CMEA, although with some nuances. For example, the GDR supported eventual convertibility for the transferable ruble, higher interest rates for CMEA transactions, and a reduction in the number of CMEA Permanent Commissions. Until the end of 1989 Bulgaria and Czechoslovakia plotted cautious, middle-course positions. Each initiated moderate reform programs, with most of the adjustments put off into the next decade, and each followed events in the Soviet Union closely to divine the political fate of perestroika. They supported reform proposals the Soviet Union put forward, but not very energetically, and they did not join their Hungarian and Polish colleagues in criticizing Soviet concessions. The conciliatory tone of Rudolf Rohliček's comments in the round-table meeting following the 123d Ispolkom session was typical:

The recommendations we have just agreed on in the Draft Proclamation of the Forty-third Session of the Council, in my opinion, correspond to the Czechoslovak principles of perestroika of the economic mechanism.

[22]"Stenogramma 123 zasedaniia Ispolnitel'nogo Komiteta Soveta Ekonomicheskoi Vzaimopomoshchi, Plenarnoe zasedanie," 6.4.1987, CMEA Archive, p. 49.

What is the most important way in which they correspond? In the fact that it is necessary, in order that we can make the effort in general, not to adopt the kind of decisions that will be fully realized by tomorrow. It is essential that we begin reconstruction, so that in all productive spheres, and both as exporters and consumers, we might orient ourselves on the basis of a deeper understanding of our partners' needs.

I do not intend to polemicize, but I believe that free movement of goods and services is not at all in contradiction with the planlike management of the national economy.[23]

The Czechoslovak delegation was alone among the CMEA countries in expressing approval of the compromise text at this point in its development, which, on the one hand, is a good sign of the Czechoslovak side's acceptance of reform, and on the other, lack of ambition on its behalf. Rohlíček struck a moderate posture, arguing against impetuous reforms but simultaneously seeking to soften the East German contention that reform was incompatible with central planning. Vladislav Cihlař, who had helped to shape the radical Czechoslovak position on the Comprehensive Program in 1968 and was still advising the premier in the late 1980s, explained the reticent Czechoslovak position on reform in the 1980s in this way:

[General Secretary Miloš] Jakeš opposed reforms. At this point, the CSSR wanted some weakening of the monopoly of foreign trade, wanted to join the IMF, and wanted to consider weakening the links between enterprises and the Planning Commission. Our recommendations at the CMEA level were very similar to our domestic reforms. If you compare the two, they did not go further. We were in a difficult position, because we knew that our political leadership did not want any changes in the political structure. We felt that there was no sense in proposing more than we were in a position to carry out in our own country; that was just pragmatic.

It was impossible to struggle with them [the Party leadership]. If we could not make particular changes at home, we did not recommend them at the CMEA. Experience showed there was no use in making proposals we could not really carry out. Take the Russian approach, for example. There were CMEA Sessions where the Comprehensive Program, the KP NTP, and the Long-Term Target Programs were agreed on. Experience demonstrated sufficiently that without domestic reforms, reforms at the CMEA level meant nothing. That is why Poland and Hungary were able to make more radical proposals than we. You can only propose what you plan to do at home, nothing more.

. . . Going to negotiate at the CMEA was like the reverse of Dante. He wrote that the gate to Hell bears the inscription, "Entering here, forget whence you

---

[23]"Stenogramma vstrechi postoiannykh predstavitelei stran v SEV," 6.5.1987, CMEA Archive, p. 67.

came." Instead, going to the CMEA, you had better not forget that you have to go home![24]

On one level, this explanation of the Czechoslovak position accurately characterizes the considerations that divided the East European countries over reform. Domestic coalitions had been built in different countries around different mixes of policies, and negotiations over CMEA-wide reform brought these differences to the fore. However, when it came to translating general ideological postures into reform proposals, an important element of opportunism crept in. Almost every reform proposal was pregnant with implications for the terms of trade between the various countries and the USSR, and the satellites crafted their proposals to make them as advantageous as possible. The experts advising the Soviet negotiators described a wide range of positions on reform in the CMEA, but they argued that the material interests of the CMEA countries were the paramount concern.

> Practically all the European countries are apprehensive that the impending changes proposed by the Soviet side may break the model of relations with the USSR that has arisen over time, and which is very comfortable and customary for those countries: receiving Soviet raw materials and fuels in exchange for their own far-from-first-class manufactured goods. Such a model can only be carried out under centrally organized cooperation at the intergovernmental level. Only at this level is it possible to depart from economic trade criteria, make administrative decisions, and employ the instruments of political pressure on one's partner.[25]

Several of the Soviet proposals seemed to jeopardize the trade subsidy, such as moves to reduce the number of goods involved in coordination of planning and to decentralize trade negotiations. Such changes, the East Germans and Romanians feared, could lead to a less favorable trade structure, since they would lose the Soviet guarantee to buy enough machinery to balance their imports of energy and raw materials. This seems to have been the primary consideration behind the categorical East German and Romanian opposition to relaxing the quota system. Concern about the trade subsidy, however, did not automatically translate into principled support for quotas. Some of the other countries, which supported the Soviet proposal, apparently hoped they could turn it to their own advantage. The Czechoslovak negotiators, for example, had long been trying to get the Soviets to agree to expand the use of value-based quotas for certain kinds of machinery and consumer goods, since that would allow them to improve their export profiles within those broad categories.[26] The chief adviser to the Polish premier on CMEA affairs admit-

[24]Interview with Vladislav Cihlař, 6.17.1992.

[25]Shastitko and Nekipelov, "Pervoocherednye zadachi formirovaniia obedinennogo rynka SEV," 1988, IMEPI Archive, IEMSS report, p. 1.

[26]Interview with Zdeněk Šedivý, 6.30.1992.

ted that Poland supported a relaxed system of quotas primarily because it was believed that the new system would allow Polish negotiators to improve their trade profile in just this way.[27]

In the financial realm, the key issue of contention was the Hungarian demand for partial convertibility, and it did not seem accidental to anyone that Hungary was the country advancing the proposal. As in 1968, when Hungary first put forward the proposal, in the late 1980s Hungary ran a substantial surplus in its trade with the Soviet Union and its negotiators hoped that the introduction of partial convertibility would net Hungary a substantial windfall.[28] The idea was that a portion of annual trade balances would be converted into hard currency and paid to the surplus country; this should create incentives to balance trade, while shifting the burden from the surplus country to the deficit country. In principle, at least, this should encourage countries to balance their books by increasing exports, which would have a salutory influence on trade flows. In fact, however, the instrument seems to have been selected as much for its short-term as for its long-term benefits. As the trade surplus with the Soviet Union widened at the end of the 1980s, Hungary made a strategic gamble that the Soviet Union would eventually pay off its trade debts in hard currency, and continued to expand its exports rather than cut production.[29]

The area of reform most obviously related to the trade subsidy was price reform, since it was the skewed prices of finished and primary goods that produced the subsidy. It is not surprising, therefore, that the most intense negotiations concerned the principles for setting foreign trade prices. The controversies surrounding foreign trade pricing do not lend themselves to a neat division into pro- and antireform positions, because the unilateral interests of particular countries were always too close to the surface, and none of the alternatives under discussion was a clear improvement from the point of view of reform. The chair of the working group that negotiated the text on prices reported four major areas of dispute: (1) the time period to be used as an average for establishing contract prices (five years, three years, or one year); (2) the basis for negotiating prices for components involved in direct ties (either a share of the world price of the analogous final product, or the world price of the analogous component); (3) whether to extend the accepted procedure of setting contract prices to all sorts of services; (4) and whether to apply subsidies to prices of agricultural and high-technology goods in order to stimulate their production.[30] In each of these issues, substantial financial interests were at stake, but none of the proposals would have meant a clear-cut victory for reform. For example, using any period of time as a basis for averaging

[27]Interview with Alfred Siennicki, 5.18.1992.

[28]Interviews with Jozsef Marjai, 9.10.1992, and György Gilyan, 9.10.1992.

[29]Interview with Janos Czibula, 8.25.1992.

[30]"Stenogramma 123 zasedaniia Ispolnitel'nogo Komiteta Soveta Ekonomicheskoi Vzaimopomoshchi, Plenarnoe zasedanie," 6.4.1987, CMEA Archive, pp. 85–87. The chairman is identified as Comrade Komin.

prices was a departure from the objective of making CMEA prices reflect real world scarcities, but each country urged adoption of the average period that its own estimates indicated would be most advantageous.

Similarly, using any accepted standard for negotiating prices in direct ties undercut the purpose of freeing the enterprises to set mutually acceptable prices, but the discussion revolved around which standards to use, rather than whether to do away with such benchmarks altogether. When a product was jointly assembled by several countries, the Czechoslovak negotiators argued, the world prices of particular components should be used to calculate the prices of intermediate goods, rather than shares of the finished product price. The Czechoslovak interest was transparent: Western prices of components were always proportionately higher than Western prices of finished products, and Czechoslovakia exported substantial quantities of components to the USSR for final assembly.[31] Along the same lines, none of the Eastern European reformers would have argued seriously that the existing method of setting prices for goods was an adequate basis for calculating the prices of services, but it was a long-standing complaint that the Soviet formula used to calculate the amount of work done by East European construction contractors failed to cover their costs, making joint investments unprofitable. The Poles complained about their investments in natural gas, the Hungarians about their investments in cellulose, and all the countries sought to avoid further investments in iron ore production. Extending the accepted principles for setting prices to services, therefore, would substantially improve terms of trade for the satellites.[32] Finally, it was clear to the reformers that applying subsidies to certain selected products, although this might temporarily stimulate their production, would simply replace one set of bureaucratic distortions with another. Yet each of the East European countries had a list of goods that were candidates to receive a subsidy: all these goods, of course, were those they produced for export. The Bulgarians proposed a subsidy for wine, the Hungarians for beef, and the Czechoslovaks for agricultural goods and high-technology machinery. These were the practical issues the countries wrangled over, and the stakes were clear. All the negotiators had their eyes firmly fixed on the bottom line, and both the reformers and the hard-liners made every effort to nudge the proposed reforms in a profitable direction.

NEGOTIATING THE UNIFIED MARKET

Following the 1986 summit meeting, the Soviet Union initiated a series of bilateral contacts with East European countries throughout the spring and

[31]"Postanovlenie' 'O perestroike mekhanizma,'" Protokol of the Forty-third (Extraordinary) CMEA Session, 10.13–14.1987, IMEPI Archive, p. 19. This proposal was in line with long-standing Czechoslovak negotiating positions for exporting parts of Tatra trucks, according to Zdeněk Šedivý, interview 6.30.1992.

[32]Interviews with Długosz, 5.7.1992; Czibula, 8.25.1992; and Šedivý, 6.30.1992.

summer of 1987, and simultaneously introduced detailed proposals to the CMEA Executive Committee. The objective was to prepare a programmatic statement on CMEA reform that could be adopted by the Forty-third CMEA Session in October. The Permanent Representatives of the CMEA countries met in April, and at the June Executive Committee meeting, they discussed a Soviet draft of a document entitled, "On Perestroika of the Mechanism of Multilateral Cooperation, Socialist Economic Integration, and the Activity of the Council for Mutual Economic Assistance." This draft encountered severe opposition, which was subsequently described in an IEMSS report.

> The entire course of negotiation over the positions taken by the states of the commonwealth (important stages of which were the Conference of Permanent Representatives of the member countries of the CMEA that took place on April 27, and the 123d Session of the Ispolkom that followed) has shown that in regard to both the general direction and the depth of the proposed changes in economic cooperation between the fraternal countries, none of the unity exists that is needed to adopt an integrated and internally consistent document.[33]

The report goes on to provide an unusually candid account of the process of negotiation, which underlines the weakness of the Soviet bargaining strategy. In the process of editing the draft, the East European countries practiced the same sort of delaying tactics that were observed during the negotiation of previous programs, seeking to force the Soviet delegation to compromise by drawing out the process of discussion.

> The traditional way out of the situation that has emerged is to attempt to achieve agreement by any means on a text of the draft of the CMEA Session Proclamation in question. In fact, that was the path the work in the International Editing Commission took. In the draft presented for consideration to the 123d CMEA Ispolkom Session, one could find a whole series of compromise formulas on controversial topics. At the same time, the mutual concessions on the text of the document did not express any real convergence of the countries' positions on the core issues of perestroika in the activity of the CMEA.
>
> Under these conditions, the real possibility exists that a document will be introduced for the Session's consideration that is eclectic in its essence, and unable to exert genuine influence over the course of mutual cooperation. One should keep in mind that our CMEA partners, aware of the USSR's devotion to "documents of large-scale dimensions," have perfected the method of emasculating those points that appear unacceptable to them for any reason in the editorial process. As a result, the terminological vocabulary of the Council contains concepts behind which no real phenomena or processes stand (convergence of economic mechanisms, joint planning, etc.).[34]

[33]Nekipelov, "O khode i perspektivakh sovmestnoi rabote stran-chlenov SEV po perestroike integratsionnogo sotrudnichestva," to the CPSU Sekretariat, 1987, IMEPI Archive, IEMSS report, pp. 1–2.
[34]Ibid., pp. 4–5.

The degree of formalism involved in this process is astonishing to the non-specialist. Somehow the formal unity of the bloc had become so sacrosanct that the Soviet delegates would sacrifice almost any principle in order to reach agreement. The CMEA countries, well aware of this Soviet propensity, took advantage of it, transforming such central concepts of CMEA ideology as joint planning into empty words. The same process, IEMSS experts warned, threatened to "emasculate" Soviet plans for perestroika in the international realm.

The Polish delegation watched in dismay as the International Editing Commission, which worked between Ispolkom sessions, whittled the document down to the least common denominator of agreement. At the 123d Ispolkom session, Polish Deputy Premier Władisław Gwiazda criticized the process that led to such a toothless text.

> I declare with regret that we have not carried out the mandate we were entrusted with. In the name of my government, I wish to express unease with the results of the International Editing Commission's work comprising the document we have received. It is particularly disillusioning that we began work by proceeding with what, in our opinion, was a good draft decision prepared by the Soviet side. It even contained a series of innovative points, which we believed corresponded to our present needs and capabilities. We expected that it would be enriched and refined as a result of the Commission's work, in accordance with the thoughts and comments of all the countries. However, in our opinion, this has not taken place.
>
>   . . . The various compromises contained in the draft decision emasculate the document, on the one hand, turning it into a mere series of interesting suggestions. On the other hand, [these compromises] have opened the way for the text to be artificially filled with formulas that repeat documents adopted earlier.[35]

Turning his attention to the particulars of the text, Gwiazda argued that although the section headings had been retained, the points under the headings had been so modified that they no longer added up to significant reform.

> The formulation at the heading of this section promises perestroika of the mechanism of cooperation, but at the same time the detailed formulations that have been agreed on in that very same section guarantee no such perestroika. So, for example, in the part concerning coordination of plans, if you compare the formulations, there is practically nothing new except for the declaration that coordination will be based on a collective conception and that the results of coordination will be collated in a single document. Even the none-too-courageously expressed formulation about "increasing the role of value-based quotas" was not adopted.[36]

[35]"Stenogramma 123 zasedaniia Ispolnitel'nogo Komiteta Soveta Ekonomicheskoi Vzaimopomoshchi, Plenarnoe zasedanie," 6.4.1987, CMEA Archive, pp. 48–50.
[36]Ibid., p. 52.

This "none-too-courageously expressed" clause did make it into the final draft, but that did not begin to answer Gwiazda's objection.[37] The point was that the weakened form of the document did not commit the countries to really go ahead with fundamental reform. Its spirit, as well as its wording, was consistent with minor tinkering to maintain the status quo.

The Hungarian delegation shared the low Polish estimation of the document that emerged from the editing process. Jozsef Marjai, the Hungarian deputy premier for foreign and economic affairs, argued that the present draft could not be expected to improve cooperation substantially.

> I am compelled to return to particular elements of my January and April speeches. I would like to remind you of the comprehensive Hungarian draft Proclamation, which was delivered to the Editing Commission, and which must be taken into account in the course of its work. Looking over the work done up to this point, we can observe that the ideas which have been agreed on will not lead us to the sort of transformation of the system of cooperation that is demanded in order to resolve the problems that have accumulated in the course of the development of cooperation. . . .
>
> From these ideas, in our opinion, it is impossible to expect any fundamental improvement in the effectiveness of cooperation. In the document, it is essential to strive for balance and to assure harmony between the goals and the means. It was characteristic of programmatic documents adopted in the past that they advanced goals that were formulated in advance on the basis of needs, but then that was sufficient—everything that regarded the development of means and conditions that were necessary to carry them out, a full perestroika, oh, we will make provision for that in the event the resolution is adopted.[38]

In the Hungarian view, the deterioration of the draft text was symptomatic of a broader failure to follow through on CMEA decisions, which in turn reflected a formalistic approach to CMEA negotiations. The criticism of the Soviet negotiators was implicit. Hungary advanced many of the same proposals made in the initial Soviet text, so in criticizing the compromise text, Marjai criticized the Soviet negotiators who permitted their own proposals to be diluted in order to reach consensus.

Emasculated is a term that recurs in these comments, and it is perhaps a fitting description for the document that emerged from the gauntlet of CMEA negotiations to be adopted as the Proclamation of the Forty-third Session. It is significant that none of the East German objections remained as dissenting comments in the final version, although the final draft is full of dissenting opinions voiced by Romania, Hungary, Czechoslovakia, and Poland. The

---

[37]"Postanovlenie 'O perestroike mekhanizma,'" Protokol of the Forty-third (Extraordinary) CMEA Session, 10.13–14.1987, IMEPI Archive, p. 15.

[38]"Stenogramma 123 zasedaniia Ispolnitel'nogo Komiteta Soveta Ekonomicheskoi Vzaimopomoshchi, Plenarnoe zasedanie," 6.4.1987, CMEA Archive, pp. 19–20.

document's cautious tone suggests that this was because the German comments were folded into the text. One concrete Soviet objective was achieved at the Session, which was the acceptance of a three-tiered system for coordination of planning at the government level, the ministry level, and the enterprise level. This was accepted in spite of a Romanian declaration that the Romanians could not be counted on to participate. All that remained of the commitment to reduce the number of physical quotas, however, was a single weak clause:

> At the intergovernmental stage, [coordination] is to be focused on the strategic emphases of cooperation in order to solve the most important economic, scientific, and technical problems . . . and on determining the levels of deliveries of basic goods by the negotiating countries, while the interested countries simultaneously increase the role of value-based quotas.[39]

Interested countries would "increase the role" of value-based quotas, but no commitment was made to reduce the number of physical quotas, and how value-based quotas would be applied was not spelled out. The traditional approach to coordination of planning did not make a significant distinction between the two forms of quotas; since contract prices were known well in advance, and quotas were set for narrow ranges of goods, setting the quota in value terms gave the branch ministries only very narrow room to maneuver. The new element of the Soviet proposal was to set value quotas for broad ranges of manufactured goods, and delegate to the ministries and enterprises many of the concrete decisions about imports and exports. The language adopted in the Proclamation left the resolution of that issue in doubt. It was made more dubious by the insertion of the phrase "interested countries," which suggested that some countries were not interested and would not participate.

The Soviet negotiators must bear most of the blame for the deterioration of the Soviet proposal, because they failed to insist on maintaining the integrity of the Soviet text. It was typical that Aleksei Antonov, the Soviet deputy premier for CMEA affairs, simply appealed to the countries in his address to the 123d Executive Committee Session to proceed in a spirit of compromise, and congratulated them for having achieved a "significant convergence of opinions."[40] The appearance of progress, as it turned out, was illusory. As the Bulgarian delegate pointed out, the issues of dispute were still so extensive at that point that the insertion in the text of the countries' special positions increased the document's total length from twelve pages to forty-seven.[41]

The negotiations about how to reform the CMEA structure provide a useful

[39]"Postanovlenie 'O perestroike mekhanizma,'" Protokol of the Forty-third (Extraordinary) CMEA Session, 10.13–14.1987, IMEPI Archive, p. 15.

[40]"Stenogramma 123 zasedaniia Ispolnitel'nogo Komiteta Soveta Ekonomicheskoi Vzaimopomoshchi, Plenarnoe zasedanie," 6.4.1987, CMEA Archive, pp. 5–7.

[41]Ibid., p. 15.

illustration of the way the East Europeans could exploit the Soviet eagerness to reach consensus, especially as deadlines approached. The Soviet draft proposed to streamline the CMEA by dramatically reducing the number of Permanent Commissions (consultative organs meeting at the level of ministers of various branches of industry). By putting up fierce resistance on the day before the Forty-third Session opened, however, the Romanians were able to prevent several of the commissions from being abolished, although all the other countries agreed that they no longer served any useful purpose.[42] Hungary and Bulgaria insisted that the meetings were useless, and the Romanian obstinance finally provoked the Bulgarian representative, Andrey Lukanov, to exclaim in exasperation that a committee meeting required representatives of ten countries, and if only the Romanians wished to attend, they would have to form a "national Permanent Commission."[43] In the end, however, the Soviet representative, Aleksei Antonov, appealed to the other countries to reach some compromise on the number of Permanent Commissions to be retained, on any grounds, so long as the document was finished in time to be submitted to the Session the following day.

> I request that the representatives of the Bulgarian, Hungarian, and Romanian sides help find the kind of resolution that will allow us to resolve this question properly at the Forty-third Session. My single request consists in this, because if you continue to occupy contradictory positions, the only possible solution is to remove the structure of the CMEA from discussion at the Forty-third Session and carry it over to a more distant date.
>
> . . . Look, gathered here are the responsible representatives of the countries, after all, and we have to introduce a proposal to the Session. What are we going to introduce? What are our proposals? To say that we have one Romanian opinion, another opinion held by two other countries, and a third opinion held by the remaining seven countries? That would probably be incomprehensible. If the Session, the heads of government, take the same position, then the question will be removed from discussion; there is no alternative.[44]

In urging compromise, Antonov probably thought he was bowing to the impossibility of convincing the Romanians, and he certainly saved the Soviet premier, Nikolai Ryzhkov, some strenuous negotiations. At the same time, however, he threw away a Soviet bargaining position and made it clear to the other countries that consensus was more important to the Soviet side than the document's content.

The Proclamation left unresolved the most important issues of reform. Price reform remained as controversial as ever. The Soviet delegation did not

[42]"Stenogramma vstrechi postoiannykh predstavitelei stran v SEV," 10.12.1987, CMEA Archive, pp. 16–26.
[43]Ibid., p. 20.
[44]Ibid., pp. 18–19.

succeed in narrowing the range of debate by October, so the Council Proclamation simply promised that the countries would continue to study the issue. Similarly, only one Soviet proposal for currency and exchange rate reform was endorsed, that several interested countries would begin to use their national currencies to settle accounts for direct ties. All the rest was left as subjects for future studies.[45] Reports written after the Forty-third Session had to admit that very little had been accomplished. The differences between the countries had not narrowed, and their consent to embark on a dramatic transformation of trade relations in the CMEA had not been secured. All that could be identified as an accomplishment was the rhetorical acceptance of the ideology of perestroika by most of the countries. IEMSS experts provided the following assessment of the achievements of the Forty-third Session, which tried to put matters in the best possible light:

> In spite of the difficulties that have emerged in implementing the Soviet proposals for perestroika of the mechanism of cooperation and creation of a unified CMEA market, the important result of the Forty-third CMEA Session and the subsequent work of the countries on those proposals is the admission that changes are essential, which was made by practically all the countries, and the acceptance by the majority of a general ideology of perestroika. It is also significant that the Soviet Union unambiguously and firmly expressed its intention to continue along its course of perestroika, and defended the principle of "interested countries" in resolving the tasks of improving the mechanism of cooperation. This final circumstance opens the possibility of gradually attracting individual countries that are ready into the orbit of perestroika, in order to begin the implementation of practical measures leading in the general direction that has been set forth: creation of a CMEA unified market.[46]

The only positive developments the Soviet experts could identify were that the countries had adopted a common rhetorical position, and that the Soviet Union had insisted it would proceed with reforms, with or without the other countries.

In December, immediately following the Forty-third Session, an IEMSS report addressed to the Council of Ministers and the Central Committee urged that the Soviet Union abandon the attempt to achieve consensus within the CMEA. Consensus would be impossible to reach, the experts reasoned, and the attempt to forge it would simply delay necessary reforms. Instead, the Soviet Union should simply announce its intention to act unilaterally, and trust that its overwhelming economic influence would compel the other countries to cooperate.

---

[45]"Postanovlenie 'O perestroike mekhanizma,'" Protokol of the Forty-third (Extraordinary) CMEA Session, 10.13–14.1987, IMEPI Archive, pp. 18–21, 23.

[46]Shastitko and Nekipelov, "Pervoocherednye zadachi formirovaniia ob'edinennogo rynka SEV," 1988, IMEPI Archive, IEMSS report, p. 7.

The preparation for the Forty-third CMEA Session showed that the Council member countries are not prepared to the same degree to carry out the internal economic transformations that are the essential precondition for perestroika of the mechanism of international cooperation. At the same time we assume that on the strength of its economic potential and its significance in mutual economic ties, the Soviet Union has the ability to give a strong impulse to the process of perestroika in this area. Our line should consist of introducing changes in the form of our relations with our integration partners that correspond to the degree of radical economic reform that we introduce on a unilateral basis. For example, concentrating centralized planning in the USSR on the resolution of questions of a strategic character will allow, and demand, that we move away from detailed coordination of mutual exports in the course of coordination of planning. The formation of wholesale trade in the means of production makes it possible to introduce convertibility of the Soviet ruble gradually. The expansion of the economic functions of the enterprise under conditions of full financial accountability [*khozraschet*] will inevitably introduce changes in its participation in the process of price formation on the CMEA market, and so on. Under these circumstances, our partners will be compelled to adapt to the changes in the Soviet economic system and to attempt to coordinate their economic policies with ours.[47]

Over the next two years the Soviet Union launched no major efforts to forge consensus in the CMEA. The Forty-fourth CMEA Session in 1988 adopted a "Collective Conception of the International Socialist Division of Labor for 1991–2005," which was intended as the basis for coordination of plans, and was to give substance to the Soviet objective of transforming that process into an exercise in joint strategic planning. The forty-two-page document, however, was much too general to be used as a program. It contained no new reform proposals, and exacted no concrete obligations from any of the countries. Instead of using the document as a vehicle to push through their reform agenda, the Soviet negotiators allowed it to become yet another in the long line of proclamations that the East Europeans could safely sign and then ignore.[48] Work went on through the end of 1989 on an "Integrated Conception for the Perestroika of Foreign Economic Ties," whose drafts bore a marked resemblance to the original Soviet proposals advanced in 1987 for the Unified Socialist Market, but even this document failed to commit the countries to specific reforms or a specific timetable. Even had it been adopted early in 1990, it would still have come too late to influence the negotiations for coordinating plans for 1991–95, which by then were nearly complete.

[47]Grinberg et al., "Etapy perestroiki mekhanizma sotsialisticheskoi ekonomicheskoi integratsii," to A. K. Antonov, O. K. Rybakov, A. A. Reub, I. D. Ivanov, P. N. Fedoseev, 12.9.1987, IMEPI Archive, IEMSS report, pp. 1–2.

[48]"Kollektivnaia kontseptsiia mezhdunarodnogo sotsialisticheskogo razdeleniia truda na 1991–2005 gg.," Prilozhenie 2 k proektu postanovleniia Sessii Soveta (44 zasedanie), Komitet po sotrudnichestvu v oblasti planovoi deiatel'nosti, May. 1988, IMEPI Archive.

In the event, fate took a different turn. All the governments of Eastern Europe fell in the second half of 1989, and when the Forty-fifth CMEA Session met in January 1990, after repeated delays the previous year, the context of its discussions was a changed world. Gradual reform was no longer an option; most of the countries had decided to launch radical market transformations. The political underpinning of the alliance had melted as well, and in June the Soviet Union announced it would no longer subsidize its former satellites. Beginning on 1 January 1991, it would accept only hard currency in payment for its exports, which would be delivered at current world prices. The disintegration of the CMEA followed almost immediately. Interviewed in the summer of 1990, East European officials said that following the suspension of CMEA trading privileges, the only reason to delay the dissolution of the organization was to avoid embarrassing Gorbachev.[49]

Given the intervention of such world-changing events, it would be a mistake to jump to conclusions about the success or failure of CMEA reform. One can, however, assess the degree of success of the Soviet reform agenda, which was adopted in part, in terms of its reflection in the negotiations over plan coordination for 1991–95. The following section argues that most of the reform principles had already been severely compromised.

IMPLEMENTATION: NEGOTIATING THE 1991–1995 PLAN

The process of negotiating the 1991–95 five-year bilateral trade plans shows that both the Soviet and East European negotiators continued to act on the assumption that perestroika would not fundamentally change the rules of trade in the CMEA. Prices would continue to be distorted, currencies would continue to be inconvertible, and the trade structure would continue to determine the winners and losers. Acting on these assumptions, they negotiated a five-year plan that would not have brought them significantly closer to an open market. The East Europeans were indeed compelled to make serious concessions during the negotiations, but not because the Soviet Union had succeeded in reforming trade relations. Rather, the Soviet Union wrung these concessions out of the East Europeans by the traditional means. Facing increasing domestic economic difficulties, Gosplan drove a hard bargain that locked in a more favorable trade structure. Meanwhile, the process of bilateral bargaining was not transformed by the introduction of new procedures, because the underlying interests and expectations remained the same.

The implementation of reforms in the CMEA was frustrated from the beginning by the fact that Soviet foreign economic policy had lost much of its

---

[49]Interview with Petr Hanzal, 8.15.1990; Milan Čižkovský, 8.24.1990; and Jerzy Rutkowski, 8.7.1990.

credibility. As the Hungarian delegate (cited above) made clear, too many CMEA programs had been announced, poorly developed, and then promptly abandoned. It is telling that one of the first warnings issued by Soviet advisers in the reformist camp was about the credibility of the Soviet Union's own commitment to reform:

> It is of overriding importance that the recommendations we propose correspond adequately to the state of the system of management of the USSR's national economy that has been reached at the respective time, since, in the opposite case, trust in the seriousness of our intentions may become seriously undermined.[50]

Soviet officials were right to be concerned about this, since in fact most of the satellites never did become convinced of the seriousness of the Soviet commitment to economic reform. According to an IEMSS report,

> The countries that refuse to accept our proposals in principle (the GDR, Romania, and in part Cuba) essentially do not hide their opinion that perestroika in economic relations within the USSR may not take place in quite the way in which it was formulated at the June 1987 Plenum of the CC CPSU. Insofar as those countries are retaining their centralized command systems of management and have no intention of changing them, they consider perestroika in the international mechanism of cooperation to contradict their interests, and they are making efforts to obstruct its implementation as much as possible.
>
> Several countries that support the general conception of renewal of the economic mechanism of relations in the CMEA have likewise made their doubts known about the Soviet Union's readiness to carry out the recommendations . . . that it itself has proposed. This to some degree explains the reserved attitude of Czechoslovakia and Hungary toward certain aspects of our proposals—in particular, on monetary and price issues.[51]

It was not only the opponents of perestroika who doubted the seriousness of Soviet intentions, and this goes a long way to explain the short-term approach that most of the countries took to implementing reform. If reform is unlikely to succeed in any case, it is unwise to take risks on its behalf, and particularly unwise to jeopardize one's own trade profile. Indeed, a number of East European officials who considered the steps taken toward reform in the Soviet Union to be very positive nonetheless had serious doubts about their long-term prospects.[52] It is hardly surprising, therefore, that although the countries took a reformist stance in international forums as long as the discussions were general, they nevertheless occupied conservative positions in bilateral relations once the issues became concrete, and reforms came attached to costs.

[50]"K razdelu 'Rekomendatsii' doklada 'Mir sotsializma,'" 4.20.1988, IMEPI Archive, IEMSS report, pp. 1–2.

[51]Shastitko and Nekipelov, "Pervoocherednye zadachi formirovaniia ob'edinennogo rynka SEV," 1988, IMEPI Archive, IEMSS report, p. 6.

[52]Interview with Cihlař, 6.17.1992; Długosz, 6.8.1992; and Zsolnai, 9.1.1992.

The extensive records of bilateral trade negotiations maintained by the Czechoslovak State Planning Commission indicate that, despite a formal commitment to liberalizing trade, the most important Czechoslovak objective in negotiations for 1991–95 was to lock in quotas for machinery exports. A briefing paper for the Collegium of the SPK written in 1987 outlined two possible scenarios for developing Soviet-Czechoslovak trade relations, explaining that the fall in energy prices and the deterioration of the Soviet economy would create a shortfall in demand for Czechoslovak machinery exports.

> A comparison of the two scenarios shows that one of the main problems for the Czechoslovak economy after 1990 will be finding an outlet for machine-building production, in particular. As long as a radical change does not occur in the structure of Czechoslovak production from the point of view of more specialization, a higher technical level, and greater reliability of manufactured machinery (which applies to the other CMEA member states as well), and involving the sort of perestroika of the whole mechanism of integration that would lead to an improvement of the conditions of the socialist market and greater reliability in its functioning, the surplus of Czechoslovak machine-building production can be quantified as more than 50 billion krone in the Ninth Five-Year Plan and probably 120 billion Krone in the Tenth.[53]

In view of the seriousness of the problem, the report concluded, the State Plan for 1991–95 should be based on the assumption that machinery exports to the Soviet Union would not increase. In fact, offering to increase imports of machinery might be necessary in order to maintain Czechoslovak exports at their customary levels.

For their part, the Soviet trade negotiators were also motivated by traditional considerations, rather than by attempts to liberalize trade. Facing a declining economy and a growing trade deficit with most of Eastern Europe, the Soviet Union sought to reduce its subsidy at the end of the 1980s by narrowing the gap between machinery imports and exports. The Soviet negotiators quickly moved to confirm Czechoslovak concerns that it would be impossible to retain the traditional level of lucrative machinery exports. In September 1987, in unofficial conversations following a trade negotiating session, Soviet officials warned their counterparts that Czechoslovak machinery exports would have to be reduced after 1990, and that Czechoslovakia would have to accept more imports of Soviet machinery.[54] In October the blow finally fell. In a negotiating session between machine-building experts from the

[53]Svobodá and Kollert, "Kvantifikace rozvoje vnějších ekonomických vztahů ČSSR po roce 1989 do roku 2000," January 1987, SPK Archive, p. 3.

[54]Černý, "Konzultace o svodných otázkách hospodářské spolupráce s SSSR na obdobi po roce 1990," 9.4.1987, SPK Archive, p. 7. The document is a memo summarizing a meeting that took place between representatives of the Czechoslovak and Soviet central planning organs on 8.24–28.1987. Comrade Svoboda led the CSSR delegation, and Comrade Prusov led the USSR delegation.

two planning commissions, the Soviet side insisted that the Czechoslovak export quota for machinery be limited to a range of 19.2–20.4 billion rubles for 1991–95, as opposed to a Czechoslovak proposal to export 24 billion rubles. Meanwhile, the Soviet negotiators demanded that Czechoslovakia import in the range of 9.5–10.7 billion rubles of machinery, more than double the level of the previous five-year plan. The Czechoslovak negotiators went so far as to propose a further increase in machinery imports to 11 billion rubles if the Soviet Union would accept Czechoslovak exports of 24 billion, but the Soviet negotiators held their ground.[55] At the subsequent negotiating session, in November, the Czechoslovak delegation repeated its proposal for a 24-billion-ruble machinery quota, and again the Soviet delegation rejected the request.[56] Clearly both sides believed that the customary rules of trade negotiations remained in force. The size of the subsidy, rather than reform, was dictating their bargaining positions, and the results of the bargaining continued to distort their trade profiles.

The Czechoslovak negotiators were compelled to accept the Soviet parameters, but the bargaining was far from over when the proportions of trade had been set. The internal structure of machinery imports and exports was perhaps as important as the overall proportions, and each side sought to assure certain conditions while they were still negotiating at the Gosplan level. For the Czechoslovaks, the primary goals were to assure exports for which there was no alternative market, and to make the reductions fall mainly in exports of material-intensive products, such as boats and heavy steel equipment. The following excerpts from a briefing paper indicate the main Czechoslovak objectives for an approaching negotiating session (the italicized comments and emphasis are textual notations made by the first deputy chairman of the State Planning Commission, J. Voraček):

—Consent to the reductions of Czechoslovak exports for items that correspond to the Czechoslovak proposal, delivered to the Soviet side during the meeting of SPK Chairman Comrade Potáč with USSR Gosplan Chairman Comrade Talyzin in October 1988;

—*Agree in principle* with the new Soviet proposals to reduce Czechoslovak exports, with the exception of several items that for various reasons are difficult to sell in other countries or employ within the CSSR;

—Insist on the original Czechoslovak proposal *to reduce* Czechoslovak exports of Avia cargo trucks *by 1,000 annually. And more!*

. . . Regarding the agreed-on principle for the export-import orientation in

[55]Prchlík, "Jednání expertů ústředních plánovacích orgánů ČSSR a SSSR," to the Chairman, SPK, 9.10.1987, SPK Archive, pp. 1–2. The meeting took place 10.5–9.1987.

[56]Prchlík, "Jednání ústředních plánovacích orgánů ČSSR a SSSR k problematice spolupráce v oblasti strojírensví," to the Chairman, SPK, 11. 25.1987, SPK Archive, p. 2. The document is a report of a meeting of experts from the Czechoslovak and USSR planning organs on 16–20 November 1987.

exchange of machinery, we will proceed from the readiness of the CSSR to *increase* Czechoslovak machinery exports to *at least 23–24 billion rubles*.

During the meeting at the expert level, we will also endeavor to reduce the nomenclature of Czechoslovak exports of material-intensive products (as per the Czechoslovak *downsizing programs*). At the same time, of course, we will *take into consideration the issue of coupling exports of Czechoslovak machinery and equipment to imports of raw materials.*[57]

This does not sound much like a reformist manifesto. The Czechoslovak bargaining position remained, as it always had been before 1988, essentially determined by the skewed prices in CMEA trade. First, the negotiators would make every effort to maximize the share of their exports falling in the machinery category. If they failed to do so by setting a high proportion of machinery exports, they would seek to win concessions on a point-by-point basis. Next, they turned their attention to optimizing the structure of machinery exports, using categories that make sense only in the context of distorted prices, such as "material intensity." In the case of trucks, which were profitable exports for which the Soviets had an almost unlimited appetite, the Czechoslovak strategy was to reduce the quota in order to hold something in reserve for which concessions could be won later. Finally, the machinery that the Soviet negotiators most desired to obtain would be linked to countertrade agreements for raw materials. The satellites endeavored to distort their trade profiles in any way that would take advantage of the distortions in CMEA prices.

The Czechoslovaks, as is true of all the East European trade negotiators, were much less successful in achieving their goals for 1991–95 than they had been during any previous five-year plan. They were compelled to accept reductions in key commodity imports across the board, substantially reduce their surplus in machinery exports, and extend credits to cover a growing Soviet deficit. The Soviet economy was perceptibly sliding into decline by 1988, and reducing the subsidy to Eastern Europe suddenly became a priority. Polish and Czechoslovak documents from 1988 and 1989 show an unusual pattern, in which the Soviet negotiators overturned successive agreements, imposing further reductions in scarce commodity exports each time, and the East Europeans were continually compelled to retreat. In each negotiating session, the Soviet officials apologetically referred to the disastrous state of their economy.

Despite this unaccustomed firmness from their Soviet partners, the East Europeans managed to win a number of key concessions of their own.

[57]Prchlík, "Směrnice pro postup specialistů Státní plánovací komise při jednáni o koordinací NHP pro období 1991–1995 v oblasti strojírenství a elektrotechiky," 5.19.1988, SPK Archive: č.j. 61 435/88, pp. 1–2. The document is a briefing paper for the negotiators for the 6–10 June 1988 Moscow meeting of experts from the central planning organs of the CSSR and USSR for coordination of plans for 1991–95 in machine building and electronics. The Czechoslovak delegation was led by M. Samonil.

Czechoslovakia was finally able to extricate itself from the second stage of construction of the costly Krivoi Rog iron-ore complex, after repeated categorical statements from the Soviet side that the CSSR must participate. In the end the refusal to participate cost Czechoslovakia only a moderate decline in its iron-ore imports, at a time when the country was trying to scale down its production of steel in any case. The Soviet negotiators insisted that Czechoslovakia agree to pay for iron ore with particular types of machinery in return for extending the 1975 long-term agreement on iron-ore exports, but a Czechoslovak analysis still showed that the deal cost only 43 percent as much as buying the ore on the world market.[58] Meanwhile, Czechoslovakia won a major victory by reducing its steel exports. Czechoslovakia had long been a significant exporter of steel to the Soviet Union, an arrangement that was markedly unprofitable. Given the price relationships in the CMEA, the most profitable arrangement was to import iron ore from the Soviet Union, produce steel, and export it to the West.[59] Czechoslovakia managed to negotiate a gradual phasing out of its CMEA exports of steel, and the Soviet response was limited to small reductions in exports of iron ore and manganese. Finally, high-level intervention in the negotiations at several points won Czechoslovakia a reprieve from Soviet intentions to cut oil exports to 5 million tons annually, and to further reduce the Czechoslovak export quota for machinery to 14–15 billion rubles over five years. After personal intervention by the Czechoslovak premier, Ladislav Adamec, oil exports were stabilized at 6.6 million tons, and the final quota for machinery was set at 18 billion rubles.[60]

It would be incorrect to argue, however, that the principles of reform failed primarily because of East European victories at the bargaining table. The record shows, on the contrary, that Soviet trade negotiators made no effort to implement their own reform principles, and in fact violated them whenever doing so could be tactically advantageous. To take a glaring example, for two decades Czechoslovakia had been seeking Soviet consent to replace its quantitative quota for shoe exports with a qualitative quota. This would be beneficial to Czechoslovakia, since it would then be possible to export higher-quality shoes at a higher price and save the cost of wasted raw materials. The proposal was in

[58]Kopečný, Prchlík, Marcinov, "Výsledky konzultace plánovacích orgánů ČSSR a SSSR o koordinací plánů v oblasti hutnictví a strojírenství," to the Chairman, SPK, 6.30.1989, SPK Archive, pp. 2–3. Also distributed to Josef Pancíř, Deputy Minister of Foreign Trade, and L. Vodražka, Deputy Premier and Minister of Metallurgy.

[59]Interview with Jozef Ružička, 6.30.1992.

[60]A letter from Adamec to Ryzhkov emphasized the serious crisis that could befall the Czechoslovak economy if the Soviet Union carried out its intentions to cut raw material exports and to reduce its imports of machinery (Kubíček, "Svodná konzultace plánovacích orgánů ČSSR a SSSR," 12.16.1988, SPK Archive). At a subsequent meeting with Adamec, Ryzhkov agreed to moderate Soviet reductions in oil exports (Dr. Nad', "Protokol z jednání předsedy vlády ČSSR L. Adamec a předsedy rady ministrů SSSR N. Ryžkova," 1.23, 1989, SPK Archive, p. 3). The meeting between Adamec and Ryzhkov took place on 17 January 1989.

line with the reformist principle of increasing the flexibility of the trade plan to reduce costs and create incentives for improving quality. As they had done for twenty years, however, the Soviet negotiators rejected the proposal, insisting on receiving a greater quantity of low-quality shoes.[61]

It is difficult to judge which were more harmful to the interests of reform: Soviet bargaining successes, or Soviet failures. Soviet concessions, which left Czechoslovakia with a substantial quota for machinery and obligated the Soviet Union to continue the majority of its raw material exports under the current conditions, tied in a very substantial bloc of trade that was protected from liberalization. On the other hand, Soviet victories obligated Czechoslovakia to double the quota of machinery that it imported from the USSR, which internal Czechoslovak State Planning Commission memos acknowledged from the outset would be outdated and unsuited to the needs of the Czechoslovak economy.[62] One of the major Soviet innovations in the 1991–95 negotiating round, born of desperation, was to overcome the traditional institutional inertia and link exports of raw materials to Czechoslovak exports of selected types of machinery and consumer goods.[63] Yet this, a tactic well suited to centralized bargaining between state monopolists, was a profoundly illiberal development, which could only set back attempts to develop initiative at the enterprise level. When it came to negotiating about trade, rather than about reform, Soviet officials remained locked in their institutional routine. They focused on the bottom line, and ignored their putative reformist principles.

One outcome of the 1991–95 trade negotiations was positive from the point of view of reform: the 1991–95 Plan bound only 40 percent of the projected USSR-CSSR trade turnover in obligatory quotas.[64] However, all that this meant in practice was that the five-year plan was less comprehensive than it had been in the past, not that the other 60 percent of trade would be liberalized. Since the underlying interests and strategies of the players had not changed, the three-tiered negotiating system simply put off much of the struggle until a later date. The scramble for unilateral advantage that took place during the first phase of negotiations leaves little reason to believe that the central planning agencies would have given their enterprises freer rein in future rounds than they had in the past.

Instead, even the most reform-minded East Europeans made it clear that in

[61]Svobodá, "Informace o výsledcích jednání," to the Council of the SPK, 5.30.1989, SPK Archive, p. 6.

[62]Svobodá et al., "Kvantifikace rozvoje vnějších ekonomických vztahů ČSSR po roce 1989 do roku 2000," January 1987, SPK Archive, p. 3.

[63]Svobodá, "Informace o výsledcích jednání," to the Council of the SPK, 5.30.1989, SPK Archive, p. 3.

[64]"Sprava o výsledcích první etapy koordinace národohospodářských plánů s členskými státy RVHP na léta 1991–1995," to B. Urban, First Deputy Chairman, Council of Ministers, Chairman, SPK, 6.9.1989, SPK Archive, p. 3. The report was background material for a report to the Council of Ministers.

the absence of far-reaching reform—which they did not expect the Soviet Union to implement—it was not in the national interest to expand the freedom of their enterprises to conduct trade. The top Hungarian negotiators, Jozsef Marjai and Istvan Hetenyi, for example, pointed out that because domestic and foreign trade prices did not necessarily reflect the true costs of production, enterprises that were guided by them could make decisions harmful to the national interest, such as exporting domestically subsidized goods. In addition, it was generally easier for East European enterprises to import from the West and export to the East, and prices often did not provide adequate incentives for them to balance their trade.[65] Consequently, even the reformist Hungarian government had long been putting strict controls on its enterprises in their trade with the other CMEA countries, which undermined its own attempts to promote direct ties. Hetenyi explained that Soviet negotiators had approached Hungarian enterprises directly on several occasions: "They saw that our firms had free capacity, and they went to our factories. Baibakov would say, 'I was at Icarus, and they said that they can produce another two thousand busses! Why doesn't the planning office tell us that?' We responded, 'Yes, Icarus can do it, but no one can afford the dollar input that is necessary.'"[66] Because of the hidden costs of production, the Hungarian Planning Commission forbade the enterprise from increasing its exports.

Vladislav Cihlař explained that Czechoslovakia took essentially the same approach. Although consistently supporting calls for expanding direct ties at the CMEA level, Czechoslovakia in fact carefully restricted them in order to prevent a hemorrhage of subsidized goods and an artificial inflation of the enterprises' budgets for foreign travel.

> We, too, supported the Polish position on this issue, but in practice we did not allow all our enterprises to make these ties. We made a decision allowing some enterprises to do so, expanding the number. Only those that were prepared to carry out this kind of activity were allowed to do so; otherwise, the decisions of inexperienced agents could harm national interests.
>
> . . . The enterprises developed proposals, and the government approved them. The decision depended on the merits of the case. It was better to have only one direct tie, but a good one, than to introduce wide freedom.
>
> . . . The regional Party first secretaries kept trying to increase the number of enterprises involved in foreign economic relations in their regions because this reflected well on them—they were carrying out the Comprehensive Program.
>
> . . . The [ministries'] main concern was to make sure that there were economic reasons for the direct ties. Every enterprise wanted to be involved, because it meant opportunities for travel. We called it a "state Čedok" [CSSR travel agency]. It was wasteful, nonproductive activity.[67]

[65]Interviews with Hetenyi, 9.8.1992, and Marjai, 9.10.1992.
[66]Interview with Istvan Hetenyi, 9.8.1992.
[67]Interview with Vladislav Cihlař, 6.17.1992.

Cihlař was as reform-minded as any official in the Czechoslovak government in the 1980s, so his testimony is evidence of the gulf between the reformers' aspirations and the practical business of maximizing national utility from trade.

The following internal memo from the Czechoslovak State Planning Commission illustrates the limits that Czechoslovakia imposed on direct ties in 1989, at the same time that it was agreeing to formal language at the CMEA level intended to remove barriers to direct cooperation between national enterprises. The Soviet Ministry of Heavy Machine Building signed an agreement with a Czechoslovak construction enterprise to build a factory in the USSR, and the Czechoslovak State Planning Commission decided that the deal was inconsistent with state interests.

> Regarding the demand of the USSR minister of heavy machine building, Comrade Velichek, of 9.29.1989, it appears that already during the meeting of the working group of experts of the central planning organs of the CSSR and USSR in the area of machine building, which took place in Moscow during 25–27 July 1989, the Soviet side referred to a meeting that had taken place between the USSR Ministry of Heavy Machine Building and the Czechoslovak organization Hutní Stavby of Košice concerning the participation of that organization in the construction of a factory to produce polygraphic equipment in the USSR. It is in this connection that the Soviet side requested the State Planning Commission to take a position on this matter.
>
> It was possible to obtain a copy of the protocol . . . of this meeting through direct contacts. It emerges from the text of the protocol that the meeting was conducted incompetently (for example, prices for the work and the delivery are not referred to) and furthermore, questions regarding the reimbursement for Czechoslovak participation were not resolved.
>
> One cannot consent to the action of the Czechoslovak organization Hutní Stavby. First, it is already obvious that there will be a deficit of construction capacity in the Czech Socialist Republic in the Ninth Five-Year Plan, and meanwhile a surplus in the Slovak Socialist Republic. Further, in consideration of the current development of the balance of payments between the CSSR and the USSR, and of the tendencies predicted for the period of the Ninth Five-Year Plan (a moratorium on the export of construction work to the USSR according to CSSR Government Decree 201/89), one must not allow the export of construction work to the USSR, because it is notably unprofitable.
>
> . . . It is therefore recommended to send a message to the USSR Ministry of Heavy Machine Building along the following lines during Comrade Voraček's meeting: the enterprise has exceeded its authority according to our legal norms, and it is currently charged with other tasks in the CSSR.[68]

[68]Dr. Naď, "Informace pro s. místopředsedu Petříčka k problematice dovozu stavebních prací do SSSR—s. p. Hutní stavby Košice," to Deputy Chairman Petříček, SPK, 10.13.1989, SPK Archive.

In the view of the Czechoslovak State Planning Commission, the enterprise was not in fact in the best position to judge the profitability of its own business. Because of lack of experience with foreign trade, the enterprise director had failed to settle all the important terms before agreeing to take on an assignment, an oversight that could potentially prove costly to the state budget. More important, however, were other considerations about which the director had no way of knowing. It was inconvenient to tie up construction firms in the Czech part of the country because of a projected shortage; Czechoslovakia was already expected to run a trade surplus with the Soviet Union in 1991–95; and, most important, internal and external prices were distorted, so an agreement that might seem profitable from an enterprise's point of view was in fact unprofitable. The enterprise was forbidden to carry out its agreement, and the Soviet partners were informed that it had exceeded its authority. When it came to concrete cases, the principles of reform were less important than considerations of unilateral advantage.

CONCLUSIONS

The Soviet Union developed a coherent program to reform the CMEA under Mikhail Gorbachev, a program flexible enough to provide some hope of realization but specific enough to enable a critic to show that even its short-term objectives were never achieved. The East European countries opposed the program to varying degrees, and from various motivations: some opposed reform, others believed it did not go far enough, and still others did not believe the Soviet Union was committed to carrying it out. Beneath the overlay of ideology and rhetoric, however, each of the East European countries maneuvered during the negotiations about reform to assure itself a maximum share of the Soviet trade subsidy. Some did this by opposing particular points in the Soviet program, such as relaxing trade quotas; others by inserting points of their own, such as introducing limited convertibility of trade debts; and still others by inserting self-serving clauses into the details of price reform.

Although able to prevail on the satellites to endorse general statements of principles, the Soviet Union never succeeded in translating its program into official CMEA legislation, despite attempting to do so for three years. Some of the basic principles of the program were retained in various CMEA documents, and a general rhetoric of reform was created, but the East European countries, and particularly the GDR and Romania, were able to blunt the thrust of every document that was adopted. No document was ever adopted that required the countries to carry out a systematic reform. Much of the blame for this rests with the Soviet delegations, which failed to push the Soviet point of view consistently. In some instances, it was more important to Soviet negotiators to reach consensus—on any grounds—than to reform the CMEA trading system.

The early stages of implementation of reform in the CMEA, before it was swept away by the historic events of 1989, lead one to believe that the Gorbachev trade reforms would have remained mired in uncertainty and inertia had they not been superseded by more significant developments. The negotiations over the 1991–95 Five-Year Plan, which were almost complete by the end of 1989, demonstrated that the countries did not believe in perestroika, and were not prepared to risk their shares of the trade subsidy to make it come about. Negotiating on the assumption that the rules of the game would not substantially change, the countries struck compromises that balanced unilateral advantage against unilateral advantage, but that did not advance the cause of reform. Even the most reform-minded governments closely monitored their enterprises, ready to rein them in if they struck any agreement that was rendered unprofitable by the distorted prices prevailing in the CMEA.

Meanwhile, the Soviet negotiators proceeded with their routine objectives. They won a number of important concessions from the East Europeans at the macroeconomic level: running a large trade deficit, shifting the balance of machinery exports, and cutting exports of key commodities. These late-blooming victories, however, were indicative of a broader malaise in the Soviet bureaucracy. Only when the problems in the Soviet economy took on crisis proportions were the Soviet negotiators finally able to drive a hard bargain. Even so, the East Europeans won a number of quiet victories at the microeconomic level, and they were still able to use intervention by high-level officials to undercut the bargaining positions of the front-line Soviet negotiators. The most important failure of the Soviet bureaucracy, however, was that it proceeded unimaginatively with trade negotiations as they had always been conducted in the past. In the absence of accountability, and in the midst of uncertain politics in Moscow, it was safer to continue according to routine. Consequently, the reform principles hammered out by the Central Committee were never implemented by Gosplan.

As the four case studies have shown, multiple attempts were made to rejuvenate the CMEA, each of them employing ingenious strategies. None of these strategies succeeded, however, and the reasons are fundamentally the same in each case: each program conflicted with entrenched East European interests, and no program had the whole-hearted support of Soviet officialdom. In each case, the East Europeans developed cunning strategies to avoid the implications of the Soviet-sponsored reforms. In each case, the Soviet bureaucracy was too paralyzed by the incentive structure in which it was embedded to act with a single, unchanging will. Compromise, neglect, and routine were easier paths, and they were chosen consistently enough to allow four major foreign-policy initiatives to fail.

CHAPTER 10

Conclusions and Reflections

NEW EVIDENCE from the archives of the former Soviet Union and its former East European satellites, and extensive interviews with participants and witnesses, provide the basis for a comprehensive reevaluation of trade politics in the Soviet bloc. This inside look dispells the official myth of a united socialist alliance striving to integrate its economies and to equalize its members' levels of development. Rather, the picture is one of covert conflict over the terms of trade and competition for shares of the Soviet subsidy, on the one hand, and extensive sabotage of joint undertakings, on the other. The new findings, however, shed equal doubt on long-held Western interpretations of Soviet–East European relations. Most observers discarded long ago the myth of a monolithic communist bloc, but few were prepared to see the fundamental weakness behind Soviet policy or the bureaucratic paralysis that allowed the Soviet satellites to plot their own orbits, and to maneuver deftly to avoid Soviet integration initiatives.

Soviet policy toward Eastern Europe failed because the artificial prices employed in CMEA trade created compelling incentives for the East Europeans to shirk their international obligations. They consciously undermined integration programs by negotiating for loopholes, filling trade plans with outdated goods, and resisting organizational reforms that were intended as confidence-building measures. In the implementation phase of each undertaking, they cheated on product quality and investment in joint projects. Meanwhile, the perverse incentives created by Soviet institutions prevented the Soviet Union from pursuing a responsive and coordinated policy. Soviet officials failed to bargain with resolve, to forge credible commitments, to make strategic linkages, and to enforce their partners' obligations. The satellites ran circles around Soviet negotiators, and became a growing drain on the Soviet economy. The rational pursuit of private interest—by the socialist states of Eastern Europe and by the officials of the Soviet bureaucracy—led to results that substantially undermined the viability of the system.

This chapter will attempt to abstract from the details of the previous discussion in order to lay bare the fundamental arguments of the book. Two major themes run throughout: first, that trade politics in the Soviet bloc is best portrayed as distributional conflict motivated by distorted prices, and second, that Soviet policy toward the satellites was crippled by domestic institutional failures. Under each of these headings, a number of specific propositions have been advanced; this chapter pulls them together systematically and assesses how well they have been tested. Ideally, I would like to present a formal estimate of the uncertainty of my empirical findings, but to do so here would require me to plunge back into the details.[1] Instead, this chapter summarizes the evidence presented in the previous chapters, pointing to the contributions that individual chapters have made to the overall argument. For the casual reader, this will serve to weave the arguments made earlier into a coherent whole. For the technical reader, this chapter highlights which pieces of my argument rest on which pieces of evidence, presenting a sort of reader's guide for the unfriendly critic. The best impressionistic estimate that can be made of the uncertainty of this study's findings will be based on the reader's own careful weighing of the evidence presented in the previous chapters.

In order to assess the persuasiveness of my argument, finally, the reader should evaluate the contribution that individual chapters make to a coherent research design. The research design sought to test the implications of distributional conflict and institutional failure in a series of divergent contexts. Part 2 tested the propositions against new evidence about bilateral trade negotiations, subjected them to statistical tests, and examined them in light of Soviet interventions in East European domestic politics. The four case studies presented in part 3 span a period of more than twenty years, and represent initiatives in fields as diverse as industrial organization, energy and raw materials production, scientific and technological development, and monetary and price reform. These four cases represent the major Soviet efforts to reform the CMEA, and cover the gamut of possible solutions to the crisis in Soviet–East European relations. I claim that the appearance of similar patterns in such divergent contexts is strong evidence on behalf of the interpretation that I advance. Distributional conflict and institutional failure capture the essential features of Soviet–East European economic relations.

RULES OF THE GAME: THE POLITICS OF SUBSIDIZED TRADE

The first major argument of this book has been that trade politics in the former Soviet bloc was fundamentally different from conventional trade politics among countries with market economies because of the distorted incentives created by artificial prices. The East European satellites planned their trade in order to maximize the Soviet trade subsidy, rather than to specialize efficiently or to exploit comparative advantage. This meant that few joint gains were to be had, and trade negotiations became a matter of maneuvering for relative advantage. From the East European point of view, there was always an incentive to economize on the quality of exports and to shirk on investment in allian-

[1] King, Keohane, and Verba, *Designing Social Inquiry*, pp. 31–32.

cewide projects. No cooperative equilibrium point existed within the dynamics of any of the areas of conflict that the Soviet Union sought to resolve. Rather, the satellites cooperated with Soviet policies only when the Soviet Union succeeded in forging effective linkages to other issues, and when the satellites' behavior could be monitored closely. Several specific arguments have been advanced in the preceding chapters:

1. There was continuous struggle over the commodity structure of trade, with each side seeking unilateral advantage defined in terms of the distorted prices that prevailed in the bloc.

2. The Soviet Union made repeated attempts to raise the quality and technical standards of East European products, and the East Europeans opposed these efforts.

3. The Soviet Union attempted to utilize its bargaining leverage by creating linkages, and the East Europeans sought to decouple these transactions.

4. The Soviet Union advanced initiatives to regularize trade relations, to promote accountability, and to achieve alliancewide objectives, and the satellites undermined these procedures.

5. The satellites used covert resistance during the process of implementation to evade Soviet demands.

As Table 10.1 indicates, the five propositions found support in a variety of contexts, and were upheld both in bilateral trade negotiations and in the four case studies. A combination of interviews and documents made it possible to reconstruct the salient characteristics of Soviet-bloc trade negotiations, and it became clear that the satellites' primary objective was to maximize their shares of the Soviet trade subsidy. The participants were aware which products were subsidized; they consistently offered to increase their exports of overpriced products and their imports of underpriced goods. Typically, the East Europeans offered a larger volume of trade than was finally agreed on, but one that would have secured more advantageous terms for themselves. When the Soviet negotiators reined in their exports of raw materials and imports of machinery, the East European response was to offer a reduced volume of trade.

Contrary to the expectations of a number of authors, East European opposition to particular integration initiatives was not driven by a desire to reduce dependence on Soviet trade.[2] The satellites did not oppose integration in principle; rather, they competed for shares of Soviet trade, and frequently expressed dissatisfaction about the limited ability of their major trading partner to expand its exports. The structure of trade, however, determined the volume of subsidized goods in each country's imports and exports, and consequently

[2]For examples of the contrary argument, see Brzezinski, *The Soviet Bloc*, pp. 456, 476–477; Garthoff, *Détente and Confrontation*, p. 498; Carrere d'Encausse, *Big Brother*, p. 260; Dawisha, *Eastern Europe*, pp. 93–94.

TABLE 10.1

Evaluation of Propositions about Subsidized Trade

Propositions	Chapter	Bilateral Relations Case Studies						
		3	4	5	6	7	8	9
1. Conflict over trade structure		•			•	•	•	•
2. Conflict over quality		•			•	•	•	•
3. Conflict over linkage		•			•	•	•	•
4. Conflict over confidence-building measures					•		•	•
5. Satellites seek to evade implementation					•	•	•	•

Note: Propositions supported by the evidence presented in a particular chapter are indicated with a bullet.

determined each country's share of the trade subsidy. This was the consideration that drove trade negotiations, and that motivated the East European maneuvers to modify Soviet integration proposals. Whenever an opportunity presented itself, the satellites modified the terms of agreements in ways that were calculated to optimize their trade profiles. The four case studies show that this led to the inclusion of traditional exports in the new specialization agreements, investment projects, and priority areas, which undermined their purpose.

There was substantial controversy over quality norms and technical standards. Soviet initiatives that would have eroded the subsidy, such as attempts to raise the technical specifications of East European machinery, provoked swift opposition. In bilateral trade negotiations, this often emerged as a subtext during discussions of the assortment of goods available for the Soviet Union to import. The East Europeans consistently proposed traditional, low-quality, standardized items, whereas Soviet negotiators preferred to substitute more advanced products that were closer in value to the stated price. The issue of quality control moved to center stage, however, in the four case studies. Each of the major Soviet integration programs attempted to improve the quality of East European manufactured goods, and in each case, the satellites made every effort to frustrate that objective.

Negotiations revolved around the issue of linkage, with Soviet negotiators attempting to link areas in which they held excess bargaining power to issues of unresolved conflict, and East European negotiators attempting to prevent these linkages from taking hold. The East Europeans were strikingly successful; indeed, a surprising finding was how ineffective the Soviet negotiators were at linking desired outcomes to Soviet power resources. Chapters 6 and 7 showed that the few concrete accomplishments of Soviet-sponsored integration programs depended on strategic linkages that the Soviet negotiators created between construction projects and exports of raw materials or energy. In each case, however, the failure to create similar linkages to motivate completion of projects in other areas led to the overwhelming failure of the program.

In each of the initiatives examined in the case studies, the Soviet Union attempted to create new procedures and institutions that would establish clear expectations about how the parties were to act in order to integrate the bloc, improve quality standards, and promote joint investments. The satellites, however, pursued obstructionist strategies. While the Soviet Union attempted to reduce uncertainty, the satellites sought to exploit any bargaining advantages that could be gleaned from it. Chapters 6, 8, and 9 demonstrated in detail how unilateral advantage dictated the countries' proposals for CMEA reform, and showed that East European opposition blocked Soviet reform initiatives. Judging that any organizational novelties introduced by the Soviet Union would reduce the East Europeans' ability to shirk undesirable obligations, and ultimately undermine profitable terms of trade, the satellites concentrated on eroding any reforms of international institutions that were proposed.

Finally, the case studies showed that the East Europeans opportunistically violated agreements whenever this would yield a short-term gain. If they had expected the Soviet Union to respond strategically in defense of its interests, the satellites would have faced incentives to adhere to agreements in order to maintain long-term cooperation. When unable to make an agreement work to their own advantage, however, the East Europeans simply failed to carry out its provisions. This behavior reveals the extent to which the East Europeans relied on Soviet paralysis. The East European negotiators, however, were circumspect in their treatment of controversial issues, seeking to create the appearance of accommodating Soviet wishes without giving up too much substance. The satellites tried to turn the discussion away from the sort of measurable progress the Soviet Union was trying to achieve, and toward the efforts they were putatively making to achieve it. Whenever possible, they sought to shift the grounds of discussion from Soviet needs and demands to their own weak political and economic situations, which limited their ability to comply. The purpose of these tactics was not to clarify, but to obscure; not to elicit a desired Soviet response, but to ward off improbable Soviet retaliation. Soviet integration initiatives succeeded only in so far as they were linked to concrete increases in the trade subsidy: increased imports of Soviet raw materials or increased exports of East European machinery.

INSTITUTIONAL FAILURE

The second major argument of this work has been that the apparent paradox of the Soviet Union's powerlessness to control its weak allies is explained by the incoherence of Soviet institutions. Soviet trade negotiators were officials in the economic bureaucracy and were embedded in the incentive structure imposed by the State Plan. The pressure to fulfill the Plan created incentives that crowded out activities other than those directed toward the achievement of quantitative indicators. As a result, Soviet negotiators displayed weak resolve, failed to make credible commitments, and neglected to monitor the East European satellites. Furthermore, the dynamics of plan revision compelled rational administrators to conceal their productive capacity, their technology, and their true requirements for inputs. As a result, vertical communication broke down, issues became compartmentalized, and Soviet negotiators failed to forge effective linkages between issues affecting different sectors of the economy. Since the Soviet strategy in trade politics depended on resolve, credibility, linkage, and monitoring, whereas the East European strategy relied on the failure of those strategies, institutional failures typical of the entire socialist world worked to the benefit of the East European satellites. The following propositions have been developed in the previous chapters:

1. Failure of resolve. Low-level officials faced weak incentives to display resolve in bargaining with the satellites, so the East Europeans could exploit inconsistencies in the Soviet bargaining position at different levels in the hierarchy.

2. Crisis of credibility. Low-level officials faced incentives to shirk tasks that were not well specified in the Plan, so higher-level officials were unable to make credible commitments that such objectives would be met.

3. Failure of linkage. Vertical communication was stifled, which compartmentalized issues and restricted the Soviet Union's ability to make strategic linkages between its power resources and its objectives.

4. Failure to monitor. Soviet officials faced weak incentives to monitor the satellites, so the bureaucracy was unable to enforce East European performance of agreements.

Table 10.2 indicates propositions supported by the evidence presented in previous chapters.

The incentive problems in the Soviet economy have been documented by others, so this study did not seek to test the hypothesized crowding-out effect, or ratchet effect. Instead, the contribution of this study is to show that these incentives have profound implications for foreign policy. The four propositions I have developed argue that incentive problems caused failures of Soviet bargaining strategy. In the course of extensive archival and interview research in Moscow, Warsaw, Prague, and Budapest, it was possible to reconstruct the process of negotiation to show where bargaining failures occurred both in bilateral relations and in the four case studies. In bilateral trade negotiations, Soviet failures of resolve and linkage played the central role, and it was particularly variations in the Soviet ability to apply linkage strategies that explained the patterns of success and failure. The issues of credibility and monitoring moved to center stage in the case studies, because of the increased complexity of Soviet objectives and the long time required to implement

TABLE 10.2

Evaluation of Institutional Failures

Propositions	Chapter	Bilateral Relations Case Studies						
		3	4	5	6	7	8	9
1. Failure of resolve		•			•	•	•	•
2. Failure of credibility				•		•	•	•
3. Failure of linkage		•	•	•	•	•	•	•
4. Failure of monitoring					•	•	•	•

Note: Propositions supported by the evidence presented in a particular chapter are indicated with a bullet.

them. Where the Soviet Union was able to make the most credible commitments and exert the most resolve, such as in large, visible projects that were easily quantifiable, the Soviet Union was most successful in achieving East European cooperation. When monitoring was difficult and resolve and credibility were lacking, as in endeavors to raise quality standards and promote technical development, the results were much more meager.

Resolve. A common pattern emerged in the record of Soviet–East European negotiations: agreements that had been reached tortuously at higher levels unraveled when lower-level officials descended upon the details. Subordinates in the Soviet hierarchy simply had no incentive to insist on central priorities. The weak incentives to bargain vigorously were illustrated by Soviet negotiators' surprising vulnerability to time pressure. Doing something "according to plan" meant doing it on time and filing the proper paperwork, and since Soviet management methods put such emphasis on timing, Soviet negotiators were particularly vulnerable to delaying tactics. The case studies demonstrated that the effort to complete negotiations in time to integrate their results into the Soviet five-year planning cycle compelled the Soviet negotiators to leave crucial issues undecided, to paper over important disputes, and to give in on key points.

As the model predicts, in bilateral trade and in the case studies, the resolve of Soviet negotiators was directly proportional to the tangibility of Soviet objectives. Quantitative targets were vigorously defended, because they were highlighted by the system of Soviet plan evaluation. The underlying weakness of bargaining resolve at the lower levels of the hierarchy was illustrated, however, by the pervasive failure of Soviet negotiators to insist on quality control. Although improving the quality of East European exports had been a high Soviet priority since the 1960s, Soviet negotiators in the 1970s and 1980s were quick to sacrifice quality considerations in order to meet quantitative targets. In bilateral trade negotiations, Soviet negotiators typically spent the majority of each negotiating session discussing detailed numerical quotas, and at the end made a passing reference to the importance of improving the quality of East European exports. It was clear to both sides which issue took priority. In fact, in the cases where the East Europeans saw an advantage in improving the quality of their products in order to raise their prices and reduce their quantitative quotas, their offers were often rebuffed because the Soviets needed to meet quantitative targets. The case studies confirmed this pattern. Each of the integration programs launched in the 1970s and 1980s set quality control as a top priority. In each case, however, the Soviet trade negotiators who had to fill in the details allowed the satellites to substitute lower-quality, less innovative, and more traditional exports for the new products the designers had envisioned. None of the administrative changes that the programs made altered the basic thrust of planning priorities, which was to sacrifice quality to quantitative indicators. As a result, when trade negotiators raised quality control as an issue at all, they treated it as a formality and quickly moved on.

In addition, the resolve of Soviet negotiators declined markedly as issues became more complex and detailed, because the ability of superiors to monitor the bargainers was severely attenuated. As a result, although the Soviet side dominated the initial stages of bargaining over each integration program—it was able to set the agenda, rule motions out of order, and advance its own text as the basis for discussion—it was able to prevail only at the most general and symbolic levels. As the topics under discussion became more concrete and complex, Soviet bargaining leverage slipped away. As general principles were translated into programs, the programs were refined into a series of discrete projects, and the projects were farmed out to a series of cooperating organizations, the Soviet Union gradually lost control of the process. Poor cooperation between levels of the Soviet hierarchy and between Soviet organizations was magnified as the scope of each undertaking expanded, and the already weak Soviet capacity for administrative oversight was stretched to the limit as the parameters of success and failure became more subtle and the time horizon lengthened. Thousands of organizations were involved in the negotiation of an initiative like the Comprehensive Program for Science and Technology, and the negotiating strategies chosen by those organizations in the detailed bargaining rounds recast its character.

Credibility. Low-level officials in the Soviet hierarchy faced a rigid evaluation system, based on clearly defined quantitative objectives and intense pressure to achieve them. Ironically, this system of controls ensured that subordinates could not be relied on to execute any additional burdensome directives, particularly if their efforts were not transparent to higher officials. As a result, high-level negotiators were generally unable to make credible commitments that projects would be completed on time and within specified quality parameters, which severely undermined their bargaining power. Unable to commit to carry out their own obligations, they were unable to convince other countries to contribute to joint projects. Collective-action problems, which were serious in any case, became intractable when the central player consistently failed to keep its commitments.

My research confirmed two patterns of variation in Soviet abilities to project credibility that were predicted by the model. First, Soviet commitments should have more credibility when they could be fulfilled within a short time, were well specified in quantitative terms, and did not rely on subsidiary organizations to carry out their provisions. Soviet commitments to export particular quantities of goods or to repay trade debts, for example, did not lack credibility. Soviet threats in bilateral bargaining were undermined by communication failures in the bureaucracy, but they did have some credibility and represented a source of bargaining leverage. In the four case studies, however, we observe that Soviet credibility was severely strained by long time horizons, lack of precision about qualitative parameters, and the large number of subsidiary organizations whose activities had to be coordinated. Furthermore, the model predicts that Soviet credibility should steadily decline over time. Research on the four case studies showed that as time went on, East Europeans frequently referred to the failure of past programs as a reason to expect new initiatives to be fruitless. As a result, Soviet bargaining power deteriorated dramatically; the USSR achieved fewer of its objectives in each successive initiative.

Linkage. The chapters on bilateral trade negotiations and the four case studies demonstrate that Soviet bargaining performance suffered from a persistent failure to forge advantageous linkages between issues. The Soviet practice of escalating plan targets to exceed the maximum level of past performance created incentives for organizations at all levels to hide information from their superiors. As a result, vertical communication broke down between levels of the bureaucracy, and issues became compartmentalized. Since critical information tended to pool at the lowest levels, that was where operational decisions had to be made. Most detailed trade negotiations were delegated to specialized agencies, which were evaluated according to their performance of narrow tasks. Consequently, no one in the system was left with both the opportunity and the inclination to defend a comprehensive view of the national interest. The political consequence was that the Soviet Union could not make efficient use of its subsidy, because it was unable to forge linkages between areas of excess bargaining leverage and issues of unresolved contention. This was made particularly clear in chapters 4 and 5. Chapter 4 used statistical tests to show that the distribution of the subsidy was inconsistent with the hypothesis of an active linkage strategy, and chapter 5 used case studies of Czechoslovakia in 1968, Hungary in the 1970s, and Poland in 1981 to argue that the implicit trade subsidy was apparently not linked to the resolution of crises in the bloc.

Research results confirm the model's prediction of a pattern in the failure of linkage. The model argues that linkage was blocked by the distance between peak-level Soviet decision makers and the subsidiary organizations that hoarded the information needed to make operational decisions. That distance was relatively small within Gosplan, which managed the aggregate bilateral trade negotiations; it increased when ministries had to be brought in to discuss particular projects, such as direct investments on Soviet territory; and it increased further in the initiatives covered by the case studies, when thousands of organizations became involved in various stages of negotiation. Linkages were difficult to forge even at the aggregate level, but some linkages did take hold in bilateral trade negotiations, and concentrated effort could make them stick. In the Comprehensive Program and the Target Programs, similarly, Gosplan negotiators were able to forge certain linkages between East European participation in raw material development and increased Soviet exports; these linkages explain the few areas in which the programs were successful. In each of the case studies, however, linkage strategies quickly broke down because of the great number of organizations involved.

Monitoring. The Soviet Union was able to monitor the satellites' performance of their treaty obligations in only the most rudimentary ways. Again, there is a pattern here. The Soviet Union was perfectly capable of monitoring the quantities of goods delivered according to annual trade protocols, and it permitted no deviations from the Plan on that score. Soviet planning penalized agencies that failed to procure the proper quantities of goods. Parameters of cooperation that were not well reflected in the Soviet Plan, however, were generally neglected, since the pressure to meet quantitative targets crowded out all other efforts. As a result, the case studies show that the East Europeans routinely failed to implement the elements of integration agreements that they found onerous. In a particularly candid example, Polish documents demonstrate a deliberate policy of nonimplementation of projects in the Comprehensive Program for Progress in Science and Technology that were not expected to create a net increase in Polish machinery exports. Each of the case studies shows a pattern of general subversion of agreements on specialization, which had been intended to improve the quality of East European exports. In each case, the Soviet Union appeared powerless to affect the substance of its allies' policies, despite achieving formal consent to its priorities.

DIRECTIONS FOR FUTURE RESEARCH

The Soviet monstrosity ultimately failed its own test: it could not vindicate itself in materialist terms, and the forces of history left it behind. This book has explored one dimension of this story. The infrastructure of empire collapsed at many points; one of the first was the system of economic arrangements that sustained the East European periphery. Many contributions remain to be made before a theorist of institutions will be able to claim a comprehensive explanation for the failure of the Soviet experiment, but this book might be seen as a first step. I have traced the theoretical connections between the incentive structures created by Soviet central planning and the many failures of Soviet foreign economic policy. If the analysis presented here is sound, similar policy failures, with similar antecedents, should have abounded in other areas of Soviet public policy.

A question that may occur to the reader is whether the foreign policy of the Soviet successor state, the Russian Federation, is likely to be plagued by the same bargaining failures. In the aftermath of the Soviet collapse, large-scale economic reform, and the reshuffling of political alliances, many of the causal mechanisms that are central to this analysis have passed into history. Central planning of the economy is no longer practiced in any of the countries covered in this study, and with it have gone the perverse incentives associated with quantitative quotas. Central planning no longer generates a crowding-out effect, which for so long prevented innovation and investment in quality; nor does it produce a ratchet effect, which induced economic units at all levels to curtail their performance and conceal information from superiors. This suggests that Russia will not face the same problems as its Soviet predecessor, since the mechanisms that spawned those problems—the crowding-out effect and the ratchet effect—were features specific to the central planning process. Although the negotiators are the same in many cases, they will be operating in a different institutional context, and that should make all the difference. The Russians have continued to subsidize their neighbors, but the implication of this analysis is that the political benefits of doing so should be more tangible than in the past.

Principal-agent problems, however, have not gone away, and they continue to be rooted in the recurring problems of asymmetric information: moral hazard and adverse selection. In a time of simultaneous economic and political transition, when policies are in flux and institutions are being destroyed and created, information problems will be exacerbated. These old problems arise in three new policy areas in Russia and Eastern Europe that underscore the continued importance of principal-agent analysis: fiscal stabilization, privatization, and regulation of monopolies.

An extensive literature has grown up around the dilemmas that asymmetric information creates for monetary and fiscal policy. Policymakers suffer from time inconsistency, which means that it is usually optimal to act one way *ex post* (to inflate the economy) and to promise to do something else *ex ante* (not to inflate the economy). If the promise is believed, wages and prices will rise more slowly, and a surprise inflation shock will increase employment. This generally becomes known over time, however, so the trick cannot be repeated. Worse, the threat that such a trick might be employed fuels the inflationary spiral, and sends policymakers scrambling for some way to make a credible commitment. The consequences are institutions, such as independent central banks, and rules, such as fixed exchange rates, which reduce policy-makers' freedom to exercise discretion.[3] The problem, however, is that the instruments of monetary and fiscal policy are so complex, and the exigencies that might influence the optimal array of policies at any time are so numerous, that it is impossible write a complete contract governing them. This makes it difficult for the government to commit to an anti-inflationary policy. In fact, the greater the information advantage that the government has over the markets for labor and capital, the more severe is the dilemma, and the more difficult macroeconomic stabilization is likely to be. The complexity of the transition from planning to markets is likely to accentuate the government's informational advantage, exacerbating the temptation to cheat, and undermining the commitments that are necessary to stabilize the economy.

Privatization, too, involves dilemmas related to asymmetric information. A short-lived Polish minister of privatization has been quoted as saying that "privatization is when someone who doesn't know who the real owner is, and doesn't know what it's really worth, sells something to someone who doesn't have any money."[4] This is a classic example of adverse selection. The buyer inevitably has more information about the viability of an enterprise and the value of its assets than the government, particularly when the buyer is the previous management. Consequently, reformers intent on promoting privatization have been forced to sweeten the deal by undervaluing assets and extending lavish government subsidies. There is some evidence that in Russia these policies have helped to perpetuate the soft budget constraint that privatization was intended to abolish.[5] Furthermore, the transition period from state to private ownership is fraught with perverse incentives. If the enterprise will be sold to insiders, those insiders have a strong incentive to deflate the enterprise's performance in order to lower the price of its shares. On the other hand, if the managers are not the prospective buyers, they face a powerful moral hazard. Unable to share in future profits, why should they attempt to protect the value of the firm's assets?[6] Regardless of the privatization strategy chosen, the transition from public to private ownership on a massive scale will create perverse incentives related to asymmetric information.

Adding complexity to a difficult transition, the landscape of the former Soviet Union and Eastern Europe is dotted with huge enterprises that dominate their particular lines of products. In the context of market reform, therefore, monopoly power becomes a serious concern. Government regulation of

---

[3]A number of the seminal articles on the subject are collected in Persson and Tabellini, *Monetary and Fiscal Policy.*

[4]Attributed to Janusz Lewandowski, who was minister of ownership transformation in Poland for a short time.

[5]Sutela, "Insider Privatization"; Clarke et al., "The Privatization of Industrial Enterprises."

[6]For an early discussion of the problem of "asset stripping," see Lipton and Sachs, "Privatization in Eastern Europe."

monopolists, however, is no simple matter, and inappropriate forms of regulation can lead to broad shirking by inefficient managers (because of moral hazard) or to excessive government subsidies to more efficient ones (because of adverse selection). In addition, there will be recurring problems of predatory pricing to deter entry into markets and collusion to fix prices. There is, furthermore, a trade-off between the cost of exploitation by unscrupulous monopolists and the costs of political corruption created by the attempt to regulate them. The market failures associated with monopoly power will necessitate extensive government intervention in the economy, but this will create opportunities for industry to capture the regulators, and cause the costs of political patronage to mount.

Principal-agent analysis continues to capture fundamental dilemmas facing policymakers in the former Soviet Union and Eastern Europe, and can be expected to generate fruitful lines of inquiry long into the future. Macroeconomic stabilization, privatization, and regulation of monopolies represent only a few of the possible applications. The dilemmas created by asymmetric information, in turn, will certainly be exported into Russian foreign economic policy. In the highly interdependent states that have emerged from the ruins of the Soviet Union, Russian policy choices will take on great significance. Furthermore, the success of Russian aspirations to lead the Commonwealth of Independent States will depend in large measure on Russia's success in resolving the dilemmas of stabilization, privatization, and regulation. The specific manifestations of principal-agent problems in the political economy of Russia and Eastern Europe provide a rich agenda for future research.

Poland

Adam Barszczewski
Long experience of CMEA affairs in the Ministry of Foreign Trade; Adviser to the Minister, Ministry for Foreign Economic Cooperation.

Dr. habil. Prof. Paweł Bożyk
1962–72, Researcher, Instytut Koniunktur i Cen Handlu Zagranicznego; 1972–77, Scientific Adviser to PUWP First Secretary Edward Gierek; 1977–80, Head of Team of Scientific Advisers to PUWP First Secretary; Professor, GSPiS, 1979–; PUWP member.

Anatol Dikij
Early 1970s–, Specialist, then Deputy Director, Department for the World Economy, Planning Commission; dealt with CMEA affairs until 1982, when he was charged with bilateral relations with the Soviet Union.

Stanisław Długosz
1966–72, Deputy Department Director, Ministry of Foreign Trade; 1972–80, Deputy Minister of Foreign Trade; 1980–90, Podsekretarz Stanu (Deputy Chairman), Polish Planning Commission; PUWP member.

Dr. Paweł Glikman
Economist, with extensive publications and CMEA experience; worked with a group of Polish experts that prepared materials for the CMEA Economic Commission in the 1960s; Member of the Institute of Economic Sciences, Polish Academy of Sciences.

Dr. habil. Stanisław Góra
1960s–early 1970s, Specialist in the Instytut Koniunktur i Cen; 1962–71, Specialist on the CMEA Economic Commission; worked on the Polish proposal for the Comprehensive Program; early 1970s–78, worked in the international CMEA institute, MIEP MSS; 1978–, Professor at GSPiS, Warsaw.

Ryszard Grabas
Early 1970s–79, Specialist in Planning Commission, Department for Relations with Socialist Countries; 1976–79, Secretary of the Polish-USSR bilateral International Commission for Coordination of Plans and Scientific and Technical Cooperation; 1979–82, First Secretary, Polish Embassy to the USSR for economic affairs; 1982–85, Specialist, Ministry of Foreign Trade, working on relations with the USSR, joint investments, and the Polish debt; 1985–87, trade attaché in Albania.

Dr. Wiesław Grudzewski
Specialist in the Planning Commission; 1985–88, Director, Department for Cooperation with Socialist Countries, Komitet Nauki i Techniki, and Podsekretarz stanu (Deputy Minister), UPNTiW.

Władysław Gwiazda

1964–, staff member of Ministry of Foreign Trade; 1971–73, Ambassador to USSR; 1973–81, Deputy Minister of Foreign Trade; 1985–87, 1988–89, Deputy Chairman, Council of Ministers, and Permanent Representative to CMEA; 1987–89, Minister of Foreign Economic Cooperation; PUWP member.

Dr. Andrzej Karpinski

Deputy Chairman, Planning Commission, dealt with long-term planning; late 1970s, dealt with CMEA affairs; Professor, Polish Academy of Sciences; author of numerous publications.

Maciej Król

Official in the Planning Commission; late 1980s–, Adviser to the Minister, Central Planning Office.

Dr. habil. Stanisław Kuziński

Soldier in Peoples' Guard, then Peoples' Army during World War II; 1954–56, Inspector, PUWP Central Committee; 1956–57, Secretary, Warsaw PUWP Committee; 1959–64, Deputy Director, Economic Department, PUWP Central Committee; 1964–73, Director, Economic Department, PUWP Central Committee; 1972–80, Chairman, Central Office for Statistics (GUS); PUWP member.

Marja Laskowska

Official in the Department of the World Economy, Planning Commission.

Dr. Andrzej Lubbe

Academic consulted by the Central Planning Office; 1991–, Deputy Chairman, CUP.

Zbigniew Machula

Deputy Director, Department for Foreign Cooperation, Committee for Scientific Research (KBN, successor to UPNTiW).

Dr. habil. Zbigniew Madej

1959–64, Staff member, Economic Department, PUWP Central Committee; 1964–71, Director, Economic Department, Committee for Science and Technology; 1972–75, Deputy Head, then Head, Economic Department, PUWP Central Committee; 1975–80, Podsekretarz Stanu, Ministry of Finance; 1980–June 1981, Deputy Chairman, Planning Commission; June 1981–October 1982, Chairman, Planning Commission; June 1981–November 1983, Deputy Chairman, Council of Ministers, and Permanent Representative to CMEA; PUWP member.

Jan Mazur

1950–83, official in the Planning Commission; 1969–74, posted to the CMEA, Department for Integrated Economic Work; 1974–80 Director, department for the CMEA, Planning Commission; 1980–83, PUWP Economic Department representative and Party First Secretary in the Planning Commission; 1983–87, Polish trade representative in Yugoslavia.

Dr. Jozef Pajestka

1958–62, Director, Economic Research Center, Planning Commission; 1962–72, Director, Planning Institute; 1968–81, Deputy Chairman, Planning Commission; 1968–81, PUWP Central Committee member.

Piotr Pajestka

1986–, Specialist and then Director, Department of International Cooperation,

UPNTiW, and Committee for Scientific Research (KBN); involved in the realization phase of the KP NTP.
Andrzej Pelczarski
    1953–, Specialist in the International Economic Department, Polish Council of Ministers.
Dr. habil. Maciej Perczyński
    Academic economist and political observer; author of numerous publications on the CMEA; brief service on Gomułka's Economic Council in the 1950s.
Dr. Jerzy Rutkowski
    Director, Economic Department, Ministry for Foreign Economic Cooperation.
Alfred Siennicki
    Early to mid-1970s, CMEA Economic Research and Statistics Department; mid-1970s–84, Director of the Department for Foreign Economic Cooperation, Planning Commission; took part in meetings of the KSOPD working group for the Long-Term Target Program in Energy; 1984–88, Polish trade representative to Yugoslavia; 1989–91, Director, Department for International Economic Affairs, Council of Ministers.
Dr. Jozef Soldaczuk
    Influential Polish reform economist; chaired the group of economists who drew up the Polish position paper for the Comprehensive Program; Professor, Instytut Koniunktur i Cen.
Stanisław Sudak
    Deputy Director, Department for the World Economy, Central Planning Office.
Dr. Eugeniusz Tabaczyński
    Polish reform economist; Professor, Instytut Koniunktur i Cen.
Dr. habil. Konrad Tott
    1982–, Director, Institute of Aircraft in Warsaw; 1985, Planning Commission member; 1985–87, Minister and Head of UPNTiW; author of numerous scientific works on aeronautics.
Ewa Wacowska
    Official, Planning Commission.
Ryszard Ziółkowski
    1970s–early 1990s, Specialist, Deputy Director and Director, Department for Foreign Cooperation, Ministry of Metallurgy and Machine Industry.

Czechoslovakia

Bedřich Bašta
    Consultant, Projekčni a konsultačni služby; Specialist on hydroelectric power.
Miroslav Černý
    Until 1972, worked in a machine-building enterprise; 1972–92, State Planning Commission, later Federal Ministry of the Economy; 1972–78, worked on CMEA affairs; 1978–92, Specialist, then Director of the Subdepartment for the USSR, which was subsequently expanded to cover all the CMEA countries, then Deputy Department Director.
Zdeněk Chalupský
    Director, Department for CMEA Affairs, Institute of Economics, Czechoslovak

Academy of Sciences; worked closely with the Planning Commission, and was present at numerous CMEA meetings; author of several publications.

Vladislav Cihlař

Until 1969, worked in the CMEA; 1970–90, Specialist, later Director, Department for Relations with Socialist Countries, Czechoslovak Council of Ministers.

Dr. Milan Čížkovskí

Academic commentator on CMEA affairs; 1968, fired from Prognostic Institute, Czechoslovak Academy of Sciences, then returned under Komarek; 1990–, Director, Department for Integration and Territorial Policy, Ministry of the Economy.

Anton Fábik

Until 1983, Ministry of Foreign Trade; 1983–92, CMEA; 1992–, Price Department, Ministry of Foreign Trade.

Petr Hanzal

1972–76, Legal Department, CMEA; 1976–, legal adviser in the Department for Relations with Socialist Countries, Council of Ministers.

Zdeněk Holas

Engineer in a heavy chemical plant; Specialist, Ministry of Industry; 1978–84, Director, Management Department, Ministry of Industry; 1984–, Adviser, Planning Commission of the Czech Republic.

Vasil Hrinda

1974–88, Specialist, Department for Relations with Socialist Countries, Ministry of Finance; 1988–91, Monetary-Financial Department; 1991–, Director, Department for Relations with Socialist Countries.

Dr. Lidia Klausová

Economist, Institute of Economics, ČSAV; wife of Václav Klaus, Prime Minister of Czechoslovakia, then of the Czech Republic.

Dr. Miroslav Kolanda

Department Director, Research Institute for Foreign Economic Ties (VUVEV).

Milan Kopecký

Specialist in the State Planning Commission; Director, Subdepartment, Council of Ministers.

Václav Kotouč

1953–63, Specialist, Department for the Local Economy, Planning Commission; 1963–80, subdepartment for relations with socialist countries other than the USSR; 1980–, Director, subdepartment for CMEA affairs.

Jaroslav Kozáčík

Director, Institute for Economic Policy of the Ministry for Economic Policy and Development of the Czech Republic.

Václav Kupka

First Deputy Minister, Ministry for Economic Policy and Development, Czech Republic; Specialist, investment policy.

Hugo Kysilka

1972–83, Specialist, international relations, Price Office; 1983–87, Price Department, Ministry of Foreign Trade; 1987–89, Prognostic Institute, Czechoslovak Academy of Sciences; 1989–92, Deputy Czechoslovak Permanent Representative to CMEA.

Eva Lašová

> 1971–81, Specialist; 1981–85, Director, Department for Relations with Socialist Countries, Ministry of Foreign Trade; 1985–90, attached to the international commissions for coordination of planning with European CMEA countries excluding the USSR; 1990–92, Director, Price Department, Ministry of Foreign Trade.

Ladislav Mindoš

> Until 1983, Ministry of Foreign Trade; 1983–88, CMEA; 1988–, Price Department, Ministry of Foreign Trade.

Dr. Alena Nešporová

> Deputy Director, Prognostic Institute, Czechoslovak Academy of Sciences.

Josef Pancíř

> Deputy Minister of Foreign Trade.

Jaromír Prchlík

> Specialist, State Planning Commission, later Federal Ministry of the Economy; long experience in negotiations with the Soviet Union over trade in machinery.

Jozef Ružička

> Until 1970, Specialist, Department for Relations with Socialist Countries, Council of Ministers (fired); 1970–89, Researcher, Scientific Research Institute for Metallurgy; 1989–, Research Institute for Foreign Economic Ties (VUVEV).

Zdeněk Šedivý

> 1965–69, Specialist, State Planning Commission; 1969–83, Deputy Chairman, Department for Relations with Socialist Countries, State Planning Commission; 1983–90, Director, Central Institute for Economic Research (UUNV); 1990–, Research Institute for Foreign Economic Ties (VUVEV).

Pavel Štěpanek

> Deputy Minister of Finance.

Dr. František Stranský

> Until 1969, Secretary, Commission for Foreign Economic Ties, Council of Ministers (fired); Researcher, then Deputy Director, Research Institute for Foreign Economic Ties.

Dr. Zdeněk Vitvar

> Long experience in bilateral trade relations in the State Planning Commission; Director, Department for Relations with Former Socialist Countries, Ministry of the Federal Economy.

Hungary

Ferenc Bacsi

> Director, Foreign Economic Policy Department, Ministry of Finance.

Dr. Akos Balassa

> 1957–65, Specialist in CMEA affairs, Department for Machinery, National Planning Commission; 1965–69, Specialist, Economic Department, which prepared the State Plan; 1969–70, Head, Integrated Subdepartment of the Economic Department; 1970–78, Deputy Head, Economic Division, which took on five-year planning as well at this time; 1978–89, Head, Economic Division; 1989–92, Deputy Chairman, National Committee for Technological Development, member

of Government Commission for Economic Reform; 1992–, Managing Director, National Bank of Hungary.

Dr. Bela Csikos-Nagy

1941–45, Secretary of Finance, Ministry of Finance; 1945–47, Deputy Secretary, Hungarian Government Economic Committee; 1947–51, Department Chief, Economics Planning Board; 1951–55, Deputy Minister, Local Light Industries, and Chairman of Prices Board; 1956–67, Chairman of Prices and Materials Board; 1967–, Undersecretary of State; 1967–, HSWP member; author of numerous publications.

Janos Czibula

1971–75, Specialist on the CSSR, Department for International Economic Relations, National Planning Commission; 1975–80, Council of Ministers Secretariat, Department for International Economic Relations; Secretary, bilateral Hungarian-CSSR Commission for Coordination of Plans and Scientific-Technical Cooperation; 1980–85, Deputy Commercial Counselor to the CSSR; 1985–87, Deputy Head, department for socialist countries excluding the USSR, Ministry of Foreign Trade; 1987–89, Commercial Director, Hungarian Optical Works; 1989–92, Head, department for socialist countries excluding the USSR, Ministry of Foreign Trade; 1992–, President, Limpex Co., Ltd.

Robert Geist

General Director, Ministry of Foreign Trade; 1992–, Adviser to the Chairman, Commercial and Credit Bank Ltd.

György Gilyan

Head of Department for Relations with Former Socialist Countries, Ministry of International Economic Relations.

Dr. Istvan Hetenyi

1948–, HSWP member; 1958–64, Head of Department for Long-term Planning, National Planning Office; 1964–73, Deputy Chairman for CMEA affairs, National Planning Office; 1973–80, First Deputy Chairman and State Secretary, National Planning Office; 1980–1987, Minister of Finance; Professor, Budapest University of Economics.

Jozsef Marjai

1943–, Hungarian Communist Party member; 1953–56, Chief of Departments in Ministry of Foreign Affairs; 1956–59, Ambassador to Switzerland; 1959–63, Ambassador to the CSSR; 1966–70, Ambassador to Yugoslavia; 1970–73, Deputy Minister of Foreign Affairs; 1973–76, First Deputy Minister of Foreign Affairs; August 1976–April 1978, Ambassador to USSR; April 1978–1987, Deputy Premier and Permanent Representative to CMEA.

Dr. Peter Medgyessy

1966–, staff member, Ministry of Finance; 1982–86, Deputy Minister of Finance; 1986–, Minister of Finance; 1987–89, Deputy Premier and Permanent Representative to CMEA.

Rezsö Nyers

1940–, Social-Democratic Party member; 1957–, HSWP Central Committee member; 1962–March 1974, Secretary (economics portfolio), HSWP Central Committee; 1962–66, Candidate Politburo Member; 1966–March 1974, Politburo Member; 1974–, Director, Institute of Political Economy, Hungarian Academy of Sciences; May 1988, Politburo Member and HSWP Secretary; author of numerous publications.

Gabor Oblath

Economist, Institute for Economic and Market Research and Information (Kopint-Datorg).

Laszlo Pal

Electrical Engineer and Economist; 1968–88, Head, Main Department, National Committee for Technological Development (NCTD); 1988, Head, First Division, NCTD (computers and telecommunications); Secretary of State, Ministry of Industry, Nemeth government; 1991–, Member of Parliament (Socialist).

Tamas Szabo

1969–, Official, National Committee for Technological Development; 1969–72, worked on Hungarian Automation and Computer Program; 1972–, NCTD Representative to CMEA; 1986–, Deputy General Director, Department of International Relations, NCTD.

Dr. Janos Szita

1946–48, economic expert with the Communist Party of Hungary; Deputy President, National Planning Bureau; 1955–56, First Deputy Minister of Finance; 1961–68, Secretary, Institute for International Relations; 1968–80, Head, Department of International Economic Relations, Ministry of Foreign Affairs; 1968–78, Deputy Foreign Minister; 1980–, Ambassador to Italy; author of several publications.

Dr. Matyas Szürös

1951–, Hungarian Communist Party member; cofounder, Hungarian Young Pioneers Movement; 1962, joined diplomatic service; 1965–75, staff member, then Deputy Head, Foreign Politics Department, HSWP Central Committee; 1975–78, Ambassador to the GDR; 1978–, HSWP Central Committee member; 1979–82, Ambassador to the USSR; 1982–83, Head, Foreign Politics Department, HSWP Central Committee; 1983–89, Secretary for Foreign Affairs, HSWP Central Committee; 1990–, Vice President, Hungarian National Assembly (Socialist).

Andras Zsolnai

Until 1977, Senior Adviser, National Planning Commission; 1977–87, Head, Department for Integrated Economic Work, CMEA; 1987–, Head, Department for Relations with Socialist Countries, National Planning Commission; Specialist, Ministry of Foreign Trade.

Note: All biographical information on East European officials not gathered from the respondents themselves is from Juliusz Stroynowski, ed., *Who's Who in the Socialist Countries of Europe* (Munich: K. G. Saur, 1989).

USSR

Dr. Oleg Bogomolov

1950–, CPSU member; 1956–62, Sector Chief, Scientific Research Institute for Economics, USSR Gosplan; 1962–69, Consultant, then Head of the Group of Economic Consultants, Department for Liaison with Socialist Countries, CPSU Central Committee; 1969–, Director, Institute for the Economy of the World

Socialist System, renamed Institute for International Economic and Political
Studies.

Dr. Aleksandr Bykov

Professor, Sector Head, IEMSS, specializing in science and technology policy in
the CMEA since the 1960s.

Dr. Boris Chumachenko

Akademik, USSR Academy of Sciences; General Director, International Scientific Research Institute for Problems of Management; Professor of cybernetics,
and laureat of the USSR State Prize for his work in that field.

Vladimir Ezerov

Head of laboratory, MNIIPU.

Dr. Ruslan Grinberg

Department Head, IEMSS, specializing in CMEA affairs and macroeconomic
policy.

Dr. Stanislav Iovtchouk

Head of Department, International Institute for Economic Problems of the World
Socialist System (MIEP MSS), CMEA.

Dr. Konstantin Ligai

Section Head, IEMSS.

Iurii Kormnov

1960s, Integrated Department (Svodnyi Otdel), Gosplan, under Sorokin; 1971–
78, Deputy Director, IEMSS, in charge of the General Economic Department;
1978–, staff member, Office of the USSR Permanent Representative to CMEA.

Vladimir Korsun

Senior Researcher, MNIIPU.

Leonid Krasnov

1960s–77, Economic Consultant, Department for Relations with Socialist Countries, CPSU Central Committee; 1977–88, Specialist, Office of the USSR Permanent Representative to CMEA; 1988–92, Deputy USSR Permanent
Representative to CMEA, and Head of the Integrated Economic Department.

Konstantin Lavrov

Until 1992, Senior Researcher, MIEP MSS; 1992–, Senior Researcher, MNIIPU.

Dr. Vladimir Leont'ev

Director, aeronautics factory; Division Director, State Committee for Science and
Technology.

Dr. Aleksandr Nekipelov

Deputy Director for international economic integration, IEMSS.

Dr. Igor' Orlik

Sector Head, IEMSS; historian, specialist in Balkan countries.

Iurii Pekshev

1949–60, Researcher, Institute for Foreign Trade (NIKI MVT); 1960–68, Head,
Subdepartment for branch-level cooperation, Gosplan; 1968–78, Consultant,
then Head of the Group of Economic Consultants, Department for Relations with
Socialist Countries, CPSU Central Committee; 1978–79, Head, Department for
Integrated Economic Work, CMEA; 1979–85, Head, Department for Foreign
Trade, and Collegium Member, Gosplan; 1986–91, staff member and unofficial

deputy chairman, Gosekonom komissiia of the Council of Ministers; 1992–, Advisor, Vneshekonombank.

Oleg Rybakov

1954–57, Specialist, Ministry of Foreign Trade; 1957–, State Committee for Economic Cooperation; Researcher, Gosplan Research Institute; 1964–74, Deputy Department Head, Gosplan; 1974–77, Consultant, Department for Relations with Socialist Countries, CPSU Central Committee; 1977–86, Sector Head, Department for Relations with Socialist Countries; 1986–89, Deputy Department Head; 1989–, Deputy Department Head, International Department (after the merger of the two departments); President's staff, USSR.

Iurii Shkarenkov

Researcher, IEMSS, since mid-1960s.

Dr. Stepan Sitaryan

1960–, CPSU member; 1970–74, Director, Scientific Research Institute of Finance; 1974–83, Deputy Minister of Finance; 1983–86, Deputy Chairman, USSR Gosplan; 1986–89, First Deputy Chairman, USSR Gosplan; 1987–, Akademik; 1989–91, Deputy Chairman, USSR Council of Ministers and Permanent Representative to the CMEA.

Dr. Viktor Starodubrovskii

Director, MNIIPU.

Dr. Alla Yaz'kova

Historian, Researcher, IEMSS.

Dr. Ruben Yevstigneev

Late 1960s–, Researcher, then Deputy Director, IEMSS.

Note: Biographical information on Soviet officials was taken from Alexander Rahr, *A Biographical Directory of 100 Leading Soviet Officials* (Boulder, Colo.: Westview Press, 1990).

Selected Bibliography

Published Literature

Akerlof, George. "The Market for Lemons." *Quarterly Journal of Economics* 54 (August 1970).

Alesina, Alberto, and Allan Drazen. "Why are Stabilizations Delayed?" *American Economic Review* 81 (1991).

Ausch, Sandor. *Theory and Practice of CMEA Cooperation.* Budapest: Akademiai Kiado, 1972.

Axelrod, Robert. *The Evolution of Cooperation.* New York: Basic Books, 1984.

Baldwin, David, ed. *Neorealism and Neoliberalism: The Contemporary Debate.* New York: Columbia University Press, 1993.

Beissinger, Mark R. *Scientific Management, Socialist Discipline, and Soviet Power.* Cambridge, Mass.: Harvard University Press, 1988.

Berliner, Joseph. *Factory and Manager in the USSR.* Cambridge, Mass.: Harvard University Press, 1957.

Bogomolov, O. T., ed. *Mirovoe sotsialisticheskoe khoziaistvo: voprosy politicheskoi ekonomii.* Moscow: Ekonomika, 1982.

Bożyk, Paweł, ed. *Raporty dla Edwarda Gierka.* Warsaw: Panstwowe Wydawnictwo Ekonomiczne, 1988.

Brzezinski, Zbigniew K. *The Soviet Bloc: Unity and Conflict.* Cambridge, Mass.: Harvard University Press, 1967.

Bunce, Valerie. "The Empire Strikes Back: The Evolution of the Eastern Bloc from a Soviet Asset to a Soviet Liability." *International Organization* 39, no. 1 (Winter 1985).

Calvert, Randall L. "The Rational Choice Theory of Social Institutions: Cooperation, Coordination, and Communication." Paper presented at the Center for International Affairs, Harvard University, 17 November 1993.

Carrere d'Encausse, Helene. *Big Brother: The Soviet Union and Soviet Europe.* New York: Holmes and Meier, 1987; Cambridge: Cambridge University Press, 1988.

Childs, David. *The GDR: Moscow's German Ally.* London: Unwin, 1983.

Chukanov, O. A. "Integratsiia kak faktor intensifikatsii ekonomiki stran SEV." *Kommunist* 17 (1982).

Chumachenko, B. A., V. B. Ezerov, and V. S. Korsun. *Problemy organizatsii upravleniia realizatsiei i obnovleniem Kompleksnoi Programmy Nauchno-Tekhnicheskogo Progressa stran-chlenov SEV.* Moscow: MNIIPU, 1989.

Chumachenko, B. A., and K. P. Lavrov. *Kompleksnaia programma nauchno-tekhnicheskogo progressa stran-chlenov SEV do 2000 goda (sostoianie; problemy, perspektivy).* Moscow: Gosudarstvennyi Komitet SSSR po nauke i tekhnike, 1990.

Čížkovský, Milan, and Karel Matějka. *ČSSR a Komplexní program vědeckotechnického pokroku členských států RVHP do roku 2000.* Prague: Československá Obchodní a Průmyslová Komora, 1987.

Clarke, Simon, Peter Fairbrother, Vladim Borisov, and Peter Bizyukov. "The Privatization of Industrial Enterprises in Russia: Four Case Studies." *Europe-Asia Studies* 46, no. 2 (1994): 179–214.

Colton, Timothy J. *The Dilemma of Reform in the Soviet Union.* New York: Council on Foreign Relations, 1986.

Csaba, Laszlo. *Eastern Europe in the World Economy.* Cambridge: Cambridge University Press, 1990.

Dawisha, Karen. *Eastern Europe, Gorbachev and Reform: The Great Challenge.* Cambridge: Cambridge University Press, 1988.

Dixit, Avinash K., and Barry J. Nalebuff. *Thinking Strategically: The Competitive Edge in Business, Politics and Everyday Life.* New York: Norton, 1991.

Eatwell, John, Murray Milgate, and Peter Newman, eds. *The New Palgrave: Game Theory.* New York: Norton, 1989.

Fainsod, Merle. *How Russia Is Ruled.* Cambridge, Mass.: Harvard University Press, 1967.

Fearon, James. "Cooperation and Bargaining under Anarchy." Paper presented at the Center for International Affairs, Harvard University, 3 November 1993.

Friedrich, Carl J., and Zbigniew K. Brzezinski, *Totalitarian Dictatorship and Autocracy.* Cambridge: Harvard University Press, 1956.

Fudenberg, Drew, Bengt Holmstrom and Paul Milgrom, "Short-Term Contracts and Long-Term Agency Relationships," *Journal of Economic Theory* 51 (June 1990).

Gaddis, John Lewis. *Strategies of Containment: A Critical Appraisal of Postwar American National Security Policy.* Oxford: Oxford University Press, 1982.

Garthoff, Raymond L. *Détente and Confrontation: American-Soviet Relations from Nixon to Reagan.* Washington, D.C.: The Brookings Institution, 1985.

Gilpin, Robert. *War and Change in World Politics.* Cambridge: Cambridge University Press, 1985.

Gowa, Joanne. "Bipolarity, Multipolarity, and Free Trade." *American Political Science Review* 83 (December 1989).

Griffith, William, ed. *Central and Eastern Europe: The Opening Curtain?* Boulder, Colo.: Westview, 1989.

Góra, Stanisław et al., ed. *Puti i metody kompleksnogo sovershenstvovaniia sistemy tsenoobrazovaniia v torgovle stran-chlenov SEV.* Moscow: Sovet Ekonomicheskoi Vzaimopomoshchi, 1977.

Gwertzman, Bernard, and Michael T. Kaufman, eds. *The Collapse of Communism.* New York: Times Books, 1990.

Heller, Mikhail, and Aleksandr Nekrich. *Utopia in Power: The History of the Soviet Union from 1917 to the Present.* New York: Simon and Schuster, 1986.

Hirschman, Albert. *National Power and the Structure of Foreign Trade.* Berkeley: University of California Press, 1945; 1980.

Hewett, Ed. *Reforming the Soviet Economy: Equality versus Efficiency.* Washington, D.C.: The Brookings Institution, 1988.

Holzman, Franklyn D. "Soviet Foreign Trade Pricing and the Question of Discrimination." *Review of Economics and Statistics* (May 1962).

———. *Foreign Trade under Central Planning.* Cambridge, Mass.: Harvard University Press, 1974.

————. *International Trade under Communism—Politics and Economics.* New York: Basic Books, 1976.

Jaruzelski, Wojciech. *Stan wojenny dlaczego . . .* Warsaw: Polska Oficyna Wydawnicza "BGW," 1992.

Kaminski, Antoni Z. *An Institutional Theory of Communist Regimes: Design, Function and Breakdown.* San Francisco: ICS, 1992.

Karpinski, Andrzej. *40 lat planowania w Polsce: problemy, ludzie, refleksje.* Warsaw: Państwowe Wydawnictwo Ekonomiczne, 1986.

Kaser, Michael. *Comecon: Integration Problems of the Planned Economies.* 1st ed. London: Oxford University Press, 1965.

Kennan, George F. *Memoirs, 1925–1950.* Boston: Little, Brown, 1967.

Keohane, Robert O. *After Hegemony: Cooperation and Discord in the World Political Economy.* Princeton, N.J.: Princeton University Press, 1984.

Keohane, Robert O., ed. *Neorealism and Its Critics.* New York: Columbia University Press, 1986.

Keohane, Robert O., and Joseph S. Nye. *Power and Interdependence.* 2d ed. Glenview, Ill.: Scott, Foresman, 1989.

Khrushchev, Nikita S. "Nasushchnye voprosy razvitiia mirovoi sotsialisticheskoi sistemy." *Kommunist,* no. 12 (1962): 3–27.

King, Gary, Robert Keohane, and Sidney Verba. *Designing Social Inquiry: Scientific Inference in Qualitative Research.* Princeton, N.J.: Princeton University Press, 1994.

"Kompleksnaia programma nauchno-tekhnicheskogo progressa stran-chlenov SEV do 2000 goda, Osnovnye polozheniia." *Problemy Teorii i Praktiki Upravleniia* 1 (January 1986).

Kormnov, Yurii. F. *Mezhdunarodnaia sotsialisticheskaia spetsializatsiia i kooperatsiia.* Moscow: Economika, 1981.

Kormnov, Yurii F. *Specialization and Co-operation in the Socialist Economies.* Moscow: Progress, 1980.

Kornai, Janos. *The Socialist System: The Political Economy of Socialism.* Princeton, N.J.: Princeton University Press, 1992.

Krasner, Stephen D., ed. *International Regimes.* Ithaca, N.Y.: Cornell University Press, 1983.

Kreps, David M. *Game Theory and Economic Modelling.* Oxford: Oxford University Press, 1990.

————. "Corporate Culture and Economic Theory." In James Alt and Kenneth Shepsle, eds., *Perspectives on Positive Political Economy.* Cambridge: Cambridge University Press, 1990.

Laffont, Jean-Jacques, and Jean Tirole. *A Theory of Incentives in Procurement and Regulation.* Cambridge: MIT, 1993.

Lavrov, K. P., ed. *Dokumenty SEV po voprosam nauchno-tekhnicheskogo sotrudnichestva.* Moscow: Sekretariat SEV, 1986.

Lax, David, and James Sebenius. "Negotiating through an Agent." *Journal of Conflict Resolution* 35 (September 1991).

Leont'ev, Vladimir, Vladilen Prokudin, Boris Chumachenko, and Vladimir Ezerov. "Kompleksnaia programma nauchno-tekhnicheskogo progressa stran-chlenov SEV:

metodologicheskie aspekty formirovaniia i upravleniia realizatsiei." *Problemy Teorii i Praktiki Upravleniia* 3 (1983). Moscow: Mezhdunarodnyi nauchno-issledovatel'skii institut problem upravleniia.

Lexikon RGW. Leipzig: VEB Bibliographisches Institut Leipzig, 1981.

Lipton, David, and Jeffrey Sachs. "Privatization in Eastern Europe: The Case of Poland." *Brookings Papers on Economic Activity* 2 (1990).

Madej, Zbigniew. *Zwroty na Polskiej drodze: rozważania o polityce i gospodarce.* Warsaw: Panstwowe Wydawnictwo Ekonomiczne, 1988.

Marer, Paul. "The Political Economy of Soviet Relations with Eastern Europe." In Sarah Meiklejohn Terry, ed., *Soviet Policy in Eastern Europe.* New Haven, Conn.: Yale University Press, 1984.

Marrese, Michael, and Jan Vanous. *Soviet Subsidization of Trade with Eastern Europe: A Soviet Perspective.* Berkeley: University of California Press, 1983.

Martin, Lisa L. *Coercive Cooperation: Explaining Multilateral Economic Sanctions.* Princeton, N.J.: Princeton University Press, 1992.

———. "Interests, Power and Multilateralism." *International Organization* 46 (Fall 1992).

Mendershausen, Horst. "Terms of Trade between the Soviet Union and Smaller Communist Countries." *Review of Economics and Statistics* (May 1959).

Milgrom, Paul, and John Roberts. *Economics, Organization and Management.* Englewood Cliffs, N.J.: Prentice Hall, 1992.

———. "Information Asymmetries, Strategic Behavior, and Industrial Organization." *American Economic Review* 77 (May 1987): 184.

———. "The Efficiency of Equity in Organizational Decision Processes." *American Economic Review* 80 (May 1990).

———. "An Economic Approach to Influence Activities in Organizations." *The American Journal of Sociology* 94 (July 1988).

Moe, Terry M. "The New Economics of Organization." *American Journal of Political Science* 28 (1984): 165–79.

———. "Interests, Institutions, and Positive Theory: The Politics of the NLRB." *Studies in American Political Development* 2 (1987): 236–99.

———. "The Politics of Structural Choice: Toward a Theory of Public Bureaucracy." In Oliver E. Williamson, ed., *Organization Theory: From Chester Barnard to the Present and Beyond.* New York: Oxford University Press, 1990.

Morgenthau, Hans. *Politics among Nations: The Struggle for Power and Peace.* 4th ed. New York: Knopf, 1967.

Nash, John. "Equilibrium Points in n-Person Games." *Proceedings of the National Academy of Sciences USA* 36 (1950).

North, Douglass. *Institutions, Institutional Change and Economic Performance.* New York: Cambridge University Press, 1990.

Nove, Alec. *The Soviet Economic System.* 2d ed. London: George Allen & Unwin, 1984.

Oblath, Gabor, and David Tarr. "The Terms-of-Trade Effects from the Elimination of State Trading in Soviet-Hungarian Trade." *Journal of Comparative Economics* 16 (1992): 75–93.

Olson, Mancur. *The Logic of Collective Action.* 2d ed. Cambridge, Mass.: Harvard University Press, 1971.

Pajestka, Jozef. *Polskie frustracje i wyzwania*. Warsaw: Polska Oficyna Wydawnicza "BGW," 1991.

Pekshev, Iurii Aleksandrovich. *Dolgosrochnye tselevye programmy sotrudnichestva stran-chlenov SEV*. Moscow: Izdatel'stvo Nauka, 1980.

Pekshev, Iu. A., and Iu. F. Kormnov. *Sotsialisticheskaia ekonomicheskaia integratsiia: itogi i perspektivy*. Moscow: 1974.

Persson, Torsten, and Guido Tabellini. *Monetary and Fiscal Policy*. Volume 1: *Credibility;* Volume 2: *Politics* (Cambridge, Mass.: MIT, 1994).

Putnam, Robert. "Diplomacy and Domestic Politics." *International Organization* 32 (Autumn 1978).

Riley, John. "Strong Evolutionary Equilibrium and the War of Attrition." *Journal of Theoretical Biology* 82 (1980).

Schelling, Thomas C. *The Strategy of Conflict*. Oxford: Oxford University Press, 1960.

Schwarz, Hans-Peter. *Vom Reich zur Bundesrepublik*. Neuwied: Hermann Luchterhand Verlag GmbH, 1966.

Sebenius, James K. "Negotiation Arithmetic: Adding and Subtracting Issues and Parties." *International Organization* 37 (Spring 1983).

Shapiro, Leonard. *The Communist Party of the Soviet Union*. New York: Random House, 1971.

Shepsle, Kenneth A. "Studying Institutions: Some Lessons from the Rational Choice Approach." *Journal of Theoretical Politics* 1, no. 2 (1989).

Skachkova, S. A. *Postroeno pri ekonomicheskom i tekhnicheskom sodeistvii Sovetskogo Soiuza*. Moscow: Mezhdunarodnye Otnosheniia, 1982.

Skilling, Gordon H. *Czechoslovakia's Interrupted Revolution*. Princeton, N.J.: Princeton University Press, 1976.

Sobell, Vladimir. *The Red Market: Industrial Co-operation and Specialization in Comecon*. Guildford, U.K.: Gower, 1984.

Sovet Ekonomicheskoi Vzaimopomoshchi. *Dokumenty SEV po voprosam nauchnotekhnicheskogo sotrudnichestva*. Moscow: SEV, 1986.

———. *Osnovnye dokumenty Soveta Ekonomicheskoi Vzaimopomoshchi*. 4th ed. 2 vols. Moscow: CMEA, 1981.

———. *Statisticheskii ezhegodnik stran-chlenov soveta ekonomicheskoi vzaimopomoshchi* (Moscow: Finansy i statistika, 1971–89).

Stein, Arthur A. "The Politics of Linkage." *World Politics* 33 (October 1980).

Sutela, Pekka. "Insider Privatization in Russia: Speculations on Systemic Change." *Europe-Asia Studies* 46, no. 3 (1994): 417–35.

Terry, Sarah M., ed. *Soviet Policy in Eastern Europe*. New Haven, Conn.: Yale University Press, 1984.

Van Brabant, Jozef M. *Socialist Economic Integration: Aspects of Contemporary Economic Problems in Eastern Europe*. Cambridge: Cambridge University Press, 1980.

Weitzman, Martin. "The 'Ratchet Principle' and Performance Incentives." *Bell Journal of Economics* 11, no. 1 (Spring 1980).

Wettig, Gerhard. *Entmilitarisierung und Wiederbewaffnung in Deutschland, 1943–1955*. Munich: R. Oldenbourg Verlag, 1967.

Williamson, Oliver E. *Markets and Hierarchies: Analysis and Antitrust Implications*.

A Study in the Economics of Internal Organization. New York: The Free Press, 1975.

————. *The Economic Institutions of Capitalism: Firms, Markets, Relational Contracting.* New York: The Free Press, 1985.

————, ed. *Organization Theory: From Chester Barnard to the Present and Beyond.* New York: Oxford University Press, 1990.

Zubkov, A. I, Iu. F. Kormnov, and S. I. Pomazanov. *Otraslevaia sotsialisticheskaia integratsiia.* Moscow: Nauka, 1976.

Unpublished Sources

Soviet Materials

Alampiev, P. M., S. I. Pomazanov, O. I. Tarnovskii, Iu. S. Shkarenkov, S. M. Iovchyk, and A. B. Miroshnichenko. "O razvitii i ukreplenii ekonomicheskogo sotrudnichestva sotsialisticheskikh stran i sovershenstvovanii form etogo sotrudnichestva." 6.18.1965. IMEPI Archive, IEMSS report.

AN SSSR, Vremennaia komissiia po vneshneekonomicheskim problemam razvitiia narodnogo khoziaistva SSSR. "Razvitie vneshneekonomicheskikh sviazei Sovetskogo Soiuza do 1990 g." 1.2.1973 (ten copies). IMEPI Archive.

Bautina, N. V., A. D. Leznik, N. I. Promskii, S. P. Petukhova, N. B. Sterlin, and B. A. Afonin. "Ob itogakh pervogo etapa koordinatsii narodnokhoziaistvennykh planov SSSR s drugimi stranami-chlenami SEV na period 1976–1980 gg. (predvaritel'nyi variant doklada)." 3.19.1974. IMEPI Archive, IEMSS Report 14306/254.

Bogomolov, O. T. "Materialy k XXV Sessiia SEV." Draft speech addressed to Iu. S. Firsov, USSR Council of Ministers. 7.16.1971. IMEPI Archive, IEMSS report.

Bogomolov, O. T., I. I. Orlik, and A. N. Bykov. "Sotsialisticheskaia ekonomicheskaia integratsiia i ee mezhdunarodnoe znachenie." To G. E. Tsukanov, CC CPSU, 1.10.1974. IMEPI Archive, IEMSS report.

Bogomolov, O. T., and Iu. S. Shiriaev. "O dolgosrochnykh tselevykh programmakh sotrudnichestva." 4.6.1976. IMEPI Archive, IEMSS report.

Bogomolov, O. T., Iu. S. Shiriaev, V. M. Shastitko, V. N. Gavrilov, L. I. Tsedlin, and K. M. Ligai, "O perspektivakh razvitiia vneshneekonomicheskikh sviazei SSSR s sotsialisticheskimi stranami v period do 1990 g." 10.27.1972. IMEPI Archive, IEMSS report.

Bogomolov, O. T., A. I. Zubkov, Iu. S. Shkarenkov, I. D. Kozlov, and E. K. Shmakova. "O nekotorykh voprosakh povysheniia effektivnosti sotrudnichestva stran SEV v reshenii syr'evoi problemy." To Mikhail A. Lesechko, Deputy Chairman for CMEA Issues, Council of Ministers, 2.16.1971. IMEPI Archive, IEMSS report.

Bykov, A. N. "Integratsiia stran SEV v oblasti nauki i tekhniki: itogi i perspektivy" (nauchnyi doklad). 1980 IMEPI Archive, IEMSS report.

Bykov, A. N. "K voprosu o soglasovannoi nauchno-tekhnicheskoi politike stran SEV." 8.29.1974. IMEPI Archive, IEMSS report, vol. 7.

Chumachenko, B. A., and V. B. Ezerov. "Nekotorye soobrazheniia o razrabotke Kompleksnoi programmy nauchno-tekhnicheskogo progressa stran-chlenov SEV." MNIIPU, January 1984.

Dudinskii, I. V., ed. "Razvitie mirovoi sotsialisticheskoi sistemy v period posle XXIII S'iezda KPSS." 6.25.1970. IMEPI Archive, IEMSS report.

Ezerov, Vladimir. "O perestroike struktury i mekhanizma upravleniia KP NTP SEV." Date unknown. MNIIPU Archive.

Gorizontov, B. B. "Mezhdunarodnye kommunikatsii—uzkoe mesto integratsii." 10.7.1974. IMEPI Archive, IEMSS report, vol. 8.

Gorizontov, B. B., A. D. Leznik, and L. S. Semenova, eds. "Osnovnye tendentsii v razvitii mezhdunarodnoi spetsializatsii i kooperatsii v obrabatyvaiushchei prom-yshlennosti" (nauchnyi doklad). 1.21.1974. IMEPI Archive, IEMSS report, vol. 1.

Gosplan USSR. "O sovershenstvovanii sistemy upravleniia i planirovaniia v SSSR (razdel I razvernutogo plana raboty rabochei gruppy I)." To Working Group I, 3.2.1970. CMEA Archive, TsGANKh, Fond 561, Opis 15, Delo 95.

Grinberg, R. S., M. S. Liubskii, G. G. Mazkov, and A. D. Nekipelov. "Etapy per-estroiki mekhanizma sotsialisticheskoi ekonomicheskoi integratsii." To A. K. Antonov, O. K. Rybakov, A. A. Reub, I. D. Ivanov, and P. N. Fedoseev, 12.9.1987. IMEPI Archive, IEMSS report.

Iakyshin, A. "O razrabotke dolgosrochnoi tselevoi programmy sotrudnichestva po ob-especheniiu ekonomicheski obosnovannykh potrebnostei stran-chlenov SEV v os-novnykh vidakh topliva i energii." 4.5.1976. IMEPI Archive, IEMSS report.

Iokhin, V. "Nekotorye voprosy ekonomicheskogo sotrudnichestva SSSR so stranami SEV v mashinostroenii." 8.12.1976. IMEPI Archive, IEMSS report.

"K razdelu 'Rekomendatsii' doklada 'Mir sotsializma v kontse 80 godov. Tendentsii i perspektivy razvitiia' (v chasti, kasaiushcheisia perestroiki integratsionnogo sotrud-nichestva)." 4.20.1988. IMEPI Archive, IEMSS report.

Kaie, V. A., "K sovremennomu ekonomicheskomu polozheniiu v Chekhoslovakii." 11.28.1972. IMEPI Archive, IEMSS report.

"Kompleksnaia programma nauchno-tekhnicheskogo progressa stran chlenov SEV: Osnovnye polozheniia kontseptsii. Struktura, poriadok i sroki razrabotki." MNIIPU Archive, February 1984.

Kormnov, Iu. F. "Mezhdunarodnye dolgosrochnye tselevye programmy: neobkhodi-most', soderzhanie i realizatsiia." 5.17.1976. IMEPI Archive, IEMSS report.

Kormnov, Iu. F. "Nekotorye voprosy razvitiia kooperatsii proizvodstva SSSR s drug-imi stranami SEV na baze pouzlovoi, podetal'noi i tekhnologicheskoi spetsializat-sii." 5.20.1974. IMEPI Archive, IEMSS report, vol. 5.

Kormnov, Iu. F. "Razrabotka problem sovershenstvovaniia ekonomicheskogo mekh-anizma sotrudnichestva sovetskimi ekonomistami." 3.2.1976. IMEPI Archive, IEMSS report.

Kormnov, Iu. F. "Zamechaniia k materialu o sovershenstvovanii sistemy vneshnetorg-ovykh tsen v otnosheniiakh stran-chlenov SEV." 8.15.1974. IMEPI Archive, IEMSS report, vol. 7.

Kormnov, Iu. F., I. D. Kozlov, and A. A. Yakushin. "Poiasnitel'naia problemnaia zapiska k MDTsP 'Toplivo-energiia.'" 8.23.1976. IMEPI Archive, IEMSS report 14306/665.

Kormnov, Iu. F., and A. D. Leznik. "Analiz prichin voznikaiushchikh trudnostei v spetsializatsii i kooperirovanii mashinostroitel'nogo proizvodstva i opredelenie pu-tei ikh ustraneniia." 9.2.1974. IMEPI Archive, IEMSS report 14306/717, vol. 7.

Kormnov, Iu. F., and A. D. Leznik. "Obespechenie uslovii, neobkhodimykh dlia de-iatel'nost mezhdunarodnykh khoziaistvennykh organizatsii," 8.15.1974. IMEPI Ar-chive, IEMSS report, vol. 7.

Kormnov, Iu. F., Iu. P. Shintiapin, and B. E. Frumkin. "Vozmozhnye puti resheniia prodovol'stvennoi problemy v ramkakh SEV na osnove razvitiia ekonomicheskoi integratsii v agrarno-promyshlennoi sfere." 8.14.1974. IMEPI Archive, IEMSS report 14306/664.

Kormnov, Iu. F., A. I. Zubkov, and B. E. Frumkin. "Skhema mezhdunarodnoi dolgosrochnoi tselevoi programmy sotrudnichestva stran-chlenov SEV v komplekse otraslei promyshlennosti." 7.23.1976. IMEPI Archive, IEMSS report.

Kozlov, I. A., and A. A. Iakushin. "Poiasnitel'naia problemnaia zapiska k MDTsP 'toplivo-energiia.'" 8.23.1976. IMEPI Archive, IEMSS report.

Kozlov, I. A., and A. A. Iakushin. "Skhema MDTsP sotrudnichestva stran-chlenov SEV v toplivno-energeticheskikh otrasliakh." 8.23.1976. IMEPI Archive, IEMSS report.

Nekipelov, A. D. "O khode i perspektivakh sovmestnoi rabote stran-chlenov SEV po perestroike integratsionnogo sotrudnichestva." 1987. IMEPI Archive, IEMSS report.

Nekipelov, A. D., et al. "Predlozheniia Sovetskoi storony k Tselostnoi kontseptsii perestroiki mekhanizma mnogostoronnego sotrudnichestva i sotsialisticheskoi ekonomicheskoi integratsii i deiatel'nosti SEV." 3.31.1989. IMEPI Archive, IEMSS report 14306/402.

NIKI [Nauchno-issledovatel'skii kon'iunkturnyi institut] MVT SSSR. "Doklad o perspektivakh razvitiia vneshnei torgovli SSSR do 1990 g." Moscow: Minvneshtorg, 1972.

Mikhliaev, A. G. "Programmy v planovoi praktike Evropeiskikh stran SEV: Nauchnaia zapiska." 1974. IMEPI Archive, IEMSS report, vol. 5.

Orlik, I. I., and A. N. Bykov. "Sotsialisticheskaia ekonomicheskaia integratsiia i ee mezhdunarodnoe znachenie." 1.10.1974. IMEPI Archive, IEMSS report, vol. 1.

"Predlozheniia po sisteme upravleniia realizatsiei Kompleksnoi programmy nauchno-tekhnicheskogo progressa stran-chlenov SEV." 1986. MNIIPU Archive.

Shastitko, V. M. "K itogam razvitiia vzaimnykh vneshneekonomicheskikh sviazei stran SEV v 1971–1975 gg." 2.3.1976. IMEPI Archive, IEMSS report.

Shastitko, V. M. "O perspektivakh razvitiia vneshneekonomicheskikh sviazei SSSR s sotsialisticheskimi stranami v period do 1990 g." 1976. IMEPI Archive, IEMSS report, Pervyi otdel.

Shastitko, V. M., K. M. Ligai, B. A. Kheifets, and A. D. Nekipelov. "Tezisy vystupleniia 'O dolgosrochnoi strategii razvitiia vneshneekonomicheskikh sviazei SSSR so stranami SEV.'" To O. A. Chukanov, CC CPSU, 11.28.1985. IMEPI Archive, IEMSS report.

Shastitko, V. M., M. S. Liubskii, R. S. Grinberg, K. M. Ligai, Iu. G. Naido, V. N. Gavrilov, and A. D. Nekipelov. "Materialy po osnovnym problemam razvitiia integratsionnogo sotrudnichestva stran-chlenov SEV i napravleniiam ego sovershenstvovaniia." 10.25.1988. IMEPI Archive, IEMSS report.

Shastitko, V. M., and A. D. Nekipelov. "Pervoocherednye zadachi formirovaniia ob'edinennogo rynka SEV." 1988. IMEPI Archive, IEMSS report 14306/640.

Shiriaev, Iu. S. "V komissiiu Prezidiuma soveta ministrov SSSR po voprosam Soveta Ekonomicheskoi Vzaimopomoshchi." 4.14.1972. IMEPI Archive, IEMSS report.

Shiriaev, Iu. S., V. M. Shastitko, V. N. Gavrilov, L. I. Tsedlin, and K. M. Ligai. "O perspektivakh razvitiia vneshneekonomicheskikh sviazei SSSR s sotsialisticheskimi stranami v period do 1990 g." 10.27.1972. IMEPI Archive, IEMSS report.

Shiriaev, Iu. S., A. N. Bykov, G. A. Vlaskin, V. Sitnin, N. I. Promskii, and K. I. Popov. "Materialy po vneshneekonomicheskim aspektam sovershenstvovaniia sistemy upravleniia nauchno-tekhnicheskim progressom: 'Sovershenstvovanie sistemy upravleniia nauchno-tekhnicheskim progressom v oblasti vneshneekonomicheskikh sviazei'; 'Predlozheniia k proektu postanovleniia'; 'Printsipy i organizatsionnye formy realizatsii za rubezhom nauchno-tekhnicheskikh novshestv. Litsenzionnaia politika.'" 5.2.1976. IMEPI Archive, IEMSS report 14206/112.

Sokolov, A. I. "Ob uchastii stran-chlenov SEV v mezhdunarodnoi spetsializatsii i kooperirovanii proizvodstva." 6.29.1976. IMEPI Archive, IEMSS report.

Akademia Nauk SSSR, Vremennaia komissiia po vneshneekonomicheskim problemam razvitiia narodnogo khoziaistva SSSR. "Razvitie vneshneekonomicheskikh sviazei Sovetskogo Soiuza do 1990 g." 1.2.1973. IMEPI Archive.

Zubkov, A. I. "Nekotorye predlozheniia k materialam Gosplana SSSR po dolgosrochnoi tselevoi programme stran SEV v oblasti topliva, energii, syr'ia i materialov." 4.5.1976. IMEPI Archive, IEMSS report.

Zubkov, A. I, and Iakushin A. A. "Nekotorye voprosy sovershchenstvovaniia sotrudnichestva stran SEV v razvitii toplivno-energeticheskogo khoziaistva." 10.4.1974. IMEPI Archive, IEMSS report, vol. 7.

Zubkov, A. I., Iu. S. Shkarenkov, I. D. Kozlov, and E. K. Shmakova. "O nekotorykh voprosakh povysheniia effektivnosti sotrudnichestva stran SEV v reshenii syr'evoi problemy." 2.16.1971. IMEPI Archive, IEMSS report.

CMEA Materials

Chumachenko, B. A., V. A. Koniushko, V. A. Prokudin, V. B. Ezerov, E. P. Vlasov, and V. S. Korsun, eds. "Predlozheniia po sisteme upravleniia realizatsiei Kompleksnoi programmy nauchno-tekhnicheskogo progressa stran-chlenov SEV." 1984. MNIIPU Archive.

"Kollektivnaia kontseptsiia mezhdunarodnogo sotsialisticheskogo razdeleniia truda na 1991–2005 gg." Prilozhenie 2 k proektu postanovleniia Sessii Soveta (44 zasedanie), Komitet po sotrudnichestvu v oblasti planovoi deiatel'nosti, May 1988. IMEPI Archive, Pervyi otdel.

"Kontseptsiia Tsentral'nogo Komiteta Bolgarskoi Kommunisticheskoi Partii i Pravitel'stva Narodnoi Respubliki Bolgarii sotrudnichestva dlia predstoiashchego Soveshchaniia na vysokom urovne." Circulated by T. Tsolov, Deputy Chairman of the Council of Ministers, Permanent Representative of Bulgaria to the CMEA, to N. V. Faddeev, Secretary of the CMEA, 31 January 1969. CMEA Archive, TsGANKh, Fond 561, Opis 53s, Delo 5, No. pp. 6.

"Memorandum Politbiuro TsK SEPG i Prezidiuma Soveta Ministrov Germanskoi Demokraticheskoi Respubliki po voprosu o razvitii sotsialisticheskogo ekonomicheskogo soobshchestva Soveta Ekonomicheskoi Vzaimopomoshchi." Circulated by G. Weiss to N. V. Faddeev, 4 October 1968. CMEA Archive, TsGANKh, Fond 561, Opis 53s, Delo 5, No. pp. 6.

"Napravleniia i metody integratsii stran-chlenov SEV." [Polish Position Paper for the Comprehensive Program.] Warsaw, March 1968. CMEA Archive, TsGANKh, Fond 561, Opis 53s, Delo 5, No. pp. 6.

"O printsipakh, poriadke, organizatsionnykh, ekonomicheskikh i pravovykh predposylkakh i povyshenii material'noi zainteresovannosti i otvetstvennosti pri ustanovlenii neposredstvennykh sviazei na osnove dogovornykh otnoshenii, a takzhe o vozmozhnykh organizatsionnykh formakh i funktsiiakh mezhdunarodnykh organizatsii, sozdavaemykh zainteresovannymi stranami." Prilozheniie 3 k Pamiatnoi zapiske Soveshchaniia ekspertov stran, uchastvuiushchikh v rabote rabochikh grupp I i 7 i v Postoiannoi Komissii SEV po ekonomicheskim voprosam, po podgotovke materialov po p. 10 postanovleniia XXIII sessii SEV. 1.12–15.1970. CMEA Archive, TsGANKh, Fond 561, Opis 15, Delo 94.

"O problemakh ekonomicheskogo sotrudnichestva stran-chlenov Soveta Ekonomicheskoi Vzaimopomoshchi (Pledlozheniia Sovetskogo Soiuza)." Circulated by M. Lesechko to N. V. Faddeev, 12.31.1968. CMEA Archive, TsGANKh, Fond 561, Opis 53s, Delo 5, No. pp. 6.

"Osnovnye printsipial'nye polozheniia Dolgosrochnoi tselevoi programmy sotrudnichestva po obespecheniiu ekonomicheski obosnovannykh potrebnostei stran-chlenov SEV v toplive i energii." Prilozhenie 3 k pamiatnoi zapiske soveshchaniia ekspertov stran-chlenov SEV po podgotovke materialov dlia Rabochei gruppy po razrabotke DTsPS v oblasti topliva, energii i syr'ia i Biuro Komiteta SEV po sotrudnichestvu v oblasti planovoi deiatel'nosti. 7.18–22.1977. CMEA Archive, TsGANKh, Fond 561, Opis 21c/pp, Delo 50.

"O sovershenstvovanii sistemy upravleniia i planirovaniia v SSSR (razdel I razvernutogo plana raboty rabochei gruppy I)." Gosplan USSR, 3.2.1970. CMEA Archive, TsGANKh, Fond 561, Opis 15, Delo 95.

"Pamiatnaia zapiska soveshchaniia ekspertov stran-chlenov SEV po podgotovke materialov dlia Rabochei gruppy po razrabotke DTsPS v oblasti topliva, energii i syr'ia i Biuro Komiteta SEV po sotrudnichestvu v oblasti planovoi deiatel'nosti," 7.18–22.1977. CMEA Archive, TsGANKh, Fond 561.

"Postanovlenie 'O perestroike mekhanizma mnogostoronnego sotrudnichestva i sotsialisticheskoi ekonomicheskoi integratsii i deiatel'nosti Soveta Ekonomicheskoi Vzaimopomoshchi.'" Protokol 43. (Vneocherednogo) zasedaniia Sessii Soveta, Moscow, 10.13–14.1987. IMEPI Archive. Pervyi otdel.

"Predlozheniia ekspertov stran-chlenov SEV po krugu voprosov dlia razrabotki dolgosrochnoi tselevoi programmy sotrudnichestva po obespecheniiu soglasovannogo na dvustoronnei i mnogostoronnei osnove razvitiia mashinostroeniia na baze glubokoi spetsializatsii i kooperirovaniia proizvodstva." Prilozhenie No. 5 k protokolu zasedaniia rabochei gruppy Biuro Komiteta SEV po sotrudnichestvu v oblasti planovoi deiatel'nosti. 12.16–18, 1975. CMEA Archive, Fond 561, Opis 15 pp, No. pp. 61, Delo 40–36.

"Prilozhenie k protokolu shestogo zasedaniia Rabochei gruppy po mashinostroeniiu Komiteta SEV po sotrudnichestvu v oblasti planovoi deiatel'nosti." 9.12–15, 1978. CMEA Archive, TsGANKh, Fond 561, Opis 18s/pp, No. pp. 64, Delo 232.

"Prilozhenie 3.2 k protokolu vos'mogo zasedaniia Rabochei gruppy po mashinostroeniiu Komiteta SEV po sotrudnichestvu v oblasti planovoi deiatel'nosti." 1.9–11.1979. CMEA Archive, TsGANKh, Fond 561, Opis 18s/pp, No. pp. 66, Delo 232.

"Protokol soveshchaniia ekspertov planovykh organov stran-chlenov SEV i ekspertov SFRIu, MXO 'Interatomenergo' i Sekretariata SEV po dorabotke prilozhenii 1,2, i 3 k proektu Soglasheniia o mnogostoronnei mezhdunarodnoi spetsializatsii i kooperirovanii proizvodstva i vzaimnykh postavok oborudovaniia dlia AES na period

1981–1990 gg." 1.4–5.1979. CMEA Archive, TsGANKh, Fond 561, Opis 65s, No. pp. 140, Delo 232.

"Protokol soveshchaniia ekspertov zainteresovannykh stran-chlenov SEV po razrabotke proekta raspredeleniia zatrat mezhdu uchastnikami sovmestno finansiruemykh rabot po nauchno-tekhnicheskomu sotrudnichestvu, a takzhe po vyrabotke predlozhenii o sozdanii sovmestnykh nauchno-proizvodstvennykh firm na khozraschetnoi osnove." 8.7–9.1984. CMEA Archive, TsGANKh, Fond 561, Opis 5 pp, No. pp. 665.

"Protokol soveshchaniia polnomochnykh predstavitelei stran-chlenov SEV po razrabotke predlozhenii po konkretizatsii prav i obiazannostei Golovnoi organizatsii-koordinatora rabot po probleme Kompleksnoi programmy nauchno-tekhnicheskogo progressa stran-chlenov SEV do 2000 goda." 2.4–5.1986. CMEA Archive, TsGANKh Fond 561, Opis 5 pp, Delo 665.

"Protokol, 31. Zasedaniia Komiteta po Nauchno-Tekhnicheskomu Sotrudnichestvu." 12.6–7.1984. Moscow. MNIIPU Archive.

"Protokol zasedaniia rabochei gruppy Biuro Komiteta SEV po sotrudnichestvu v oblasti planovoi deiatel'nosti po podgotovke materiala 'Soobrazheniia po soderzhaniiu i krugu voprosov dolgosrochnykh tselevykh programm sotrudnichestva, a takzhe metodicheskie polozheniia (v t.ch. primernye skhemy, formy, pokazateli) po ikh podgotovke.'" 12.16–18.1975. CMEA Archive, TsGANKh, Fond 561, Opis 15pp, Delo 61.

"Rabochaia zapis' zasedaniia redaktsionnoi komissii 25 iiulia 1975." Twenty-ninth Session of the CMEA. CMEA Archive, TsGANKh, Fond 561, Opis 61c, Delo 2.

"Rabochaia zapis' soveshchaniia ekspertov stran-chlenov SEV po podgotovke dolgosrochnykh tselevykh programm sotrudnichestva." 7.18.1977 CMEA Archive, TsGANKh, Fond 561.

"Soglashenie o mnogostoronei mezhdunarodnoi spetsializatsii i kooperirovanii proizvodstva i vzaimnykh postavkakh oborudovaniia dlia atomnykh elektrostantsii na period 1981–1990 gg." Protocol of the Ninth Meeting of the Working Group for Machine-Building of the CMEA Committee for Cooperation in Planning (KSOPD), 5.14.1979, CMEA Archive, TsGANKh, Fond 561, Opis 18s/pp, Delo 232, No. pp. 67.

"Soglashenie o mnogostoronei mezhdunarodnoi spetsializatsii i kooperirovanii proizvodstva i vzaimnykh postavkakh oborudovaniia dlia atomnykh elektrostantsii na period 1981–1990 gg." Protocol of the Tenth Meeting of the Working Group for Machine-Building of the CMEA Committee for Cooperation in Planning (KSOPD), 6.7.1979, CMEA Archive, TsGANKh, Fond 561, Opis 18s/pp, Delo 232, No. pp. 68.

"Soglashenie o mnogostoronnei mezhdunarodnoi spetsializatsii i kooperirovanii proizvodstva i vzaimnykh postavkakh oborudovaniia dlia atomnykh elektrostantsii na period 1981–1990 gg." Appendix 3 to the Protocol of the Sixth Meeting of the Working group for Machine-Building of the CMEA Committee for Cooperation in Planning (KSOPD), 9.12–15.1978. CMEA Archive, TsGANKh, Fond 561, Opis 64s, No. pp. 135.

"Soobrazheniia po soderzhaniiu i krugu voprosov dolgosrochnykh tselevykh programm sotrudnichestva, a takzhe metodicheskie polozheniia (v t.ch. primernye skhemy, formy, pokazateli) po ikh podgotovke." Prilozheniia 5 k Protokolu zasedaniia rabochei gruppy Biuro Komiteta SEV po sotrudnichestvu v oblasti planovoi deiatel'nosti po podgotovke materiala. 12.16–18.1975. CMEA Archive, TsGANKh, Fond 561, Opis 15 pp., Delo 61.

"Soobrazheniia Tsentral'nogo Komiteta Rumynskoi Kommunisticheskoi Partii i Soveta Ministrov Sotsialisticheskoi Respubliki Rumynii po voprosu o sovershenstvovanii ekonomicheskogo i nauchno-tekhnicheskogo sotrudnichestva stran-chlenov SEV." Circulated by V. Bukur, Deputy Permanent SRR Representative to CMEA, to N. V. Faddeev, Secretary, CMEA, 2.28.1969. CMEA Archive, TsGANKh, Fond 561, Opis 53s, Delo 5, No. pp. 6.

"Soobrazheniia Vengerskoi Sotsialisticheskoi Rabochei Partii po ekonomicheskoi integratsii sotsialisticheskikh stran." Circulated by Apro Antal to N. V. Faddeev, 7.18.1968, p. 6. CMEA Archive, TsGANKh, Fond 561, Opis 53s, Delo 5, No. pp. 6.

Sovet Ekonomicheskoi Vzaimopomoshchi. "Kompleksnaia Programma Nauchno-Tekhnicheskogo Progressa stran-chlenov SEV, Osnovnye polozheniia (Predvaritel'nyi proekt)." 1984. MNIIPU Archive.

Sovet Ekonomicheskoi Vzaimopomoshchi. "Kompleksnaia Programma Nauchno-Tekhnicheskogo Progressa stran-chlenov SEV, Osnovnye polozheniia (Proekt)." 1985. MNIIPU Archive.

"Spetsializatsiia stran-chlenov SEV i SFRIu v proizvodstve oborudovaniia dlia AES." Prilozhenie 3 k protokolu 10 zasedaniia Rabochei gruppy po mashinostroeniiu Komiteta SEV po sotrudnichestvu v oblasti planovoi deiatel'nosti." 9.12–15.1978 CMEA Archive, TsGANKh, Fond 561, Opis 18s/pp, No. pp. 68, Delo 232.

"Stenogramma soveshchaniia predstavitelei stran-chlenov SEV po konkretizatsii prav i obiazannostei golovnykh organizatsii." 2.4–5.1986. CMEA Archive, TsGANKh, Fond 561, Opis 5 pp, Delo 716.

"Stenogramma vstrechi postoiannykh predstavitelei stran v SEV." 10.12.1987. CMEA Archive, TsGANKh, Fond 561, Opis 77s, Delo 3.

"Stenogramma vstrechi postoiannykh predstavitelei stran v SEV." 6.5.1987. CMEA Archive, TsGANKh Fond 561, Opis 77s, Delo 15.

"Stenogramma 123. zasedaniia Ispolnitel'nogo Komiteta Soveta Ekonomicheskoi Vzaimopomoshchi." Plenarnoe zasedanie, 6.4.1987. CMEA Archive, TsGANKh, Fond 561, Opis 75s, Delo 29.

"Stenogramma zasedaniia redaktsionnoi komissii XXIII Sessii SEV." 4.23–24.1969. CMEA Archive, TsGANKh, Fond 561, Opis 53s, Delo 13.

"Stenogramma zasedaniia XXIX sessii Soveta Ekonomicheskoi Vzaimopomoshchi, 24 iiunia 1975 goda." 7.24.1975. CMEA Archive, TsGANKh, Fond 561, Opis 61s, No. pp. 3, Delo 4.

"Zaiavleniie ob osnovnykh napravleniiakh dal'neishego razvitiia i uglubleniia ekonomicheskogo i nauchno-tekhnicheskogo sotrudnichestva stran-chlenov SEV." Reshenie ekonomicheskogo soveshchaniia stran-chlenov SEV na vyshem urovne, 11.10–11.1986. CMEA Archive, TsGANKh, Fond 561, Opis 15, Delo 66.

Polish Materials

Bożyk, Paweł. "Teoreticheskie problemy torgovli mezhdu stranami-chlenami SEV." Instytut Koniunktur i Cen Handlu Zagranicznego, August 1969. IKC Archive, number II-212.

Brych, Janusz. "Zamechaniia k pamiatnoi zapiske." 2.4.1985. CUP Archive, 488/6.

Bogucki, Marek, Podsekretarz Stanu, UPNTiW. Letter to Stanisław Mach, Wiceprezes Najwyzszej Izby Kontroli, 8.2.1989. KBN Archive.

Gorywoda, Manfred, Chairman, Polish Planning Commission. Letter to Wojciech Jaruzelski, General Secretary, 10 April 1985. CUP Archive, 488/6.

Janowski, Jan, Wiceprezes Rady Ministrów, Minister-Kierownik Urzędu Postępu Naukowo-Technicznego i Wdrożen. Letter to Tadeusz Hupalowski, Prezes Najwyzszej Izby Kontroli, 10.21.1989. KBN Archive.

Jaruzelski, Wojciech. "Notatki w sprawach gospodarczych Polski z Związkiem radzieckim (Pisma na najwyzszjem szczeblu)." Letter to Iu. Andropov, Polish, 18.4.1983. Reply by Iurii Andropov, Russian, 29 April 1983. CUP Archive, File 541/7.

Komisja Planowania przy Radzie Ministrów. "Ocena Realizacji Zadan Wynikających z Koordynacji Planów Między Polską a Krajami Członkowskimi RWPG do 1990 r." January 1988. CUP Archive.

Komisja Planowania przy Radzie Ministrów. "Rozmowy z ZSRR n. S. koordynacji planów na lata 1986–1990 (25–29 marca 1985 r.)." CUP Archive, 488/6.

Komisja Planowania przy Radzie Ministrów, Zespół Współpracy Gospodarczej z Zagranicą, "Pamiatnaia zapiska." 12.7.1967. CUP Archive, WG/W/2012/67.

Komisja Planowania przy Radzie Ministrów, Zespół Współpracy Gospodarczej z Zagranicą. "Sprawozdanie z konsultacji grupy zbiorczej centralnych organów planowania w sprawie koordynacji planów między PRL a ZSRR na lata 1991–1995 przeprowadzonej w Moskwie w dniach 21–25 listopada 1988 r." CUP Archive.

Konarzewski, Jan. "Informacja o wynikach kontroli realizacji wspólnych prac naukowo-badawczych i wdrożenowych podjętych przez Polskę, na podstawie porozumien między Polską a krajami socjalistycznymi." Najwyzsza Izba Kontroli, Zespół Nauki i Postępu Technicznego, 9.11.1989. KBN Archive.

Mycielski, J., W. Trzeciakowski. "Kurs złotego a rachunek efektywności handlu zagranicznego oraz system finansowy w gospodarce narodowej i w skali międzynarodowej." Instytut Koniunktur i Cen Handlu Zagranicznego, 1969. IKC Archive, number 987.

"Notatka z 3 posiedzenia Rady Koordynacyjnej d/s realizacji Kompleksowego Programu Postępu Naukowo-Technicznego krajów członkowskich RWPG do 2000 roku." 10.5.1989. KBN Archive.

Tott, Konrad, Minister-Kierownik UPNTiW. "Instrukcja w sprawie trybu i zasad współpracy Urzędu Postępu Naukowo-Technicznego i Wdrożen z ministerstwami (urzędami centralnymi) przy realizacji zadan, wynikających z Kompleksowego Programu Postępu Naukowo-Technicznego krajów członkowskich RWPG do 2000 roku (KP PNT) oraz Długofalowego Polsko-Radzieckiego Kompleksowego Programu Postępu Naukowo-Technicznego (DPRKPPNT), zwanych dalej 'Programami.'" 10.1.1986. KBN Archive.

"Uchwała Nr. 48/86 Rady Ministrów, z dnia 7 kwietnia 1986 r." KBN Archive.

Urząd Postępu Naukowo-Technicznego i Wdrożen. "Ocena realizacji Kompleksowego programu postępu naukowo-technicznego krajów członkowskich RWPG." 4.26.1989. KBN Archive.

Urząd Postępu Naukowo-Technicznego i Wdrożen. "Ocena realizacji Kompleksowego Programu Postępu Naukowo-Technicznego krajów członkowskich RWPG." March 1990. KBN Archive.

Zespól Współpracy z Zagranicą Urzędu Komisji Planowania. "Sprawozdanie z konsultacji grupy zbiorczej centralnych organów planowania w sprawie koordynacji planów między PRL a ZSRR na lata 1991–1995 przeprowadzonej w Moskwie w dniach 21–25 listopada 1988." CUP Archive.

Czechoslovak Materials

Černý, M. "Informace o výsledcích jednání mistopředsedy vlády ČSSR a předsedy Státní plánovací komise s. Potáče s I. mistopředsedou rady ministrů a předsedou Gosplanu SSSR s. Talyzinem." 10.19.1987. SPK Archive, č.j. 22 475/87.

Černý, M. "Konzultace o svodných otázkách hospodářské spolupráce s SSSR na období po roce 1990. Informace pro mistopředsedu vlády ČSSR a předsedu SPK." 9.4.19897. SPK Archive, č.j. 21 009/87.

Černý, M. "Výsledky jednání s. Potáče se s. Masljukovem. Operativní informace o jednání předsedy Státní plánovací komise s. Potače s předsedou Gosplanu SSSR s. Masljukovem." 5.30.1988. SPK Archive, č.j. 61 522/88.

Kolanda, Miroslav, and Václav Kubišta. "Náklady, výkony a chování podniků čs. zpracovatelského průmyslu na světových trzích v 80. letech." Prague: Prognostický ústav ČSAV, 1990.

"Koncepce hospodářské a vědeckotechnické spolupráce ČSSR a SSSR na příštích 15–20 let." Signed 1.17.1989 by L. Adamec and N. Ryzhkov, Moscow. SPK Archive, č.j. 24 460/89.

Kopečný, O. "Pamětní zápis z konzultace expertů ústředních plánovacích orgánů SSSR a ČSSR o koordinaci státních plánů v odvětví hutnictví železa a neželezných kovů na leta 1991–1995." 10.21.1988. SPK Archive, č.j. 62 996/88.

Kopečný, O. "Příprava jednání se sovětskou stranou o Koncepci HVTS. Stanovisko pro I. místopředsedu SPK s. ing. Šupku k informaci č. j. 62 248/88." Odbor dlouhodobe odvětvové strukturální politiky, 9.20.1988. SPK Archive, č.j. 62 248/88.

Kopečný, Prchlík, Marcinov. "Výsledky konzultace plánovacích orgánů ČSSR a SSSR o koordinaci plánů v oblasti hutnictvi a strojírenství." 6.30.1989. SPK Archive, č.j. 25 582/89.

Kubíček, J. "Svodná konzultace plánovacích orgánů ČSSR a SSSR." 12.16.1988. SPK Archive, č.j. 63 315/88.

Dr. Nad'. "Informace pro s. místopředsedu Petříčka k problematice dovozu stavebních praci do SSSR—s. p. Hutní stavby Košice." 10.13.1989. SPK Archive, č.j. 26 418/89.

Dr. Nad'. "Informace pro náměstka předsedy Státní plánovací komise s. ing. Jána Štrbu o výsledcích jednání expertů ústředních plánovacích orgánů ČSSR a SSSR." 4.14.1988. SPK Archive, č.j. 60 684/88.

Dr. Nad'. "Návrh Zásad dalšího postupu čs. ústředních orgánů státní správy při zabezpečování čs. účasti na přípravě a realizaci integračních akcí v členských státech RVHP." 5.18.1988. SPK Archive, č.j. 61 156/88.

Dr. Nad'. "Protokol z jednání předsedy vlády ČSSR L. Adamce a předsedy rady ministrů SSSR N. Ryžkova." 1.23.1989. SPK Archive, č.j. 24 461/89.

Prchlík, J. "Jednání expertů ústředních plánovacích orgánů ČSSR a SSSR." Information for the Chairman, SPK, 9.10.1987. SPK Archive, č.j. 22 607/87.

Prchlík, J. "Jednání ústředních plánovacích orgánů ČSSR a SSSR k problematice spolupráce v oblasti strojírensví." Information for the Chairman, SPK, 11. 25.1987. SPK Archive, č.j. 22 475/87.

Prchlík, J. "Směrnice pro postup specialistů Státní plánovací komise při jednání o koordinaci NHP pro období 1991–1995 v oblasti strojírenství a elektrotechiky." 5.19.1988. SPK Archive, č.j. 61 435/88.

"Sprava o výsledcích první etapy koordinacc národohospodářských plánů s členskymi státy RVHP na léta 1991–1995." Information for the Chairman, SPK, 6.9.1989. SPK Archive, č.j. 25 362/89.

Svobodá, P. "Informace o výsledcích jednání svodné skupiny ústředních plánovacích orgánů o koordinaci národohospodářských plánů mezi ČSSR a SSSR na leta 1991–1995." Material pro operativní poradu u předsedy Státní plánovací komise, 5.30.1989. SPK Archive, č.j. 25 225/89.

Svobodá, P., A. Kollert. "Kvantifikace rozvoje vnějších ekonomických vztahů ČSSR po roce 1989 do roku 2000." Materiál pro operativní poradu u předsedy Státní planovací komise, January 1987. SPK archive, č.j. 20 322/87.

Index

9 780691 095981